Where the Wasteland Ends

Politics and Transcendence in Postindustrial Society.

Theodore Roszak

Author of
The Making of a Counter Culture

Published in Association with Robert Briggs

CELESTIAL ARTS
Berkeley, California

CELESTIAL ARTS
P.O. Box 7327
Berkeley, California 94707

Cover design by Ken Scott

Library of Congress Cataloging-in-Publication Data
Roszak, Theodore, 1933–
    Where the wasteland ends: politics and transcendence in postindustrial society / Theodore Roszak.
        p.   cm.
    Reprint. Originally published: 1st ed. Garden City, N.Y.: Doubleday, 1972.
    Bibliography: p.
    ISBN 0-89087-561-8
    1. Civilization, Modern — 1950 –   I. Title.
[CB428.R67   1989]
909.82 — dc19   88-13860
                                                                                    CIP

First Printing of this trade paperback edition, 1989

1 2 3 4 5 6 — 91 90 89

Manufactured in the United States of America

Portions of Chapters 1, 2, and 7 have appeared in altered form in the *New American Review* and *New Scientist.*

Acknowledgment is gratefully made for permission to reprint from the following material:
    Portions of Chapter 7 appeared in *The Atlantic Monthly* issue of July 1972. Copyright © 1972 by The Atlantic Monthly Company. Reprinted by permission.
    "Autopsy on Science" originally appeared in *New Scientist and Science Journal* issue of 3/11/71. Copyright © 1971 by Theodore Roszak, and has been revised for publication in this volume. Reprinted by permission.
    "The Artificial Environment" originally appeared in *New American Review* No. 9. Copyright © 1970 by Theodore Roszak, and has been revised for publication in this volume. (Also appeared in *The Rotarian*)
    Excerpt from *Paths in Utopia* by Martin Buber. Copyright 1949 by Martin Buber. Reprinted by permission of The Macmillan Company and Routledge & Kegan Paul, Ltd.

The author wishes to give special thanks to the John Simon Guggenheim Memorial Foundation, whose generous grant during 1971–72 made it possible for the manuscript of this book to be completed.

CONTENTS

CONTENTS

Looking Backward: 1989 to 1969

> In fact, it seems to me quite possible that the nineteen-sixties represented the last burst of the human being before he was extinguished. And that this is the beginning of the rest of the future, and that from now on there will simply be all these robots walking around, feeling nothing, thinking nothing. And there will be nobody left almost to remind them that there once was a species called a human being, with feelings and thoughts. And that history and memory are right now being erased, and that soon no one will really remember that life existed on the planet.
>
> from *My Dinner With Andre* (1981)
> by Wallace Shawn and Andre Gregory

When this book was being written in the late 1960s, the United States was undergoing one of its great periods of social upheaval. Although at the time the media tended to exaggerate the numbers who participated in the protests of the day, the intensity of the agitation and the weight of the issues that were raised — beginning with the civil rights movement of the late fifties through the Watergate scandal of the mid-seventies — were sufficient to shake the nation's confidence in its leadership and to undermine its collective sense of identity. For that matter, major industrial societies everywhere were experiencing displays of militant discontent. Dissent was in the streets of Paris, London, Warsaw, Prague, Tokyo, seeming to portend enormous, worldwide changes.

While much of the protest was voiced by people in their teens and twenties, the grievances that were being thrust upon the public were far from mere youthful hi-jinx — though that is often the way they are now portrayed by political leaders who would prefer to bury what we now call "the sixties" beneath a landslide of ridicule and trivialization. The issues of that period included some of the most radical criticisms our society has had to face. It would have been understandable if the protest had been limited to social and racial justice, matters that had been on the American political agenda for generations and which were long overdue for attention. But things went well beyond that. The very rightness and rationality of industrial culture was being brought noisily into question by a generation of mainly middle-class children who were, curiously enough, among the chief beneficiaries of that culture: college-educated youth destined for the best jobs, the richest rewards their society had to offer. My purpose in this book was to investigate this remarkable state of affairs, to trace the discontent of that generation to its sources, and to formulate its protest as broadly as possible.

In seeking to do this, I fastened upon the image T. S. Eliot has given us in the most famous and prophetic English poem of the twentieth century. The wasteland. I set out to write a book about politics that integrated Eliot's sense of spiritual anxiety. Hence the subtitle, "Politics and Transcendence in Post-industrial Society." This I felt one had to do in order to grasp the real significance of the protests that were being raised on all sides in so rude and unruly a way. The issues of the day reached well beyond familiar matters of social equality, fairness, civil liberty. It seemed to me that the desiccation of the soul which Eliot lamented in his poem arose from forces of alienation that lay deep within the industrial process and within the scientific worldview which had provided the power behind that process. It was also becoming clear as we entered the last quarter of the century that the "wasteland" Eliot had understood symbolically might soon become a literal one as the global environment began to crumble beneath the punishing demands of our technology. Our state of soul was becoming the state of nature. The protest

of the period seemed to be declaring war upon everything industrial progress represented: its obsession with material goods, its ruthless domination of the biosphere, its extravagant urban lifestyle, its
contempt for the organic, the primitive, the traditional, the compulsive masculinity of its politics, its cool and detached vision of
nature. Never before have issues of this magnitude been raised for
political consideration.

It is instructive to compare the sixties with the two other periods
of protest that the United States has undergone in the twentieth
century—each about a generation apart. The comparison brings
out the strangeness of the sixties and may offer an insight into the
flaws that blunted its effectiveness.

At the outset of this century, the Progressive Movement, which
culminated in the presidency of Woodrow Wilson, took the trusts
and the city bosses to task in the name of the free market and an
honest ballot. The issues raised were matters of political adjustment
within the existing industrial framework. Indeed, federal regulation of the marketplace was meant to contribute to the stability and
efficiency of the economy. Regulatory agencies, clean elections, the
ballot initiative and referendum, primary elections—these were
goals that could be formulated as a party platform, taken to the
public as part of a political campaign, and finally given legislative
expression. Unhappily, those goals, once achieved, could also be
undercut by interests with enough money and cunning to take over
political parties and federal regulators. The power of the dollar is
not easily contained by laws. Nevertheless, the Progressives invented
the political tools to do the job they set for themselves; they left
behind institutions.

So too the New Deal of the Roosevelt era. Here again there were
institutions—most notably labor unions and an array of new government agencies—that could be used to curb the power of the business community and redistribute enough wealth to dig the country
out of the depression. And, like the Progressives, the New Dealers
left behind laws, programs, offices of government that permanently
reshaped our society. But just as important as the changes these

reform movements made are the things they left unquestioned. Both worked solidly within the boundaries of an urban-industrial system. The Progressives sought to clean up the cities, but not to eliminate them. The New Deal sought better means to manage the economy — mainly through a makeshift collection of Keynesian expedients — but not to undo it. Both accepted the big corporation as the principal means of providing goods and jobs; both sought prosperity through increased production; both saw progress as meaning more merchandise for more people and more profit for those who owned the economy. Both endorsed the nation state and the global hegemony of western European culture. Indeed, with the coming of World War II, the New Deal finished out its course by ushering in the military-industrial complex, that alliance of government, the major corporations, the universities which has remained the foundation of American economic life, and which represents the highest stage of urban-industrial dominance.

In stark contrast, the unstructured, many-sided protest of the sixties has left behind little in the way of laws, programs, institutions. The one great exception would be the landmark civil rights reforms sanctioned by the Warren Court, which might best be seen as the unfinished business of the New Deal and the war years. Otherwise, the dissent of the sixties tended to take little interest in standard political methods and objectives. Its major forms of expression were cultural — or rather *counter*cultural, to use the phrase I coined in 1967 for a series of magazine articles published in *The Nation*. The poetry, song, art, literature, living styles of the period struck out at established values, tastes, moral standards, sexual habits. For such purposes, rock music, satire, and overt erotic displays proved more attractive than political manifestos or party platforms. Often the protestors acted more like bohemian artists of the past than crusading cadres of a mass movement. They spoke of themselves as "tribes," "clans," "families" rather than a disciplined rank and file. The characteristic gestures of the period were not political rallies or parties, but campus teach-ins, rock concerts, Love-ins, Be-ins, communes or collectives — all of which were efforts to achieve a certain high intensity of dissent and cultural innovation that could rarely be sustained for more than brief periods.

Some of what went on in the sixties—white middle-class kids trying to live like Indians in the wilderness, dizzy experiments in participative democracy, efforts to rustify urban neighborhoods—can seem comic. Probably the quaintest and most sadly dated portion of this book are the projects mentioned in passing in chapter twelve, the communal and rural retreats that once seemed so spirited and hopeful. But behind such episodes, even when they washed away in a few short months, stood a genuine rejection of the industrial city and the massification of life it has brought with it.

For changes of this magnitude, standard political action is just useless. Our institutions are adapted, at best, to making adjustments *within* an urban-industrial order, not to overthrowing it. All too obviously, no political party could be expected to campaign on behalf of a cultural transformation so great; it would simply scare the public to death. As I suggest in the first chapter of this book, for better or worse, we are embedded in the "artificial environment" which industrialism has created. Most of us cannot even imagine any other reality than that with which the all-devouring city, its economy, its means of transport and communication surround us, no more so than our ancestors of five centuries ago could imagine a new world across the seas. "Here be monsters," they wrote at the margins of their abbreviated map of the world. That is what so many of the countercultural gestures of the sixties looked like, especially those that involved shabby dress, funky living, liberated sexuality, communal sharing, voluntary poverty and primitivism. Monstrous!

Even more threatening was the extension of this dissenting cultural style into the area of sanity itself. The sixties was the first period in which the insights of psychiatry were prominantly applied to our social affairs. Psychosis became a political category—as in the film *Dr. Strangelove,* the novel *Catch-22,* the surrealist lyrics of Bob Dylan and the Beatles, the writings of Herbert Marcuse, Norman O. Brown, R.D. Laing. In the spirit of the great Romantic artists—who had also placed themselves in opposition to urban life and industrial growth — the counterculture steeped itself in a fascination with exotic states of consciousness: madness, mystical religion, psychedelic drugs. What these experiments produced might range from zany to tragic, but there was at least a fringe of good sense attached. The argument ran as follows: industrialism is grounded in a scientific worldview; science, in turn, is grounded in a carefully restricted sensibility which has come to be regarded as monopolistically rational, practical, sane. So, if one is to raise serious doubts about industrial culture, one must transform its underlying mode of consciousness. As William Blake put it back in the early days of the "dark satanic mills," the goal is "to cleanse the doors of perception."

In the pages that follow, my contribution to that project was to update the argument which Romantics like Blake, Goethe, Wordsworth raised against the "single vision" of Newtonian science. Not that I had much hope of jarring the scientists, or the public which has come to regard their expertise as indispensible, into questioning the psychological foundations of our culture. It seems to be our destiny to press science and technology forward to the limit — which may be close at hand. The planet as a whole is fast becoming a single industrial artefact; mind and life are being maniacally computerized and genetically engineered. There may soon be nothing left to mechanize or scientize. There are some, like those I cite in the appendix to chapter seven of the book, who seem bent on rendering human life obsolete in a world of artificially intelligent, robotized systems where the computers have taken over everything, executive decision-making as well as assembly-line drudgery, play as well as work. By the last quarter of the twentieth century, the demonically anti-human aspects of science, which were once concealed by its authentic heroism, have become all too apparent. But at the same time, as André laments in the excerpt at the head of this preface, people seem to have lost the sensitivity to see the obvious.

Insofar as the protest of the sixties demanded a wrenching reappraisal of urban-industrialism, its culture and its consciousness,

it wanted too much too soon, far more than the American
public could give. That should not have been surprising. The
short-lived world of new ideals and strange lifestyles that the disaffiliated youth of an affluent and indulgent society can create
around themselves may look to their more blinkered, careworn elders
as bizarre as life on some other planet. On their political dimension, societies can experience revolutionary transfers of power that
happen overnight. But changes of perception, of sensibility, of
metaphysical conviction, these take place much more slowly; they
evolve, usually under the subtle influence of sages, seers, artists,
philosophers. If, as Shelley believed, poets are the unacknowledged
legislators of the world, they take a very long time getting their bills
passed through the parliament of mankind. Our culture has struck
a Faustian bargain for power over man and nature, and it will not
easily resign its wager. It still looks to its machines, its science, its
big economic systems for security, prosperity, salvation.

The small minority of mainly dissenting youth who made up
the bulk of the counterculture failed to allow for this. Misled
by the extraordinary attention the bemused media gave its
activities, it overestimated the numbers of the converted. Or
it was content to limit its appeal to an audience of under-thirties,
perhaps assuming that generational change by itself would
guarantee cultural revolution. In any case, in the heat and
excitement of the moment, too little was done to translate
new cultural values into real options the greater public could
understand and take seriously. Worst of all, the counterculture
grossly underestimated the power of its conservative opposition and the durability of established institutions. Vietnam and
Watergate brought down presidential administrations, but the
urban-industrial leadership simply regrouped, waited, and fought
back. When the dust finally settled, the military-industrial complex was just as solidly in the saddle, evangelical Christians
were wielding more influence than hippies or flower children
ever dreamed of having, Ronald Reagan was leading America
into the most shameless era of corporate greed since the days

of Calvin Coolidge, and middle-America was convinced that salut-
ing the flag was the highest order of public business.

Still, I am prepared to believe that our society's brief, breathless
experience of countercultural dissent may have managed to shift
the collective consciousness at least a little in the direction of a timely,
new politics. In a later book written in the late seventies (*Person/Planet:
The Creative Disintegration of Industrial Society*, which is really the
companion volume to this work) I set myself the task of deciding
what had survived out of the turbulence of the sixties that was of
enduring value. Two things, I concluded. Our society had developed a more complex and modulated sense of the self that allowed
for greater introspection and variety. It had also developed a keener
sense of its ecological responsibility. And the two, I am convinced,
are one, the personal and the planetary aspects of the culture that
awaits us on the far side of our troubled industrial adventure.

—*Theodore Roszak*
   Berkeley, California, January 1989

Where the Wasteland Ends

The Last Days were announced to St. John by a voice like the sound of many waters. But the voice that comes in our day summoning us to play out the dark myth of the reckoning is our meager own, making casual conversation about the varieties of annihilation . . . the thermonuclear Armageddon, the death of the seas, the vanishing atmosphere, the massacre of the innocents, the universal famine to come . . .

Such horrors should be the stuff of nightmare or the merely metaphorical rancors of old prophecy. They aren't. They are the news of the day, by now even growing stale (for some) with reiteration. They descend upon us, not as the will of capricious gods, but as the fruit of a politics held to be pre-eminently practical, of down-to-earth policy and tough-minded, dollars-and-cents realism. Governing elites, empowered by the consent of multimillionfold majorities, have piloted us deliberately along our way. We have not stumbled into the arms of Gog and Magog; we have *progressed* there. The peculiar genius of our culture—*"our* culture" meaning the culture of white, western masculinity and its many admiring or envious imitators—only now reaches its full height. Never before so much power, knowledge, daring, opulence, dynamism. Never so many great adventures in the making. And that is the worst of it—that even the genocidal end we prepare for our species shines with a Promethean grandeur. Who can escape being torn between the yes and the no?

This book is about the religious dimension of political life. How else to talk politics in an apocalyptic era?

The religion I refer to is not that of the churches; not the religion of Belief and Doctrine, which is, I think, the last fitful flicker of the divine fire before it sinks into darkness. Rather, I mean religion in its perennial sense. The Old Gnosis. Vision born of transcendent knowledge. Mysticism, if you will—though that has become too flabby and unrefined a word to help us discriminate among those rhapsodic powers of the mind from which so many traditions of worship and philosophical reflection flow. My purpose is to discover how this, the essential religious impulse, was exiled from our culture, what effect this has had on the quality of our life and course of our politics, and what part the energies of transcendence must now play in saving urban-industrial society from self-annihilation. By the time you and I have finished with the unlikely speculations that fill these pages, I will be content if intellect divorced of its visionary powers looks to you rather more like the mad rationality it is—and if the politics of eternity appears more relevant to the politics of time than you once found it convenient to admit.

This is as unconventional a treatment of politics as of religion. Little time is spent here on many hotly debated issues of the day; nor is there much I offer that will pass muster as orthodox sociology or economics. Instead, what follows is largely given over to the exploration of magic and dreams, science and alchemy, idolatry and the sacramental awareness, visionary poetry and the tricks of perception. I confess at the outset that I have not the head to contribute much that is original to the discussion of these august subjects. Yet they are here—because I no longer know any way to be significantly political without bringing them in; because it has become too great a strain to continue regarding the sickness of spirit so long festering among anxious artists and philosophers of our society as the private wound of a sensitive few. We are long past the time for pretending that the death of God is not a political fact.

The repression of the religious sensibilities in our culture over the past few centuries has been as much an adjunct of social and economic necessity as any act of class oppression or physical exploitation; it has been as mandatory for urban-industrial development as the accumulation of capital or the inculcation of factory discipline upon the working millions. And it has been achieved with as much ruthlessness. If we have not been accustomed to think of this harsh secularization of consciousness as a political issue, this has been—in part—because the damage suffered has overspilled the obvious class barriers; it has fallen as heavily on the social elite as on the masses, and so has lacked the invidious contrast politics normally requires. Universal evils are less actionable than partisan iniquity, though hardly for that reason less real.

Moreover, the secularization of our culture has been attended by a high idealism along its entire course; it has been seen by many of our finest thinkers not only as inevitable, but as a prerequisite of freedom. The major movements for social justice have almost without exception joined in that celebration; drawing on a legitimate anti-clericalism and a healthy cynicism for promises of pie-in-the-sky, they have been fiercely and proudly secular in their politics. The loss of the transcendent energies in our society has been taken by few radical leaders of the past two centuries to be a privation as great as any due to physical hardship or the violation of personal dignity. For the most part, it has not been experienced as a loss at all, but as an historical necessity to which enlightened people adapt without protest, perhaps even welcome as a positive gain in maturity.

Now all this is changing. There is a strange, new radicalism abroad which refuses to respect the conventions of secular thought and value, which insists on making the visionary powers a central point of political reference. This book is written against a background of significant, if as yet amorphous religious renewal in the western world. I realize there are many who prefer to denigrate or trivialize this widespread preoccupation with the varieties of religious sensibility, with communal ritual and the contemplative disciplines, with the therapeutic yogas of sensory awareness and organic integration. For the Christian establishment, much of this is a whoring after alien, antinomian gods. For conventional humanism, it is an affront to Reason and a contemptible failure of nerve. For left-wing ideologues, it is a betrayal of social conscience, if not a sign of downright bourgeois decadence. For the mass media, it is a faintly sensational fad. For the majority of middle Americans, it is a shocking offense to good manners and common sense. I think I understand the suspicion which any overt interest in occult or mystic experience evokes. At other times in my life, I have been on the side of such hostile and belittling responses. I also recognize the cheap modishness, the mindless excess, and the selfish escapism that can characterize such interests. Nevertheless . . . I am convinced that these pejorative views are mistaken, and that it is a waste of energy to let easy targets for ridicule distract attention from greater meanings.

The religious renewal we see happening about us—especially among disaffiliated young people, but by no means only among them—seems to me neither trivial nor irresponsible, neither uncivil nor indecent. On the contrary, I accept it as a profoundly serious sign of the times, a necessary phase of our cultural evolution, and—potentially—a life-enhancing influence of incalculable value. I believe it means we have arrived, after long journeying, at an historical vantage point from which we can at last see where the wasteland ends and where a culture of human wholeness and fulfillment begins. We can now recognize that the fate of the soul is the fate of the social order; that if the spirit within us withers, so too will all the world we build about us. Literally so. What, after all, is the ecological crisis that now captures so much belated attention but the inevitable extroversion of a blighted psyche? Like inside, like outside. In the eleventh hour, the very physical environment suddenly looms up before us as the outward mirror of our inner condition, for many the first discernible symptom of advanced disease within.

This book stems from the conviction that, in the course of our generation, many proud traditions of protest and reform have grown as depleted as the life-resources of that environment may soon be. It is the energy of religious renewal that will generate the next politics, and perhaps the final radicalism of our society. Already it is those who speak from the perspective of that renewal who provide the shrewdest critique of our alienated existence, the brightest insight into the meaning of liberation. What I offer here is in no sense a report on current religious manifestations; nor is it another tour of the Human Potentials Movement. That has been done well enough and often enough already. Certainly I am not out to give a blanket endorsement to every last ecstatic tremor that ripples over the contemporary scene. I am in no position either to report or endorse. Rather, this is meant as an independent contribution to the adventure of spiritual regeneration, a discussion of themes and problems of the religious sensibility that have long held my attention. Perhaps some will find in it a portion of my thought and experience that will bring a little greater clarity to their quest. At the least my hope is to give this regenerative movement some sense of cultural and sociological location so that its political intelligence may be sharpened.

The general framework in which I will be working is this:

Politics—in its principled conduct, but often in its perversions as well—draws upon culture for its sanctions, needing a good, a true, and a beautiful by which to command widespread acquiescence. *Culture* is the embodiment of a people's shared reality, as expressed in word, image, myth, music, philosophy, science, moral style. *Reality* marks out the boundaries of what might be called the collective mindscape, the limits of sane experience. Thus politics is metaphysically and psychologically grounded. Always. But as long as politics does not call the culture into question, or culture the politics, people may pay little attention to this metaphysical and psychic dimension of political life. It may only vibrate in the background like a groundtone so constant that it is only perceived as silence; nevertheless all else must harmonize with it or seem intolerably discordant.

The mindscape to which our culture has been shaping itself over the past three centuries—and with ever more decisive urgency since the advent of industrialization—is the creation of modern science. Science, in its turn, has reared itself on certain continuities of consciousness it inherits from the Judeo-Christian tradition of the west. What is important in the examination of a people's mindscape is not what they articulately know or say they believe. In that respect, our society is, at the popular level, all but scientifically illiterate. What matters is something deeper: the feel of the world around us, the sense of reality, the taste that spontaneously discriminates between knowledge and fantasy. It is in all these respects that science has become the dominant force in designing the psychological and metaphysical basis of our politics.

That is why we will be paying close attention to science in this study—especially to its odd psychology and its role in contemporary political life. Science is not, in my view, merely *another* subject for discussion. It is *the* subject. It is the prime expression of the west's cultural uniqueness, the secret of our extraordinary dynamism, the keystone of technocratic politics, the curse and the gift we bring to history. Where social thought on the dilemmas of urban-industrial life refuses to touch science critically, it betrays its essential conservatism and can only finish with shallow understanding. It has begged the big question. Its intention may still be revolutionary, but the revolution it aspires to will leave the cultural framework intact. The classic example of this kind of revolutionary endeavor is the politics of Marxist radicalism, especially as it has been practiced in the industrial west. Here, Marxism has prided itself on its realism precisely because it raises no doubts regarding the worldview of western science and the essential rightness of industrialism. "Consciousness," as Marx wielded the term, meant "class" consciousness: the outraged recognition of injustice used to intensify group loyalty. Marx laid a deadly critical edge against bourgeois social values, but his blade barely scratched the mindscape of science and industrialism. Hence, in the Soviet Union and in China today, there are no capitalists left; but, oddly enough, all the artistic banalities and crude materialist sensibilities of the nineteenth century bourgeoisie live on, now fiercely enforced by official edict. Any of John Galsworthy's philistine Forsytes might serve nicely to head up a ministry of culture in the people's republics.

On the other hand, in the industrial west, we remain heavily saddled with capitalist business and politics as usual, if lately mellowed and grown highly sophisticated in its public relations. But our culture, while dominated by science-based industrialism, has been in revolutionary ferment since the industrial economy first began to devour the landscape. The origin of this ferment lies in that tempestuous artistic outburst we call the Romantic movement. From it, we inherit a stubborn counter cultural resistance to the pre-eminence of science, to its technological elaborations and to its manifold imitators in the humanities, arts, and so-called behavioral sciences.

Significant that this rebellious opposition consciousness should have emerged most vividly in the arts—and should have largely remained there, giving us our singular tradition of the artist as outlaw, rebel, lunatic, misfit, rogue. Why should this be? Perhaps because the burden of alienation weighs most heavily on the creative powers; because the beauties of science are not the beauties of art but their antithesis. Who recognizes a cage for what it is? Not canaries of careful Reason who value well-fortified shelter, but skylarks whose song needs the space and sunlight beyond the bars. And what does it tell us about the nature of our religious tradition in the west that it should be the arts and not the churches that have produced far and away the greater number of modern martyrs, persecuted prophets, and suffering saints? A theme we shall return to many times in the chapters that follow.

If I had to summarize the purpose of this book in a sentence, I might call it an effort to work out the political meaning of William Blake's prophetic poems—especially *Vala, Milton,* and *Jerusalem.* That Blake was a fire-eating radical and the ally of the English Jacobins has long been obvious from his life and from much of his writing. But the political significance of his "mental fight" against the psychology of science and the culture of industrialism has been less appreciated—least of all in his own lifetime, when the task of keeping a minimum of skin stretched over one's bones was a full-time struggle for millions. Yet even during those first agonies of industrialization, Blake recognized there was another, darker politics unfolding beneath the surface of class conflict. He saw in the steady advance of science and its machines a terrifying aggression against precious human potentialities—and especially against the visionary imagination. The "mind-forg'd manacles" he assailed were not simply the fetters of social oppression. They were that. But they were far more. Blake's attack struck through the "dark Satanic mills"—at Newton, at Locke, at Bacon. The cause was that of Jesus the Imagination. The enemy was Urizen, Blake's mythical demon of Reason and technical power mad with his lust "to vegetate the divine vision." It is not the least evil the forces of social injustice have worked in our culture that they have for so long distracted our attention from this underlying spiritual violation by imposing upon us issues as urgent as sheer physical survival.

Blake's effort was to redesign the mindscape of an alienated culture, to return his society to spiritual realities that had vanished from its consciousness. His politics has waited a long while for its day to come. And even now, his cannot be everybody's cause. Not yet. Granted the great issue is always the size of our lives. But that issue is confronted by people on many different historical horizons. Deprived of bread or the equal benefits of the commonwealth, the person shrivels. Obviously. And that is a clear line to fight on. But when the transcendent energies waste away, then too the person shrivels —though far less obviously. Their loss is suffered in privacy and bewildered silence; it is easily submerged in affluence, entertaining diversions, and adjustive therapy. Well fed and fashionably dressed, surrounded by every manner of mechanical convenience and with our credit rating in good order, we may even be ashamed to feel we have any problem at all. Certainly from the viewpoint of the poor and excluded, we have nothing to complain about.

It would be a disservice to Blake—and the defeat of my own intentions—if this book should in the least dull the edge of anyone's revolution. The world cries out for revolution— for the revolutions of bread, and social justice, and national liberation. Not for a moment do I deny that fact (though my own pacifist and anarchist instincts make me dubious that violent militancy can for a certainty achieve those ends). But it needs the *next* revolution too, which is the struggle to liberate the visionary powers from the lesser reality in which they have been confined by urban-industrial necessity. And I do deny that this liberation can be achieved automatically by a politics belonging to an earlier historical horizon. It requires a revolution in its own right. Only those of us who have reached the horizon of the technocratic society are ready for that postindustrial revolution. We alone can know the impoverishing price we have paid for the old ideals. We alone can untangle the terrible paradox of progress which gives us this world where things get worse as they get better.

Why, in our time, have societies well endowed with industrial plenty and scientific genius turned uglier with totalitarian violence than any barbarous people? Why does the moral blight of nationalist bigotry and the disease of total war continue to haunt the children of the Enlightenment, more oppressively now than in the age of Voltaire? Why do nihilism and neurosis brood over what we please to call the "developed" societies, taking as great a toll of human happiness as gross physical privation in the third world?

Is it not clear enough that these are the many twisted faces of despair? We conquer nature, we augment our power and wealth, we multiply the means of distracting our attention this way and that . . . but the despair burrows in deeper and grows fatter; it feeds on our secret sense of having failed the potentialities of human being. A despairing humanity is not merely an unhappy humanity; it is an ugly humanity, ugly in its own eyes—dwarfed, diminished, stunted, and self-loathing. These are the buried sources of world war and despotic collectivism, of scapegoat hatred and exploitation. Ugly hates beautiful, hates gentle, hates loving, hates life. There is a politics of despair. Out of despair, people rush to the counterfeit community of the totalitarian state. Out of despair, they invent themselves fantastic enemies that must be punished for their own failure. Out of despair, they grow burdened with moral embarrassment for themselves, until they must at last despise and crucify the good which they are helpless to achieve. And that is the final measure of damnation: to hate the good precisely because we know it is good and know that its beauty calls our whole being into question.

Once we fall that far, we may soon enough begin to yearn for the peace of annihilation. Then it is no trick to endorse the lunatic realism of those who undertake so methodically to build the machinery of that yearning. Even the rascals and self-serving mandarins who pilot the technocratic politics of urban-industrial society are afflicted by this despair born of diminished consciousness. They are largely the agents of a corrupted consensus; but a consensus which the makers of the *last* revolution have done as much as any to impose. It was Marx who disparaged visionary experience as "mere phantoms formed in the human brain" and religious aspiration as no better than the pain killer of long-suffering victims. It was Lenin who called religion "one of the most abominable things in the world" and who said, "while production is always necessary, democracy is not." It is Chairman Mao who, instead of socializing the long-restricted wisdom of his people's heritage, crowds it out of awareness with the cult of industrial discipline and the crude mystique of the dynamo.

True, there have been the noble stoics who, with Bertrand Russell, have lived unflinchingly by the belief that "only on the firm foundation of unyielding despair can the soul's habitation henceforth be safely built." Nevertheless, to embrace the life of alienation is to embrace a tragic illusion. And people do not live well by illusions. Rather, they will fill the vacuum in their hearts with something . . . anything . . . if need be, with the murdering worship of nation, race, class.

Perhaps it was inevitable that we should give ourselves body and soul to the scientific and industrial revolutions. The change came so suddenly and promised so much. But, properly, urban-industrialism must be regarded as an *experiment*. And if the scientific spirit has taught us anything of value, it is that honest experiments may well fail. When they do, there must be a radical reconsideration, one which does not flinch even at the prospect of abandoning the project. Surely, as of the mid-twentieth century, urban-industrialism is proving to be such a failed experiment, bringing in its wake every evil that progress was meant to vanquish. It is not the paraphernalia of that experiment which accounts for the failure, not the machines, not the technical ingenuity, certainly not the healthy human desire for a measure of ease and material security. What *is* to blame is the root assumption which has given the machines and desires a demonic animation: that the transcendent aspirations of mankind can be, *must* be translated into purely secular equivalents; that culture—if it is to be cleansed of superstition and reclaimed for humanitarian values—must be wholly entrusted to the mindscape of scientific rationality. I know there are those who believe fervently that, within the limits of that assumption, the good society may yet be built—if only our humanistic resolve is sufficiently strong. I disagree. Humanism is the finest flower of urban-industrial society; but the odor of alienation yet clings to it—and to all culture and public policy that spring from it. That is a hard judgment, and not one I have arrived at easily in my own life. No one arrives there without making a severe reappraisal of what he takes to be sane, true, and real. Surely it is an anguish of the mind and no little humiliation of the ego to be driven so far back into the rudiments of experience, behind the consensual worldview, behind the security of personal identity.

I think, at bottom, this is why the religious propensities of the counter cultural style are so slighted or scorned, even by radicals and liberal intellectuals who otherwise would endorse its social dissent. Because this is where one can feel the chasm suddenly open out between the old politics and the new. To question the sufficiency of science even as an adequate understanding of the non-human world, to reject the validity of the secular ideals from which men and women have for so long drawn their vital motivation, is to shake the stone on which our orthodox reality stands—and that cannot help but be a fearful event. One does not give over to the alternative realities without summoning up forces of nature and mind which urban-industrialism was designed to exclude, never to contain.

There are dragons buried beneath our cities, primordial energies greater than the power of our bombs. Two thousand years of Judeo-Christian soul-shaping and three centuries of crusading scientific intellect have gone into their interment. We had assumed them dead, forgotten their presence, constructed our social order atop their graves. But now they wake and stir. Something in the mode of the music, in the mind-rhythms of the time disturbs them. I am as aware as any that these dragon forces are nothing to be trifled with, even if one thinks they are no more than subjective passions. Nevertheless, to admit that urban-industrialism is erected upon a culture of alienation is like admitting that an edifice tall as the clouds and centuries in the building has been raised on a rotten foundation. Sooner or later, that foundation must be dug up and rebuilt—though the edifice should be toppled and the dragons below aroused. Let us hope they will wake to be gentle beasts after all.

It will not be my conclusion that the industrial economy should be abruptly scrapped in favor of a paleolithic primitivism. I have no idea what such a proposition even means, though it is the straw man usually pressed forward as the single alternative to the status quo by those who will hear no evil of industrial progress. Yet science-based industrialism must be disciplined if it is to be made spiritually, even physically livable. There must be a drastic scaling down and decentralizing; altogether, a renunciation of excesses of power and production which have become sick necessities for so many people—but a renunciation which is experienced as a liberation, not a sacrifice. Of course we must be selective in our winnowing out of the industrial experiment. Does that not go without saying? But selection requires a criterion of judgment. And here, the issue lies between those who believe that the culture of science can somehow generate its own principle of life-enhancing selection (the ideal of secular humanism) . . . and those (like myself) who believe that hope is bound to finish a despairing vanity.

The only standard of selection that will apply in these matters must grow from a living realization of what human destiny is. Perhaps no single mind, no single culture can grasp that destiny whole. But of this much I feel certain: that such a realization lies on a plane of experience which mainstream science does not embrace, *cannot* embrace without turning back on its own distinctive commitment. Alienation *means* being sundered from that dimension of life. And the alienated person is far too small and uneven a mirror to reflect more than a distorted portion of that destiny.

Only those who have pressed through and beyond the spell of science are capable of knowing this. Others, it sadly seems, will have first to surrender themselves to the urban-industrial imperative with fanatical conviction—as the west itself has done. Certainly the wretched of the earth are being left no choice in the matter. Those in the west who may care nothing whatever for their fate have nevertheless aroused their indignation and awakened their envy. As for the revolutionary leadership of the third world, what else can one expect its response to be to the argument of books like this but that of Dostoyevsky's Grand Inquisitor in his encounter with the risen Christ?

> Thou didst promise them the bread of Heaven, but I repeat again, can it compare with earthly bread in the eyes of the weak, ever sinful and ignoble race of man? And if for the sake of the bread of Heaven thousands and tens of thousands shall follow Thee, what is to become of the millions and tens of millions of creatures who will not have the strength to forego the earthly bread for the sake of the heavenly?

I fully expect that much of what I say here will be taken cruelly to task by the Grand Inquisitor's many disciples. And that is, I suppose, as it should be. If I did not think there were already enough to champion the Inquisitor's cause, doubtless I should do so myself, even knowing (as he knew) that it was a lie—but a lie born of compassion. Where people go hungry, to say that man does not live by bread alone is too easily misunderstood as an argument in favor of starvation.

Certainly the last voice that has any right to challenge the Inquisitor's diabolical politics is the voice of the well-fed. We must all live through our own history in sequence. At one horizon in time, the fully developed society glitters in the plains below like the promised land. At another, it proves to conceal within itself a wasteland of the spirit. Then dignity begins to mean something besides (though not instead of) a full stomach . . . and certainly something very different from equal access to an air-conditioned nightmare.

This study is pegged at that second horizon. What it discusses—dream thieving and idolatrous worship, the privation of the senses and the metaphysics of science—belongs to the radicalism of the next revolution. Blake, not Marx, is the prophet of our historical horizon.

> . . . Such is my awful Vision:
> I see the Four-fold Man, The Humanity in deadly sleep
> And its fallen Emanation, The Spectre and its cruel Shadow.
> I see the Past, Present and Future existing all at once
> Before me. O Divine Spirit, sustain me on thy wings,
> That I may awake Albion from his long and cold repose;
> For Bacon and Newton, sheath'd in dismal steel, their terrors hang
> Like iron scourges over Albion: Reasonings like vast Serpents
> Infold around my limbs, bruising my minute articulations.
> I turn my eyes to the Schools and Universities of Europe
> And there behold the Loom of Locke, whose Woof rages dire,

Wash'd by the Water-wheels of Newton; black the cloth
In heavy wreathes folds over every Nation: cruel Works
Of many Wheels I view, wheel without wheel, with cogs
   tyrannic
Moving by compulsion each other, not as those in Eden, which
Wheel within Wheel, in freedom revolve in harmony and
   peace.

One last remark before we begin. I realize that an unresolved
tension runs through this book. There are sections—mainly
the first few chapters—that are overcast with a bleak cynicism. They betray an oppressive sense of how grave our situation is and a genuine fear of the cunning and persistence of
the powers of darkness which exist not only on the social
scene but in every one of us. Other parts of the book reflect
high expectations for what the lively forces of cultural renewal now organizing themselves in the belly of the monster
may yet achieve. But these are not so much predictions as
they are one man's hope and fear presented as forcefully as it
was possible for me to give them voice. We are, as Samuel
Beckett has said, "between a death and a difficult birth." The
possibilities are clear to see. I know which I reject and
which I long to see achieved. But I trust to nobody's optimism, nobody's despair. Not yet.

To Betty
For the conversations where all
the best ideas happened.

For our contention is not with the flesh and blood,
but with dominion and authority, with the world-
ruling powers of this dark age, with the spirit
of evil in things heavenly.

Ephesians 6:12, quoted by
William Blake on the title page of *Vala*.

Crazy Horse dreamed and went into the world
where there is nothing but the spirits of
all things. That is the real world that is
behind this one, and everything we see here is
something like a shadow from that world.

Black Elk

I'd rather learn from one bird how to sing
than teach ten thousand stars how not to dance.

e. e. cummings

PART ONE

THE WASTELAND WITHIN
AND ABOUT US

How the urban-industrial revolution generated an artificial environment, and what style of politics and consciousness has followed from that environment.

Unreal City,
Under the brown fog of a winter dawn,
A crowd flowed over London Bridge, so many,
I had not thought death had undone so many.

T. S. Eliot

CHAPTER I

The Artificial Environment

> *Here is this vast, savage, howling mother of ours, Nature, lying all around, with such beauty, and such affection for her children, as the leopard; and yet we are so early weaned from her breast to society, to that culture which is exclusively an interaction of man on man—a sort of breeding in and in, which produces . . . a civilization destined to have a speedy limit.*
>
> *Henry David Thoreau*

THE FLIGHT FROM THE PRIMITIVE

For the average man and woman, enmeshed in the busy and intricate pattern of high industrial society, it doubtless requires a supreme exercise of the imagination to understand how their technologically primitive ancestors of one hundred centuries ago could have managed to survive at all, let alone survive with any passable degree of dignity. For most of us, the productivity, ease, and efficiency of our industrial economy—either as it is now or as we confidently believe it will soon become—contribute indispensably to our conception of the human condition. In their absence our health, our security, our sustaining hopes and aspirations, indeed the very meaning of our existence, would be jeopardized. When, therefore, we try to conceive of life within a simpler economic and technical order, it is difficult in the extreme to see beyond the readily apparent hardships we would then be required to suffer. As our imagination subtracts, one by one, the comforts and conveniences of modern life, we find ourselves drifting steadily toward what we can only understand to be a "backward" condition of life in which it would seem impossible for people to realize their full humanity.

So great is the technological distance between our time and even the very recent past, that we may find ourselves no less baffled to understand how those who inhabited the high civilizations of the preindustrial era could tolerate their onerous existence. By the criteria the United Nations uses to measure such matters, Athens of the Golden Age and China of the Tang dynasty were what we would now call "underdeveloped societies" which escaped only at their more aristocratic levels from a poor living not far removed from that of our contemporary peasant and primitive communities. And when we pause to consider the latter—these pathetic cultural anachronisms that struggle along in the midst of *our* world like so many anthropological sideshows—the contrast between their indigent stagnation and our superabundant dynamism seems to confirm at a glance our indisputable superiority.

While it is true that, here and there, images of a noble savagery, joyful and virtuous in the arcadian wilderness, appear in our literature and philosophy, the historical record proclaims unambiguously what western society's prevailing attitude has been toward primitive peoples. What have they ever really been for us but objects of contempt whom we have self-righteously driven to the poorest margins of existence, there to be massacred, forcibly acculturated, overwhelmed, or at best corralled into reservations for purposes of condescending protection and detached study? A few of the more sympathetic anthropologists may see something of enduring value in primitive folk; but for most others, the squalid human past which the primitives embody has but one redeeming value. It served to inch mankind, by trial and error, toward the great "take-off" point at which science and technology could come into their own to transform the earth marvelously and irreversibly. J. Bronowski only repeats urban-industrial society's death sentence upon the primitives when he concludes that

> they have failed in culture: in making a picture of the universe rich enough, subtle enough—one that they can work with and live by beyond the level of the Stone Age. They have failed because they did not create a mature view of nature, and of man too.

The words are those of a philosopher of science; they might just as well be those of any Sunday supplement . . . of the *Reader's Digest* . . . of the local Chamber of Commerce. It is one of those grand self-congratulatory judgments which great minds and small alike can endorse.

Whatever doubts our gloomier artists and intellectuals may have developed over the past few generations about the idea of progress, the average person of our day, convinced in his bones of the imperative rightness of the urban-industrial pattern of life, is immersed in a worldview that makes nothing so unthinkable as the proposition that his pre-modern predecessors or contemporaries could have anything to teach him that is humanly valuable. Despite the fact that urban-industrialism makes up but the slenderest fraction of man's experience on earth (perhaps only two tenths of 1 per cent—and that largely limited to Western European society) it is *that* culture alone which dictates for most of us not only how life ought to be lived, but must be lived. It is the manifest destiny of humankind. For who can seriously doubt that the genes in our protoplasm are there to be scrutinized and improved upon, or that the moon is there to be conquered by technical ingenuity? Which is to say that, however much science has revolutionized the life of the average man and woman, it has scarcely made their thinking less stubbornly ethnocentric than it was in the days of the paleolithic hunting camp.

THE URBAN-INDUSTRIAL IMPERATIVE

There exists a rock-solid consensus in urban-industrial society as to what is the proper measure of our progress beyond the primitive. It is the degree to which the environment we inhabit becomes more artificial, either by way of eliminating the original given by nature or by way of the predictive anticipation and control of natural forces. To be sure, the human environment must always have a touch of the artificial about it. One might almost say that the living space of human beings is destined to be "naturally artificial" to the extent that they spontaneously surround themselves with artifacts and institutions and with cautious, customary deliberations about their future. Human beings invent and plan and imaginatively embroider—and the result is culture, a buffer zone of the man-made and man-construed which it is as proper for humanity to inhabit as it is for plant and animal to reside in their sphere of tropisms and reflexes and instinctive responses. But in acknowledging the cultural capacity of human beings, we must not ignore the fact that there *is* a natural environment—the world of wind and wave, beast and flower, sun and stars—and that preindustrial people lived for millennia in close company with that world, striving to harmonize the things and thoughts of their own making with its non-human forces. Circadian and seasonal rhythms were the first clock people knew, and it was by co-ordinating these fluid organic cycles with their own physiological tempos that they timed their activities. What they ate, they had killed or cultivated with their own hands, staining them with the blood or dirt of the effort. They learned from the flora and fauna of their surroundings, conversed with them, worshiped them, and sacrificed to them. They were convinced that their fate was bound up intimately with these non-human friends and foes, and in their culture they made place for them, honoring their ways.

It would be impossible to exaggerate how important to the evolution of human consciousness this prolonged intimacy between the human and non-human was, though it is not an easy realization to recapture beyond the purely verbal-cerebral level. Unhappily, this poor, devitalized word "nature" which we must use to speak of the non-human world has lost its force by coming to mean for us an objectified realm of miscellaneous physical things and events which is outside of and other than us. We tend, for example, to think of "nature poetry" as poems that speak of daffodils or sunsets, a single possible subject matter among many, and at this point rather an outmoded one because largely irrelevant to the life of modern urban society. We forget that nature is, quite simply, the universal continuum, ourselves inextricably included; it is that which mothered us into existence, which will outsurvive us, and from which we have learned (if we still remember the lesson) our destiny. It is the mirror of our identity. Any cultural goods we produce which sunder themselves from this traditional, lively connection with the non-human, any thinking we do which isolates itself from, or pits itself against the natural environment is—strictly speaking—a delusion, and a very sick one. Not only because it will lack ecological intelligence, but because, more critically still, it will lack psychological completeness. It will be ignorant of the greatest truth mankind learned from its ancient intimacy with nature: the reality of spiritual being, with whose loss and recovery we will be much involved in later chapters.

Until well into the industrial period, the natural environment—that which was neither humanly made nor controlled—was never far removed from the routine round of mankind's daily life. Throughout much of the civilized past, even those who lived in that most humanly regulated of abodes, the city, knew that not far beyond the town limits untamed wilderness and forest held possession. The town walls of medieval Europe may have been a fair defense against the wolf; but they were useless against the plague-bearing rat, who could, even in the time of the high Renaissance in Italy, panic urban populations into mass exodus and bring great cities to a standstill. Within the city itself, until the very recent advent of modern sanitation, the tenor of life preserved much of the noisome earthiness of the rural village —to a degree that would be intolerable even in many American ghettos today. The grime and stench of animals filled the streets; the fetor of sickness, death, and human wastes was never absent. Imperial Rome, equipped with better sanitary engineering than many eighteenth-century European cities, still dumped its dead in *carnaria* just beyond the city wall. In Dr. Johnson's London, one might happen upon the decaying bodies of starved paupers in cellars and garrets; in English industrial towns until well into the nineteenth century, pigs continued to be the major street cleaners. In the New York of that day cattle were still being driven through the business district to be publicly butchered, and—in an incident no further back than 1844—a citizen out for a walk along the Bowery was gored to death by an angry bull escaped from the herd.

We take legitimate pride in whatever success we have had in eliminating such crudity and unpleasantness from our midst. But we forget that, while these afflictions freely interpenetrated life even in the shelter of the city, they served as constant, if often harsh reminders to people of their dependence upon forces of nature they could never hope to subjugate. At this existential boundary, where human self-sufficiency gave way before the indomitable and inscrutable power of the non-human environment, men and women discovered that experience of psychic contingency which they attributed to the presence of the sacred. The embrace of nature may often have been rough, even murderous, as when nature assumed the formidable aspect of Mother Kali; but it was nonetheless an embrace. Locked within it, mankind found a sense of the human limits which precluded both arrogance and that dispiriting conviction of cosmic absurdity which haunts contemporary culture.

In our time, the opportunity to live a life completely enveloped by the man-made and man-controlled has increased rapidly and enormously. We are in the way of suffering what can justly be called a cataclysm of urbanization. It was only in 1850 that England, the first industrial society, became as much as 50 per cent urban. Today, nearly 40 per cent of the world as a whole lives in urban areas; in another fifteen years, the figure will rise to over 50 per cent. In another fifty years, very nearly 100 per cent of the global population will be living in cities of over one million, with the largest megalopolitan complexes totaling well above one billion residents. These supercities will merely be the integrated versions of what we today call "urban sprawl": a Bosnywash stretching from Boston through New York and Philadelphia to Washington; a San Difranangeles running down the Pacific coast from San Francisco to San Diego.

Such headlong urban concentration, it should be clear, has nothing to do with industrial necessity and little to do with population pressure. Industrial plant, no longer anchored to inflexible, bulky steam power, could easily and with great advantage be decentralized nowadays. And the rapid urbanization of many countries in Asia, Africa, and Latin America is happening at the cost of crippling depopulation in village and rural areas still quite capable of supporting life at a higher level than is possible in the shantytowns that encircle Calcutta or Lima or Stanleyville. One could in fact make an excellent case that rapid, massive urbanization in both the developed and underdeveloped societies is extremely antifunctional—though few economists have troubled to do so. Both those who make decisions about the course of history and the millions who are their trusting publics have simply accepted urbanism as, inevitably, a key measure of development—like it or not. They have mistaken a style of life for a necessity of life. That is why urbanism must be treated, with industrialism, as a separate and parallel force in what we call the modernization of the world. The building of megalopolitan complexes is no longer a derivative of industrialization, but an imperative in its own right, because only the urban showcase serves to display the industrial pattern of life, its products and values, with maximum visibility and intimidating eminence. It is the stage on which we have chosen to enact the drama of our time; it is our collective mindscape physically embodied. The supercity alone guarantees the utmost in artificiality, which is the unquestioned goal of progress.

Already in the western world and Japan millions of city-dwellers and suburbanites have grown accustomed to an almost hermetically sealed and sanitized pattern of living in which very little of their experience ever impinges on non-human phenomena. For those of us born to such an existence, it is all but impossible to believe that anything is any longer beyond human adjustment, domination, and improvement. That is the lesson in vanity the city teaches us every moment of every day. For on all sides we see, hear, and smell the evidence of human supremacy over nature—right down to the noise and odor and irritants that foul the air around us. Like Narcissus, modern men and women take pride in seeing themselves—their products, their planning—reflected in all that they behold. The more artifice, the more progress; the more progress, the more security. We press our technological imperialism forward against the natural environment until we reach the point at which it comes as startling and not entirely credible news to our urban masses to be told by anxious ecologists that their survival has anything whatever to do with air, water, soil, plant, or animal.

Is it any wonder that they find these ecological forebodings the most difficult of all scientific expertise to accept? How much of their environment do most city-dwellers ever see and use in the raw? Remarkably little, compared to the overwhelming amount that comes to them pre-packaged, arranged, purified, remodeled, and, according to all the most reliable reports, *enriched*. How easily we forget that behind the technical membrane that mediates our life-needs, there *is* ultimately a world not of our making and upon which we must draw for sustenance. The air conditioner must still rely upon a respirable atmosphere; the chlorinated, fluoridated, piped-in water supply must still connect with potable lakes and rivers; the neatly displayed cans, jars, and cartons in the supermarket must still be filled with the nutritive fruits of the earth and the edible flesh of its animals.

I can recall still the day my daughter first realized that the meat we ate at home was the flesh of slaughtered animals. She was then eight and a half years old, city born and bred, and only learned the terrible truth when she visited her first European butcher shop. There she saw the unmistakable carcasses of cattle, pigs, sheep, and poultry openly displayed. The connection dawned upon her as a brutal shock; and as much of a shock to me to realize that she had not until then known such a basic fact of life. But then, how could she? In America, she had known meat only as something we bought at the supermarket frozen, neatly carved, and plastic-wrapped. Not a hoof or a claw or a bloody pelt in sight. These chunks of food simply emerged from a screened-off back room of the store where the gore and guts were hidden from view. She knew the meat "came from" animals; but her thought was that animals *gave* meat the way cows *gave* milk.

The incident was as instructive for me as it was for my daughter. It made me vividly aware of how remote we can become from the resources of our daily life. With the result that we grow hopelessly stupid about our relations with the natural environment. We live off land and forests, animals, plants, and minerals; but what do we know of their ecological necessities or the integrity of their being? How can we, in our ignorance, make responsible decisions about resources we can only recognize and name when they arrive to us at the end of a long line of processing?

Yet even if we were to trace our life-needs back to their ostensible origin, we would finally be confronted with insurmountable barriers of artificiality which screen off basic nature as much from those who raise and produce our food as from ourselves—so determined have we become to subordinate the natural environment. Agriculture today is largely a species of industrial mass production worked up off a soil that is little more than a chemical blotter. Increasingly, the business is swallowed up by conglomerate companies which clearly have no love or knowledge of farmcraft, but only perceive the land and its produce as so many profit and loss statistics in their ledgers. The fruits and vegetables themselves have already been predesigned to the commercial specifications of a food research industry that dictates the color, shape, size, taste, and aroma of every last grape and pea. The researchers know the natural product will be unacceptable to the eyes and palates of consumers who have learned from books, advertising copy, and canned goods what food is *supposed* to look and taste like. Our eggs are pumped out of carefully dieted battery hens that never see the light of day. Our meat comes to us from factory farms where immobilized, fast-fatted cattle and pigs are fed by the time clock and scientifically tranquilized to hold down the often violent anxiety that comes of lifelong close confinement. These beasts we eat are all but a fabricated counterfeit; we do not even grant them the dignity of setting foot in the open air once in a lifetime. For after all, what difference does *their* dignity make to *us?* Meat is meat, isn't it?

Not only does the artificial environment blind us to the paramount facts of our ecology, but we become convinced that there are human substitutes for everything we exhaust or contaminate. The scientists can manufacture vitamins and wonder drugs, can they not? They can spin cloth and building materials out of pure chemicals. Then surely, if need be, they can conjure sunshine, fresh air, clean water, nutritious foods out of their magic test tubes . . . or discover ways to cure us of the ailments that follow from their absence. Have they not already promised us programmed genetics and surgical immortality by way of major organ transplants? "We cannot duplicate God's work," a medical researcher quoted in *Newsweek* (April 24, 1967) tells us, "but we can come very close."

To lament the expanding empire of urban-industrialism is one of the oldest and seemingly most useless preoccupations of social criticism. Since Rousseau and the Romantics, hostility toward the artificial environment has run through our culture like a soft, lyrical counterpoint to the swelling cacophony of the machine. This book, in fact, will seek to associate itself in a discriminate and positive way with that great lost cause which has done so little to impede the technological imperative. Yet what chance of success can the Romantic critique enjoy as long as the gains—both material and moral—of increased artificiality are so widely and spontaneously felt to outweigh the costs? Even such imponderable values as creativity, dignity, and heroism have become inseparably wedded in the popular imagination with our power to boss nature about and to surround ourselves with the products of advanced technology. We have come to believe that mankind is never so essentially human as when it is cast in the role of *homo faber*. It is upon inventing the machine, Buckminster Fuller tells us, that "man . . . began for the first time to really employ his intellect in the most important way." And J. Bronowski echoes the sentiment: "that is where the human mind realized itself most fully: in the cities that stand at the peak of technical achievement in their time. That is where great men flower . . ."

THE GREAT DIVIDE

But if it seems cranky to lament the expanding artificiality of our environment, the fact underlying that lament is indisputable, and it would blindness to set its significance at less than being the greatest and most rapid cultural transition in the entire history of mankind. This is the historical great divide—in one sense, quite literally. In little more than a century, millions of human beings in Europe and America—and their number grows daily throughout the world—have undertaken to divide themselves off more completely and irremediably from the natural continuum and from all that it has to teach us of our relationship to the non-human, than ever before in the human past.

It is all too easy to obscure this pre-eminent truth by conjuring up a picture of the remaining wide-open spaces—the mountain fastnesses and desert solitudes, the faraway islands and jungle thickets—and then to conclude, consolingly, that the cities will never encroach upon these remote corners of the earth. But that is wishful thinking already belied by fact and supported only by a misconception about the way in which urban-industrialism asserts its dominance. True enough, urban sprawl may never swallow these outlying areas into its concrete and steel maw. But that is not the only way the supercity propagates its power.

Before industrialism, most cities stood apart as modest workshops or markets whose ethos was bounded by their own walls. They were an option in the world, one way of life among many possibilities. The supercity, however—or rather the artificial environment taken as a whole—stretches out tentacles of influence that reach thousands of miles beyond its already sprawling perimeters. It sucks every hinterland and wilderness into its technological metabolism. It forces rural populations off the land and replaces them with vast agrindustrial combines. Its investments and technicians muscle their way into the back of every beyond, bringing the roar of the bulldozer and oil derrick into the most uncharted quarters. It runs its conduits of transport and communication, its lines of supply and distribution through the wildest landscapes. It flushes its wastes into every river, lake, and ocean, or trucks them away into desert areas. The world becomes its garbage can—including the capacious vault of the atmosphere itself; and surely outer space and the moon will in due course be enlisted for this unbecoming function, probably as the dumping ground for rocket-borne radioactive refuse.

In our time, whole lakes are dying of industrial exhaust. The seemingly isolated races of Lapland and Tierra del Fuego find their foodstuffs riddled with methyl mercury or radioactivity and must appeal to civilized societies to rescue them from their plight. The Atmospheric Sciences Research Center of Scotia, New York, reported in December 1969 that there was no longer a breath of uncontaminated air to be found anywhere in the North American hemisphere and predicted the universal use of artificial respirators throughout America within two decades. Thor Heyerdahl, sailing the Atlantic on the *RA II* expedition in 1970, reported finding not one oil-free stretch of water during the crossing. Jacques Piccard, exploring the depths of the seas, warned the United Nations in October 1971 that the oceans of the world would soon be incapable of sustaining aquatic life due to lead exhaust, oil dumping, and mercury pollution, with the Baltic, Adriatic, and Mediterranean seas already too far deteriorated to be saved.

But these now well-publicized forms of pollution are not the only distortive force the artificial environment exerts upon the rest of the world for the sake of sustaining its lifestyle. A single oil pipeline across the wild Alaskan tundra is enough to subordinate its entire ecology (ruinously) to urban-industrial needs. A single superhighway built from São Paulo to Brasília deprives an entire rain forest of its autonomy. Already the land bordering the Trans-Amazonian Highway has been staked out for commercial and urban development; the beasts are being killed or driven off and the natives coerced into compliance with official policy by methods that include the strategic use of infectious diseases. The fact is, there remains little wilderness anywhere that does not have its resources scheduled on somebody's industrial or real estate agenda, less still that is not already piped and wired through with the city's necessities or criss-crossed by air traffic skylanes.

And then there is the tourism that goes out from the cities of the affluent societies like a non-stop attack of locusts. Whatever outright industrial pollution and development may spare, tourism—now the world's largest money-making industry—claims for its omnivorous appetite. There are few governments that have the stamina and self-respect to hold out against the brutal pressure to turn their land and folkways into a commercial fraud for the opulent foreigners who flatter themselves that they are "seeing the world." All the globe trotters really see, of course (or want to see), is a bit of commercialized ethnic hokum and some make-believe wilderness. Just as the world becomes the dumping ground of the urban-industrial societies, it also becomes their amusement park. And how many are there now, even among my readers, assiduously saving up for summer safaris in Kenya or whirlwind junkets of "the enchanted Orient," without any idea what a destructive entertainment they are planning—but of course at bargain prices?

The remnants of the natural world that survive in the experience of urban-industrial populations—like the national parks we must drive miles to see, only to find them cluttered with automobiles, beer cans, and transistor radios—are fast becoming only a different order of artificiality, islands of carefully doctored wilderness put on display for vacationers and boasting all the comforts of gracious suburban living. It is hard to imagine that within another few generations the globe will possess a single wild area that will be more than thirty minutes removed by helicopter from a television set, an air-conditioned de-luxe hotel, and a Coca-Cola machine. By then, the remotest regions may well have been staked out for exotic tours whose price includes the opportunity to shoot a tiger or harpoon a whale—as a souvenir of one's rugged vacation adventure. The natives will be flown in from central casting and the local color will be under the direction of Walt Disney productions. The visitors—knowing no better—will conceive of this charade as "getting away to nature." But in truth it will be only another, and a climactic aspect of the urban-industrial expansion.

What we have here is an exercise in arrogance that breaks with the human past as dramatically and violently as our astronauts in their space rockets break from the gravitational grip of the earth. And the destination toward which we move is already clearly before us in the image of the astronaut. Here we have man encapsulated in a *wholly* man-made environment, sealed up and surviving securely in a plastic womb that leaves nothing to chance or natural process. Nothing "irrational"—meaning nothing man has not made, or made allowance for—can intrude upon the astronaut's life space. He interacts with the world beyond his metallic epidermis only by way of electronic equipment; even his wastes are stored up within his self-contained, mechanical envelope. As for the astronaut himself, he is almost invariably a military man. How significant it is that so much of our future, both as it appears in science fiction and as it emerges in science fact, should be dominated by soldiers—the most machine-tooled and psychically regimented breed of human being: men programmed and under control from within as from without. Can any of us even imagine a future for urban-industrial society in which the heroes and leaders—those who explore the stars and handle the crises—are not such a breed of warrior-technician?

What is there left of the human being in our militarized space programs but a small knot of neural complexity not yet simulable by electronic means, obediently serving the great technical project at hand by integrating itself totally with the apparatus surrounding it? In this form—cushioned and isolated within a prefabricated, homeostatic life space and disciplined to the demands of the mechanisms which sustain it—the astronaut perfects the artificial environment. Here is a human being who may travel anywhere and say, "I am not part of this place or that. I am autonomous. I make my own world after my own image." He is packaged for export anywhere in the universe. But ultimately all places become the same gleaming, antiseptic, electronic, man-made place, endlessly reproduced. Ambitious "world-planners," like the students of Buckminster Fuller, already foresee a global system of transportable geodesic domes that will provide a standardized environment in every quarter of the earth. Something of such a world is with us now in the glass-box architecture of our jet-age airports and high-rise apartments. One can traverse half the earth in passing from one such building to another, only to discover oneself in a structure indistinguishable from that which one has left. Even the piped-in music is the same.

These are momentous developments. The astronautical image of man—and it is nothing but the quintessence of urban-industrial society's pursuit of the wholly controlled, wholly artificial environment—amounts to a spiritual revolution. This is man as he has never lived before; it draws a line through human history that almost assumes the dimensions of an evolutionary turning point. So it has been identified by Teilhard de Chardin, who has given us the concept of the "noosphere," a level of existence that is to be permanently dominated by human intellect and planning, and to which our species must now adapt if it is to fulfill its destiny. So too, Victor Ferkiss has described technological man as a creature on the brink of an "evolutionary breakthrough." Technology, by giving man "almost infinite power to change his world and to change himself," has ushered in what Ferkiss calls an "existential revolution" whose spirit is summarized by the words of Emmanuel Mesthene.

> We have now, or know how to acquire, the technical capability to do very nearly anything we want. Can we transplant hearts, control personality, order the weather that suits us, travel to Mars or Venus? Of course we can, if not now or in five years or ten years, then certainly in 25 or in 50 or in 100.

The Greek tragedians would have referred to such a declaration as *hubris*—the overweening pride of the doomed. It remains *hubris;* but its moral edge becomes blunted as the sentiment descends into a journalistic cliché. Moreover, we have no Sophoclean operations analyst to give us a cost-benefit appraisal of its spiritual implications. The sensibility that accompanies technological omnipotence lacks the tragic dimension; it does not take seriously the terrible possibility that a society wielding such inordinate power may release reactive forces within the human psyche, as well as within the repressed natural environment, that will never allow it to survive for the fifty or one hundred more years it needs to exploit its capabilities.

THE TECHNOLOGICAL COALESCENCE: ITS USE AND ABUSE

By far the most highly (and deservedly) celebrated aspect of urban-industrial expansion is the worldwide technological coalescence it has brought about. The physical isolation of cultures has been abolished and all people everywhere are now drawn into a common fate. No age before ours has possessed such a wealth of materials with which to draw the self-portrait of the human race. Not that we needed modern transport and communication to inspire the vision of human universality. The fellowship of mankind and the ethical energy it demands (need one recall?) have been before us as an ideal at least since the age of Buddha and the rhapsodic prophets. What technology has brought us is the superior means of shared experience and, under the threat of thermonuclear annihilation, the necessity of universal caring. It has brought the apparatus that enables us, and the crisis that forces us to turn the old vision into an historical project.

But in the very process of achieving this new world unity, we—and by "we" I here mean peculiarly the white western middle classes—have suffered a gross distortion of the sensibilities. It is as if in amassing the sheer physical energy the technological coalescence demanded of us, we have burned away our deeper awareness of the opportunity and responsibility that are uniquely ours. In the chapters that follow I hope to suggest how this degeneration of consciousness has come about in our culture.

Our technology ought to be the means of a universal cultural sharing, and we who "discovered" the rest of the world should be the most eager to share, learn, and integrate. Instead, from the outset, we have mistaken the invention and possession of this means as the self-evident sign of cultural superiority, and have at last made the technology itself (and the science on which it is based) a culture in its own right— the *one* culture to be uniformly imitated or imposed everywhere. Our technology, freighted with all the prestige the western hegemony can lend it, communicates nothing so efficiently as itself: its attendant values and ideologies, its obsession with power-knowledge, above all the underdeveloped worldview from which it derives. Though some may celebrate such ironies, what is it but the death of dialogue when the medium blocks out every message and asserts only itself? In the communist nations of Europe and Asia alone during this century, we have seen more than one third of the human race scrap its finest traditions wholesale in order to adopt a Marxist-Leninist ideology of development which is but a comic caricature of nineteenth-century bourgeois scientism.

There have been the few—the artists, the philosophers, the scholars—who have risen to the level of the age and have used the technological coalescence as a true forum where the cultures of past and present may meet as self-respecting equals. And perhaps the young people one now sees backpacking their way across the globe have tried to enter the world more authentically than the legions of tourists who bounce from one vacation paradise to another. But at this point the currents of change do not run in the direction of dialogue and sharing. The international unities that matter significantly remain those of trade, warfare, and technics: the unities of power. The world is being bound together by the affluent societies in ingenious networks of investment, military alliance, and commerce which, in themselves, can only end by propagating an oppressive urban-industrial uniformity over the earth. Yet there is no lack of "forward-looking" opinion makers who accept that uniformity as the highest expression of a world culture. They mistake the homogenized architecture of airports, hotels, and conference centers—which is as much as many jet-set intellectuals ever see of the world—for an authentic sharing and synthesis of sensibilities.

Either that, or they identify as a glorious multiplication of "options" the glossy cosmopolitan eclecticism now available to the educated and citified. But even as urban-industrial populations have the varied cultural fare of the world laid before them in their theater, television, cinema, art galleries, restaurants, supermarkets, book shops, and newsstands, urban-industrialism expands aggressively to blanket the globe, crowding out every alternative that does not agree to reduce itself to the status of museum piece. Thus, while urban-industrial society grows intellectually fat on a smorgasbord of cultural tidbits, the world as a whole is flattened beneath the weight of its appetite and becomes steadily poorer in real *lived* variety. Herman Kahn gazes into the future and sees a "mosaic society" containing innumerable alcoves and enclaves of minority taste and custom. So too Alvin Toffler sees our society as one that enjoys "an explosive extension of freedom," "a crazy-quilt pattern of evanescent lifestyles." Yes, but both the mosaic and the crazy quilt have a design—and the design is that of an urban-industrial global monopoly.

Within that cultural monopoly and on its terms, we may have a variety of nostalgic fads and eccentric novelties, hobbies and entertainments; but nothing for real and for keeps. And outside the monopoly, nothing, nothing, nothing at all. In another two generations, there will be no primitive or tribal societies left anywhere on earth—and they are not all giving up their traditional ways because they freely choose to. In another three generations, no self-determining rural life. In another four generations, no wildlife or wilderness on land or sea outside protected areas and zoos. Today there are few societies where official policy works to preserve wilderness and the old ways of life as serious alternatives to the urban-industrial pattern; at best, they are being embalmed and tarted up as tourist attractions. Of course there are those who think the accessible counterfeit is far superior to any reality one must take pains to approach and know. After all, the whole force of urban-industrialism upon our tastes is to convince us that artificiality is not only inevitable, but better—perhaps finally to shut the real and original out of our awareness entirely. It was about such corrupted tastes that Hans Christian Andersen wrote his story of the nightingale, one of the supreme parables of our time. How many still read and understand it?

As things stand now, we are apt to have a worldwide artificial environment long before an authentic world culture or an ethical community of mankind has had the chance to become more than the failed aspiration of a few sensitive, inquiring minds. The Oneness of humanity properly means communion of vision and concern, and from this a new integration of consciousness. Instead, we have settled for the artificial environment under the debased leadership of the technocratic elites we shall discuss in the chapter that follows; we have begun with a mere material sameness and physical integration, and now use that environment as the procrustean bed to whose size all values and sensibilities must be tailored.

And how rapidly it is happening. The Coca-colonization of the world within little more than a century's time, the emblems and political imperatives of urban-industrialism carried to every remote corner of the earth. How can any people be so sure about so much?

Is the alternative to the urban-industrial dominance some manner of anti-technological, anti-urban fanaticism? I think not, and, as a born and bred urbanite who craves the life of the city, I would hardly be the person to champion such an extreme position. The fact is that much of my resistance to the artificial environment stems from its poisonous effect upon the qualities I value in an authentic city life. Megalopolis is as much the destroyer of cities as of wilderness and rural society —a point we will return to in Chapter 12 where I hope to suggest a more modest and life-enhancing place for the city and the machine in our world.

DISNEYLAND IS BETTER

Until somewhere within the last few generations, the prevailing popular attitude toward untamed nature in western society was one of belligerent distrust grounded in fear. The face of nature was the face of wolf and tiger, plague and famine, insurmountable obstruction and inscrutable mystery. Nature was Goliath, oppressor and enemy against whom we held no more likely weapon than the slingshot of our monkey cunning. The odds were not in our favor.

But then, quite suddenly, the war against nature came to an end for the urban-industrial millions; it was over and decisively won. The turning point is marked by no single event, but by the stupendous accumulation of discoveries and new technical possibilities that have followed the advent of atomic energy. True, journalists may still speak of outer space as hostile territory needing to be "conquered"; a few recalcitrant diseases hold out against us; now and then we suffer a natural disaster or two. But who (besides a few worrywart ecologists) doubts that even these remaining obstacles to human dominance will in time be brought under control? And meanwhile we know how to make good the damage, rebuild to our profit, and carry on to still greater heights. Clearly the old adversary's teeth have been drawn. In the stronghold of our artificial environment, what have we any longer to fear from the non-human? All the mountains have been scaled, all the sea-depths explored. The course of great rivers and the behavior of our genes can now be redesigned to our specifications.

So nature—or at least what most of us still know of her through the mediation of technical manipulation and scientific authority—no longer wears the look of a serious opponent. Instead, she has come to seem, in her humiliation, rather pathetic and (once we puzzle out her tricky mechanisms) highly incompetent, needing to be taken in hand and much improved. There seems to be nothing she sets before us that we could not dismantle if we put our mind to it; nothing she does that we cannot find a way of doing bigger, better, faster. Even her grandeur survives only by our sufferance. Not long ago, there were those in the Pentagon who talked seriously of using the moon as a missile testing target, perhaps of knocking off a few sizable chunks. What a show of military prowess that would be!

This is the monumental novelty the artificial environment has introduced into the mindscape of our time: that the non-human world should have become for us an object of such casual contempt. As if our vision, closed in by these glass and concrete urban contours, could no longer look before and after and discern the context of our being. Of course it is only proper that people, like all living things, should strive to make a livable place for themselves in the world. Who can imagine it otherwise? But the state of soul in which we undertake the project—*that* is what makes the difference.

A personal anecdote: a sign of the times. Several years ago, on a cross-country trip, my family and I were foolish enough to visit Yellowstone National Park during the summer crush. We expected it to be crowded but hardly—as it was—more congested than downtown San Francisco. The traffic for forty miles leading into the park and all the way through was packed bumper to bumper. There was not an inch of solitude or even minimal privacy to be found anywhere during the two days we stayed before giving up and leaving. Never once were we out of earshot of chattering throngs and transistor radios or beyond the odor of automobile exhaust. We spent a major part of each day waiting in line to buy food or get water. And at night, the coming and going of traffic and crowds made sleep nearly impossible. Ah, wilderness . . .

All this was bad enough to convince me that, if any true respect for wildlife survived in me, my duty hereafter was to stay away from it and spare it my contribution to such desecration. But the worst came on the day we decided to visit Old Faithful. At the site we discovered what might have been a miniature football stadium: a large circle of bleachers packed thick with spectators devouring hot dogs and swilling soft drinks while vendors passed among them hawking souvenirs.

The center of attraction was the geyser which—as all the world must know—erupts promptly once each hour. To prove the point, a large clock stood nearby with a sign indicating exactly when the next eruption would happen. Loudspeakers were located around the area, and through them a park guide kept up a steady monologue giving every conceivable statistic about the geyser's geology and performance —as if to certify its status as a veritable marvel of nature. But most of what he said was drowned in the roar of the crowd.

Beside us on the bleacher seat we occupied was a family of five, the father and three children equipped with ornate and expensive cameras. They were extremely impatient for the show to begin. All were guzzling Coke and timing the geyser, somewhat skeptically, on their wrist watches. Finally the great event came. The guide made one loud, urgent appeal for attention, the crowd stilled momentarily, and Old Faithful went off on schedule. For all the carnival atmosphere, it was an impressive phenomenon to witness. There was even a scattering of applause and cheers as the water gushed up in several ascending spurts.

But many of the spectators, like the father and three children beside me, were far too preoccupied to ogle the spectacle. For no sooner did the geyser begin to blow than their eyes vanished behind their cameras, as if for sure the best way to have this experience was through a lens and on film. The children, eager to catch Old Faithful at its very zenith, kept asking their father throughout the eruption, "Now, Dad? Now?" But the father, apparently expecting the geyser to split the heavens, restrained them. "No, not yet . . . wait till she really gets up there."

But Old Faithful only rises so high, and then the show is over. Before this family of photographers had snapped their pictures, the veritable marvel of nature had bubbled back beneath the earth. The father's face emerged from behind his camera, frowning with disbelief. "Is that all?" he asked, with the belligerent voice of a man who knows when he is not getting his money's worth. "I thought it was supposed to go higher," his wife said. The children were no less crushed with disappointment. As they got up to leave, one of the boys sourly remarked, "Disneyland is better." And the whole family agreed.

CHAPTER 2

Citadel of Expertise

The people's trust in their new intellectual leadership is, by its very nature, totally different from that which they once placed in their theological leaders. Trust in the opinions of experts has a completely different character. The fear that there will one day be established a despotism based on science is a ridiculous and absurd fantasy. Such a thing could only arise in minds wholly alien to the positivist idea.

Claude Henri Saint-Simon

FROM LUXURY TO CONVENIENCE TO NECESSITY

When I was growing up during the 1930s, there still existed a quaint American folkway called "pleasure driving." On Sunday afternoons my family, like many another, would take off in the automobile for no place in particular to spend several hours motoring along quiet country lanes outside the city limits, stopping to picnic beside the road or to park by river, lake, or other attractive landscape. The pleasure drive was the city-dweller's chance to widen horizons and clean out the lungs, perhaps to buy some fresh vegetables from farmers along the way or to pick berries in the woods. There were families I knew that kept the car locked away all week for use only on these special occasions.

But even then, the custom was in its last days. By the late thirties the roads were already beginning to gag on their traffic. The quiet country lanes were becoming harder to find and the long drive back to town at the end of the day had become a daunting struggle. It was somewhere in the course of the Second World War, as I recall, that people stopped thinking about the car as a luxury and began to call it a "convenience"—even a *"necessary* convenience," much sought after especially by suburbanites as a supplement to overburdened commuter trains. Then, in the late forties, as public transport began to wither away or break down hopelessly throughout much of America, the car was promoted to the status of absolute "necessity"—and so it remains. In many American cities, it is now a greater necessity than food, clothing, or shelter, because it is the very means of getting to work and to market. Without a car, no job and no groceries.

In such necessities there are no joys; only troubles and expense. The pleasure drive has long since become extinct, as accessible open country round about the cities has retreated before a ubiquitous vista of busy freeways and turnpikes bordered by unsightly slurbs. One drives past such eyesores at as fast a clip as possible, seeing nothing and breathing pure exhaust. At the end of the trip, one competes for overpriced parking places in inner cities which madly cannibalize their beauties in a vain effort to move traffic and park cars. The cost of the vehicle increases, the cost of its maintenance increases, the cost of its insurance increases, the smog increases, the emotional strain of battling traffic increases, the number of fatalities claimed by the "four wheel disease" increases. What has become of the convenience? What has become of the widening horizons—in any sense other than oppressive and unengaging distances covered? These are the forgotten hopes of earlier generations. Those of us now on the road know only the crushing necessity and all the insurmountable problems accruing. We sit stewing in an expanding traffic jam and cry out for someone to speed us on our way. But the only "practical" solutions seem to come from a new species of expert called the traffic engineer, who, not surprisingly, holds a vested interest in traffic. And so his prescription involves more ambitious highways still, the widening of thoroughfares, and spectacular experiments in rerouting—all of which sacrifice more open land and urban space to the automobile. Typically, all the solutions finish by compounding the problem and elevating it to a higher pitch of urgency.

There are few articles of technological furniture in our artificial environment that have not made the same dismal transition from luxury to convenience to necessity . . . perhaps finally—like the automobile—to become an outright curse that many thoughtful people now talk seriously of eliminating from our lives altogether. We have become so technologically musclebound in so many ways that the major preoccupation of our technics is no longer to conquer the now subservient natural world, but to unscramble the chaos of its own making. In short order, the artificial environment has treacherously turned into public enemy number one and the losses threaten to cancel out the gains.

How much of what we readily identify as "progress" in urban-industrial society is really the undoing of evils inherited from the *last* round of technological innovation? In England, the cradle of industrialism, one looks in vain to find more than a handful of reforms in the period from Arkwright and

Watt down to World War I (the so-called "age of improvement") which were not essentially efforts to cancel out social dislocations born of industrialism in the first place. So in our own day, we "progress" toward scientific husbandry by way of nitrate fertilizers and hyper-lethal pesticides, only to discover the noxious ecological consequences when they are well advanced. Then we move to correct the imbalance and confidently identify this as progress too. A moribund patient flat on his back in a hospital bed can also be said to be making such progress if he is further from death today than yesterday. But he is nowhere near being a healthy person.

THE SCIENTIZATION OF CULTURE

Since Charlie Chaplin's *Modern Times,* people as the victims of their own technical genius have been a standard subject of popular comedy. But the ironies of progress are far more than laughingstock for casual satire. Even crusading reformers like Ralph Nader or Paul Ehrlich who gamely challenge each new criminality or breakdown of the system, often fail to do justice to the depth of the problem. While each failure of the technology may allow us to pillory a few profiteering culprits for incompetence or selfishness, the plain fact is that few people in our society surrender one jot of their allegiance to the urban-industrial system as a whole. They cannot afford to. The thousand devices and organizational structures on which our daily survival depends are far more than an accumulation of technical appendages that can be scaled down by simple subtraction. They are an interlocking whole from which nothing can easily be dropped. How many of us could tolerate the condition of our lives if but a single "convenience" were taken away . . . the telephone . . .

automobile . . . air conditioner . . . refrigerator . . . computerized checking account and credit card . . . ? Each element is wedded to the total pattern of our existence; remove any one and chaos seems to impend. As a society, we are addicted to the increase of environmental artificiality; the agonies of even partial withdrawal are more than most of us dare contemplate.

From this fact springs the great paradox of the technological mystique: its remarkable ability to grow strong by virtue of chronic failure. While the treachery of our technology may provide many occasions for disenchantment, the sum total of failures has the effect of increasing our dependence on technical expertise. After all, who is there better suited to repair the technology than the technicians? We may, indeed, begin to value them and defer to them more as repairmen than inventors—just as we are apt to appreciate an airplane pilot's skill more when we are riding out a patch of severe turbulence than when we are smoothly under way. Thus, when the technology freezes up, our society resorts to the only cure that seems available: the hair of the dog. Where one technique has failed, another is called to its rescue; where one engineer has goofed, another—or several more— are summoned to pick up the pieces. What other choice have we? If modern society originally embraced industrialism with hope and pride, we seem to have little alternative at this advanced stage but to cling on with desperation. So, by imperceptible degrees, we license technical intelligence, in its pursuit of · all the factors it must control, to move well beyond the sphere of "hardware" engineering—until it begins to orchestrate the entire surrounding social context. The result is a proliferation of what Jacques Ellul has called "human techniques": behavioral and management sciences, simulation and gaming processes, information control, personnel administration, market and motivational research, etc., —the highest stage of technological integration.

Once social policy becomes so determined to make us dance to the rhythm of technology, it is inevitable that the entire intellectual and moral context of our lives should be transformed. As our collective concern for the stability of urban-industrialism mounts, science—or shall we say the scientized temperament?—begins its militant march through the whole of culture. For who are the wizards of the artificial environment? Who, but the scientists and their entourage of technicians? Modern technology is, after all, the scientist's conception of nature harnessed and put to work for us. It is the practical social embodiment of the scientific worldview; and through the clutter of our technology, we gain little more than an occasional and distorted view of any other world. People may still nostalgically honor prescientific faiths, but no one—no priest or prophet—any longer speaks with authority to us about the nature of things except the scientists.

The scientists are no doubt what John Ziman has called them: "humble practical men who have learnt from experience the limitations of their arts, and know that they know very little." Caution and diffidence are the classic characteristics of the scientific personality. But Ziman goes on:

> Why should we even want to decide whether a particular discipline is scientific or not? The answer is, simply, that, *when it is available,* scientific knowledge is more reliable, on the whole, than non-scientific. . . . In a discipline where there is a scientific consensus the amount of *certain* knowledge may be limited, but it will be honestly labelled: "Trust your neck to this," . . .

The humility we are confronted with here is not unlike that of Undershaft's son in Shaw's *Major Barbara*. The modest young man had nothing more to say for himself than that he knew the difference between right and wrong.

If we lose sight of the arrogance that lies hidden in Ziman's "humble practical men" of science, who simply happen to know the difference between what is reliably so and what isn't and who possess the only means of telling the difference, it is doubtless because their claim makes such perfect sense to us. All the metaphysical and psychological premises of that claim have become the subliminal boundaries of the contemporary mindscape; we absorb them as if by osmosis from the artificial environment that envelops us and which has become the *only* environment we know. The scientists simply work within this universally endorsed reality. They search for what that reality defines as knowable and—with strict professional integrity—feel obliged to entertain no alternative realities. Scientific knowing becomes, within the artificial environment, the orthodox mode of knowing; all else defers to it. Soon enough the style of mind that began with the natural scientists is taken up by imitators throughout the culture. Until we find ourselves surrounded by every manner of scientific-technical expert, all of them purporting to know as the scientist knows: dispassionately, articulately, on the basis of empirical evidence or experiment, without idiosyncratic distortion, and if possible by the intervention of mathematics, statistics, or a suitably esoteric methodology.

In urban-industrial society, nothing enjoys much chance of being dignified as knowledge which does not proceed from such an epistemological stance. Therefore, we must have objective and specialized scrutiny of all things, of outer space and the inner psyche, of quasars and of sex, of history and of literature, of public opinion and personal neurosis, of how to learn and how to sleep and how to dream and how to raise babies and how to relax and how to digest and how to excrete. Take up the catalog of courses issued by any of

our great multiversities—the mills of our "knowledge industry"—and there you find the whole repertory of expertise
laid out. And does it not cover every inch of the cultural
ground with scientized specialization? What is there left
that the non-expert can yet be said to know? Name it—and
surely it will soon be christened as a new professional field
of study with its own jargon and methodology, its own
journals and academic departments.

THE SYSTEMS APPROACH

Given the extent of this empire of expertise, it might seem
at first glance incomprehensible that urban-industrial society
has any serious problems left at all. With such a growing
army of trained specialists at work accumulating data and
generating theory about every aspect of our lives, we should
surely have long since entered the New Jerusalem. Obviously
we have not. But why? The answer most commonly forthcoming in recent years is that our expertise has simply not
been properly co-ordinated; it has been practiced in too
narrow, disorganized, and myopic a way. So we begin to
hear of a new panacea: the "systems approach"—and in years
to come, we shall undoubtedly be hearing a great deal more
about it.

Systems analysis, derived from World War II and Cold
War military research, is the attempt to solve social problems
by ganging up more and more experts of more and more kinds
until every last "parameter" of the situation has been blan-
keted with technical competence and nothing has been left to
amateurish improvisation. The method is frequently mentioned nowadays as the most valuable civilian spin-off of our
aerospace programs. We are told that the same broad-gauged

planning, management, and decision making that have succeeded in putting a man on the moon can now be used to redesign cities and reform education. In brief, systems analysis is the perfection of Ellul's "human technique." To quote the military-industrialist Simon Ramo, one of the great boosters of the approach, it is the effort to create a "multiheaded engineer," a "techno-political-econo-socio" expert

> who must include in "his" head the total intelligence, background, experience, wisdom, and creative ability in all aspects of the problem of applying science, and particularly, who must integrate his total intelligence . . . who must *mobilize* it all—to get real-life solutions to real-life problems.
>
> In this sense, then, a good systems-engineering team —and we have begun in the United States to develop such groups—combines individuals who have specialized variously in mathematics, physics, chemistry, other branches of physical science, psychology, sociology, business finance, government, and so on.

Notably, the good systems team does not include poets, painters, holy men, or social revolutionaries, who, presumably, have nothing to contribute to "real-life solutions." And how should they, when, as Ramo tells us, the relevant experts are those who understand people "as members of a system of people, machines, matériel, and information flow, with specific well-described and often measurable performance requirements"? Above all, the experts are those who can place "quantitative measures on everything—very often, cost and time measures."

One might well ask at this point: but is this "science"? —this doctrinaire mathematicization of the person and society, this statistical manipulation of human beings as if they were so many atomic particles? In later chapters, I will try to trace the genealogy which does, in fact, make Simon Ramo and the terrible systematizers legitimate offspring of Galileo and Newton. But as far as contemporary politics is concerned, the question is wholly academic. Such behavioral engineering is taken without question to be science by those who practice it, by those who subsidize its practice, and by most of those upon whom it is practiced. And the promised reward for such unquestioning deference to scientific expertise is glowing indeed; no less, in Ramo's words, than a "golden age."

> Once most people are wedded to creative logic and objectivity to get solutions to society's problems, the world is going to be a lot better. Then maybe we can say an important thing, namely, that science and technology are then being used to the fullest on behalf of mankind.

The message is clear. The ills that plague urban-industrial society are not techno-genetic in essence; they are not the result of a radically distorted relationship between human beings and their environment. Rather, they result from an as yet incomplete or poorly co-ordinated application of scientific expertise. The province of expertise must, therefore, be broadened and more carefully administered. Urban-industrial society, having hopelessly lost touch with life lived on a simpler, more "primitive" level, and convinced beyond question of the omnipotence of technical intelligence, can do no other than trust to ever greater numbers of experts to salvage the promise of industrialism. Accordingly, the principal business of education becomes the training of experts, for whom progressively more room is made available in government and the economy. From our desperate conviction that the endangered artificial environment is the *only* livable environment, there stems the mature social form of industrial society: the technocracy.

THE CITADEL OF EXPERTISE

The continuities of tradition, ideology, and inherited institutions—severely ruptured though they have been by the urban-industrial revolution—may never allow a perfect technocracy to come into existence in any society. Certainly the pure technocratic system that Francis Bacon heralded in his *New Atlantis* and which Saint-Simon, Auguste Comte, and Thorstein Veblen were later to champion, is best regarded as no more than an ideal type of what Saint-Simon called "the administrative state"—the society beyond politics to which social engineers like Simon Ramo might aspire. If one were to declare oneself foursquare for such an institutionalized regime of the experts, the reaction from most citizens and politicians would doubtless be hostile. "Technocracy Incorporated," the American political movement of the 1920s and 1930s which openly advocated such an H. G. Wells government of the technicians, attracted only a meager following—and understandably so. Our national societies are committed one and all to the preservation of ideals, symbols, and rhetoric left over from the preindustrial past or from nineteenth-century ideologies which spoke the language of class struggle and political economy, not technics. These cultural remnants are still very much with us, and there is no denying that in various ways they retard the speedy and open maturation of the technocracy. Politics must still wear a political costume; it must have somewhat to do with elected representation, ethical debate over policy, and competition for office. At least for the sake of appearances, the hands on the levers of power must be those of politicians —and the politicians must continue to pretend they serve the general will of the citizen body as expressed by conventional electoral means.

Yet it is the essence of social criticism to enumerate the ways in which the democratic intention of such political principles has been utterly subverted with one degree of subtlety or another by those possessing money or guns, property or bureaucratic privilege. The language and iconography of democracy dominate all the politics of our time, but political power is no less elitist for all that. So too the technocracy continues to respect the formal surface of democratic politics; it is another, and this time extraordinarily potent means of subverting democracy from within its own ideals and institutions. It is a citadel of expertise dominating the high ground of urban-industrial society, exercising control over a social system that is utterly beholden to technician and scientist for its survival and prosperity. It is, within modern society, what the control of the sacramental powers was to the medieval church—the monopoly of all that people value and revere: material plenty, physical power, a reliable and expanding body of knowledge. To be an expert or (as is more often the arrangement) to *own* the experts in the period of high industrialism is to possess the keys to the kingdom, and with them a power that neither guns nor money alone can provide, namely mastery over the artificial environment, which is the only reality most people any longer know.

Contemporary politics tends toward technocracy wherever the mystique of industrial expansion or the zeal for development come to dominate the hearts and minds of people— and that means just about everywhere on earth. Whether we are dealing with societies as superindustrialized as America or as underdeveloped as many new African and Asian states, competent, realistic, responsible government means a crisp air of bustle and forward-looking dynamism, with a steady eye on the growth rate and the balance of payments. It means much confabulation with the statistical enigmas of the economic index and a sober concern for the big technological inevitables to which one's society *must* without question adapt. It means, therefore, being smartly in step with the best technical and economic expertise money can buy. "Like a national flag and a national airline," E. J. Mishan observes, "a national plan for economic growth is deemed an essential item in the paraphernalia of every new nation state."

Even the surviving sheiks and shahs of the world must cloak their public relations in pretensions of technological glory; they must be able to pose confidently for pictures against a background of hydroelectric projects, freeways, air terminals. Everywhere it is the appearance (if not always the reality) of change, newness, efficiency that legitimates political control. Nothing else will qualify in the eyes of the world as a proper claim to power and privilege. Even where the state is barbarically repressive, the governing regime will seek to gild its image with the evidence of economic progress. Think, for example, of how our state department justifies its support for dictatorships in Brazil and Spain, Taiwan and South Korea. These, we are assured, are progressive, development-oriented governments. We need only be told that the growth rate in Brazil in recent years has been above 9 per cent, and enough said. Justice, freedom, dignity are almost unanimously understood to be the automatic results of successful development . . . in time. That is not true; but an intimidating world consensus believes it to be true. Even those who are clear-sighted enough to recognize that growth is of no guaranteed benefit to the wretched, for the most part limit their politics to the hard task of winning the excluded a secure place in the artificial environment. They do not question the desirability of that environment, and less so its necessity.

This is the sense in which contemporary politics is technocratic politics—even when what the experts themselves might

define as optimal rationality is thwarted by those who enlist
their services. Which is more often the case than not. In
practice, the experts work within limits not of their own
making. They are the chief employees and principal legitima-
tors of power, not its possessors. The well-designed technocracy must have on tap experts who are eager and able
to do *everything* technically feasible; but precisely what will
at last be done is seldom of the experts' choosing—though
their influence is far from negligible. Their chance to do
their thing much depends upon their talent for being loyal
employees. It is as Jean Meynaud has remarked in his study
Technocracy. Successful experts know how to combine "technical boldness" with "social conservatism." Their guiding light
is an ethically neutralized conception of "efficiency."

> Efficiency means putting facts before preconceived
> ideas. . . . Respect for the facts, which are always in
> advance of ideas, is one of the qualities often attributed
> to technicians, and one which they are always quick
> to claim. . . . Even when realities are irksome or ugly,
> the technician does not rebel against them. Technicians
> take the world as it is, without yielding to nostalgia
> or useless recriminations. . . . In a capitalist regime
> . . . technicians undoubtedly work towards consolidat-
> ing the whole system of powers exercised by owners
> and managers of the means of production, although it
> is true that many of them make the public good their
> criterion.

This does not mean that, like conscienceless automatons, the
experts surrender all capacity to criticize or dissent. There
may well be hot debate among them about options and
priorities and, quite sincerely, about "the public good." It
is simply that their debate does not reach very deep, nor is
it heard far off. Their disagreements do not extend to advocating major reallocations of social power, nor do they

challenge the cultural context of politics. Above all, good experts confine their dissent to the seminar table and the corridors of power where their peers can understand the jargon and where they can avoid the painful simplifications of popular controversy. It is the one overarching value all experts share: the preservation of intellectual respectability against those who would vulgarize the mysteries of the guild.

THE VARIETIES OF TECHNOCRACY

For the near future, as urban-industrialism assimilates the ethnic continuities and economic conditions of different societies, we are apt to see a variety of bastardized technocracies spread across the world's political landscape. I say "bastardized" because none of these industrial states is apt to measure up to the Baconian ideal type, in which the scientist-technician was fully in charge. Rather, they will be societies that tailor their rationality to suit the interests of dominant commissars or capitalists or bureaucrats. All the technocracies we see abuilding in the world today are in the hands of what Veblen called "saboteurs"—those who undertake a "conscientious withdrawal of efficiency" from the industrial process for their own selfish advantage. What Veblen did not foresee is that such sabotage can, with the aid of enough co-opted expertise, become remarkably "efficient" in its own right—certainly at mystifying the public and defending vested interests, but even at jacking up the economic index to dazzling levels of performance.

At present, the most prominent types of bastardized technocracy to be found in the world are the following:

1. In America, Western Europe, and Japan, *the suave technocracy*. This style is the ultimate expression of a mature,

administered capitalism, whose corporate structure has been so skillfully woven into the fabric of public life that it is impossible to imagine there was ever a time when AT&T or Dupont or GM did not exist. Surely they were installed in the universe by God along with the sun and the moon—and surely they must endure as long. Already the major American corporations and conglomerates are quasi-political institutions with a stability (not to mention a control of capital, people, and resources) that shames many governments. By way of the great military-industrial boondoggle, they share handsomely in the $75–90 billion the federal government now lays out annually for wars and weapons—always the fattest slice of the budget. The federal treasury (mainly the Department of Defense) contributes $16 billion alone to the total $28 billion currently (as of 1971) being spent by American corporations on the Research and Development which keeps their innovative capacities racing well ahead of public comprehension or criticism. The "think tanks," which generate the most daring R & D, brainstorm everything from Styrofoam eggs to counterinsurgency warfare; but mainly they serve to quarter a well-salaried and -exercised reserve army of experts who may always be called up to certify official and corporate policy.

The world influence of the major corporations grows by the year as their multinational organization overlaps political frontiers and undercuts the authority of nation states. Professor Howard Perlmutter has predicted a degree of global consolidation among the corporate giants that will, by 1985, place the bulk of the world's economic power in the hands of two hundred multinational firms, possibly by then incorporated under the United Nations or the World Bank. Many of these firms will be tied into "trans-ideological mergers" with socialist governments—like the recent agreement of the Soviet state insurance agency to underwrite American investments in the third world against the risk of expropriation or the much-rumored Russian-American-Japanese venture to exploit Siberian oil—and so will have more to do with the shape of world affairs than the official foreign ministries. Their bookkeeping will be the real story of international relations.

Given this Olympian stability (especially of the one hundred American corporations that now control half the nation's manufacturing assets) the suave technocracy can well afford to be benign (relatively speaking) and pluralistic. It is therefore—at least potentially—far more open to reform than other forms of technocracy. In dealing with dissent, its strength lies in having learned to substitute the absorbency of the sponge for the brute force of the truncheon. That is, I should think, a welcome measure of civilized progress by anybody's standards—though it guarantees nothing about democratic vitality. The suave technocracy knows how to accommodate much divergence—but without significantly redistributing power or changing the direction of main line social policy. It is even willing to flirt with social protest for the sake of cozening it. It can let long hair grow in high places. It knows how to swing.

The suave technocracy is much like the cybernated industrial systems it watches over; it is a well-programmed software machinery aimed at achieving precision control with little sweat and a minimal use of energy. It specializes in pervasive manipulation rather than top-down dictation, managing deftly to coax a national order out of the seeming chaos of inherited institutions. For example, in America the educational system—a critical component of the technocratic society—is, at the local level, a baffling confusion of school boards and PTAs. But by way of the major universities—where the influences of the government, the corporations, the military, and the foundations converge—a serviceable standard of "excellence" imposes itself on high-achieving students and their families. Draft deferments, college entrance requirements, competition for scholarships and jobs work together to insure a steady supply of the right kinds of brains. No need to commandeer the entire system; bribery and careful pressure at the periphery will do the trick. Doubtless, in the decade ahead, the major public and private corporations that undergird the European Economic Community (the Common Market) will find similarly unobtrusive ways to override the troublesome and outmoded national parliaments of the member states. Decisions of great consequence will simply unfold as matters of inexorable economic necessity —as interpreted by the Brussels-based bureaucracy of the EEC. The near non-existence of popular control over the Common Market's Council of Ministers and its economic planners promises to make the EEC the most effective suave technocracy in the world. For how else to compete with the dynamism of the American corporate establishment?

The suave technocracy has its secret police and its agencies of surveillance and intimidation; but these are of marginal importance in maintaining social cohesion within the mainstream. Much more effective is the ethos and economic manipulation of the big corporations which permeate the fabric of national life, controlling jobs, careers, markets, resources, tastes, habits of consumption, self-images. The corporations tie into politics and opinion making at all levels, from the local newspaper and chamber of commerce up to the secret paramilitary agencies which patrol their foreign investments and to the prices and incomes machinery of the Nixon New Economic Policy. All along the line they have generally succeeded in identifying their interest with the national interest. Among contemporary sociologists Herbert Marcuse has perhaps been most perceptive in uncovering the subtle psychic stratagems by which state and corporate elites befuddle discontent, cover up failures, and outflank dissent before it can make headway. His studies—like *One-Dimensional Man* —are a shrewd critique of the way in which subliminal techniques of persuasion (advertising, public relations, mass media imagery) work to make the status quo seem the best of all possible worlds.

The assimilative flexibility of the suave technocracy is both its greatest strength and weakness, and I confess to being totally uncertain how things will go in the societies where it predominates. As all the world knows, social protest within America, Japan, and Western Europe is now intense, widespread, and becoming more experienced by the year. Obviously if I did not think America was capable of significant radical change, I would not be writing this book. But in the swinging society, it is growing progressively more difficult to know who is outsmarting whom, so clever have the means of denaturing dissent become. It may well be that the technocrats will yet have their way with us, outwit or outlast their opposition, and speed us into the Brave New World well ahead of any other society.

2. The collectivist societies will probably continue for some while to be *vulgar technocracies,* grim-faced, heavy-handed, and much more overtly given over to a monolithic scientistic orthodoxy that recalls the English Benthamites. Under Russian influence, they inherit a weakness for the secret police methods of the Holy Alliance and have been weighed down intellectually by dim-witted, often vicious party hacks whose tastes are a musty legacy from the court of the Czars. If the suave technocracy resembles the delicacy of cybernation, the vulgar technocracy is the political analogue of steam power and the sweatshop; it relies on ponderous social controls coupled with an unrelenting ideological hard sell. It surely lacks finesse—as did those bourgeois *nouveaux riches* of the last century whose philistinism and paleotechnic materialism the vulgar technocracy continues to champion as the true proletarian culture.

Do the Chinese belong in this category? I don't know.

They are a puzzle. If one can believe official propaganda like that I come across in *Red Flag*, the Chinese are dedicated to development by sheer peasant cunning. One reads accounts of machine tools and jet aircraft being improvised seemingly out of little more than baling wire, rubber bands, and the thoughts of Chairman Mao. Surely this is only the folklore of primitive accumulation. Granted the objective of the Cultural Revolution has been to de-emphasize elitist expertise and move toward decentralized, small-scale, local industry that stays close to rural life. But this may only be making a virtue of current necessity. Ultimately China is determined to possess its "people's bomb" and ICBMs and moon rockets; it is dead set on measuring up as a superpower and has the pressing example of Japan to match. Perhaps as China opens up to the world, the pressure of the urban-industrial imperatives will mount irresistibly there as well.

3. One of the remarkable features of the twentieth century has been the capacity of advanced technical expertise to ally with the most benighted forms of racist and nationalist megalomania—and so to produce *the teratoid technocracy*. Nazi Germany pioneered the social form as a push-button-controlled witch's kitchen where racial mumbo-jumbo bubbled in the same caldron with sleekly efficient social administration and avant garde technology. Even there, the mystagogy of the *Reich* was far from irrationality run riot; it was calculated psychological manipulation. Behind the mock hysteria of the *Führer* there stood the echelons of cold-blooded bureaucrats, the Albert Speers and Adolf Eichmanns, toiling away at the engines of Juggernaut.

Stalin's Russia was much the same sort of nightmare, though far less economically efficient. Brazil and South Africa are the foremost contempory examples of the tradition. In both societies, the technocrats bed down with torturers and fanatics. South Africa boasts to the world of its industrial progress, military sophistication, and contributions to open-heart surgery, while the governing Nationalist Party remains committed to racist superstition and Calvinist moral theology. The Brazilian military junta also celebrates its growth rate and advertises itself throughout Latin America (with increasing effect) as the "economic miracle" for all to imitate. The technocracy there (the name is openly and prominently used) is, in fact, the direct descendant of a transplanted nineteenth-century European positivism. But meanwhile the Brazilian secret police apply the latest electronic tortures to their many political prisoners, and government-endorsed "death squads" gun down their opposition in back alleys.

Surely these societies, where the think tank overlooks the concentration camp, are the most grotesque hybrids of the urban-industrial world.

4. Finally, we must mention those *comic opera technocracies* that arise in many underdeveloped societies where an eager leadership struggles against impossible odds "to enter the modern world." A smattering of foreign technicians, a few high-rise office buildings and hotels in the capital, a vast pretentious bureaucracy, an air force of cast-off jet fighters from the Great Powers, an ambitious (but chronically half-finished) development project for which funds are forever being solicited . . . perhaps that is as far as these minor league technocrats will get over the next few generations— until at last the Russians, Americans, or EEC move in to integrate the economy into theirs. But these too are part of the great urban-industrial expansion, even if their role is no more than to launch in their societies a revolution of rising expectations that others will complete and profit from.

*   *   *

It would be foolish to suggest that there are not significant differences between the several technocratic styles. In my mind, at least, there is a valuable distinction between a society that jails its dissenters in hellholes and there electrifies their genitals, and a society where dissent fills the Broadway theater and the best-seller lists. My point is that the differences oscillate around similarities of value and high policy that have more to do with shaping contemporary history than even many radical critics realize. What concerns me here is the technocratic groundtone that underlies the differences and which will, I think, more and more become the forward issue of politics as time goes on. The differences between the several technocratic styles are very likely to diminish, especially as the giant-sized enterprises of the developed societies work out their advantageous mergers and spheres of influence. The ideological rhetoric of the Cold War may continue for some time; but the main course of world affairs will flow toward a grand urban-industrial homogeneity, spreading outward from five or six increasingly suave centers of technocratic power: the United States (dominating most of the western hemisphere), the European Economic Community (well tied into several Near Eastern and former colonial African economies), Russia and her East European satellite empire, Japan (probably increasingly integrated into southern Asia), and China. If things continue on the course they now follow, it is likely that for those looking back from a century or so in the future the most prominent feature of our time will be the global consolidation of the artificial environment, carrying with it the cultural dominance of western science and the politics of technocratic elitism.

THE NEW SHIP OF STATE

Even if, in all superficial aspects, the ship of state in which an urban-industrial society sails should look much as it did in the preindustrial era, even if the same political and social

leadership should still be on hand to serve as captain and
crew, nevertheless there is a decisive difference. In the era
of mature industrialism, the ship rapidly becomes a supremely
sophisticated instrument. We are no longer in an age when the
amateurish citizen, knowing a little ordinary seamanship, can
adjust the rigging, read the sextant and compass, and take
over the helm. Instead, the quarter-deck begins to look like
the cockpit of a spaceship. What do all these dials and
gauges and meters mean? What untutored passenger can
make sense of the strange charts, computer print outs, and
implements that fill the navigator's cabin? Who can understand the working of the mysterious engines down below?

It is precisely to deal with this esoteric apparatus that we
have experts on board, hired to serve our needs by the
government, the corporation, the party. They understand the
mechanisms of the ship—and we do not. If we ask for explanations, they answer us in incomprehensible technologisms.
Even when we talk social policy with them, they speak of impenetrable procedures, methodologies, and statistical factors.
Where people arguing politics used to talk of justice, freedom,
and moral rights and wrongs, the new expertise talks of "pa-
rameters," "trade-offs," "interfaces," "inputs," "optimiza-
tions," "cost-benefits," and "cross matrix impact analyses."
Nothing is any longer simply and straightforwardly accessible
to the layman. Everything—economics, foreign policy, war
and peace, city planning, education, environmental design,
business administration, human psychology—now requires the
benefit of professional training to be comprehensible. Or so
the technocrats insist; and often enough—given our conditions
of life—they are correct.

For example, within the last eighteen months, as a citizen
of mid-twentieth-century America, I have been confronted
with the task of making an intelligent judgment about the
following issues. The list could be much extended to include
local and regional problems that have come my way; but it

should suffice to suggest what absurd demands the artificial environment makes of citizens who would participate in the politics of the day.

— Is the supply of atmospheric oxygen rapidly diminishing due to the destruction of oceanic phytoplankton by industrial pollution?

— If a five-megaton nuclear bomb is detonated at the Amchitka Island underground test site, will it produce serious earthquakes and tidal waves along the Pacific coast?

— Is the methyl mercury in seafood within safe limits for human consumption, or should its sale be banned?

— Will there be world famine by 1975? 1980? 1985? Will the "Green Revolution" head off disaster in the nick of time or are Green Revolution methods themselves destroying the long-term crumb structure of the topsoil?

— Will supersonic transport severely change the ozone content of the stratosphere and so alter the world weather pattern?

— Is it true that within the next generation electric power will have to increase twice over to meet demand in America? And if so, can we trust that the attendant radiation leakage of nuclear generators and their wastes will be kept within tolerable limits? Can we trust the Atomic Energy Commission when it tells us that we need the power and that nuclear generators are the "cleanest" source of electricity available?

— Is the Operations Research Society of America correct in saying that several dissenting scientists confused the public during the 1970 debate on the Safeguard anti-missile missile by issuing defense analyses that were "misleading or factually in error"?

— Does the concentration of nitrates from the run-off of chemical fertilizers pose a serious threat to the survival of aquatic life in the oceans as Rachel Carson and Barry Commoner have argued? Or is Nobel prize agriculturalist Norman Borlaug correct in calling the environmentalist position "vicious, hysterical propaganda"?

— Is our public education system operating on a false and detrimental premise by assuming an equality of intelligence among the races? Can we trust the psychological testing experts who claim to have proved that Negroes are, genetically, the intellectual inferiors of whites? And shall we therefore revise our entire educational policy accordingly? On this issue, one major authority states that the relevant mental measurements have to be understood in the light of a "simple formula" or two, like the following:

$$r_{12} = r_{tt} \sqrt{\frac{CA_1}{CA_2}}$$

— What to do about the economy? Can we believe the President's experts when they tell us that the New Economic Policy will simultaneously halt inflation, stimulate growth, improve the balance of payments, increase liquidity, boost exports, and stabilize the dollar—all without scrapping the two-tier gold system or violating any principle of social justice? Is the NEP really necessary? Is it properly timed and scheduled? Is it coherent and sensible? Is it legal? Is it workable? One economist I turn to for help begins his analysis of the balance of payments problem from the premise: Since

$$\varepsilon_F = \triangle X \cdot P / \triangle P \cdot X, \ \triangle X \cdot P = \varepsilon_F \triangle P \cdot X \equiv \varepsilon_F \triangle P / P \cdot (XP)$$

. . . which means precisely nothing to me. But he does reach a conclusion about growth policy I rather like. Shall I endorse his analysis and act as if I know what it's all about?

None of these issues seems to me to be of only marginal

importance to my life. But on all of them, the official and corporate experts have been (often heatedly) challenged. I am tempted to conclude, therefore, that on each question we should opt for caution, slow down to a walk and collect our thoughts, stop and talk it over before we make any rash commitments. Well and good. But look at this roster of questions again. If we *do* look before we leap, does that not very nearly amount to suggesting that we *stop the entire system?* And what chance is there of that?

Now, as this book seeks to suggest, there may be a viewpoint that makes the conflicting expertise surrounding these questions strictly secondary, if not irrelevant—provided we are prepared to give the discussion of social framework and philosophical first principles precedence over matters of immediate policy. But for many responsible citizens caught in the raging thick of things this is bound to seem "unrealistic." For here are these great issues coming at them daily like bullets fired point blank. They *must* decide . . . and yet how *can* they decide? The world is just no longer their size.

We live, says Kenneth Boulding, in the age of the "superculture"—"the culture of airports, throughways, skyscrapers, hybrid corn and artificial fertilizers, birth control and universities. It is worldwide in its scope. . . . It even has a world language, technical English, and a common ideology, science." An age, in short, built hopelessly beyond the scale of the ordinary citizen. For most of us that language and that ideology are what the Latin of the mass was to the medieval peasantry: the hocus-pocus of social domination. If, then, the experts tell us that the ship of state must be steered along a certain course, at a certain speed, that it *must* go here and *cannot* go there . . . who are we to say them nay? And if we mutiny against them, who among us will pilot this complicated craft and keep it off the shoals? Better, then, to affirm the decisions of those who claim to understand the experts and not rock the boat.

THE STRATEGY OF COUNTERVAILING EXPERTISE

Or is there, perhaps, another solution? Might the citizenry not smuggle aboard its own skeleton crew of experts who will advise and criticize independently, resisting the advantages of serving the wealthy and powerful? It is a strategy that must be seriously considered, for it has been advocated from numerous thoughtful quarters and put into practice in many limited ways. Over the past generation, no publication or organization working for peace, disarmament, social justice, or ecological sanity has been able to do without a contingent of experts to provide reliable counsel and argue its cause before the public.

The number of scientists, technicians, and scholars who have devoted themselves to such citizenly service has been great, and one can have nothing but admiration for these conscientious men and women. They have done much good on many issues and, taken as a whole, their activity has clearly borne witness to the corruptions of technocratic politics. Here we have knowledgeable people, experts in their own right, who have made it indisputably clear that those who function as the official experts—those who take public money and purport to be serving the public interest by way of counseling the holders of elective office—cannot be trusted.

And yet we must ask troubling questions about this strategy of democratic defense. Does it not, by its very nature, further enforce the public's reliance on expertise? Does it not ultimately leave the citizen still in the hands of experts whose words he must take on faith, trusting that they have his best interests at heart and provide the wisest counsel? Does our democracy not continue to be a spectator sport in which the general public chooses up sides among contending groups of experts, looking on stupidly as the specialists exchange the facts and figures, debate the esoteric details, challenge one another's statistics, and question one another's prognostications? It is difficult to see that, in the long run, such a counterbalancing of expertise can be a real victory for the democratic autonomy of ordinary citizens. They remain expert-dependent.

The strategy of countervailing expertise, while undeniably well intentioned and capable of stopgap success on specific political issues, leaves wholly untouched the great cultural question of our time. It does not challenge the universally presumed rightness of the urban-industrial order of life. Therefore it cannot address itself to the possibility that high industrial society, due to its scale, pace, and complexity, is *inherently* technocratic, and so inherently undemocratic. At most, it leaves us with the hope that the bastardized technocracies of our day might yet be converted into ideal technocracies. Presumably, then, in such a Veblenesque Utopia, only the requirements of industrial efficiency and the well-being of mankind—the two perhaps conceived to be one and the same—would govern the uses of technology. Like good physicians, the virtuous experts would advise, counsel, educate, and employ their skills with no other end in view but their patients' benefit. So we would begin to approach the "administrative state," where, amid the industrial abundance, conflict could stem only from misunderstanding or ignorance—and the function of the principled expert would be to undertake the research and analysis that undoes such intellectual snarls.

Even if such an ideal technocracy were desirable (and I would not find it so) there is every reason to doubt that it could ever be brought into existence, despite the strenuous efforts of many public-spirited scientists, technicians, and scholars. It is far more likely that the fire of their high principles will be stolen by the existing power elites of state and corporation, who are not apt to let themselves be outmatched in mustering the greater expertise or in persuading the populace that their decisions represent the true, well-researched, and scientifically sound interests of the public. The state will always enjoy the advantage of being able to pose as the official guardian of the social good. Where, in league with the productive apparatus of the economy, it can provide sufficient affluence to avoid gross physical privation, there is little chance that the great majority of the society—mesmerized by images of a life filled with merchandise, sybaritic leisure, and creature comfort—will contemplate revolutionary politics. Every advertisement which holds forth the promise of fun, luxury, sexual fulfillment, ease, and opulence is an integral part of technocratic politics. It tells us: "behave and all this can be yours too; obey and the fat life is within your grasp."

THE ARSENAL OF WONDERS

Where such material promises—and we should recognize that they need not be false promises, given the real productivity of industrial society—are coupled with a display of prodigious technical competence, why should the citizen not take the course of least resistance: believe, endorse, and obey? After all, if the government can so manage things as to land astronauts and cosmonauts on distant planets, then clearly its capabilities are godlike and it can be trusted, *must* be trusted to realize the earthly paradise. Like the subconscious manipulations of our advertising, such technical and scientific spectaculars are of the essence of technocratic power. Technicians and scientists who may be through and through apolitical, convinced that their pure research has no political significance, nevertheless make their all-important contribution to technocratic social control. The successes of their research may seem to them to represent the pursuit of knowledge for the sake of knowledge. But in reality they help, with each sensational discovery and breakthrough, to augment the technocracy's arsenal of wonders. They celebrate the omnipotence of the new industrial state by heaping up scientific and technical splendors before a citizenry that cannot avoid being reduced to a sense of helpless awe and dependence.

The televised expedition of America's Apollo 11 in 1969 was precisely such a subliminal glorification of the established social order, a crushing assertion of overbearing official competence linked to nationalistic vanity. Carefully scheduled to culminate on a Sunday afternoon, the great event became a bedazzling technological circus staged for the onlooking public. Homes across the land were filled with images of the Houston Mission Control Center where a disciplined battalion of technicians waited in attendance upon incomprehensible instruments. Strange computer data and Buck Rogers simulations were flashed across the screen. The voices of flight controllers droned out an endless litany of esoteric mathematics. Sage experts, all on the government payroll, struggled to simplify the weighty technicalities and boldly brainstormed about even more outré uses of our technology. Here was the full panoply of technocratic authority—and how could any ordinary citizen seriously contemplate challenging those who were capable of such magnificent feats? Did not the President himself designate this the most momentous achievement since the creation of the universe? Did not the greatest of America's space technicians, our own Wernher von Braun, call it (a shade more modestly) the most important evolutionary advance since life emerged from the sea? And such things are done by *our* social system! Yours and mine. Under the tutelage of omnipotent experts, we become like gods by the simple act of paying taxes and providing applause. There is even the possibility that we shall all share in these cosmic adventures. Within a week of the historic moon shot, Pan-Am airlines had already informed a roster of opinion-making notables that their passage to the moon had been reserved on an early commercial flight.

To what lengths will public faith in the wisdom and prowess of the technocracy extend? This need not be a matter of conjecture. That faith has already demonstrated itself to be without limit or qualification. How else is one to interpret public compliance, both in the west and in the Soviet bloc, with the policy of thermonuclear deterrence? Here is a technological system—the balance of terror—on which we allow our very survival as a species to depend. It is a reckless commitment, predicated upon a willingness to do genocide which is the moral scandal of the age. Yet we take both the hazard and the ethical obscenity of the matter in stride. Assured by the experts that the system is technically infallible, morally permissible, and politically realistic, we accept it as a prospectively permanent feature of our lives. A society that will grant technical expertise this much leave to be the arbiter of its conscience and its survival, has stretched its trust as far as it can possibly extend. Did any people ever place more faith in their gods than we have in the infernal machines of our strategists and technicians?

Where such a mighty consensus exists in support of technocratic authority, it is not surprising that, with the exception of the recent student rebellions on our campuses, the most disruptive social movements in the society should be essentially efforts on the part of the dispossessed to claim their place in the Great Society and share its plenty. The black revolution has rocked middle America with militant agitation, angry denunciation, and violent insurrection. But the object of the agitation is nevertheless cultural assimilation, if not always social integration. The excluded and exploited minorities do not by and large call for an end to technocratic capitalism, but for jobs, for "black capitalism," and for greater access to the multiversities so that they too can rise in the meritocracy. With few exceptions, Black Power is a demand for the control of those institutions which will insure social mobility within the technocratic system. Given the incredible seductiveness of industrial affluence, and the all-inclusiveness of the worldview that supports the artificial environment, it is hardly those who live poor in the midst of imbecile plenty who can fairly be expected to deny their most urgent needs while they develop a deep critique of the technocracy. Their dignity demands that they be allowed into the system. Only then perhaps will they—like many disaffiliated white middle-class young—begin to feel the pinch of social controls far more subtle than police brutality and the privations of the ghetto.

DETOURS AND DEADENDS

It is important to recognize, of course, that not even the technocracy—for all its expertise and advance planning—can completely dominate the infinite hitches and quirks of history. At least, not yet. There are ways in which our society might be deflected from the kindly regime of paternalistic social engineers toward which it tends—though the most immediate obstacles that come to mind within the near future are far from pleasant. Most obviously, there is the hideous possibility that thermonuclear war will ambush us in the jungles of our power politics, despite the supposedly infallible logic of the deterrence system. Or, if anxious ecologists

like Barry Commoner and Rene Dubos are to be taken seriously in their warnings, there is the danger of catastrophic
environmental collapse at some point within the next generation: the rapid and irreparable exhaustion of the atmosphere, the global water supply, the topsoil.

There is also the chance that the militant dissent of young
blacks and white disaffiliates, demanding more change more
rapidly than the bulk of our society can tolerate or even
imagine, will produce a sharp reaction toward the most brutal
forms of police-state repression. Within recent years heavy
champions of reaction like Governor Reagan of California
and Vice President Agnew have managed to improvise an
entire politics out of racist anxiety and a pervasive hostility toward the radical, dropped-out young. In some campus
communities, at any rate, we have reached the point at which
anything remotely resembling a student can, in time of crisis,
be gunned down, gassed, and bayoneted by the authorities with
impunity, indeed, with the applause of millions of voters.
Black Panthers and hippies have become for cynical oppor-
tunists like Governor Reagan the scapegoat equivalent of
Hitler's Jews.

With respect to the young white drop-outs: if they persist
resourcefully and aggressively in their present course, there
will really be nothing most of our high industrial societies
can do to meet the standards they set for the quality of life,
except to repeal the urban-industrial dominance. But as for
the demands of the black and poor minorities for admission
to the American mainstream, it is clear enough that the
heights of the technocracy—the federal government, the federal courts, the military, the major corporations, the big
foundations, the universities and the liberal intellectual establishment—are prepared to accept steady if leisurely movement
toward integration. Why not? Their interest is in the well-
oiled social machine, where coercion gives way to manipula-

tion, where everybody co-operates nicely because everybody is happy to the point of euphoria, and where we all advance together into the consumer's heaven—which will look, for sure, like a collage of advertisements (liberally sprinkled with black models and mannequins) cut from *The New Yorker, Playboy,* and *Mademoiselle.*

But one cannot rule out the possibility that, should racial integration not come fast enough to blunt the appeal of the most aggressive forms of black militancy, an even angrier racist backlash than we have so far known might ensue in America. It would take its momentum from the outrage and festering anomie of the white "working poor," the fretful suburbanites, the downtown merchants and worried realtors, the local police, the gun clubs and law-and-order patriots; its bankroll could come from any number of self-made millionaires who, like the southwest oil magnates, still view the world from that cockeyed pre-Keynesian perspective which makes labor unions and "big government" look like the shipwreck rather than the ballast of capitalism. Add an anticommunist crusader or two and a strong-stomached demagogue . . . and, under sufficient pressure, here is indeed a volatile mix.

While it is true that the technocracy progressively dominates more and more of our life in the contemporary industrialized societies, one need not go to the tribes and villages of the underdeveloped world to find those whose emotional adjustment to the technocracy's official conception of rationality borders on the precarious. They abound among us, the dispossessed and bewildered millions who obey and co-operate, but uncertainly, sullenly. The John Birch chauvinists, the decency legionnaires, the hard hats, the embattled squares and cranks and quacks who vindictively brood over moralities and bigotries that the swinging society subjects to ever crueller ridicule . . . undeniably, the technocracy skyrockets into the world of Flash Gordon dragging behind it a bizarre baggage train of such atavistic types. Their desperation, should it ever congeal into a mass movement, might yet drive our suave technocracy along a route it would prefer not to travel. It is not with the likes of George Wallace or Archie Bunker that our cosmopolitan business and government elites care to share power. Indeed, it is primarily by way of contrast with our surviving political Neanderthals that the technocrats enjoy their most gratifying sense of enlightenment. Still and in spite of themselves—or rather for lack of courage and essential humanity—the technocrats and their employers might be tempted to make the cynical detour through fascism that the German governing classes took during the 1930s, when they joined forces with vulgarians and wild men they despised, but whom they felt confident they could ultimately use to their advantage. Then we in America might also find ourselves sinking into the teratoid technocracy, where all the trains run on time, including those bound for the concentration camps.

It is one of the troubling follies of much New Left radicalism that it tends to make so light of this terrible possibility. In their eagerness to vilify the society they loathe, many superheated radicals frequently lump all their opponents together —as if there were no difference to be made between the John Birch Society and the Presidential Council of Economic Advisors, between the National Gun Club and the National Security Council. They proceed apparently on the assumption that the stronger the backlash, the nearer we come to a major social explosion. And from such an explosion, one gathers, all good things are expected to follow. The ghettos will produce battalions of disciplined black guerrillas; a heroic and radicalized working class (now in hiding) will pour into the streets to proclaim the socialist commune; and the entire American middle class with its cops and soldiers will go into exile.

THE AIR-CONDITIONED NIGHTMARE

Thermonuclear holocaust, environmental collapse, the mad rapid slide into fascism. These are the more obvious ways in which urban-industrialism in America and western society generally could have its history cut short or might fail to achieve the smooth integration its technocratic leadership aspires to. But even if these disasters should be avoided, the technocracy is bound to find that the flawless social efficiency at which it aims is, like fairy gold, unattainable. As the artificial environment becomes denser, more precision-engineered, more global in its organization, more intricately woven into every least detail of daily life, it is certain to become an intractable social machinery. There are limits not only to what the environment can gracefully support, but also to the scale of things which human ingenuity can bring under control. All the more so when the experts must work within the corrupted priorities which the self-interest of existing elites in the state, corporations, and military dictate. But the result would be little better under ideal conditions. When the body politic grows so hypertrophic, the sharpest systems engineering in the world cannot keep it healthy.

I suspect that what the suave technocracy may finally have to settle for will be (to borrow a phrase from Henry Miller) "an air-conditioned nightmare" of endemic malfunction and slapdash inprovisation. Glowing advertisements of undiminished progress will continue to rain down on us from official quarters; there will always be well-researched predictions of light at the end of every tunnel. There will be dazzling forecasts of limitless affluence; there will even be much *real* affluence. But nothing will ever quite work the way the salesmen promised; the abundance will be mired in organizational confusion and bureaucratic malaise, constant environmental emergency, off-schedule policy, a chaos of crossed circuits, clogged pipelines, breakdowns in communication, overburdened social services. The data banks will become a jungle of misinformation, the computers will suffer from chronic electropsychosis. The scene will be indefinably sad and shoddy despite the veneer of orthodox optimism. It will be rather like a world's fair in its final days, when things start to sag and disintegrate behind the futuristic façades, when the rubble begins to accumulate in the corners, the chromium to grow tarnished, the neon lights to burn out, all the switches and buttons to stop working. Everything will take on that vile tackiness which only plastic can assume, the look of things decaying that were never supposed to grow old, or stop gleaming, never to cease being gay and sleek and perfect. It will be the look of Jean-Luc Godard's Alphaville in the ghastly concluding portion of the film. Much of the air terminal and high-rise architecture built only a decade ago already wears this look of sudden, embarrassed dilapidation. Like Dorian Gray, it is magnificently unblemished one moment, and a deteriorating horror the next. The photoelectric cells go haywire, the air conditioning bogs down, the piped-in music begins to blur and wheeze, the escalators jam. The buildings were never meant to age and mellow; they can only become instant junk.

But let us make no mistake. Such a precarious state of affairs by no means implies the end of the artificial environment or the technocracy. As I have suggested, in and of itself technological breakdown only strengthens the social power of expertise and licenses the next round of research and development. When the internal combustion engine becomes an intolerable nuisance, the proposal will be that we retool and replace it with an electric motor—which also provides the neat advantage of selling everybody an automobile all over again. When public education collapses under the weight of its own coercions and futility, the systems teams will step forward to propose that the schools invest in electronicized - individualized - computerized - audio - visual - multi - instructional consoles. When industrial pollutants finally make the air unbreathable, we will be advised to cover the cities over with plastic domes and air-condition them. Technological optimism is the snake oil of urban-industrialism. Each new application buys time, fast-shuffles the dissenters, and rubs the addiction to artificiality deeper into the collective psyche.

Moreover, as time goes on, the technocracy is bound to grow exquisitely adept at distracting protest and tranquilizing anxiety. Our government and the big corporations have already learned that it is easier to appoint a blue-ribbon committee, launch a corrective non-program, and change the image of policy than to change the policy itself. Perhaps the bulk of our brainpower and governmental energy will one day be employed concocting cover stories, propagating ingenious alibis, and applying public relations. At the top of our society there will be a vast mandarin establishment of professional obfuscators; the whole art of governing will finally be a matter of skillfully papering over the cracks in the artificial environment, making gestures of confidence, and assimilating opposition. Already the mass media, in league with the advertising industry, have discovered ways to type our shaggy drop-outs and student radicals in the public consciousness so that they might also have their quaint and innocuous role as marginal, if often obstreperous, eccentrics. They are even given a "functional" dignity: their ad-mass images become a new gimmick to sell aspirin, deodorants, and automobiles.

More significantly, the leading think tanks are well advanced in researching ways to oil disaffiliated youth and other divergent types into the social apparatus. Here, for example, is Herman Kahn, director of the Hudson Institute, replying to a British reporter who has asked his opinion on hippies.

> Instantly, from one of his seven briefcases, he pro-
> duced a report the size of a telephone directory analyz-
> ing the future of hippies. "It's all in here," he said,
> "your late fifties beat, your early sixties anti-family
> hip, your pathological flower kid. We're moving into a
> post-industrial mosaic society where machines will do
> all the routine jobs and the hippies will be absorbed
> into the general relaxation . . ."

(What a marvelous conception this is: "the general relaxation"! No doubt it comes just before *rigor mortis*.)

The business community is not far behind the systems engineers. *Fortune* magazine, in an issue of January 1969 dealing
exclusively with "American Youth" and focusing on the drop-
out problem, gives reason to believe that the more quick-
witted members of the corporate establishment are already
adjusting their image in ways that will permit them to re-
cruit all but the most obstinately disaffiliated young people.

> . . . the search for meaning and purpose [writes
> *Fortune*] is a serious matter to many young men and
> women.
> Our hope about most such youths must be that the
> search will be directed into constructive endeavors.
> . . . We can also hope that most such youths will at
> some point make the discovery that quite a few busi-
> ness careers entail socially constructive ventures. Many
> have in fact made this discovery already; furthermore,
> many have learned that they are in demand in busi-
> ness . . . and that . . . they can go a long way quite
> rapidly in business—and be in a position themselves
> to determine policies.
> It is important that businessmen now determining
> those policies do everything possible to make young

men aware of the opportunities that await them in the corporate world—and to expand the horizons of that world.

Does this sound like the prospectus for a cynical con job? Perhaps it is. But perhaps—and this is more likely—the technocrats begin to aspire with all their hearts to an ideal of public service which will make their wealth and privilege the well-deserved perquisites of a burdensome social responsibility. It would be an invaluable image. In time, they, like the imperial masters of old Rome, may even find a Virgil to commemorate them for the indefatigable curators of power they are; doubtless he will be a young university poet, working under a Guggenheim grant or quartered at RAND.

And surely they will merit the epic praise, since they will be no parasitic patrician class. As the indispensable experts and decision makers who stand behind the programs that stand behind the computers, they may well become the most toilsome members of the cybernated society, the last embodiment of an obsolescent work ethic. Do they not labor backbreakingly among us already? We have all seen them, these harried and care-worn men of affairs. We catch sight of them bustling through at airports or glimpse them on television newscasts, scurrying from international conference to secret briefing to congressional hearing, rushing by motorcade to connect with departing jet liners, struggling heroically amid the heat and press of crisis to explain, to clarify, to decode the mysteries of state to the great lay public . . . but never quite succeeding. They are the heroic few for whom the man-killing world of the hot line, the nanosecond data bank, the methedrine breakfast, and the SST has been designed. And for whom do they work themselves to the point of nervous collapse but for you and for me? We may not have requested their self-sacrificial service; but who else is there to tend the industrial leviathan?

THE SWEET AND SWINGING LIFE

It would be a mistake, I think, to assume that such a system could not be, despite its fraudulence and persistent malfunction, a viable social order capable of careering along its madcap course indefinitely. People adjust to the most seemingly impossible situations—especially when they are told by authority and expertise that they have no realistic choice but to learn to live with the little complications which are "the price of progress," "the cost of success." They will be told by those who know best that there is no alternative but to be where they are, and they will believe there is no alternative, because the blade of the Reality Principle will be at their throats. Perhaps they will take extension courses in crisis-coping and in time forget what the computers were ever supposed to be more efficient than.

Moreover, there will be improved therapies of adjustment and many "future shock absorbers" to ease the pain. In June 1968, as part of a British Broadcasting Corporation documentary film, a leading member of the National Health Service spoke of the growing need for a "Ministry of Well-Being" (he did not wince to quote from Orwell), whose task it would be to adjust the recalcitrant to an ever more demanding social reality. In time, he predicted, this may be the major function of the NHS. In the Soviet Union, the confinement of political malcontents like Natalya Gorbanevskaya and Zhores Medvedev in psychiatric hospitals is even now officially called "therapeutic isolation."

Of special interest among such technocratic lubricants is the "futures industry" that already thrives in several American think tanks and which claims an ever greater power to predict all the social results of every possible invention and line of policy. This would conveniently allow objections and anxieties to be planned for even before they had dawned upon the public consciousness. Ideally, in the view of Alvin Toffler, we shall have a new profession of Value-Impact Forecasters, "armed with scientific tools," busily "drawing up their reports in forms that can be taken into account in cost-benefit appraisals." They will be "located at the hot-center of decision-making" as "part of every corporation, research laboratory, government agency and foundation whose output includes technological innovation." What these ethical engineers will know of "value" (Old Style: the meaning of life) may of course be only a computer simulation of a statistical illusion gleaned from questionnaires whose unreality crudely approximates a moral imbecile's conception of an ethical decision. But in time perhaps the whole urban-industrial population will come to regard values as just such a higher nonsense. So the technocracy will be able to assure us that its decisions are indisputably compatible with the good, the true, and the beautiful, expertly researched and objectively measured.

Above all, there will be the real and assured abundance with which the technocracy has to work. And we are only beginning to learn how much compliance, if not passionate loyalty, can be coaxed out of a society by the distractions of widespread affluence. I sometimes think most middle Americans finish each day of their life too bone-weary with consuming things and shuffling their credit cards to voice any grievances they may harbor. Surely it is a folly to assume, in an economy where such prodigious surplus value is extracted from the industrial apparatus and not from human labor, that a sophisticated capitalism cannot undertake to clean up its ghettos, integrate the excluded minorities, and distribute the guaranteed annual income. As for the non-capitalist technocracies of the world, gifted as they are with a superior co-ordination and an absence of crass profiteering hang-ups, they may find it even easier to move toward stabilization by way of the same humanitarian mellowing. So one might expect the next generation of Soviet leaders to liberalize as the nation fattens, laying aside its worst coercions in favor of seduced acquiescence.

Between them, then, the great capitalist and collectivist technocracies might collaborate to blanket the world with a soft despotism of beneficent expertise so well rationalized and so clearly well intentioned that to extol its glories would become the whole meaning of sanity; to question its sufficiency, the essence of madness. Within this global Pax Technocratica, science would flourish, knowledge accumulate, technical prowess achieve ever greater perfection, abundance multiply. What more can Reason, Freedom, and Happiness require?

Perhaps there would still be tender souls who, sensing that all is not well in the urban-industrial Shangrila, would continue to drift off into bohemian limbos. These might well be the society's most gifted young. Such a seeping away of competence might seem, at first glance, to be a great loss to the technocracy. But the defaulting first-raters would quickly be replaced by second- and third-raters, who bring with them the advantage of cruder sensibilities and greater docility. Indeed, the technocracy will find itself better served by routineers who are less capable of seeing beyond the official priorities. And being fabulously wealthy, it can easily subsidize the recurrent failures of such mediocrities and glorify their products until they too begin to assume the stature of great scientists, scholars, technicians.

Provided its Reality Principle holds as the criterion of official sanity, the mature technocracy need not lack for a remarkable amount of superficial cultural variety. Within the "mosaic society" any number of prescientific atavisms can find their place—off the public scene. Perhaps atheist Presidents will continue to swear their oaths of office upon the Bible and astronauts will still read us Scripture from outer space. Millions will flock to church on Sunday; the paperback sales of great religious classics will remain high. Such pious gestures will pose no problem to the expansion of technocratic culture as long as, whenever people exclaim, "Will wonders never cease!" most of them mean the wonders of officially subsidized human ingenuity, not the wonders of God. At pricey resorts and spas patterned after the west coast Esalen, exotic forms of therapeutic self-indulgence will be merchandised. Our burgeoning creative leisure will include psychedelic artistry, amateur string quartets, the cultivation of *bonsai,* and finger painting. Encounter grouping will become a national ritual practiced from the White House on down as a means of filling the existential vacuum with instant intimacy and push-button friendship—on conveniently short-term arrangements. Sexual gratification, once ideally inseparable from love and a personal commitment to the beloved, will be available in a marvelous variety of erotic participations by way of the avant-garde theater, the mate swap, the group grope party, the weekly love-in at the local public park.

As long as their practitioners settle for co-existence, none of these private pleasures and avocations need disturb the technocracy's definition of reason and reality. There is not one of them that cannot be co-opted and integrated. Indeed, they can even make their important contribution to the preservation of emotional stability. Gradually then, we shall become a polished society of well-rounded warrior and technician humanists. The ruling patriciate will quote to us from the one hundred great books in its public statements. Our bankers and brokers will hang the walls of their boardrooms with the works of the most promising young painters. Our modern samurai will decorate the subterranean bunkers from which they protect the peace with choice old masters and will while away the hours contemplating the beauties of the chrysanthemum.

From the viewpoint of the well-integrated, what could possibly be wrong with such a social order? Within its embrace, few—perhaps none—will lack for at least minimal security. There will be high cultural tone. Science and scholarship will grow from strength to strength, filling our lives to surfeit with the fruits of their learning. The technology will flourish. And are these not the essential criteria of the good society: that there shall be no (visible) dearth, nor (detectable) death, nor (olfactable) decay? That there shall be cultivated taste and the limitless acquisition of knowledge for its own sake? True, the suave technocracy will not be a democratic society. But do not democratic formalities become a fetish where all the ends toward which democracy was the means seem to have been adequately realized? Where the fat life is available to all (or very nearly all), where scholar and scientist toil diligently amid the finest research facilities, where the artist is generously subsidized, above all where the cultural consensus in behalf of scientific advance and technological elaboration is so solidly founded, have not the labors of citizenship become obsolete? I fear there are many who will say so. Perhaps, then, this is the final and highest blessing of urban-industrial progress. Having resolved all conflict by way of efficiently distributed abundance and cultural totalitarianism, it renders the duties of citizenly vigilance not only impracticable, but unnecessary. The common man may understand less and less of the intricacies of his artificial environment, but the guardians of the citadel of expertise will relieve him of the need to do so by filling his life with the merchandise and marvels of scientific progress.

Who could ask for anything more?

The answer is: no one who does not know that more exists; no one who does not *know* it so vividly, so poignantly, so painfully that neither the easeful distractions of industrial plenty nor the stern authority of science can stifle the vital desire to reside in the greater reality. Ultimately, it will only be those who experience the agony of a psychic claustrophobia within the scientific worldview who will be able to take radical issue with the technocracy—and they will do so on matters that vastly transcend the issues of conventional social justice with which the radicalism of former times filled its now obsolete ideologies. They will see that the expertise we bow before derives from a diminished mode of consciousness. They will recognize that the ideal of scientific objectivity is our common disease of alienation grandly disguised as respectable epistemology. They will come to understand, in their pursuit of a reality justly proportioned to the full dimensions of our human nature, that it is the culture of science from which we must liberate ourselves if we are to be free spirits.

For what science can measure is only a portion of what man can know. Our knowing reaches out to embrace the sacred; what bars its way, though it promise us dominion, condemns us to be prisoners of the empirical lie.

Caliban, having acquired the higher mathematics and devised him a clever machinery, hastens to counterfeit his master's magic. Our politics must become that of the poet . . . of Blake, whose brave perversity counsels us

To cast off Bacon, Locke, & Newton from Albion's covering,
To take off his filthy garments & clothe him with Imagination.

CHAPTER 3

Waking Up, Being Real: The Mindscape of Single Vision

What seems to Be, Is, To those
to whom
It seems to Be, & is productive of
the most dreadful
Consequences to those to whom it
seems to Be, even of
Torments, Despair, Eternal Death . . .

William Blake

PSYCHE AND SOCIETY

Every society claims a portion of the private psyche for its own, a piece of our mind from which it fashions an orthodox consciousness adapted to what Freud called the Reality Principle. In Freud's view, the Reality Principle was the result of a latent activity called "reality testing," the purpose of which was to fix the frontier between objective and subjective. A confirmed nineteenth-century positivist, Freud took the objective to be nature as defined by science, the *real* external world of empirical fact and mechanistic determinism. The subjective, on the other hand, was a mixture of two elements:

sexuality—the playful, non-utilitarian "pleasure principle"; and fantasy—a broad category in which Freud included dreams, myths, reveries, religion, and art. In so far as the latter were not acting as sexual disguise, they were mere wishful thinking and essentially infantile. They must, therefore, Freud thought, be outgrown in adulthood or at least subordinated in their influence. He was, for example, proud of his daughter because in her childhood she had never believed in fairy tales.

What Freud never wished to face squarely was the fact that the line we draw between the world Out There and the world In Here must be predicated on metaphysical assumptions that cannot themselves be subjected to scientific proof. Such assumptions are grounded in capacities of consciousness which may differ widely from age to age, culture to culture, person to person. Different experiences, different metaphysics; different metaphysics, different realities. Freud chose the course of least resistance. He simply endorsed the prevailing worldview of scientific positivism and went on from there. Art was mere wish fulfillment. Religion was an "illusion" that had no future. External reality was recalcitrant and inhuman. Alienation was man's fate. Sanity was "acquiescence in fate."

For many later psychotherapists, the issue has been far more complex. Early on, Jung developed serious reservations about the Reality Principle. As a criterion of sanity, it began to look suspiciously arbitrary. It condemned to the status of mere fantasy too much that is indubitably precious to culture and essential to creative growth. It refused to recognize experiences that are universally meaningful without being scientifically empirical. Such misgivings throw psychiatry into exactly the metaphysical turmoil Freud wanted to avoid; yet no psychotherapist worth regarding seriously can ever again sidestep these ultimate questions now that they have been raised.

For our society generally, however, the Reality Principle Freud borrowed from the urban-industrial culture around him remains in force. We have fewer crusading positivists about today and there is somewhat less certainty in philosophical circles about the validity of paleotechnic materialism; but no matter. As the artificial environment moves toward consolidation with a ponderous momentum, it carries with it a greater commitment to the culture of science than any other social form in history. Allegiance to the scientific Reality Principle has grown steadily more deep-seated and routine as a matter of industrial necessity. But since that allegiance forms the boundary condition of awareness, its arbitrariness is apt to be felt by most people only as an elusive, embarrassing deficiency which words cannot describe. Nothing is more difficult to name than what is present to the mind only as an absence, though such a vacancy in our life can become terrifying enough to break us spiritually and physically.

In this study I will be calling the orthodox consciousness of urban-industrialism by the name William Blake gave it—single vision. It was his term for that narrowing of the sensibilities we often refer to as "alienation" today. My main interest is in the cultural transformations from which this psychic style stems and the force it exerts upon our politics. But before we enter into this history and sociology of consciousness, it may be best to work up at least a rough sketch of how single vision acts upon our experience of the world in "normal" life. Only in this way can we begin to understand how deeply the artificial environment penetrates the personality. This is especially important since it has become something of a current fashion to play fast and loose with trivial conceptions of consciousness, many of which come down to being little more than impressionistic reportage about tastes and social conventions. But what is most important about consciousness is that which remains *unconscious* at the core of the mind, subliminally shaping our powers of perception and intellection, screening, filtering, censoring without making its presence known. This is the level at which society most decisively governs the psyche, and the only level at which a discussion of consciousness has significance. Until we realize, at least dimly, what portions of our personality lie buried, forgotten, perhaps ruined in this submerged quarter of the mind, there is no chance of changing our quality of consciousness, no chance of challenging the official reality.

To probe these foundations of the personality by way of all too ordinary language poses no small problem. Consciousness is the universe of personal awareness; and anyone's universe, being a totality, admits of no relations outside itself. The familiar logic of comparison and contrast will not apply. What authentically escapes our awareness, we are free to dismiss as unreal, nonexistent. Yet my contention is that the universe of single vision, the orthodox consciousness in which most of us reside most of the time and especially when we are being most "wide awake" and "realistic," is very cramped quarters, by no means various and spacious enough to let us grow to full human size. But how to convince people that their totality is less than the whole? How to awaken them to limits within a universe they regard as infinite?

Those who have enjoyed the benefit of successful psychotherapy, some affective education, or perhaps a bit of disciplined meditation will doubtless by now have ventured at least a few steps across the boundaries of single vision. I may have less to tell them than they would have to tell me about the world outside our matchbox-sized sanity. And then there are the hallucinogenic drugs, an even more prominent and facile technique of psychic jailbreak, though one whose value is uncertain. Turning on is so easily done, and often has no connection with a comprehensive discipline of life. It therefore frequently degenerates into an obsession or an entertainment and so loses its potential philosophical significance. "Every day on the road to God *is* God," said Saint Theresa—meaning, I suppose, that our road does not become the true road until we pass up the shortcuts in favor of the long way around.

In any event, though this chapter may have little to offer those who have had access to depth therapy or the drugs, its approach may yet be of interest to them. I have said the orthodox consciousness of our culture is a much diminished reality. Let me then try to give at least a provisional idea of how diminished a mind our normal life within the artificial environment requires. And where better to begin than within your own awareness here and now, as you take up this book to read?

DARK MIND AND DREAM THIEVING

> Some say that gleams of a remoter
>   world
> Visit the soul in sleep—that death
>   is slumber,
> And that its shapes the busy thoughts
>   outnumber
> Of those who wake and live.
>
> *Shelley*

> But now is it worthwhile bother-
> ing about what sort of account
> one is going to give of dreams?
> They are very peripheral things.
> . . . If you like to say that I
> haven't given a full and clear ac-
> count of dreaming or of seeing
> things in the mind's eye, I'm per-
> fectly happy to say: "No, indeed
> I haven't."
>
> *Gilbert Ryle*

Suppose I were to ask that you now pause and try to recollect all you can of what you dreamed last night. It is a safe assumption that few of you could salvage more than some faded fragments of your dreams. You might even be convinced that you did not dream at all. But you did. Contemporary sleep research finds that all of us dream prodigiously each night and give the fact away by the fluttering of our eyeballs beneath their sleeping lids. Last night, as on all the nights of your life, you dreamed much and magnificently, moving in an alternative reality of your own invention whose imaginative magnitude (for all you know) may have rivaled the creations of Homer and Shakespeare. Yet there are many people who would insist that their nights were wholly dreamless, if there did not exist behavioral evidence—electronically calibrated and recorded—to show them otherwise. Strange, is it not, that even in such matters, we should need to invoke the authority of experts . . . as if our very dreams were not our own?

As for the abyss which lies beyond the edge of dreams, that interlude of the dark mind we call sleep—how do you look back upon it now? As a succession of empty holes punctuating your life with lost time? Do you give it any thought at all, this daily retreat to oblivion? Perhaps you assume—"simply"—that you pass through this eclipse of ordinary consciousness only because of some obvious form of physical fatigue. If that were so, then sleep could well be viewed as a bothersome necessity imposed by the limitations of our organism, a flaw we must surely repair when we know better how to manipulate the chemistry of the body. There are those in the advance guard of medical research who predict the event with no little enthusiasm . . . and technicians too who eagerly anticipate the abolition of night by way of orbiting space-mirrors. The prospect has been called "an all-out war on sleep." After all, sleep *is,* economically speaking, a dead loss. Not until it is eliminated, then, can we expect the utopia of round-the-clock, non-stop consumption and active leisure.

The common assumption: we sleep because we grow tired. But in what way "tired"? In the muscles . . . in the blood . . . in the nerves . . . Yes, the fatigue makes itself felt there physiologically. But why will simple immobility and relaxation not do to rest us? Why the radical change of consciousness? For sleep is not mere relaxation; not mere *un*consciousness either, but a rich dream life that spirals down through ever deeper levels of the dark mind. How deep? James Joyce, in his *Finnegans Wake*, leads us across a dreamscape that reaches to the dark running river of collective remembrance. Is that perhaps what lies waiting in those depths of tranquility that will not yield the sleep researcher's electrodes the least behavioral twitch? If that were so, then what should we make of this irrepressible need for sleep? Perhaps that it is the claim upon us of another dimension of experience—a longing for alternative consciousness built into the circadian rhythm of all animal life. Seen in this light, sleep might well be the most rewarding of all "natural highs," and the most universal—compared to which the psychedelic drugs bring only a poor substitute. For what if Joyce was right? (And always best to take poets more seriously than laboratory psychologists in such matters.) What if, without resort to artificial technique, the dark mind broadens of its own accord into universality and we re-enact each night the mythical identities of man?

What if . . . ? A question that cannot expect an answer. In what spirit can I raise the point with you but as an interesting speculation? The adventures of the dark mind are among the most commonplace facts of daily life. Yet no sooner do we probe their meaning than we find ourselves brought to a halt at the utmost limits of awareness; and nothing I can say here will take you across that shadowy frontier. Let the fact take hold before you read further: by no act of will no matter how strenuous, can you now reclaim from all your life more than a few scraps of your dreams.

You *cannot*. If I were to suggest that in your dreams miracles
of self-discovery have taken place, that in the ocean bottoms
of sleep you have found your way to sacred ground . . .
if I were to submit that this had happened to you—to *you*,
last night—you would be incapable of verifying or refuting
the suggestion. That is what it means to be at the boundaries
of consciousness—or rather of *orthodox* consciousness. Here,
in part, is what our alienated normality requires of you, this
scornful neglect of the dark mind which leaves you a stranger
to so much of your own experience, and which, even now,
may be counseling you to pay these trivial matters no attention . . . these senseless dreams . . . this vacuum of existence called sleep.

You might, with some philosophical sophistication, con-
tend at this point that the discussion is meaningless, since
scious and so unverifiable in principle. But in fact what I
it requires of you an awareness of what is naturally uncon-
suggest is no more than the possibility of amnesia: episodic,
habitual amnesia. To tell an amnesiac dancer who had
lost his talents that he once danced like a god would hardly
be meaningless, though the artist could not for the life of
him recall more than fleeting images of his forgotten achievements. The mad Nijinsky was, in his catatonic later years, just
this sort of tragic figure. Yet *we* would know what lay hidden
from remembrance in the shadow of the artist's life. Just
so, there are those who know what our collective amnesia con-
ceals. We call them "mystics" and I shall have more to say
of their role before this chapter ends.

It may be extremely difficult for most of us to draw back
the amnesiac curtain that parts us from the bulk of our
dreams. But with a little care, it is at least possible to brighten
our awareness of the repressive act that daily drives the dark
mind into unconsciousness. In the normal course of things,
all of us come awake by way of dream thieving, a psychic
discipline of great severity. Each morning, systematically but

quite subliminally, we steal from ourselves and sequester every remnant of our prewaking awareness. We have all learned to carry out this exercise in self-impoverishment with a precise and automatic thoroughness. The alarm rings, and instantaneously an axe falls across the continuum of consciousness, sharply dividing awake from asleep. Wakefulness points forward into the bright light of the *real* world: the world of office buildings, factory floors, classrooms, city streets, shopping centers, yesterday's worries, this morning's news. Responsibility, ambition, decision are upon us at once, monopolizing our attention. While behind us, dotted here and there with dream images like failing embers, the dark mind is fast becoming an undifferentiated waste where we discern nothing that resembles knowledge or achievement. Yet cultivate even a small measure of psychic plasticity, and it becomes possible to prolong the process of waking, at least to a degree, to feel how pre-emptorily the waking mind deals with the dark mind. Rapidly, efficiently, the dreams are dispersed from memory and our sharply outlined, compacted, daytime identity is precipitated out of the shape-shifting self we were in our sleep, a creature of cloud, a creature of water. All within moments. An hour after we awake, for most of us the dreams are gone and today has blended into yesterday without interruption or distraction.

It requires a nimble attentiveness during just that first crucial interval of the morning—but if the effort is successful, one gains from it a sense of how reluctantly the dark mind slides away from us . . . as if it had more to tell, as if it were not yet ready to surrender our attention and would call us back. And what we then take away into the waking world can be a distressing sense of mutilation.

But here is an obvious question. Do not all people wake to deal with the dark mind as we do? The answer is no. It is among the marked characteristics of all prescientific cultures that the dream life is treated with great, but commonplace respect and that oneirologists are given prominent status. Alfred Kroeber, the anthropologist, once cited this as a key measure of the "backwardness" of primitive people. "To them," he remarked, "a child or a hawk or a stone seen or heard in a certain kind of dream or trance is much more important than a physical child or hawk or stone that one can touch or handle, because it is the possible source of much more power. . . . Certain things we classify as unreal, the primitive considers super-real—with the result that his world seems 'surrealistically' fantastic to us." In some primitive cultures, like that of the Senoi of Malaya, dream exploration is a highly sophisticated skill and a form of pedagogy; indeed, Senoi oneirics makes our own poor psychology of dreams seem sadly immature by comparison. For the American Plains Indians, the more impressive dream visions of a gifted medicine man like the Sioux Black Elk could become the occasion for magnificent tribal ceremonials in which the dream was re-enacted in careful detail, a striking anticipation of what the Gestalt psychotherapist Frederick Perls has, in our own time, recreated as "existential dream interpretation."

In most high civilizations of the past, dream meanings were granted a similarly high status. In the yoga tradition of India, students were counseled to watch for the appearance of great teaching masters who would come in dreams to instruct them. Dreamless sleep was also accorded a special dignity as the unconscious version of the supreme illumination (*samadhi*). In effect, the yogi's objective was to achieve a form of wakefulness within the sleeping state—a condition for which our culture cannot find words remotely appropriate. In ancient Sumer, it was the standard practice of high priests to search their dreams for the design of their temples. Perhaps we skeptically reject the claim that architecture can be thus dreamed up, but the claim itself is significant. The dream was accepted as an indisputable principle of authority. The gods made themselves known in dreams, and even crowned heads would be foolish not to heed them. One need only recall how young Joseph made his way to the top of Egyptian political life and why it was that Neb ᵢ hadnezzar abased himself before Daniel and showered him with favors.

We in the contemporary west may wake each morning to cast out our sleep and dream experience like so much rubbish. But that is an almost freakish act of alienation. Only western society—and especially in the modern era—has been quite so prodigal in dealing with what is, even by the fictitious measure of our mechanical clocks, a major portion of our lives. And what becomes of those who break under the strain of such a spendthrift sanity—for many do? Does not our psychiatry return them to their dreamlife to recover a portion of what they have squandered? Yet, ironically, "normal" men and women rise every morning of their adult lives to dose themselves on caffeinated drinks whose purpose is to expunge their dream experience. Many are driven by the demands of their work to intensify the waking state and prolong it well into the night by a punishing regimen of pep pills and "uppers." The business life and politics of the artificial environment are transacted exclusively by men and women in just such a condition of exaggerated alertness. Sad victims of a grueling addiction—yet they enjoy high regard for being practical, productive, "wide awake."

It is no mere coincidence that coffee, tea, and chocolate— the repertory of stimulant beverages to which western society has become habituated and without which the compulsive wakefulness of our daily routine would be inconceivable— entered our society simultaneously with the scientific revolution. Lewis Feuer has suggested (though in a different context) that modern science takes its origin from the coffee-houses of seventeenth-century England. There is an important truth hidden in that fact. Caffeine has been the chemical adjunct of one of the most dramatic transformations of consciousness the human race has experienced. It has helped press the razor-sharp edge of wakefulness mercilessly against the mind; still today, only the pain of that blade will serve to convince most of us that we are alive and awake in the real world.

Since Freud, psychotherapy has been much concerned with the dream's symbolic vocabulary. But even Freud, though he was daring enough to take dreams seriously in an era of hyperrealism, confined himself to examining how repression shapes a few motifs of the dreaming mind: the sexual and aggressive elements which are among the most easily recoverable. Similarly, Jung, in his study of the archetypal unconscious, was primarily interested in the *contents* of dreams, more so than in the dream as a peculiar medium of experience. True enough, we forbiddenly make love and war in our dreams; we may also delve to the collective, archetypal levels of the psyche. But *whatever* is taken up by the dark mind is molded by the dream as a freely imaginative medium respecting no conventional order of space, time, identity, or logic. What is most important about the dream is the way it perversely makes sport of such "realities" as if they did not much matter, thus indulging in what is, for the waking mind, an unpardonable heresy.

And so it is a heresy. Let me at this point suggest only briefly what I believe the offense is for which our dreams are censored—and then return to the subject in a later chapter. Dreaming begins with the free play of metaphorical fantasy— that fascination with the infinite plasticity of things and events which Joyce sought to capture by way of his "portmanteau" puns. In dreams, all durability, solidity, logical coherence are mischievously defied. By way of such imaginative play, we surround ourselves with an environment of shifting symbolic surfaces; and at last, as the dream deepens, we move toward the dramatized participation of those symbols. This is so very singular and important a mode of experience that modern psychology, despite its scientific pretensions, has been forced to treat dreams in a strikingly special way. In our wakeful awareness, most of us in the modern west quite automatically address the world about us with the questions "How does it work?"; "What caused it?" But when we confront our dreams, such questions have no satisfying sense to them. Instead, we put a question of an entirely different order, one which our ancestors habitually asked of their experience as a whole, awake or dreaming. We ask, *"What does it mean?"* For we at once recognize in our dreams a symbolic presence which makes what is before us other and more than it seems.

Here is a mode of experience that returns to us in waking life as art—especially poetry, drama, and the visual arts. In what artists lay before us there is the residue of a reality we first learned in sleep. As Walter Abell has observed, artists are "dreamers of the collective dream." In the supreme images of art, as in our dreams, there is the same sense of a world bordering on transparency: images, situations, people, adventures that want to reveal more than lies on the surface of things. Is that not what we mean when we call something "dreamlike" . . . that there is an eerie *unreality* to the appearances immediately before us? So in our dreams, the reality is not in the appearances, but behind them. The dream invites us *into* the experience, would have us *penetrate,* enter, be lost, be still, and at last (here is the heart of it) annihilate time. And we *do* enter, and we *do* become lost, and time *does* stop . . . and that might be the knowledge of eternity. But for us the experience is censored. We recall it only as the blank stupor called sleep, because the waking mind's time is, ideally and of necessity in our artificial environment, clock time and will not be made plastic or suffer annihilation. It is the physicist's time we march to, time as time would be if there were no living thing to transform existence into experience; time such as machines can measure out in the lockstep of equal and abstract measures. The most threatening heresy of the dark mind lies precisely in this: that it brings us to the still center of time's axis, where the turning wheel no longer turns.

So then, it is not any particular dream content that is most significantly repressed by the waking mind, but *dreaming itself* as an uncompromised, essentially poetic mode of experiencing. It is just this lawless defiance of literalness and necessity that the intolerant waking mind rejects; for here is the dark mind thrusting forward a rival Reality Principle, and, in the course of each night's adventures, gaining our acquiescence. Psychiatry has learned to salvage this and that from the rich contents of the dream. But until it integrates the dream as medium of experience into our lives, it has not reconciled the antagonism that divides the soul most radically, that between the contending realities of the waking and dark minds.

THE SPECTATOR SENSES

Consider another aspect of your present state of awareness. You see the book you are holding as an object located outside yourself and at a distance, with every conviction that you see it where it is and as it is, something separate and external. Tap the book with your finger, and again you immediately locate the sound at a distance from yourself—at what is surely its source. Without the least awareness of so doing, you reflect sight and sound away and so are conscious of seeing and hearing only as they take hold of objects external to eye and ear. With respect to what you see and hear, you are in the position of a spectator witnessing things that exist outside and away from yourself.

The advantages that flow from this capacity to isolate one-self as a spectator within the field of experience are too obvi-ous to mention. But that capacity is nonetheless a well-rationalized illusion and ought to be recognized for what it is. In reality, both sight and sound take place internally. Phys-iologically, they would be located at the rear of the eyeball, at the surface of the eardrum. They happen inside the head, just as a smell happens in the olfactory organs, or a taste in the buds of the tongue, or the sensation of touch within the depressed surface of the skin (and, seemingly, just be-neath the outer layer of flesh). In all the latter cases, you are aware of the personal intimacy of the experience; you are aware of lively action within your organism. The experi-ence presses against you and into you—and there is a sense of participation in the event that makes it difficult if not impossible to disentangle yourself from what you are ex-periencing. We take the source of an odor to be as much outside of us as the source of a sound. Yet we do not spontaneously distance an odor; we first experience it inside the head . . . and *then* we look about with our eyes to locate its source. The nose breathes in experience; the eyes auto-matically trace experience out and away to a "cause." It re-quires a painfully bright light to sting our eyes, a startlingly loud sound to jangle our ears and thus remind us that we also see and hear internally. Otherwise, and for the most part, our eyes and ears are numb to their own act of feeling. We know nothing of their internal action, but only the cerebral representation of things Out There.

Again, see if this is not so. How possible do you find it to feel the light in your eyes, the sound in your ears? Can you hold the representations there and savor them . . . as you might hold a flavor in your mouth? Can you imagine your eyes as mouths *tasting* the light and color, the shape and shadow that fill them? Or do you not, despite the effort, re-flect these representations away to a source outside?

In the sensory make-up of the human being, the eyes and ears (especially the eyes) predominate, vastly overshadowing the other senses. This is a distinctive feature of our sensory evolution. The senses that lend themselves to the illusion of distancing experience press despotically to the fore; the intimate senses recede and grow weak. Most notably, the human power of smell, which remains so vibrantly alive in other mammals, degenerates—although Freud's disciple Georg Groddeck speculated that our olfactory powers had not so much degenerated as been repressed. At the unconscious level, he believed a vocabulary of odors continues to be secretly exchanged, a possibility which recent research in human pheromones seems to support. In any case, our conscious relations with the world have become almost exclusively those of a spectator looking on and listening in from a hypothetical vantage point which has the feeling of lying outside the experience. It is in no sense "wrong" that we should employ our eyes and ears in this way; this is also a possibility to be explored and used. But it is clearly a violation of reality to forget that we permeate the experiences of vision and hearing, and that there is no more clear distinction between us and a sound or sight representation than there is between us and an odor.

Of course we *do* forget; our entire evolutionary development helps us to forget. And the significance of this evolutionary quirk cannot be overestimated. Doubtless, the predominance and attendant benumbing of eye and ear are related to the rise of linguistic intelligence with its habit of naming things and substituting cerebral imagery for immediate experience. All these belong together as so many useful means of holding off experience, surveying the ground, choosing among options, in a word, of *controlling* action within the field of possibilities. Still, below the act of static, cerebral representation, and preceding the distancing thrust of our anesthetized eyesight and hearing, the intimate and enveloping flow of experience continues, the vital continuum from which we cut and tailor our picture of the world. In many cultures, a deal of ritual, often involving powerful "mind-blowing" techniques, has served to suspend temporarily the predominance of logicality and the distancing senses, perhaps by ruthlessly disorienting them. At least in spirit, some of these rituals have lately begun to reappear at the fringes of our culture. The eyeball-battering light shows and ear-splitting amplification of rock music, so prominent a part of youth culture, may seem a masochistic punishment of the sensory equipment. But they serve only to produce the sort of harsh stimulation that numbness, once sensed, calls out to experience; the effect is to drive sight and sound like nails deep into the narcotized eye and ear and awaken there the deadened potentialities of these senses so that one may then, so to speak, "smell" the light and music. Once the automatic tendency to distance visual and auditory representations has been thwarted, there is some chance to recapture the participatory powers of the dominant senses.

It is only when this experience of sensory participation has been sufficiently weakened that we find ourselves burdened with the "knowledge problem" which has haunted western philosophy so insistently since Descartes. The relations between knower and known are problematic with us because we have grown so peculiarly stupid about the way experience really happens. Even (or perhaps especially) in the work of our leading modern philosophers, discussion of the sense life is incredibly insipid; experience has neither power nor complexity for them. Empiricists and rationalists alike seem wholly ignorant of that pitch of experience which can seize and sear and dizzy the senses, of those moments when an uncanny power can descend upon the eye or ear raising their sensitivity to the magnitude of rapture. Instead, our philosophy often trails off into much bookish discussion about something called "sense data," conceived of abstractly as a uniform species of evidence that politely registers its arrival and then waits about to be accounted for in clever epistemological schemes. Rarely is any thought given to how painters and poets must perceive the world about them to grow so enamored of it, so obsessed with a single image, a single landscape. Rather, the model for the unsensuous sense data so dear to the empiricists seems to be a scientist reading a thermometer as part of a not very eventful experiment—surely the most minimal exercise of the sensory abilities.

In later chapters, when we deal with the Romantic poets, we will see how our senses, if cultivated with proper discipline and respect, hold powers that empirical philosophy never dreamed possible. But to realize this, one must no longer pattern one's understanding of the senses upon the long-distancing habits of the anesthetized eye and ear. For these faculties, the representations of the world do indeed seem to loom up as a congeries of objects and events Out There; we do not perceive them as vibrations within a field that involves us *inextricably.* Then, having isolated ourselves from the experiential continuum, we are left to wonder how knowledge can safely leap the sensed gap between world and mind. There are many ingenious solutions to the problem, though none that an uncompromising solipsism will not devastate. But the simplest solution and the most true to life is that which denies the problem by closing the dichotomy —by closing it *experientially,* and not merely in epistemological discourse.

To deny, however, that there is an In Here distinct from an Out There is to become—as in the case of those who will not let their dreams be thieved—"mystical." Still, the seventeenth-century poet Thomas Traherne was convinced that a vividly participative sensory life is the innate human condition—the "Pure Primitive Virgin Light"—and thus the depth dimension of a true normality. In that condition, knower and known merge; the eye ingests the object and tastes it internally.

This made me present evermore
    With whatso ere I saw.
An Object, if it were before
My Ey, was by Dame Natures Law,
    Within my Soul. Her Store
Was all at once within me; all her Treasures
Were my Immediat and Internal Pleasures,
Substantial Joys, which did inform my Mind.

    The utmost Star,
    Tho seen from far,
Was present in the Apple of my Eye.
    There was my Sight, my Life, my Sence,
        My Substance and my Mind
        My Spirit Shind
Even there, not by a Transeunt Influence.
The Act was Immanent, yet there.
The Thing remote, yet felt even here.

An *interesting* way of seeing things, we might say. But for
Traherne, much more than that. For him, the virgin senses of
childhood experienced a different reality. "Eternity was Manifest in the Light of the Day, and som thing infinit Behind
evry thing appeared," he tells us. "All Time was Eternity,
and a Perpetual Sabbath. Is it not Strange, that an Infant
should be Heir of the World, and see those Mysteries which
the Books of the Learned never unfold?"

THE DEATH-IN-LIFE OF THE BODY

Our sense of being isolated from the field of experience is
not due entirely to the dominance of the anesthetized eye
and ear. If that were so, the boundary of our sense of self

would likely be the perimeter of the body. Out There would then begin just beyond the skin surface to which outer ear and cornea are attached. The body is, of course, a significant limit in the drawing of our self-image; but it is not the decisive line between In Here and Out There because the body itself has become for us an alien object located Out There, the mere receptacle of our true and irrevocable identity. That identity is ultimately felt to reside at a point inside the body . . . inside the head . . . somewhere just behind the eyes and between the ears.

Again, see if this is not the case as you read—*especially* as you read. What now is the locus of your identity? Where is your awareness most brightly alert? Is it not, this reading of books, almost wholly an exercise of the waking consciousness, of the distancing eyes, of the "you" who looks alertly out through your eyes from within your skull? During such an exercise, does your body even exist for you at all? Do its messages register, except as unwelcome distractions from the business at hand? When the head is engaged in concentrated intellectual activity—especially dealing intensely in syntax or measurements—notice how like a castle it becomes, separated from the body as if by battlements.

Here, once more, we are dealing with a distinctive feature of our animal evolution. Our posture has developed toward being comfortably, gracefully erect. Even when moving, we need not—like the other primates—bend earthward and lope. It becomes difficult, abnormal, for us to sweep the ground with our nose and mouth; instead, the hands raise food and water to the head, which now rises up like a watchtower to scan the surrounding landscape. What a prodigious achievement this has been, this erection of the human frame. A triumph of anatomical architecture. How much of the human character has been shaped by this interplay of risky balance and gravitational discipline. But once achieved, uprightness alters dramatically the relations of the senses. Most obviously, the olfactory powers atrophy when the nose is removed from its intimate connection with the ground. Instead, the eyes and ears become the watchtower's dominant faculties. Concurrently, there is the marked tendency for proprioception within the body to grow dim, inexact, and heavily censored. The head begins to grow away from the body, to detach and become domineering—as if obsessed by its own position as the body's crown, protector of the fantastically elaborated cerebral cortex. With dismal regularity, therapeutic work in sensory awareness discovers this hypercapitated picture of the body to be the chief obstacle to organic wholeness.

In our single-visioned culture most people have taken up exclusive residence in their heads; they are at home nowhere but among the wakeful, logical processes. For them, the head becomes *headquarters,* the body's command and control center. Forgetting the innate competence of the body, they even seek to run their organism from the top down. They think up (or inanely adopt from their surroundings) a baseless conception of "normality" and then impose it on the body, regulating their waking and sleeping, their digestion and excretion, their alertness and relaxation and sexual drives by a regimen of pharmaceutical concoctions and by a clock-time schedule.

The significance of the body's repression extends far beyond Freud's concern for sexual deprivation. As in the case of dreams, Freud's first conclusion was plausible but superficial. He decided that it is sexuality which is repressed by the Reality Principle. But in fact the sexual drive, while deflected this way or that (but more often ritualized than really censored) is perhaps the *least* repressed element in the body's constitution—for obvious reasons. A prudish society may ban discussion of the subject, but sex remains brightly visible in most people's awareness, so close to the surface that any slip of the tongue or double entendre at once betrays its presence. Even the so-called perversions have always found their many illicit outlets. Sexuality may be driven into furtiveness; its pleasures may be much dimmed; but it cannot be repressed in any widespread way. What is made furtive is only forced into secrecy; what is truly repressed is forced totally out of awareness. Later in his work, Freud came to recognize this and became optimistic that sexual censorship might become progressively less onerous, as indeed it has. But by then he had seen there was a far darker secret locked away in the body, and this he named Thanatos, the body's need to live out its organic destiny, to ripen and die.

This insight shifts the entire discussion of the body to a much deeper level. At once we see that what is most repressed—and surely more so in our culture than in any other —is the body's organic nature, which is the body's whole reality. Sex only suffers in the wake of this general act of repression—and far less so than other aspects of the body's activity. Indeed, that is why we are so acutely aware of sexual repression: because sexuality is still alive and fighting within us. It is still sensitive to pressure; it can hurt and protest. In contrast, what is numb or dead (like the potentialities of the senses) no longer feels pressure; its battle for survival has been lost. It is *organism* which the estranged cerebral cortex cannot tolerate and seeks to forget, obliterate, subjugate. Organism is spontaneous self-regulation, the mystery of formed growth, the inarticulate wisdom of the instincts. Single vision cannot understand such a state of being, let alone trust it to look after itself. Rather, it seeks to *imperialize* the body, in much the same way that, in the world at large, civilized cultures seek to imperialize primitive cultures. (And that is more than a purely metaphorical comparison.) Worst of all, from the viewpoint of the alienated head, the body is mortal; it dies. It dies, of course, because the whole meaning of organism is to fulfill the cycle of life, leave seed, and make way for new growth. But organic time—the time of maturating cycles —is an absurdity to the head, and death a shattering defeat.

Head is death-denying far more so than sex-denying. In our contemporary swinging society, the orthodox consciousness gives ever more ample place to sexuality and allows the young to crusade obstreperously for erotic freedom. But the fact of death remains far more of an obscenity than sex. No doubt, in the fully permissive society, we shall all—every man, woman, and child of us—know fifty-seven clever ways to fuck long before we know one humanly becoming way to die.

Our proud, presumptuous head speaks one language; our body another—a silent, arcane language. Our head experiences in the mode of number, logic, mechanical connection; our body in the mode of fluid process, intuitive adaptation; it sways to an inner purposive rhythm . . . doubtless as deeply buried in nature as the spontaneous need of quarks and sub-nucleons (or whatever the ultimate dust may be) to take the first rude shape of matter. It may seem that to speak this way is to deal in a crude dichotomy of human nature. It is. The dichotomy that tears at our personality *is* crude; but I did not invent it. I have only inherited it, like you, from the anti-organic fanaticism of western culture. Consider for a moment: since we were children, what have we been taught to regard as the quintessential image of loathing and disgust? What is it our horror literature and science fiction haul in whenever they seek to make our skin crawl? Anything alive, mindless, and gooey . . . anything sloppy, slobbering, liquescent, smelly, slimy, gurgling, putrescent, mushy, grubby . . . things amoeboid or fungoid that stick and cling, that creep and seep and grow . . . things that have the feel of spit or shit, snot or piss, sweat or pus or blood . . . In a word, anything *organic,* and as messy as birth, sex, death, and decay. We cringe from anything as oozy as the inside of our body and look for security to what is clinically tidy, hard-edged, dry, rigidly solid, odorless, aseptic, durable. In another word, anything *lifeless*—as lifeless and gleamingly sterile as the glass and aluminum, stainless steel and plastic of the high-rise architecture and its interiors that now fill the urban-industrial world.

But how remarkable it is, that we should shrink from what is most akin to the vital processes of the body, preferring what is patently unalive and artificial. And yet how serviceable to the urban-industrial ethos. It is almost as if we might wish to disconnect from the meat and juice of our organism and become disembodied intelligences. And how many members of our culture would not trade in their natural body tomorrow for a guaranteed deathproof counterfeit? How many already pay a high price to be expertly embalmed and buried in caskets that will keep them (so they hope) eternally undecayed? As if that should be the final insult to their integrity. Perhaps in all human cultures there has been some tendency to subordinate or bully the body. But I doubt there has been such a hostile breakdown of communications between head and body, such an ingrained, generalized asceticism, as in ours—and without even an occasional ritual means of getting back in touch with organic reality. Again to quote Alfred Kroeber on the primitives: "retarded cultures seem infantile . . . in their unabashed preoccupation with bodily functions. . . ." The primitives, he observes, persist in "the gratuitous obtrusion into public recognition and the social order of physiological happenings, including blood and death and decay, which we tend to regard . . . as unpleasant and useless." In contrast to the childlike messiness of primitive people, civilized societies possess what Kroeber calls "adult attitudes toward physiological function."

Yet what strange problems come of this bourgeois fastidiousness Kroeber identifies with "civilization." So obnoxious has organic reality become within the artificial environment that we can only conceive of our own wastes and garbage as a repulsive nuisance to be washed down the disposal or neatly sealed up in plastic bags. Determined to repress the sight and smell of putrefaction, the urban-industrial societies destroy the rich and cheap organic fertilizers that could, with a little care, be reclaimed by way of municipal composting. Then, having cast away this valuable organic waste, they become progressively more dependent on ecologically damaging chemical fertilizers, which, in turn, produce an even more pallid, plastic-flavored food requiring artificial "enrichment." Remarkable, is it not, how efficiently the artificiality of our lifestyle compounds itself?

Only within recent years have we begun to sense how diseased this squeamish rejection of the organic is. Accordingly, a host of new post-Freudian therapies have grown up whose purpose is to salvage the wisdom of the body, many of them deriving from the bioenergetics of Wilhelm Reich. Gestalt therapy, sensory awareness, non-verbal communication, structural integration, psychosynthesis . . . The techniques are many, but the project is the same: to reclaim our identity as organisms. The degradation of the body which results from the head's intolerance for the organic can of course play havoc with personal health. But I raise the point here because it leads to a more far-reaching liability. The sense we have of being so exclusively drawn up into our heads and sealed off from the body determines fundamentally the way in which we address the world, the way in which we *feel* the reality around us. Intolerance for the organic begins with the body, but it spreads from there to the environment at large. The body is nature nearest home; it is *us* as we take part in the self-regulating processes of form and growth that sustain the universe.

When, therefore, our powers of proprioception dim, it is more than a personal misfortune. It is also the foreclosure of our ability to know nature from the inside out. Or, to put it another way, it is the beginning of that scientific objectivity whose extreme has been reached with western society's total conversion to mechanistic reductionism. It is also the beginning of our infatuation with the artificial environment. That is why any significant change in our body-consciousness might well amount to cultural revolution. For to know nature and the body from the inside cannot be the sort of knowing that goes on within the precincts of the isolated, domineering head. It has little to do with accumulating more biological data. It is nothing that can be acquired by academic research. Rather, it is a knowledge that must come through the body and be accepted on the body's own terms as a lesson not to be learned elsewhere or otherwise: an organic message, organically integrated.

A REVOLUTIONARY MYSTICISM

This has been only a brief, preliminary inventory of the privations required by our culture's orthodox consciousness. But what I have mentioned—the censoring of the dark mind, the sensory predominance of the anesthetized eye and ear, the undoing of organic sensibility—seem to me the cruelest wounds of our personal alienation. Taken together, they describe the major contours of the psychic wasteland we carry within us as we make our way through the "real" world of the artificial environment. It should be clear enough toward what grim end such alienative tendencies point. Deprive the person of dreamlife, of sensuous participation in experience, of organic plasticity, and what is there left? The bare, obedient mechanisms of cerebration and behavior: the *biocomputer,* which it is no great trick to mimic with clever electronic substitutes, since the machines are then only imitating the imitation of a machine. That end—the complete crystallization of life which Roderick Seidenberg has predicted as the fate of "posthistoric man"—may not be humanly attainable even at the cost of psychotic self-distortion. But cultural ideals

may elude complete achievement and still command our aspirations. We would not be the first people to find ourselves
trapped in a toxic culture . . . though we could be the last.

There might be little hope that the privations mentioned
here could be sensibly discussed at all, if it were not that a
significant number of people have clearly begun to grow
restive with this diminished self we have become. A minority,
yes; but a minority whose presence is like a mirror held up
to the society at large. I speak of the wide-ranging Human
Potentials Movement encamped in its many Growth Centers
across America. Over the past generation, this "eupsychian
network" (as Abraham Maslow called it) has borrowed
heavily on yogic, Taoist, and Tantric sources to propagate a
variety of techniques for expanding personality. No question
but that the promise of the movement is great. Yet there has
often been a haunting ambiguity about its intentions, which
I sense is only lately finding resolution.

The interest of both teachers and students in these new
psychic disciplines can be purely therapeutic in the very
narrowest sense (*"limbers you up . . . makes you feel
better"*)—and, during its early days, the movement for the
most part carried its members no further than such "emotional nourishment." In this respect, the Gestalt master Frederick Perls was typical of the movement's founding generation.
A gifted healer, Perls would never agree that his work should
reach beyond the mending of disintegrated organisms. But,
as a growing number of contemporary therapists realize, their
work goes much deeper. To enlarge consciousness may be an
exhilarating, even a life-saving personal adventure; but more
important by far are the metaphysical implications of these
psychic experiments. Potentially at least, there is a religious
dimension involved in the work of reshaping consciousness;
for originally these techniques were invented to illuminate a
transpersonal reality. Once recognize that, and therapy gives
way to the perennial mystic quest.

If you will, therapy is mysticism with all the metaphysical

commitments drained off; it can end in a kind of splendid psychosensory athleticism, with all the emotional knots untied and the kinks carefully smoothed away. One meets people like this in the movement. They tune their psyches with marvelous self-indulgence until there is not an inhibition, not a frustration left to ruffle their calm. They are much like the body-builders who fastidiously train every last little muscle and tendon to perfection. Who can tell? Perhaps someday we shall have a National Psychic Development Competition with awards for Mr. and Miss Ataraxy . . . But what was the warning the wise Zen master gave his pupil? "Now that you have achieved total perfection enlightenment, you may expect to be just as miserable as ever."

Mysticism is an ungainly word to bring into the discussion; it is wrapped in such an exotic air. Yet that very sense of the exotic is a telling measure of how estranged we are from essential portions of our personality. The mystic quest very likely begins no further off than just the other side of the commonplace, daily repressions we have been reviewing here. So near . . . and yet so far. If we know the mystical only in its most extravagant forms, it is because we are like children raised wholly in the metropolis. We are more likely to have seen tigers in the zoo than barnyard cows, more apt to have seen hothouse orchids than ordinary wild flowers. Yet the truth is what Shelley, like Traherne before him, recognized it to be. One discerns in children the visionary normality which is largely cast off in adulthood . . . or perhaps buried alive.

> Let us recollect our sensations as children. What a distinct and intense apprehension we had of the world and of ourselves. . . . We less habitually distinguished all that we saw and felt from ourselves. They seemed as it were to constitute one mass. . . . There are some persons who, in this respect, are always children. Those who are subject to the state called reverie feel as if

their nature were dissolved into the surrounding universe, or as if the surrounding universe were absorbed into their being.

The same doors of perception are in us all; but some manage to hold them open, others by habit pass them by and never look through. In our culture, we have nailed the doors shut and plastered them over. That is what life in the artificial environment demands of us. And this makes us indeed a unique people. No prescientific society is even imaginable without its mystic contingent, its oracles and seers, yogis, medicine men, and shamans, always there in the thick of life moving among the populace as casually as the fish among the waves. (But note that I speak here of the prophetical not the priestly tradition, of Bergson's "dynamic" as opposed to his "static religion.") Even when the holy men chose to retire into solitude, not a person remained behind in the world but knew that the woods and mountains round about, the caves and desert places were filled with saints who waited there to teach the other reality. St. Anthony, try as he would, could never withdraw so far into the Egyptian wastes but that townsfolk and villagers would follow to bring him food, and the young men to study his example; even the Roman emperor himself sent his solicitations after the great hermit. It is the paradox of the mystical tradition that it has managed to be at the same time peripheral and central, reclusive yet pervasive. Why should this be so?

It is because, though the gifts of mystics might be special, the reality in which they trafficked was, at least to a degree, widely shared, usually by way of collective ritual. It existed as a fact, an undisputed and central fact of the common awareness. Is this not precisely what we have for so long identified as the "superstitiousness" of prescientific cultures? Only when that reality ceases to be generally, if but tenuously shared, does the mystical become what it peculiarly is with us: exotic . . . abnormal . . . cranky.

We have lost that reality because it has no public place in the urban-industrial world. Our diminished consciousness is cut to fit the reduced psychic dimensions of that social form. Given the scale on which it has wrought its changes and the pace at which it has undertaken to homogenize the cultures of the world within its uniform, artificial environment, the urban-industrial revolution could hardly make do with less than a radical reconstruction of the personality. And nothing has suffered more in the turbulent transition than the mystical capacities. They are indeed the great obstacle, because the mystic vision has always denied the finality of history, the self-sufficiency of man.

In times past, a widespread respect for mystical insight has obviously guaranteed nothing about the material well-being, justice, or decency of any society. The afflictions and corruptions of the world are many, and it has not been the role of the mystic to heal them all. This is in spite of the fact that the ethical sensibility of the mystics, counseling as it does compassion, gentleness, and the selfless community of all living things, has always been totally at odds with the way of the world. For the great yoga master Pathanjali, it went without question that the first step toward enlightenment (long before instruction in the postures, the breathing exercises, and the rest began) was a life which was pure of violence, exploitation, greed, and falsehood. And yet, by and large, the mystical tradition has chosen to achieve its purity by quietism and withdrawal, not by active resistance to evil. There is one notable exception of course. Jewish prophecy has never hesitated to bring its full rhapsodic and visionary powers to bear against the injustice of its times. From this strain of mysticism, we derive that ethical zeal which echoes through the words of a George Fox, a Blake, a Tolstoy, and which even reaches down to Gandhi who, under Tolstoy's influence, brilliantly assimilated Hindu mysticism to militant political action.

Along these lines, prophetical mysticism has made a contribution of inestimable value to our political life; but there is an irony to the matter. Since the time of the French Revolution, while the moral surface of prophetical protest has been skimmed by modern radicalism, its religious vision has been transmuted into purely secular ideologies. The thunder of Amos still reverberates in the pronouncements of Marx—but now the poetic ecstasy has been flattened into power political prose. Having borrowed the moral fires of rhapsodic prophecy, modern radicalism has placed them at the service of a fiercely anti-religious politics. Even Gandhi's synthesis has been rapidly undone by activists who appropriate the "tactic" of *satyagraha,* but discard its animating vision. And then, usually, the tactic becomes a *"mere"* tactic and is soon dispensed with.

There is of course an undeniable justification for the radical's mistrust of mysticism. Prophetic protest is clearly exceptional within the mystical tradition. For the most part, the mystics have settled for playing the part of fire-tenders in the midst of a troubled humanity. They have contented themselves with saving individual souls, and have rarely sought to transform society. Those of us who are more political animals may find it difficult to appreciate such a quietistic strategy. But we might at least recognize that, from the mystic's viewpoint, it was based on a sort of victory. While the authority of mystical insight has frequently been perverted by church and state, it has never in the past been denied its reality. The state has in fact employed the priest precisely to co-opt prophetical vision. But by that very act of piracy it has had to affirm the sanctity of that vision. And so there was always hope that the fire, if faithfully tended, might yet grow bright enough to light the world. As long as the throne leaned itself cynically upon the altar for support, no earthly power could afford to dry up the sources of mystical religion. Kings have been known to butcher saints, only to finish by raising shrines to them. Hypocritical gestures no doubt; but hypocrisy must in spite of itself honor the ideal it defiles.

However one may regard this long-standing accommodation between the world and its charismatic holy men, that *modus vivendi* is now at an end. More and more, the imperatives of urban-industrial society close out visionary consciousness, replacing the sacramental worldview with the desacralized universe of modern science. For the first time in history, governing elites in the world's developed and developing societies labor to detach themselves even from the most denatured religious conventions of the past; they rule in the name of another ideal entirely. The high principle that has motivated this epoch-making secularization of life is familiar enough; no need here to praise liberal humanism for its brave intentions and many achievements. Nevertheless, under the pressure of that secularizing thrust, the role of mystical consciousness in our culture now alters fundamentally. It is no longer simply the mystic's moral perfectionism that runs contrary to the world; even more so it is the metaphysical meaning of his vision. The biologist Jacques Monod, who would have done once and for all with the entire religious heritage, has posed the issue with fierce honesty. "The scientific attitude," says Monod, "implies what I call the postulate of objectivity—that is to say, the fundamental postulate that there is no plan, that there is no intention in the universe." This, he maintains, is "the essential message of science," which must replace "the ancient animist covenant between man and nature, leaving nothing in place of that precious bond but an anxious quest in a frozen universe of solitude."

> Modern societies accepted the treasures and the power that science laid in their laps. But they have not accepted—they have scarcely even heard—its profounder message: the defining of a new and unique source of truth, and the demand for a thorough revision of ethical premises. . . . If he accepts this message—accepts

all it contains—then man must at last wake out of his
millenary dream; and in doing so, wake to his total
solitude, his fundamental isolation. Now does he at
last realize that, like a gypsy, he lives on the boundary
of an alien world. A world that is deaf to his music,
just as indifferent to his hopes as it is to his suffering
or his crimes.

Monod is wrong, I think, in believing that many values
seriously at variance with his postulate of objectivity any longer
get taught in the mainstream of the developed societies. But
in any case, far more important than the values and traditions to which people pay lip service are the underlying
sensibilities that animate their lives, the Reality Principle to
which they are bound in their perception and intellection. And
at that level of consciousness, most of us, by way of the
psychic privations this chapter discusses, are already well advanced toward becoming the biocomputer Monod's postulate
of objectivity—"the *only* authentic source of truth"—demands.

The artificial environment of urban-industrialism needs
only that dream-bereft fraction of the human whole. The
rest—so rich a part!—it leaves to wither or take refuge in the
coward heart; its Reality Principle aggressively seeks to crowd
all others from sane awareness. Does this not force mysticism
toward a revolutionary role? Either that or a bad end as a
mere therapeutic amusement of alienated man. As, progressively, all the earth becomes an industrial artifact, not even the
withdrawal into solitude remains as an option. Once, perhaps,
the God-intoxicated few could abscond to the wild frontiers,
the forests, the desert places to keep alive the perennial wisdom that they harbored. But no longer. They must now become a political force or their tradition perishes. Soon enough,
there will be no solitude left for the saints to roam but its air
will shudder with a noise of great engines that drowns all
prayers.

PART TWO

SINGLE VISION AND NEWTON'S SLEEP:

The Strange Interplay of Objectivity and Alienation

How the psychology of single vision, beginning as a defense of the sacred, was carried by Christianity into the Scientific Revolution, and how an alienated natural philosophy, after achieving cultural supremacy in the modern world, has betrayed its brightest ideals.

> *Now I a fourfold vision see,*
> *And a fourfold vision is given to me;*
> *'Tis fourfold in my supreme delight*
> *And threefold in soft Beulah's night*
> *And twofold Always. May God us keep*
> *From Single vision & Newton's sleep!*

> William Blake

CHAPTER 4

The Sin of Idolatry

I was born a thousand years ago,
born in the culture of bows and
arrows . . . born in an age when
people loved the things of nature
and spoke to it as though it had
a soul.

Chief Dan George

IN THE EYE OF THE BEHOLDER

As a phase in the history of consciousness, the building of the artificial environment may best be understood as an ever deepening condition of idolatry. Note that I do not say a *form* of idolatry, but idolatry itself, pure and simple; the term is used here in no metaphorical sense as, for example, when we speak of the "idolatry" of nationalism. Nor is it employed as by the preacher in the pulpit when he castigates his flock for whoring after the false gods of money or material possessions. I intend no ethical usage. Rather, I refer to a state of consciousness, a condition of our powers of perception and intellection which has only an indirect, and far from obvious relationship to moral behavior. (In fact, taking the word as it will be used here, many of the most hardened idolators I know, personally or by reputation, have led lives of exemplary moral character.) It is in respect to the quality of our experience that we have become an idolatrous culture . . . and in fact the *only* idolatrous culture in the history of mankind.

Now, this is paradoxical indeed. For no culture has been at greater pains to search out and eradicate the sin of idolatry than those touched by the Judeo-Christian heritage. As a category of religious thought, idolatry unfolds peculiarly out of the Jewish religious sensibility. In no respect is Judaism more unique than in its uncompromising insistence on God's unity, invisibility, and transcendence. It is the first commandment imposed upon the nation: that God should not be idolized, nor any idol (whether man-made or natural object) be deified. Christianity carries forward the same hot intolerance for nature worship and the pagan use of imagery. In Protestantism especially, hostility toward the slightest idolatrous inclination becomes obsessive. At times, the word even broadens to include any deviation from orthodox belief or practice. Thus the seventeenth-century English divine Henry Hammond warns in his tract *Of Idolatry* (1646)

> . . . if still our eares are open to every sect of hypocriticall professors, though never so wilde and ignorant, that brings any liberty, or proffer of carnality along with it, then sure is the title of *Christian* but ill bestowed on us, we are still the grossest idolaters in the world.

Calvin, for his part, was convinced that the "brutal stupidity" of idolatrous worship was an ineradicable symptom of man's corruption. In one form or another, it was bound always to come to the surface. "The mind of man," he held, "is . . . a perpetual manufactory of idols." One could not, therefore, guard too watchfully against this "flagitious madness," this "abomination," this "perverse superstition." Hence, the puritanical passion for making ever more refined discriminations between idolatrous and godly worship. At the extreme, any extraneous gesture, vestment, or ornament—even one candlestick too many—might conceal idolatrous intent. The western tradition of iconomachy is long and fiercely scrupulous. The stereotypic picture it offers us of primitive worshipers bowed down before sacred grove or statue still represents for many one of the most hideous examples of human degradation, one of those horrors of ignorance which it is the glory of Christian civilization to have left behind forever.

Yet—and here is the irony of the matter—it is doubtful that any such thing as idolatry has ever existed to any significant degree outside the perceptions—or misperceptions—of the Judeo-Christian cultures. What Jew, Christian, and Moslem saw and condemned in the worship of infidel peoples was not idolatry at all—not as they understood it. Rather, the sin was in the eye of the beholders. And more than in their eye, in their heart eventually to emerge as a besetting vice. From this point of view, the centuries-long Judeo-Christian crusade against idolatry has in reality been not a struggle against a real evil in the world but a guilty anticipation of the strange destiny which the consciousness of western man was to realize in our own time.

"THE HEATHEN IN HIS BLINDNESS . . ."

For the Jews, believers in the invisible God whose face was hidden even from his most favored prophet, idolatry was a simple and obvious matter. It was worship mediated by sight or touch, worship which fastened upon a tangible or visible presence. "The heathen in his blindness bows down to wood and stone." We can only wonder by what secret and ruthless process Judaism purged itself of the primeval power of the eye and hand to give witness to the divine. But so it was. And in return for this rough amputation of visual and tactile witness, the Jews acquired their incomparable ear. Their witness became exclusively, prodigiously auditory: they *heard* . . . they heard as no one else had ever heard. They became history's most alert listeners. Their God was pre-eminently a voice, one who revealed his magisterial presence by speaking into the world from beyond it. Undeniably, in this vocal God we have a mighty realization of the universality of the sacred. Manifested in the image of sound, the divine presence may span all space, be at once in all places, penetrate all barriers. Such a God can hover over the world and send his voice out vastly before him to announce his will. From such a God one does not hide or run away, because he is no spatially delimited being to be left behind in the distance. Nor need he, like a physical image, suffer to be constantly on display. He alone may choose to be revealed or withdrawn, to speak or keep silent. The Jews beyond all other cultures seized upon the spiritually potent symbolism of sound: that which is present in the world ubiquitously, but intangibly. Or rather, they seized upon *articulate* sound. The sound to which the Jewish ear was tuned was far removed from the primal groundtone of the Hindu and Buddhist mantra, the "seed-syllable" from which the worshiper evokes an immediate awareness of the divine. The mantra is a hypnotic murmur; it entrances . . . and then consumes. But the word of the prophetical God instructs; it is intelligible speech.

Here was what Judaism uniquely discovered: that God *spoke*. Adopting human language, he could speak through the mouths of human beings. This was the point at which the Jewish prophetical consciousness abandoned the shamanistic tradition from which it derived—and so broke with that

ancient religious lineage which Judaism has taught us ever
since to regard as "primitive." To be sure, behind the rhapsodic prophets there stands the Hebrew *nabi,* the babbler, the
mutterer, the speaker with tongues, whose only "message" is
his undecipherable yammer, which proclaims authentic possession by the sacred. But the prophetical tradition moves
beyond its origin. The intoxicated blather becomes language
which can be recalled, *re*-spoken, written down, treasured up
and preserved. So Judaism becomes the religion of the word
and the book.

It is a great question: did God's decision to exchange
ecstatic yammering for rhapsodic speech represent a maturation of the word . . . or a "talking down"? One liability
is surely clear. When the prophetic utterance has at last
cooled on the page and in the memory, it easily falls prey to
small-minded literalism. It becomes the word which is not the
spirit, and which kills the spirit. It congeals into law, and at
last it lends its lifeless carcass to the creed makers and theolo-
gians.

In any event, it was inevitable that the Jew, as the devotee
of a God who was to be heard and not seen, should view the
traditional worship of the infidel as debased. For what were
the infidel's gods? Mere *things,* natural objects *in* the world,
contained and made small by the space of that world, minute
in relationship to all earth and the heavens, time-bound and
perishable, vulnerable to accident or abuse. Worse still, perhaps these objects were things made by the worshiper's own
hand and then set up before him for devotion. For the Jew,
such an act of worship could only seem grotesque. Thus,
Isaiah:

> The carpenter stretcheth out a line; he marketh it
> out with a pencil; he shapeth it with planes, and he
> marketh it out with the compasses, and shapeth it
> after the figure of a man, to dwell in the house. He

> . . . strengtheneth for himself one among the trees
> of the forest; . . . He burneth part thereof in the fire;
> . . . yea, he warmeth himself and saith, Aha, I am
> warm, I have seen the fire; and the residue thereof
> he maketh a god . . . He falleth down to it and wor-
> shippeth, and prayeth unto it and saith, Deliver me;
> for thou art my God.
>
> (Isaiah 44:13–18)

Later, with equal spleen, St. Augustine would speak of the use of icons as "mankind tyrannized over by the work of his own hands." The mockery is cruel. But worse than that, it is un-justified. It assumes, incorrectly, that the infidel's perception of the sacred lodged *wholly in* the object before him and traveled no further. The infidel "is not ashamed," says the Book of Wisdom, "to speak to that *which hath no life*." If that were so, then the spiritual consciousness of the infidel would indeed be pathetically flawed. But we have no reason to believe that the Hebrew interpretation of idolatry is correct. As Edwyn Bevan observes:

> It is hardly possible that anyone thought of the deity
> worshipped as simply the image he saw and nothing
> more. The personality of the deity was not confined
> to the image in the sense in which my personality is
> confined to my body. The deity was certainly con-
> ceived of as a person active in the world apart from
> the image. . . . The image was not the one body of
> the god.

Rather, the object on which the so-called idolater fixes his devout attention is transparent to the senses that contemplate it. It is a window, both seen and seen through, a material medium where perception and revelation mingle and are mar-ried. An American Indian explains his act of worship in this way:

Everything as it moves, now and then, here and there, makes stops. The bird as it flies stops in one place to make its nest, and in another to rest in its flight. A man when he goes forth stops when he wills. So the god has stopped. The sun, which is so bright and beautiful, is one place where he has stopped. The trees, the animals, are where he has stopped, and the Indian thinks of these places and sends his prayers to reach the place where the god has stopped.

In Owen Barfield's terminology, such temporary resting places of the divine are "participated" by human perception. They *open* to experience and escort the witness through to sacred ground beyond themselves. Participation, as Barfield puts it, is "the sense that there stands behind the phenomena, *and on the other side of them from man,* a represented, which is of the same nature as man." But, he continues, "it was against this that Israel's face was set." Instead, the Jews undertook, as their distinctive historical project, an "ingathering withdrawal from participation."

This reductive Jewish interpretation of nature worship and graven images passed over into early Christianity to become one of the fiercest elements in the rejection of Greco-Roman paganism. The pagans, St. Paul charged, had "changed the glory of the incorruptible God into an image made like to corruptible man, and to birds, and four-footed beasts, and creeping things." For the Church Father Clement of Alexandria the rejection carried even further. It extended to the plastic arts generally, all of which seemed to him a kind of madness since they diverted attention toward an even more derivative reality than that of the surrounding world of nature. The argument is strongly Neoplatonic. Even as nature is but a reflection of the supreme reality of God, so art is but a reflection of nature, a mere shadow of a shadow. But in early and medieval Christianity, the monophysite iconoclasts were the only sizable group to carry the objection to imagery nearly so far in their worship. Only they, arguing that it insulted the unbounded God to confine his image within a material object, were to join the Jews and Moslems in categorically prohibiting any representation of the deity. Fortunately for the art history of the west, mainstream Christianity rapidly accommodated itself to the pagan need for visual imagery. Its compromise was to accept the image as *nothing but* a statue, a mere symbol deprived of sacred personality. Thus the Christian image (at least in official theology) ceased to be of any magical character—though in practice, the images and relics of the Church have repeatedly been invested with an enchanted aura by what we should be forced to call the "superstitious masses." Natural objects were, of course, wholly banned from official worship.

What this adamant rejection of pagan worship failed to grasp (and we must assume it was for lack of the ability to experience the fact) was precisely the capacity of an icon or natural object to be enchanted, to be transmuted into something more than itself. What our tradition refers to as idolatry is a variety of magic, and magic, in its pristine form, is sacramental perception. The function of any so-called idol, authentically perceived, is to give local embodiment to the universal presence and power of the divine. It gathers up that presence as a lens gathers up light diffused in space and gives it a bright, hard focus. But of course the light vastly envelops the lens; so too the supposed idolater understands attendant divinity to envelop all being. To know this is to understand how any portion of nature, even the most unaccountable things or indeed nature as a whole, can quite suddenly assume the radiance of a magical object. To this psychic dimension of idolatry, however, Christianity was as firmly closed as Judaism.

Interestingly, the point I raise here was acknowledged by Calvin, who agreed that no heathen could ever conceivably have been stupid enough to believe that a lump of wood or stone was "god." Admittedly then, said Calvin, the pagans in fact worshiped "the Divinity that invisibly dwelt in" the object. Yet even this insight could not mitigate the sin of idolatry for him; it remained an impermissible act of "corporeal adoration" which lacked "spiritual knowledge." But what an extraordinarily revealing line of argument this is. Calvin is able—intellectually—to make out the distinction between idolatrous and participative consciousness. But it makes no difference to him! Why? Because he is, obviously, cold to the experience. He *knows* it, but he does not *feel* it. He has no experiential sense of what it means to discover divinity dwelling invisibly within—a striking example of how remote head knowledge can be from visionary realization.

What we find being rejected here as idolatry by Jews, Christians, and Moslems is the form of worship anthropologists have called animism or naturism, usually with the unmistakable suggestion that this is the crudest, most rudimentary level of religious sensibility. But such scholarly condescension is only another reflection of the doctrinaire prejudice we inherit from the Judeo-Christian past; it is surely a questionable interpretation of the animist experience. Why, one wonders, should it be thought crude or rudimentary to find divinity brightly present in the world where others find only dead matter or an inferior order of being? And with what justification do we conclude that this thing we call animism is a false experience of the world? Even if they have observed such worship at close range, what members of our culture have ever entered sufficiently into the animist sensibility to judge its existential validity?

Prejudice and ethnocentrism aside, what we know for a fact is that, outside our narrow cultural experience, in religious rites both sophisticated and primitive, human beings have been able to achieve a sacramental vision of being, and that this may well be the wellspring of human spiritual consciousness. From that rich source there flow countless religious and philosophical traditions. The differences between these traditions—between Eskimo shamanism and medieval alchemy, between Celtic druidism and Buddhist Tantra—are many; but an essentially magical worldview is common to them all. I will from time to time be referring to this diverse family of religions and philosophies as the Old Gnosis—the old way of knowing, which delighted in finding the sacred in the profane—and I will be treating it with no little respect, since I regard it as the essential and supreme impulse of the religious life. This is not, of course, religion as many people in our society know it. It is a visionary style of knowledge, not a theological one; its proper language is myth and ritual; its foundation is rapture, not faith and doctrine; and its experience of nature is one of living communion. It will not be the least eccentric aspect of this book that I will so often be taking my bearings in the discussion of religion from this supposedly defunct tradition, perhaps even suggesting that its resurrection is an urgent project of the times.

THE DEATH OF MAGIC

Just as the Church found it possible (or rather absolutely necessary, given its mission to the Gentiles) to accommodate religious imagery in its worship, so too it turned a more liberal eye than Judaism toward magic. Here, however, the accommodation had to be far more painstaking. The Church had to be careful not to compromise the unity, aloofness, and sovereignty of God the Father, as well as the specialness of the revelation in Christ. For Christian orthodoxy, in all history there has been only one physical embodiment of the divine, only one path to communion with God: the incarnation of the Word in Jesus. Christian authority could not, therefore, tolerate any access to the sacred that it did not monopolize. Hence its crusade against the magical worldview.

It is from the early Church that we inherit our commonplace skepticism toward all magicians, our conviction that they are nature-fakers one and all worthy of no higher status than that of entertainers. We find among early Christian writers treatises as astringently critical of magicians as anything ever produced by the Society for Psychical Research. For example, in the third century A.D., Hippolytus, a disciple of the Church Father Irenaeus, produced a tract, "The Refutation of All Heresies," which offers a deft exposé of the "juggleries" performed by noted miracle workers of the day—all the more amusing because a good number of the tricks it covers remain the stock-in-trade of stage magic today. But not all magic could be disposed of so easily by Christian critics; not all of it was vulnerable to simple debunking. For Tertullian, pagan magic was "a second idolatry" that involved not hoax but a veritable trafficking with evil spirits. For Augustine, magic was "a criminal tampering with the unseen world." Such illicit necromancy had to be clearly distinguished from true Christian miracles, especially those of Jesus. Only the latter were performed by God and they were used for no selfish advantage.

This critical distinction between good and bad magic is epitomized in the opposition between Jesus and that ominous figure who haunts the early Church like the anti-Christ himself: Simon Magus, the most infamous of the black magicians. There were few Christians who denied his extraordinary powers, few who did not feel the menace of his reputation. Simon too claimed to be virgin-born and an incarnate divinity worthy of worship; he too raised the dead. In fact, his inventory of wonders far outstrips that of Jesus. He is credited with animal transformations, the powers of flight and invisibility, and the secret of making gold. But Simon is remembered only as the shadow of Christ, because his powers, being derived from demons, were used for self-aggrandizement, not for the saving of souls. Simon restricted access to the miraculous for the sake of personal gain. Hence the sin of "simony," the prime offense against the Holy Spirit. Perhaps Simon was the villain Christian tradition makes of him, for there *are* bad magicians. But perhaps also there is more than a little partisan slander in the matter, a spiteful desire to denounce the sort of formidable rival Simon typifies—the free magician who resisted the Church's effort to monopolize the occult powers.

The Christian response to the competing magicians and idolaters of the Church had the advantage of offering simplicity and order. It restricted the authentically miraculous to a single tradition (biblical history and the life of Jesus) and to a single institution and its loyal members. Thus God worked miracles through his prophets and saints; Jesus was the unique instance of the sacred made incarnate; and in the sacraments of the Church, the faithful could legitimately participate in magic ceremonial. But only within these well-defined boundaries was the once wide-ranging sacramental consciousness to be accommodated. Beyond lay demonology or pure fakery, the realm of bad magic.

Doubtless this strategy of delimiting and institutionalizing magic saved the Christian believer from being inundated by a deal of superstition and crass charlatanry. Certainly much of what Christian critics saw about them in the cultic life of the Hellenistic world was nothing better than cheap prestidigitation, a sadly debased substitute for authentic religion. It was indeed a teeming, chaotic age of nature-faking and occult inanity. The repertory of Simon Magus, for instance (animal transformations, magical flight, invisibility), is largely that of primitive shamanism. In a stable, tribal context such practices can assist in invoking a deep, collective experience of the sacred. But in the dislocated society of the early Christian period, tribal culture was dead. What remained of its magical perception of nature—especially among the deracinated masses of the metropolitan areas—was little more than the superficial gestures of shamanist technique, the sort of diversion we today call "tricks." Then, as now, magic disconnected from the shared sacramental consciousness of a well-knit community quickly degenerates into "playing tricks" on people, cheap mystification suited only to the carnival stage.

The Church, in effect, stepped forward as a new cosmopolitan community—or rather, a community within the cosmopolis made up of the human ruins of collapsed empire. It provided the protective shell within which a purified, if much restricted sacramental consciousness could survive. Most important, the Church preserved the eucharistic supper carried over from the mystery cults as an ever renewed experience of God's miraculous embodiment in the natural world. In the sacrament of the mass an act of ritual enchantment as old as human religious consciousness survives. Here, a worldly object, a piece of ordinary bread made by human hands, is transformed by magical utterance and gesture into a real manifestation of the sacred. How does this consecrated bread then differ from the participated objects which pagan and infidel select for worship? Only with respect to the exclusiveness which the Church claims for it.

Yet Christian doctrine requires that there *must* be a genuine difference, since Catholicism inherits from Judaism the misconception of infidel idolatry. So the Church must condemn the idolaters and exclude their rites. Yet it must maintain that the eucharistic host is *not* an idol. This leads to a curious and unstable resolution. Like Judaism and Islam, Catholicism is required to prejudge the religious perception of infidel people and to conclude that they worship dead and unsanctified things, *mere* objects. But the Church shelters in its heart a rite which is psychologically indistinguishable from what it condemns as infidel idolatry. It knows that the bread, once magically transubstantiated, is not a mere object, but the veritable person of Christ. Thus the Church cannot—simply—forbid the exercise of participative consciousness. Instead, it must demand that the whole strength of that consciousness be concentrated in this one institutionalized mystery. *Only* this piece of enchanted bread can be the body of God; nothing else, nothing beyond. But whether this is true or not is something that only the capacities of human consciousness can decide, not doctrine. For how if, like Sri Ramakrishna (or Francis of Assisi), one begins to find the sacred vividly alive and calling in the fire, the water, the bird, the tree, the rock? Is one to say that God *cannot* so embody his presence? Is one to forbid this livelier, greater awareness of the divine to experience what in fact it experiences? God forbid.

To say that the Church's sacramental theology is an "unstable" resolution obviously does not apply to the Catholic societies of the world. But within Christendom as a whole, the Church's effort to straddle sacramental consciousness and the Judaic tradition of iconoclasm was bound to prove offensive to doctrinal purists. Too much of what the Church had assimilated from the pagan world—including the eucharistic supper—might easily fall under suspicion of idolatry. Magic must bring the sacred perilously close to the profane, always with the hope that the profane will, at its touch, reveal the hidden wonders it contains; always at the risk that the sacred will be diminished into some lesser manifestation which can legitimately be called an idol. For those who were quick to spy out idols (even where idols did not exist except in their own suspicion) there was a safer strategy for saving the sacred from idolatrous degeneration. This was to ban magic from the world entirely, thus to deny nature its authentic enchantment. The strategy is already anticipated by the fourth-century Christian polemicist Lactantius in his *Divine Institutes*. Here Lactantius, mocking his own simple-minded misconception of paganism, systematically attacks the supposed divinity of rivers, mountains, plants, beasts, etc. Obviously none of these are God, he concludes; nor is nature as a whole to be regarded as God. Rather, nature is a lesser object created by God and existing wholly apart from him.

> Therefore, the world is neither God nor living, if it has been made: for a living creature is not made, but born; and if it has been built, it has been built as a house or ship is built. Therefore, there is a builder of the world, even God; and the world which has been made is distinct from him who made it. . . . If, therefore, it has been constructed as an abode, it is neither itself God, nor are the elements which are its parts; because a house cannot bear rule over itself, nor can the parts of which a house consists. . . . For a house, made for the purpose of being inhabited, has no sensibility by itself and is subject to the master who built or inhabits it.

Thus nature is pronounced dead and desacralized. But where then in this morbid waste is the place of man, who is obviously a spiritual being? Significantly, Lactantius does not locate man inside this inanimate world; rather, in an ultimate expression of human estrangement, he concludes that man is existentially *outside nature* and only temporarily in residence during his mortal life.

> . . . the world does not produce man, nor is man a part of the world. For the same God who created the world, also created man from the beginning; *and man is not a part of the world,* in the same manner in which a limb is a part of the body; for it is possible for the world to be without man, as it is for a city or house.

This is a fateful ontology. Pressed to its ultimate conclusion, it yields a world in which nothing can be held sacred or companionable, a world disenchanted in root and branch into which man has been intruded like a cosmic freak. We are within earshot of Pascal's cry of sheer existential terror: "Cast into the infinite immensity of spaces of which I am ignorant and which know me not, I am frightened!"

ICONOCLAST FURY AND THE KALI YUGA

It remained for the Protestant Reformation to bring icono-clast Christianity to its fever pitch of intensity. So zealous has been the Protestant crusade to purify itself of what it took to be "accursed idolatry" that one feels impelled to conclude that we are dealing here not simply with a divergent inter-pretation of Christian doctrine but with a strange new stage in the history of human consciousness. Protestantism revised Christian orthodoxy because the *experience* of its founders and followers had shifted into a radically different key from that of their Catholic rivals. Their sensibility harked back to the desert prophets of Israel. In them we find the same in-tolerance for sensuous imagery and magic, the same fanatical determination to segregate the sacred from the profane that the two might at no point touch. It is an event of unparalleled importance that this old prophetical animus against magic should be reborn in a society as expansively energetic and as technologically proficient as Western Europe in the age of the discoveries. For now, in its search for a purified Christian-ity, Protestantism carried the desacralization of nature to its annihilating extreme, and so conceived a world into which the extraordinary dynamism of the west could flow freely and aggressively to work its will.

"Protestantism," observes Paul Tillich in *The Protestant Era,* "asserts that grace appears *through* a living Gestalt which remains itself what it is. . . . A Gestalt of grace is a transparent Gestalt. Something shines through it which is more than it." Tillich's principle of transparency is an extremely important religious category. Perhaps with its help Christians might have found it possible to distinguish pagan worship from what they mistook idolatry to be. What is a "Gestalt of grace," after all, but an object participated by sacramental contemplation? But, tragically, Tillich's Protestant precursors were incapable of trusting *any* Gestalt of grace to remain transparent—as if the psychology of participation had weakened drastically among them to the point of becoming a risky venture. As if the sacramental visibility of the world about them were closing down, and all things were fast declining to the status of mere objects, opaque and unilluminated. Nothing then could be trusted as a receptacle of the sacred. Excepting Luther's ambiguous idea of consubstantiation, Protestantism insisted that the traditional sacraments of the Church must be denied all magical efficacy. For Calvin, transubstantiation becomes a "monstrous notion," a "fictitious illusion" based on the "stupid notion" that the consecration of the host is "a kind of magical incantation." Even the ecclesiastical ornaments, artwork and liturgy of the faith became suspect, for they too had grown too dense and lusterless to transmit the act of worship beyond themselves. How else to describe radical Protestantism, then, but as a relentless stripping down operation directed against every object or gesture upon which sacramental consciousness might light?

At the extreme, in a very fury of iconoclasm, there were puritan divines like William Perkins, who, in his *Warning Against the Idolatrie of the Last Times* (1603), was even prepared to attack mental pictures and representations as "idols." True worship, he insisted, had to be totally imageless, totally devoid of visual content or sensual appeal, an abstraction made up of concepts and words. For "a thing faigned in the mind by imagination is an idol." Here we can discern the religious sanction behind that peculiar, pitiless war upon the imaginative powers which philosophy, both empiricist and rationalist, would wage for the next two centuries. When Blake, in defense of the poetic powers, finally proclaimed that "the Eternal Body of Man is the Imagination, that is, God himself the Divine Body," he was pitting himself against a formidable tradition.

The torturous transformation of consciousness we discuss here can be found mirrored throughout the art, decor, and costume of Protestant Society. The drabness of puritan life is usually taken to be an outgrowth of thrift and moral austerity. But even more so, the darkness, sobriety, and oppressive weightiness of the puritan style betoken a perceived *thickening* of the world's substance, as if the very gravity of matter were on the increase. Indeed, this is the point in time at which, as Ernst Lehrs points out, the traditional conception of levity (the polar opposite of gravity) rapidly fades from scientific thought, as if it had become an unthinkable notion. Simultaneously, in the painting of the period, especially that of Rembrandt and the Dutch masters, the light rapidly fails; it is poured over with the "brown sauce" of heavy oils. The atmosphere of landscapes grows gross to the point of impenetrability. Weight . . . shadow . . . thickness . . . density . . . opacity . . . We have in this Calvinist perception of things the sense of a world that has become ponderously material, *real* in its own right as we would understand the meaning of "real" today . . . a world whose gravity hauls at the mind, drawing down attention, forcing people to take time and matter seriously. Nothing possesses the brightness to reflect, the clarity to transmit perception beyond itself. The spiritual transparency of the earth clouds over; the questing vision gets *stuck in things*. Such a world is obviously no place for the sacred to reside.

We are at the point where, in Tillich's words, "Protestant protest has . . . brought to the verge of disappearance the sacramental foundation of Christianity, and with it the religious foundation of the protest itself." It is, in Vedic terminology, the advent of the Kali Yuga, the age of darkness.

Under such conditions of consciousness, what choice did Protestantism have but to resort to an absolute iconoclasm? In its darkening perception, the things of this world possessed far too much *gravity* to be trusted with sacramental significance; they would weigh down, crush to themselves, imprison, and diminish. Recall the mission of Judeo-Christian iconoclasm: to rescue the sacred from those who would reduce it to something small, dead, and undeserving. The sin of idolatry is to believe that one has captured all the sea in a cockleshell. Then smash the shell, and turn the idolater's eyes back to the ocean deep! Protestantism, hearing the cry of the sacred for rescue in a world where all the traditional Gestalts of grace had darkened into idols, undertook to fix between God and the world that protective gulf which Kierkegaard was to call the "infinite qualitative difference." God, infinitely removed from fallen nature, became that cosmic bouillon cube in which all holiness was now to be concentrated for safekeeping. In effect, this is a scorched earth strategy aimed at placing between heaven and earth a barrier of waste terrain, a no-man's-land . . . or rather, a no-god's-land.

But what becomes of a world purged of its sacramental capacities? It dies the death of the spirit. It may retain for some its pleasing aesthetic surface, but that is of little significance. Beauty cut loose of its sacramental base is a decadent pleasure, and a vulnerable one. For most, the desacralized world is doomed to become an obstacle inviting conquest, a mere object. Like the animal or the slave who is understood to have no soul, it becomes a thing of subhuman status to be worked, used up, exploited. Potentially, the relationship of such a devitalized nature to its creator is that of excrement to the civilized human being: inert and contemptible stuff left behind. I say "potentially" because, before the world descended in our regard to this excremental level, there was a phase in western history—in the wake of Newton's great synthesis—when nature stood forth as a marvelous and divine contrivance, much to be praised for as long as its intricacy surpassed that of any man-made mechanism and seemed to defy all improvement. But this was only an episode. With the advance of industrialism, it rapidly passed. Steadily, the artificial environment has crowded out the wonders of nature; the clockwork universe has long since depreciated in the minds of most people. Through the haze and bright lights of the city, few can any longer keep track of even the phases of the moon, let alone the stately procession of the stars . . . had they time to do so in the first place. And then, at last, the world does become God's dunghill, waste matter abandoned in a far corner of the cosmos.

But excrement, as we know, is metaphorical money in the poetry of the unconscious . . . or money is perhaps metaphorical excrement. And has this not become our predominant way of viewing the world: as so much raw material there but to manure the growth of economies? Today, when "realistic" people look at nature around them—mountains, forests, lakes, rivers—what is it they see? Not divine epiphanies, but cash values, investments, potential contributions to the GNP, great glowing heaps of money, the crude shit-wealth of the world that only exists to be taken manfully in hand and made over into something human greed will find "valuable." As Lynn White has aptly observed, in its relations with nature, "Christianity is the most anthropocentric religion the world has even seen. . . . By destroying pagan animism, Christianity made it possible to exploit nature in a mood of indifference to the feelings of natural objects."

Conservationists who can say nothing against these depredations but that they are short-sighted or wasteful or ugly—or more pathetically still that such despoiling deprives people of recreational space—have no argument that will find any sizable audience, not when the chips are down, not when the alternative turns out to be as horrendously unthinkable to urban-industrial society as to do without a freeway or enough electrical power to keep the picture tube well lit. The despoilers then win every time, because the assumption that nature is "ours" to remake as *we* see fit—so much dead and recalcitrant stuff to be shaped to our standards—already concedes the key line of defense.

In the Protestant universe, there survives only one spiritually valuable remnant: the buried spark of longing that lingers in the human soul and by virtue of which man makes his "leap of faith" *out* of the abyss of nature. It of course requires stupendous fortitude to live by such a bleak and despairing vision. There is an undeniable drama in the Protestant's spiritual travail. One is tempted by the sheer heroism it demands to conclude that only Protestantism has known the full, dread seriousness of the search for salvation. But then we are dealing here with religion exiled from the magical worldview, the religion of single vision, and this is perhaps more pathetic than heroic. Its historical repercussions, however, have been a calamity—and not only for the Protestant societies. For there was one terrible possibility that the Protestant founders failed to anticipate in their fierce hunger for iconoclastic purity. They did not foresee that the eclipse of God might grow so dark and last so long that men and women would lose their eyes for the light. They did not realize that, like any disused faculty, sacramental consciousness too might atrophy, allowing the human condition to drift into radically divergent lines of development, perhaps toward a permanently irreligious, totally secularized culture, a culture in which the capacity for transcendence would become so feeble that, at last, people, confronted with the great historical projections of sacramental experience, might only wonder what these exotic symbols really meant . . . once upon a time . . . and then undertake sophisticated reductionist "interpretations."

It is as if Protestantism, having interposed Himalayan obstacles of self-abnegation, despair, and dread between God and man—all for the sake of preserving the transcendent sovereignty of the sacred—had at last succeeded in making the separation too vast ever again to be bridged. One might almost imagine a Kafkaesque story dealing with the theme. Over many generations a people busy themselves hiding a treasure. They become obsessed with the devising of safe-guards, pitfalls, snares, barriers. Finally, the treasure is in-geniously sequestered, but so well that not even the people themselves can find it . . . nor can they any longer remember what it was they hid. *And then,* there arises a generation which begins to doubt that there ever was a treasure in the first place! So they ask, "Were our ancestors not perhaps badly mistaken about the existence of these riches?"

The thrust of Protestantism is to make the sacred wholly *super*natural—something beyond nature, not in it, not in any least measure, except as a longing in the souls of the elect. But everything one says about the *super*natural is doomed to the category of "mysticism"; it becomes a philosophically sloppy hypothesis for which there is no evidence. And how should there be? Where sacramental consciousness has atro-phied, there can be no confirming epiphanies. We are left then to translate the rhapsodic reports of the past into mere doctrines and credos, the obituaries of religion. Or perhaps, more condescendingly, we undertake to salvage what we can from this quaint heritage in the way of ethical inspiration, or psychotherapy, or the faintly evocative symbolism of cer-tain schools of art and literature. But among those who wish to be enlightened, rational, scientific, the secular skeptic is bound to have it all his own way. And so he does. "Well then," he announces "enough of this pious nonsense! Are we a scientific age or are we not? This palaver about super-

natural entities is the baby talk of the human race. Only
children and weak-minds attend to such distractions. Away
with it all. There is no future for this illusion. It is time
we grew up, grew strong, and grew rational."

THE DEGRADATION OF MYTH

One more respect in which Protestantism carried Judeo-Christian iconoclasm to its pathological extreme. From Judaism,
Christianity inherited a passionate concern for the historicity of belief. In a way that contrasts sharply with the mythopoeic consciousness of all other religions, Judaism embeds the
heroes and prodigies of its tradition in a worldly chronology.
Even the stories of the creation and of Eden—outside the
Jewish mystical movements—lack that sense of being located
in the "dream-time long ago" which is the necessary dimension
of myth. To be sure, Judaism preserves enough poetic sensibility to value the imaginative qualities of folklore and legend,
and to avoid the worst inanities of fundamentalism. Nonetheless, Judaism is essentially the history of a people; the God of
the Bible has no knowable existence outside that history;
his word and his deed are events in history. This is what
guarantees the uniqueness of his covenant with Israel. What
happens in historical time (so Judaism asserts) *really* happens
—in a way that reduces myth to fiction and strips it of its
entire validity. Moreover, it happens once and is, specifically,
some one event or fact peculiarly related to certain people
at a certain place at a certain time; it defines a unique
tradition that can clearly be distinguished from all the rest of
the world.

Myths, on the other hand, are like the motifs of dreams.
They elude the logic of contradiction; their happening is

transhistorical, leaving no imprint on time. One cannot ask of them "when" or "where," because they are, in their essence, ever present. The narrative surfaces of myth are unimportant; the truth of mythical thought is not a matter of fact, but of perennial insight, which may be cast in a thousand forms. So the tendency is for myths to blend and identify, rather than to exclude one another. Myth makers, unlike historians, are able to say to each other, "You tell the story this way, I tell it that way. But *both* are true." The meaning of myths lies in the vision of life and nature they hold at their core. Either one re-experiences that vision, or one has missed the message—in which case the myth is bound to become an empty literal shell, a fiction, a lie; it loses its magic and becomes an idol.

For Christians, this inherited prejudice in favor of historicity became the very foundation of their soteriology. While other mystery cults might teach the myth of the suffering and resurrected savior, Christianity alone could claim historical validity for its gospel. It alone taught the Word become flesh—at one time, at one place, in one human personality. That was what made Christ *real*, and condemned Mithra, Tammuz, Osiris, the Gnostic Primal Man to unreality. Christ belonged to history; his rivals were *mere* myths. Clearly, there occurred with the advent of Christianity a deep shift of consciousness which severely damaged the mythopoeic powers—far more so than was the case even in Judaism. In Christianity uniquely, matters of fact became the basis for articles of belief and doctrine—as if no other reality than that of the historical record could hold truth. Here, within the religious life of the west, was the origin of that fanatically secular sensibility which would, in time, turn back upon Christianity itself, skeptically demanding more historical evidence than the sources could ever supply. That, of course, is the liability of historicity. Myth can be relived endlessly; its symbols can be called up in visionary experience and so can have their validity renewed. History happens once; not even the Holy Spirit can make the past happen again. A religion tied to history must therefore ground itself in a strenuous act of faith, for one can only strive to *believe* what cannot be known as immediate experience.

But, again, the early and medieval Church remained pliable enough to accommodate to some degree the widespread need for myth. The major manifestation of this was the cult of the Virgin, which elevated the inconsequential figure of Mary to a stupendous symbolic stature. Here was the Mother Goddess Christianity lacked, worked up out of the meagerest historical material by the mythic imagination—a triumph of collective visionary power at times so sweeping that the Virgin nearly crowded out the official trinity. Of course, the theology of the Church deftly delimited Mariolatry; but that had little meaning at the level of popular worship or artistic creation, where the Virgin rapidly occupied the psychic ground that had always been held by Isis, Cybele, Magna Mater, and their ageless sisterhood. After all, how poor and unbalanced a religion it is that does not find place for the divine mother.

But with the advance of Protestantism, this residual, popular mythology was seared away at the roots; it too was identified as idolatry. Myth, like sacramental symbolism, fell under the iconoclastic ban. Nothing was to remain as a support for faith but the remote scriptural narrative, a cold, increasingly literal commitment to historical fact which would finally produce the higher criticism, the quest for "the historical Jesus," and programs (like that of Rudolf Bultmann) for the total "demythologization" of Christianity.

It is only within the past few generations—thanks to the inspiration of Romantic art and the daring of psychoanalysis—that myth has been salvaged from the positivist and agnostic slag heap. It now begins to enjoy its proper dignity as a depth dimension of the human mind. We have been a

long time finding our way back to the old wisdom: in the
words of Kathleen Raine, that "fact is not the truth of
myth; myth is the truth of fact."

IDOLATRY AND DAMNATION

Again to draw upon Owen Barfield's analysis, an idol is
"a representation which is collectively mistaken for an ultimate. . . . More particularly, idolatry is the effective tendency to abstract the sense-content from the whole representation and seek that for its own sake, transmuting the admired
image into a desired object." Idolatry is not a moral failing; it
is a mistaken ontology, grounded in a flawed consciousness.
It is the substitution of a lesser for a greater reality. The prophets of Israel, seeing the infidel worshiping before a tree, a rock,
a figurine, were convinced they had seen the divine degraded
to the level of an ordinary object. Yet if this object was participated, it was not an idol; it was the medium of an epiphany.
But desacralized nature, *our* nature, lacking sacramental transparency, *has* become an idol, an objectivized reality held to be
final and self-sufficient: the highest reality, the *only* reality.
One need only ponder what people mean in our time when
they counsel us to "be realistic." They mean, at every point, to
forgo the claims of transcendence, to spurn the magic of imaginative wonder, to regard the world as *nothing but* what the
hard facts and quantitative abstractions of scientific objectivity make it out to be. Only when translated downward
into such terms does anything become a something "real."
That, in its deepest sense, is what it means to say that
science has become the contemporary religion. Not that we
praise and glorify scientists; we *may* do that, but that is
not the essence of the matter. Science is our religion because

we cannot, most of us, with any living conviction *see around it*. Religions are built at the boundaries of consciousness. We live in a world whose consciousness of reality ends at the scientific perimeter, hence a world growing more idolatrous by the hour—in the name of Realism, in the name of Reason. Idolatry is the inversion of the hierarchical realities.

It is only after Protestant iconoclasm has at last rooted sacramental perception out of our culture that we arrive, for the first time in history, at a condition of true idolatry. All knowledge becomes a single-visioned knowledge of mere objects, an *objective* knowledge from which, we feel certain, mastery, security, affluence flow. Again the psychic metaphors tell the story. Nature as excrement means money means power. These are tempting prizes, sufficient to induce non-Protestants to join the iconoclast cause. Ours is indeed "the Protestant era"—in the sense that societies everywhere, of all religious and irreligious persuasions, have appropriated just enough of the Protestant project to give them a desacralized cosmos susceptible to scientific analysis and technological exploitation.

And the idolatrous momentum carries further. In the midst of a nature as deprived of magicality—perhaps even of immediate visibility—as that which industrial urbanites know, more and more it is only the works of man that command admiration. The technological repertory of the artificial environment takes the place of the miraculous, like so many brilliantly fascinating figures against a drably alien ground. Machines, gadgets, devices, techniques monopolize attention and high esteem. They take our breath away as nothing else does and command our abject dependence. Consider the computers, the data banks, the great cybernated systems, the remembering machines and predicting machines, the controlling machines and deciding machines on which ever more of our daily survival depends . . . is it not with us as the prophet said of the heathen? "For life he beseecheth that which is dead, And for aid he supplicateth that which hath least experience." How is it again that Augustine described idolatry? "Mankind tyrannized over by the work of his own hands."

"Worship," it may seem, is too strong a word for this relationship between man and his artificial environment. After all, worship is always conditioned by its object. The technological paraphernalia of our society, for all its prowess, may not carry religious contemplation far, not beyond a sort of low-grade amazement and routine applause. *But* . . . as far as it carries the mind is as far as we go. This is as great an exercise of worship as the prevailing Reality Principle permits. And we settle for it . . . most of us.

I think perhaps this is what damnation means: to live out one's days imprisoned in this idolatrous realm, the infinite universe which Pascal could only experience as "a little prison cell." But we have made a great discovery. Namely, that hell can be an *interesting* place! The world may indeed be God's dunghill; but there is much to be discovered and reclaimed therein. It can be *worked*. It can be made neat and productive. The life's energy of generations can be expended *developing* the thing, covering it over with concrete and plastic and sprawling supercities, finding faster ways to travel over and across its surfaces, consuming its substance and inventing substitutes for its depleted elements. In this busy way the time may be passed, and we shall get used to the idolatrous life. We shall make ourselves at home in it. Milton's fallen angels toyed with just such a strategy for enduring the unendurable. Significantly, it was Mammon, the demon of affluence, who devised a program for progress among the damned.

> . . . Our greatness will appear
> Then most conspicuous, when great things of small,
> Useful of hurtful, prosperous of adverse
> We can create, and in what place so e'er

Thrive under evil, and work ease out of pain
Through labor and endurance. This deep world
Of darkness do we dread? How oft amidst
Thick clouds and dark doth Heav'n's all-ruling Sire
Choose to reside, his Glory obscur'd . . . .
As He our darkness, cannot we His Light
Imitate when we please? This Desert soil
Wants not her hidden lustre, Gems and Gold;
Nor want we skill or art, from whence to raise
Magnificence; and what can Heav'n show more?
Our torments also may in length of time
Become our Elements, these piercing Fires
As soft as now severe, our temper chang'd
Into their temper; which must needs remove
The sensible of pain.

TRANSCENDENT SYMBOLISM

Throughout this chapter I have sought to avoid using the
word "symbol" in speaking of idolatrous and sacramental
awareness, though it has slipped in a few times anyway. At
several points it would have been tempting to distinguish the
two modes of awareness by observing that, for primitives and
pagans, natural objects and icons "symbolize" the divine.
That is, I assume, the way in which most people would
now make sense of such worship, and it would not actually
have falsified my meaning to say so . . . *except* that the concept "symbol" has become so denatured that it does more to
becloud than clarify. Yes, the trees and rivers and rocks once
were symbolic of the divine—but in a much deeper sense of
the word "symbol" than we now recognize. Surely in a deeper
way than the word is used by logicians and mathematical
philosophers, in whose cautious professional parlance the job

of a symbol is to be as steel-edged and unambiguous as possible. This is, in fact, the exact opposite of the tradition of symbolic consciousness I am following. Analytical philosophers rely on symbols as a mainstay of single vision. But the symbolism that interests me gains in richness from its imprecision and ambiguity, indeed its radical mystery. It is the power-language of mystics, inevitably and perversely an outrage to the logical temperament.

When most people today—and especially literary scholars —speak of a "symbol," they really mean a "cipher." A cipher is a code which, as we say, "stands for something else"—and having said that, we then go on to say *what* it stands for. We fill in the other side of the equation, in what is rather like a mathematical procedure. The essence of a cipher is that it can be *de*ciphered by a simple intellectual exercise. Thus, if we ask, "What does the white whale symbolize in *Moby Dick?*" the answer is (perhaps) "Evil in the universe." Or if we ask, "What did the rites of the Eleusinian mysteries symbolize?" the answer is (perhaps) "The regenerative forces of nature and the desire for personal immortality."

Now, the trouble with this fill-in-the-blank conception of symbolism is not so much that it is wrong, as that it is idiotically shallow. It lacks any experiential dimension beyond that of intellectual facility. It decodes the symbol, but it does not *participate* the symbol. A cipher is an intellectualized symbol, a symbol drained of life and become cadaverous. Such ciphers do indeed lend themselves to scholarly manipulation, which requires the use of flat prose and academic caution; but they are not any longer vital symbols.

True, there is much inferior literature which never gets beyond ciphers. There is, for example, a pedantic "substitute-one-word-for-another" poetry which invites learned decoding and nothing more. But it should be obvious that the mark of a great literary symbol is its unfathomable mystery; we can never get to the bottom of it, never simply substitute a form of words and have done with it. Great symbols swallow us whole. They lead us on into themselves . . . we pursue . . . but we never capture their whole meaning. Not because the symbol is mindlessly obscure (though there are literary vices of this kind too) but because it is radically, authentically enigmatic. The figures of Prospero, Ariel, and Caliban, or Beethoven's sixteenth quartet, or Rembrandt's painting of the old woman paring her nails are supreme symbols because they draw the mind beyond its limit. We might talk, argue, and analyze all our lives, but never exhaust their meaning; they can never be replaced by summary or interpretation. The artist has given us something absolute and irreducible. At last, such symbols survive in their own being as the only possible way of saying what they say. What Archibald MacLeish once said of poetry may be said of the symbol. A symbol "must not mean but be."

True symbols transcend intellectual deciphering, calling forth another level of consciousness which eludes words. They are, as it were, doors leading into dark chambers of reality, like the entranceways of the old mystery cults. We must take our whole life in with us and be prepared to be totally transformed. A true symbol must be *lived into*. That is how its meaning is found. Only then does its magic take effect. *A symbol is a magical object.* It is known (in Ananda Coomaraswamy's words) "by seeing in things material and sensible a formal likeness to spiritual prototypes of which the senses can give no direct report." That is the essence of the matter. And the great artists are magicians, the best and truest we have left from the tradition of the Old Gnosis. They are conjurers with the sacramental consciousness of the race, reality makers or unmakers.

The religious rites which Jews and Christians and Moslems perceive as idolatrous *are* symbolic, but in ways that our literalist, deciphering habits of mind can only barely understand. Take for example the American Plains Indian use of the "peace pipe." For a people like the Sioux, the pipe was a sacred object, a kind of consecrated altar about which elaborate rites took place. For the Christian, the pipe is therefore an idol par excellence. But a sympathetic scholar who takes the trouble to decipher this and that about the sacred pipe can at least give us some hint of the spiritual beauties and profundities of these rites. Joseph Epes Brown tells us that the grains of tobacco represent "the myriad forms of creation"; the filled pipe is the cosmic totality; "when the fire of the Great Spirit is added, a divine sacrifice is enacted in which the universe and man are reabsorbed within the Principle, and become what in reality they are." Such explanations are a bare beginning and, realizing as much, Brown finishes with a wise reticence: "The mysteries of the peace pipe are so profound that it is not too much to say that the rite of smoking for the Indian is something very near to the Holy Communion for Christians." In short, the pipe and its uses are not an idol, but a true symbol, never to be exhausted by study, demanding a commitment to total experience . . . for all one's life is worth. If we take the matter at any lesser value, we turn the symbol into a cipher. Then we may make much talk, but it will all be the sort of talk Lao Tzu mocks in the familiar paradox "those who speak do not know."

We have seen that this was the way in which Calvin disposed of pagan idolatry. He turned it into a cipher, and then coldly, non-participatively deciphered it. This is what Protestantism undertook with all the traditional sacraments. They ceased to be mysteries; they became decipherable ciphers. Then one could *talk about* what they *meant*. The sacrament was no longer an experience of magical transformations; it became a talking point. The Protestant thrust is always toward didactic preaching, interpretation, and loquacious explaining. The pulpit crowds out the altar.

Our habit in the modern west—especially in the academy

—is to denature all symbols on contact, the better to keep them safely isolated at the cerebral level. This is our way of being objective about what cannot be objectified. We substitute dead language for living experience. An idolatrous culture will have nothing to do with magic, an act of absolute rejection which leads to much learned folly. There is a prodigious scholarship on myth, ritual, religion, rite, mostly by experts who have never *lived* their way into these things for a moment. Yet it would seem, judging by the quantity and pretentious tone of the literature on these subjects, that there really are anthropologists who know more about, say, Australian aboriginal worship than the natives themselves, none of whom could compose a single explanatory paragraph about what it all means.

So there are ways of knowing and there are ways of knowing. And if there is any magic to be found in the great sacramental symbols of human culture, it is certain *our* orthodox way of knowing will never find it out. So much the worse for us.

We will return in later chapters to the discussion of transcendent symbols. Their re-emergence is destined to play a major part in liberating us from the death grip of single vision.

CHAPTER 5

A Dead Man's Eyes

> *That the state of knowledge is not prosperous nor greatly advancing; and that a way must be opened for the human understanding entirely different from any hitherto known, and other helps provided, in order that the mind may exercize over the nature of things the authority which properly belongs to it.*
>
> *Francis Bacon*

THE SCIENTIFIC REVOLUTION: IDOLATRY TRIUMPHANT

It is a familiar human vice. We project the sins that reside in our hearts, locating them far off, in others, in adversaries whom we then assail and persecute for our own guilt. For centuries, the tendency toward idolatry in Judeo-Christian culture was externalized as scorn for pagan worship and the reproof of heresy. Still today, the discussion of idolatry would be thought of as an old religious subject matter, a dead controversy no longer part of our lives. At the superficial level of intellectual history, that is true enough. But within the evolution of consciousness, it is a different story. Idolatry has come into its own not within the mainstream religious life of the west, but as the psychic style belonging to a wholly new and domineering cultural enterprise—a "New Philosophy" as Francis Bacon called seventeenth-century science.

Here is the subterranean link between the religion and science of the western world. The two are far from being antagonists—as one might suspect when one notices, especially in the Protestant societies, how smoothly science took its place in the seventeenth and eighteenth centuries alongside the prevailing religion, and indeed what very devout men the early scientists were. There *was* a "scientific revolution" during the age of Galileo, Kepler, and Newton; but it was a revolution for which Christianity had long since been making ready the psychic ground. The melodramatic confrontation between Galileo and the Church (usually misread), often obscures the truth of the matter. What was most revolutionary about the revolution was not the struggle with Christian religious psychology, but with its overlay of inherited Aristotelian concepts. And what was the great obstacle that the pagan Aristotle posed? Simply that his study of nature preserved, if only as a weak residue, too much of the Old Gnosis, too much of the sense of nature alive and infused with purpose, nature aglow with seductively sensuous qualities. This was nature as it had been known in pagan worship—philosophically intellectualized by Aristotle, yet nonetheless a nature that concealed divinity never far below the surface of appearances. These remnants of a degraded pagan naturalism were the *ancien régime* that had to be overthrown by single vision before Christian society could produce its own peculiar natural philosophy. What science did was to extract from western man's religious psychology its well-developed idolatrous disposition and to elaborate the experience of na-

ture that lay within it—at first with every expectation that
this fresh worldview would serve piety, not detract from
it.

Let us, in this chapter, trace this transition in some detail
as we find it in the work of Francis Bacon, the most precocious
mind of the scientific revolution.

BLAKE . . . OR BACON

"To cast off Bacon, Locke, & Newton . . ."
I closed an earlier chapter with this snatch of Blake: the
unholy trinity which the poet marked out as the prime enemies
of visionary power, the founding fathers of single vision.
And surely the strangest of these three is Bacon. Far more
so than Newton the mathematician and physicist or Locke
the rigorous empiricist, Bacon qualifies as moralist and man
of letters, philosopher and humanist. More so than Newton
or Locke, he embroiders his thought with a brooding religiosity, a puritanical sense of the soul's travail in the midst of
temptation and worldly corruption. There is a passion and
elegance to Bacon that one does not often find in the literature of science or its philosophy. There is also a rhetorical
splendor that is easily misconstrued for simple lack of rigor.
For this reason, Bacon—despite the importance Blake attributes to him—figures only marginally in conventional studies
of the philosophy or the history of science. Few philosophers
of science any longer take seriously the facile view that credits
Bacon with having invented the logic of induction or the
experimental method. He is therefore normally made to stand
in the shadow of his greater contemporaries. Galileo bulks
larger in the development of experimental science, Descartes
in the mainstream of modern philosophy. If Bacon is studied

at all, it is apt to be for his literary talents. We think of him more in the company of Montaigne and the great Elizabethan stylists; he survives as an intellectual adventurer of the high Renaissance, projector of titanic ambitions, author of an imposing wisdom literature.

Yet for Blake there was no doubt that Bacon must be numbered among the great betrayers of the human spirit, as one who gives "Good advice for Satan's Kingdom." And he insists we must choose: Blake . . . or Bacon. It is not a choice we prefer to have thrust upon us. We may wonder if Blake has not been unjust in choosing Bacon—a man whose style of thought could lead some to mistake him for a Shakespeare, but never for a Newton—as one of his weightiest metaphysical opponents. Or we may wonder if Blake's error does not lie in giving far too much credit to one whom the science and philosophy texts of our day mention hardly at all. In either case, we may well ask if the hard judgment Blake pronounces on Bacon is justified.

I will argue here that it is, and that it is a particularly shrewd judgment—though one that requires far more elaboration than Blake ever gave it. In Blake's writing (especially in *Milton* and *Jerusalem*) Bacon stands as little more than a synonym for all that the poet despises. But the choice of that synonym is right and telling. Bacon, properly studied, is far more than an eccentric fellow traveler in the history of science. True, we find no "hard science" in Bacon's work that will compare with the accomplishments of Harvey, Kepler, or Galileo. But we find what is far more important to the future of science in our society; we find the moral, aesthetic, and psychic raw materials of the scientific worldview. They are all there in his writing—the bright hopes and humanitarian intentions, obscurely mingled with hidden forces of dehumanization, the promise and the curse of the New Philosophy. More than any other figure in the western tradition, it was Bacon, writing in the first generation of the scientific revolution, who foreshadowed—but ironically, unintentionally—the bleakest aspects of scientized culture: the malaise of spirit, the nightmare of environmental collapse, and the technocratic *machine à gouverner*. They brew and swirl darkly in his rich sensibility, elemental motifs within a primordial chaos.

It is by now an academic commonplace that in many respects Bacon was neither so radical nor so original as he assumed himself to be. Careful study shows more Aristotle lingering on in his work than Bacon would have cared to admit; more too of the medieval alchemists. It is most likely from the more vulgar alchemists that Bacon acquired his taste for a knowledge that yields power over nature and, from this in turn, the flamboyant claim that his New Philosophy would reach out to transform the world marvelously.

Pry a little beyond the grandiose façade of Bacon's philosophical edifice, and his entire project begins to totter and creak like a jerry-built tenement. Under close study, the intellectual categories and compartments he designed in his famous Advancement of Learning soon lose definition and sink into a morass of elusive terminology. The logic of Bacon's classifications is frequently so obscure and his scope so encyclopedic that one almost despairs at moments of discovering what Bacon is really writing about after all. Bacon's *scientia* (usually used by him in the Latin plural *scientiae*) is surely not *our* natural science in the most compact, professional sense. By *scientia* he means "knowledge," in a sense that blankets all human intellectual activity. The enormous number and fluidity of categories Bacon finds within this nearly boundless province only serves to remind us both of his breadth of mind and of the antique traditions to which he was still beholden.

And yet, perhaps even this uncertainty as to where the boundary is to be drawn in Bacon's writing between science and non-science hints of a remarkably prophetic conception of science. For when Bacon at last concludes that his *novum organum* shall apply "not only to natural but to *all* sciences" (specifically including ethics and politics), that it is to "embrace everything," does he not anticipate the modern intellectual obsession to create a totally scientized culture? In his *Advancement of Learning* Bacon actually envisions such a "universal science" to which all knowledge will contribute and from which "axioms" will flow that apply to ethics, physics, mathematics, theology, medicine . . . Ultimately, he could find no way to exclude any form of knowledge—save perhaps (and tactfully) the mysteries of faith—from the expansive province of the New Philosophy. In Bacon's ambitious "everything" there lie the dim origins of laboratory psychology and the behavioral sciences, operations research and systems analysis, general value and utility theory. So it was that within Bacon's own generation his disciple Thomas Hobbes would undertake the first exploration of a rigorously mechanistic behavioral and political science, an effort that stemmed from Hobbes's conviction that the mind of man is "*nothing but* the motions in certain parts of an organic body."

Bacon, a lesser natural philosopher than he fancied himself to be, was the keenest trailblazer of the imperialistic career science would pursue in time to come. The Royal Society of England may have done Bacon the honor of adopting him as its inspirational founder; but Bacon's dream of a New Philosophy aspired to realization on a far vaster scale. The society, a modest association of gentlemen scientists, tinkerers, and good conversationalists, could really never be more than a way station along the great highway of Bacon's vision. For Bacon the *novum organum* led to the New Atlantis, our earliest significant anticipation of the technocratic state. When William Harvey, discoverer of the circulation of the blood, commented sardonically that Bacon wrote about science "like a Lord Chancellor," he paid greater tribute to Bacon's precocity than he intended. He could scarcely have realized how gracefully his amateurish Lord Chancellor would take his place three centuries hence in our contemporary discussion of science and society.

If Bacon's thought preserves its freshness, it is largely because it comes down to us bearing the intellectual imprint of a philosopher who was also a public man. For Bacon, the busy and battle-scarred man of affairs, it was unthinkable that his New Philosophy should become the exclusive property of dilettante investigator or professional coterie. Rather, it was to be the intellectual base of a major political institution, a collective public enterprise uniting thought and action, and requiring the collaboration of the state. In the *New Atlantis,* Bacon's most ambitious projection of the proper destiny of science, we have our earliest blueprint of the think tank, the House of Solomon. And we find this primitive version of the RAND Corporation at the governing center of Bacon's Utopia. In Bacon's ideal society, the beneficent administration of inquiry and invention supplants the dismal futilities of traditional politics with the promise of peace, abundance, and enlightenment. From this perspective, the centuries that separate the House of Solomon from the technocratic elitism of our own time shrink to no more than a moment. We pass smoothly from Bacon's priestly regime of technicians to C. P. Snow's "new men." For both Bacon and Snow, the scientist makes his home in the corridors of power. For both, power is the scientist's talisman and his license to public preferment.

THE NOVUM ORGANUM

Whatever his seeming failures as epistemologist and natural philosopher, Bacon has never been denied his place as the unsurpassed booster of the New Philosophy. Charles Gillispie has called him a "prophet" *not* of science, but of "an image of scientific progress which has been vastly more popular than science itself can ever think to be." The prophetic title is well deserved. Bacon was among the first Europeans to iden- tify the secular future as the New Jerusalem. And only a society that has come to accept Bacon's "argument of hope," his summons to an open and improvable future could ever be as relentlessly up and doing as ours. If Bacon had done nothing more than dedicate his rhetorical genius to leading cheers for the strenuous life, his influence upon us might be great enough.

But to see Bacon as no more than the propagandist of progress diminishes the richness of his thinking. Bacon did not simply celebrate worldly activity in the abstract or trust in the optimistic possibilities of the future with a blind faith. He had confidence in human effort because he had devised a special and specific activity, a form of knowledge gathering which he believed could reach forward in time, which could bind the future to the past, thus giving history a palpable sense of development. With Bacon we arrive at the pregnant idea that there is a kind of knowledge which grows incre- mentally and systematically over time, not as the result of hit- and-miss discovery or lucky accident, but as the product of a deliberate activity of the mind. Such knowledge is bound to be greater in volume and coherence tomorrow than it is today, because what we know today is the basis for what we will discover tomorrow. Above all, this knowledge will not be sim- ply contemplative. It will be capable of "closing with nature," of asserting power over the world. That, indeed, will serve as its validation as true knowledge. So we arrive at the great Baconian dictum that in a true natural philosophy "human knowledge and human power meet in one." Bacon bothers to develop no other criterion of truth than the bluntly opera- tional one: if it works, it is true. "Truth," he insists, "and utility are here the very same things."

These, then, are the distinctive features of Bacon's revolutionary new conception of knowledge. Knowledge is that which yields a steady increase of human control over the environment, which grows incrementally and systematically as time passes, and which is forthcoming upon deliberate exercise of the will to know. As Bacon clearly recognized, this intoxicating vision of what knowledge ought to be was enough, if he went no further, to open a new world of intellect. To cross the threshold of that world was to leave behind the haphazard sort of knowledge that comes of endlessly assembling and reassembling elements of custom and tradition. It was also to leave behind the airy extrapolations of all philosophy and theology which end in passive meditation upon a cosmic order held to be fixed and unalterable. With Bacon, knowledge gathering becomes an on-going collective project in which the present can contribute to the future. And in this— at least so Bacon thought—lay the secret of the power he sought. Baconian knowledge would pool the efforts of people over time. As Bacon put it,

> this Instauration of mine . . . is by no means forgetful of the conditions of mortality and humanity, for it does not suppose that the work can be altogether completed within one generation but provides for its being taken up by another.

In Bacon, there is no recognition that man's knowledge of nature might progress by dramatic breakthroughs or revolutionary transformations. He makes no allowance for the radical new departure or the epoch-making insight. Rather, he banks his hopes on "a gradual and unbroken ascent" to the truth, a step-by-step development through "progressive stages of certainty" to which all people can contribute their modest portion. The human race need not wait for the blinding flash of individual genius to light the way forward; it can rely instead upon the myriad candles passed on from generation to generation by ordinary people whose only talent is that of persistent application. So Bacon gives his audience of self-reliant gentlemen, merchants, and entrepreneurs the counsel it was most willing to hear.

> You will never be sorry for trusting your own strength if you but once make trial of it. You may be inferior to Aristotle on the whole, but not in everything. . . . Are you of a mind to cast aside not only your own endowments but the gifts of time? Assert yourselves before it is too late. . . . Be not for ever the property of one man.

It is this conception of cumulative knowledge which makes it sensible to Bacon—and more than sensible, imperative—to conceive of the New Philosophy as an institution of the state. What yields such great worldly power clearly requires the supervision of the state and merits the large public expenditures Bacon prescribes as the basis for continuing research. By the same token, only what the state fosters can enjoy the continuity of finance and high prestige necessary to long-term achievement. The ideas interlock: cumulative knowledge—power—state sponsorship.

In our own day, it is second nature for us to think of science as being that field of intellectual endeavor that grows and progresses over time. We take science to be unique in this respect—so much so that we might almost define "science" as any study that achieves incremental and systematic development. What progresses as a body of knowledge holds scientific status; what fails to progress is something other than science. As the anthropologist Max Gluckman puts it, "a science is any discipline in which the fool of this generation can go beyond the point reached by the genius of the last generation."

This cumulative aspect of scientific knowledge accounts for the peculiar way in which the sciences are taught. It is, in fact, the essence of their pedagogy. In the sciences, there is held to be a knowledge that can be condensed and distilled as time goes on, supposedly without loss. This means that each new generation of scientists can rapidly assimilate decades, even centuries of theory and research within perhaps a few years of undergraduate study. Any high school physics student can claim to know more about physics than Galileo, Newton, or Faraday. This is not, of course, because the student is a greater physicist; the talent to discover knowledge is of a distinctly higher order than the ability to record its existence. Nevertheless, there is a meaningful sense in which any scientific neophyte may be said to know more about his field than any of its great founders. He knows how the field has progressed up to the present; he knows where the discoveries of the great scientists have led; he knows where their work has been modified or superseded. Moreover, his path has been cleared of the many pitfalls and misconceptions that obstructed even the finest scientific minds of the past; he need waste no time over them. After all, even Galileo had to struggle for years to get the mathematics of gravitation reasonably correct; today, every schoolchild learns the concept in the first few minutes of an introductory science course —and learns the point exhaustively. One could hardly argue that Galileo in some way possessed a more mature and intimate knowledge of gravity than the mathematics contains. Indeed, the whole achievement of Galileo lies in his historic decision that the mathematics *is* the phenomenon.

The same situation hardly obtains in literature or the arts —to take an obvious contrast. There is no way in which these can be distilled without losing their entire value. For this reason, there is no sense in which any ordinary student can be said to know more about the aesthetic interplay of light and air than Monet, or more about the myth of Faust than

Goethe. There is an autonomy, a finality about every work of art, an irreducible uniqueness which stems from the personal vision of its maker and which does not permit it to be summed up, compressed, or subsumed under the work that follows it. Each work of art—even if it is a bad work—demands attention for what it alone is. A young scientist learns everything the profession cares to teach him about Newton from one textbook chapter or a single classroom lecture. He would never be sent out to read the *Principia;* if he were, he might well find its antique mathematical style intolerably time-consuming. Such documents are, from the student's viewpoint, "old science," and to spend much time with them would be indeed a quaint assignment. But a student of literature who had never read Balzac or Tolstoy on the grounds that they were "old literature" would surely be a boor. And any teacher who tried to teach Shakespeare by way of brief textbook summations of the plays would be everybody's idea of a shameful incompetent.

It is a paradox of this distinction that, while science grows through time, storing up its past in a way that makes history of its essence, few scientists feel they need give more than minimal attention to the history of their field. One is not the least surprised to meet quite capable scientists who have never read the classics of their discipline: physicists who have never read Galileo, chemists who have never read Boyle or Dalton, biologists who have never read Darwin. They have never felt the need. The tested bulk of knowledge in their field is carried forward into the professional consensus of the present, where it is officially certified by inclusion in the current textbooks. The textbook holds a unique place in scientific pedagogy; it is the endorsed distillation of professional knowledge, and very nearly the life's blood of the discipline. What it omits is of interest only to historians of science, not to the practicing professionals.

We need only return to the past when we find there—as

we do in the arts—things imperishable and final, expressed
with an authority that time cannot significantly diminish,
qualify, or improve. It is not the task of the arts to get
"further along," but to go deep and so to relate us once more
and ever again to the essential truths of the human condition
. . . as potently as Shakespeare did, as Sophocles did, as the
cave paintings of Lascaux did. The foundation of science is
what the textbooks of the present generation have distilled out
of the past three or four centuries of inquiry and discovery in
the west. The foundation of the arts and of philosophy
properly understood is the perennial wisdom.

But what is there about the knowledge of scientists that
makes it so peculiarly capable of distillation and accumulation? The answer is, *the product of scientific thought has
been purged of its personal characteristics.* As the Baconian
ideal would have it, science is not some one person's feeling or
opinion. Rather, it derives from a kind of knowing that has
eliminated all elements of the knower's personality—taste or
feeling, moral disposition or aesthetic temperament. Even if
one recognizes, as many a scientist does, that hypotheses are
usually struck like sparks from unaccountable hunches or
quirks of the mind, from an idiosyncratic penchant for the
pleasing form or agreeable order, a hypothesis is only a beginning, not an end. The scientist does not finish there—as the
artist does, with the personally satisfying vision well expressed
and left to make its intuitive appeal. This is not to say (let me
emphasize) that scientists have no personal tastes or capacity
for dizzying inspiration. Of course they have. Nevertheless,
science presents itself professionally and publicly as that discipline in which taste, inspiration, and intuition do not *prove*
anything and are, in themselves, insufficient to constitute
knowledge.

The process of distillation which characterizes scientific
knowledge therefore begins with the individual scientist, who
normally seeks to strip his professional product of all personal

eccentricity before placing it on public display. No well-wrought scientific paper goes out to the world encumbered with the author's metaphysical speculation or ethical sentiments. If there is occasionally a stylistic flourish quaintly added, that is a liberty that must never distract from the important matter at hand—which is the material that can be suitably expressed as an impersonal finding. The effort in science writing is to achieve an abstract and facelessly formal tone. After all, one's colleagues have little enough time now to spend savoring the idiosyncrasies of the Pasteurs and Rutherfords. What should they care for the autobiographical tidbits and subjective ruminations of lesser figures? So the scientist subtracts as much of himself from his work as possible, knowing that his successors will distill his efforts even more severely as time goes on. Eventually his life's work may only survive as a point of fact or a single calibration in the textbooks: an anonymous, condensed detail.

The scientist possesses two not quite congruent identities, one personal and one professional. In his own person, he may be as quirky as any mad artist. But what his professional identity demands of him is a strict discipline of the total self, until he achieves the stance of one who possesses an impeccably impersonal grasp of reality. He must make the transition from the one identity to the other if he is to meet the standards of what John Ziman has called "public knowledge." The peculiar piece of role playing involved in this transition has proved to be of momentous cultural importance. For it has lent science a social image of self-correcting infallibility which disguises its origin as essentially a craft activity as much based on hunches, intuitive knack, personal judgment as any craft. The scientist himself may easily forget the personal basis of his professional performance as he soldiers on through his "expurgation of the intellect" (as Bacon puts it), determined to cleanse from his experience all that is purely personal. He must be careful that he does not give the name of truth to that which he merely finds subjectively pleasing. In that respect, poets, artists, prophets, and great storytellers can always go him one better, freely inventing and elaborating worlds that excite or inspire. Scientific knowing rigorously subordinates these intrusions of personal fancy and predilection. It is self-denying and puritanically disciplined. It does not wish to see with the lively, wayward eye of the artist, which allows itself to be seduced by what is charming, dramatic, or awesome—and to remain there, entranced. It seeks a neutral eye, an impersonal eye . . . in effect, the eyes of the dead wherein reality is reflected without emotional distortion.

The eyes of the dead . . . the phrase is chilling. And perhaps the scientist protests, "Will people never have done accusing us of cold-bloodedness! We also experience excitement and elation and aesthetic rapture." And that is no doubt true. The impersonal eye also has its gratifications. One suspects that those who study the world by its benefit must try to make some sense to themselves of what others have meant in speaking of wonder. But they appropriate the word for another kind of experience, for the sense of achievement that one derives from intricate measurements precisely made, from quantities and relationships given a grandiose order, from subjecting the once uncontrollable to human manipulation, from translating the once incomprehensible into a mathematical and mechanistic imagery . . . and perhaps too (dare we suggest it?) from reducing the formerly marvelous to a "nothing but." Such satisfactions are not the same as those of artistic or visionary imagination. One may wish to value the pleasures of science more highly than those of artist or seer . . . but they are not the same. We are dealing here with two orders of experience and even if the two can schizophrenically coexist in the same personality, let their antithesis be honestly declared. For the scientific mode of knowing cannot have it both ways. If scientific knowledge progresses, and if this is its distinctive claim to being the most valuable kind of knowledge, then it must be detachable; it cannot be validated by the peculiar subjective predilections of its discoverers. It is not true because it is pleasing, but because it expresses what is regarded as impersonally so. It must purport to stand free of the person by whom it was formulated. Only in this way can it rise above its age, or place, or circumstance of origin and so be liberated from those follies and blind spots which Bacon analyzes so brilliantly in the classic passages of the *Novum Organum* dealing with the "idols" of the mind.

The burden of what we call the "scientific method," then, is to achieve just such an impersonal stance in our encounter with reality. It is precisely in this act of depersonalization that Bacon placed his hope of "building in the human understanding a true model of the world, such as it is in fact, not such as a man's own reason would have it to be . . .". And he continues, "those foolish and apish images of worlds which the fancies of men have created in philosophical systems, must be utterly scattered to the winds."

Now, precisely what this "scientific method" is, or ought to be—or whether it exists at all—is the subject of long and continuing dispute among epistemologists. Few of them would any longer take Bacon's suggested method very seriously . . . or that of Descartes, which bears much the same passionate concern for impersonality and which was devised nearly simultaneously with Bacon's work. Scientists themselves may be even less certain (and probably less concerned) about their method than the epistemologists, settling for some fairly loose and homely rules of thumb. Science is actually taught and practiced more as a craft than a philosophy. For example: Sir George Thomson, the physicist, tells us that the method of science is really no more than

> . . . a collection of pieces of advice, some general, some rather special, which may help to guide the explorer in his passage through the jungle of apparently

arbitrary facts. . . . In fact, the sciences differ so greatly
that it is not easy to find any sort of rule which applies
to all without exception.

It is likely that many scientists would settle for Percy Bridg-
man's even more latitudinarian dictum that their method
"is nothing more than doing one's damnedest with one's
mind, no holds barred." For our purposes here we need go no
further in attempting a rigorous definition of this method; it
is sufficient to point out the monumentally significant fact that
impersonal method is the matter of Bacon's *Novum Organum,*
as much as it is of Descartes' philosophical tracts. Regardless
of how faulty these initial scientific methodologies of Bacon
and Descartes may now seem, both men were convinced that
an impersonal method could be invented. Together they pioneered the concept and launched it upon its historical course.
Perhaps, as Michael Polanyi has argued (and I think he is
right), the pursuit of a technique that yields impersonal knowledge is, in strict epistemological terms, hopelessly chimerical.
Nonetheless, we can give credit to Bacon and Descartes that
there exists the tantalizing assumption, basic to all scientific
work, that a depersonalized method of knowing *can* be perfected—and that *only* such a method of knowing gains access
to the realities of nature.

From the scientist's viewpoint, it is a supreme virtue of his
method that it allows an objective knowledge to be distilled
and so accumulated over time. If this were not so, think how
difficult it would be to train each new generation of scientists.
Suppose, like many novelists or poets, scientists also embedded
their work in a personal philosophy. Suppose the neophytes
had to wade through the original texts of the old masters,
pondering all the facets of Newton's religion, Faraday's
ethics, Darwin's psychic development. How little progress the
sciences would make then. How bogged down they would
become in soul-searching and moral criticism.

On the other hand, once we agree there is a form of knowledge that *can* be distilled without loss, we should be aware of the crucial step we are taking. We are agreeing that it is no loss to the scientist personally or to the culture generally to strip human thought of its most intimately personal qualities—its ethical vision, its metaphysical resonance, its existential meaning. We are agreeing that, as far as natural philosophy is concerned, these are so much excess baggage. With Bacon and Descartes, we are legitimizing an act of depersonalization, a censorship of those very qualities of mind and spirit which have always been regarded as indispensable to the health of culture. Bacon had no doubt that act of censorship would be worth what it cost. How confident can we be today that he was right?

"HERE BE MONSTERS . . ."

In Bacon, then, for all his faults and false starts, we find the paradigm of scientific work, a paradigm now so commonplace in our intellectual activity in all fields scientific and scholarly that we may easily underestimate or overlook entirely the pioneering genius that first gave it cultural dignity. On one side the observer; on the other, reality—and separating them, a mediating method which serves as a neutral filter between the two. "Neither the naked hand nor the understanding left to itself," Bacon warns, "can effect much. . . . And as the instruments of the hand either give motion or guide it, so the instruments of the mind supply either suggestions for the understanding or cautions."

> Certainly if in things mechanical men had set to work
> with their naked hands, without help or force of in-

struments, just as in things intellectual they have set
to work with little else than the naked forces of understanding, very small would the matters have been
which . . . they could have attempted or accomplished.

But convinced as he was that people can make little sense
of the universe by dint of their native and spontaneous
capacities, Bacon was nonetheless certain that there could be
devised a method—an instrument of the mind—that would
permit them to experience the world as it really is. On this
Bacon staked all: that the fallible mind can fashion for itself
an infallible technique.

Bacon's analogy here is with the making and using of tools.
As Paolo Rossi puts it, method is for Bacon "a delicate precision instrument patiently fashioned by man for predeter-
mined ends." Like a tool, it is outside and apart from its
maker, free of the subjective taint of personality. Bacon likens
the *novum organum* at several points to an instrument, a
mechanism, a ruler and compass. It will be "a new machine
for the mind," he tells us, and his high hope is that "the
business" of understanding should eventually "be done as if
by machinery." Are these only figures of speech? Perhaps . . .
though they are, as a person's metaphors and images always
are, supremely revealing. Or can we perhaps discern in
Bacon's words the first faint adumbration of one of our
peculiar contemporary projects: that of relinquishing as much
"thinking" as possible to artificial means of so-called intelligence?

The intellectual world of our own day has become so accustomed to thought mediated by impersonal methodology
that much of what Bacon says on the subject may seem
platitudinous. We take for granted the Baconian analogy between the activities of knowing and contriving. We make
nothing more basic to our higher education than careful
training in the "tools" of each intellectual discipline. A

discipline that does not have at its back an arsenal of techniques, methods, procedures—preferably tied up with a deal
of jargon and much numerology—is apt to suffer from an
oppressive inferiority complex, its practitioners suspecting that
they have no defensible reason for existing. "Methods first"
is the motto on which we establish the education of a good
professional. In some fields of the behavioral sciences, the
watchword almost seems to be "methods, first, last, and
always."

And yet, what a curious idea it is, this fear that has
haunted us since the age of Bacon, that knower and known
cannot be trusted alone in one another's company but must be
chaperoned by a sober and censorious methodology . . . lest
they should have illegitimate intercourse and produce bas-
tards of fantasy. To judge by our fierce determination to have
the knower prepared and disciplined, instructed to do this
and forbidden to do that, we would seem to fear that the
mind in search of knowledge goes forth into hostile and
treacherous terrain—much like that unknown world Bacon's
contemporaries, the great voyagers, were braving on the uncharted seas. Like them, we seem also to write upon our
epistemological maps, beyond the boundaries of our most deliberately focused logical consciousness, "here be monsters."

This is clearly the way Bacon himself envisaged the nature
that man confronted, not as a candid and helpful companion,
but as an elusive keeper of secrets, "a labyrinth . . . knotted
and entangled" and filled with "deceitful resemblances."
With such a secretive and deceptive antagonist, one must
obviously be guarded; one must lay plans and prepare strategies—for the relation of man to his environment is not at all a
natural and graceful one. "The subtlety of nature," Bacon
asserts, "is greater many times over than the subtlety of the
senses and understanding." Worse still, the natural equipment with which man has been endowed is totally inadequate
to its tasks. "The human understanding," says Bacon, "is no

dry light, but receives an infusion from the will and affections." The senses, too, are chronically incompetent, "a thing infirm and erring." We humans would seem, then, to be pathetic creatures, disastrously out of touch with the nature in which we reside. Therefore, Bacon counsels us to hesitate and think twice, to double-check ourselves at every step. As he puts it, in describing his approach to the study of nature, "I interpose everywhere admonitions and scruples and cautions, with a religious care to eject, repress, and as it were to exorcise every kind of phantasm."

To eject . . . repress . . . exorcise . . . But *who* or *what* within us is to be trusted with this grave responsibility of policing the spontaneous self? How can we be certain that it— whatever it is—is not beset by its own "phantasms"? How can we be sure this mental watchman needs no watching himself?

It is not a question Bacon answers—or even asks. Rather, he draws upon our well-developed capacity for splitting the person, for cleaving the identity into a duality of rival selves: soul against body, passion against reason, id against ego. It is our old habit of the self-doubting second thought, as old perhaps as the emergence of advanced intelligence in our evolutionary forebears. And upon that psychic rift, Bacon rears his epistemology. He knows that there exists within us the strange capacity to contract our consciousness back and away from the moment in which experience embraces us. That contraction is the essential gesture of single vision. Bacon does not pause to examine the curious act by which we create this other, non-personal self somewhere within and then decide, from that vantage point, to regard our conduct as if from a distance. Instead, into this gap between ourselves In Here and the object Out There, Bacon thrusts the *novum organum*. And so we have the essence of methodology: to distrust what is impulsive and warmly personal; to replace it with the once-removed and coldly other. In this way we achieve *objectivity,* that mode of consciousness which insures (to repeat Bacon's words) that "the mind itself be from the very outset not left to take its own course, but be guided at every step, and the business be done as if by machinery."

It was a momentous decision on Bacon's part to designate the objective consciousness as our single means of gaining access to reality. For what is this objectification of experience but the act of alienation, a breaking of faith between people and their environment, between people and their own experiential faculties? The psychic capacity to commit that act may be as old as humanity; but with Bacon—and Descartes— the capacity is at last given epistemological dignity. More than that, it is given the monopoly of knowledge. It becomes *the* means of knowing, our *only* means of knowing. And those who speak from any other stance are to be dismissed as offering us what Bacon calls "but so many stage-plays, representing worlds of their own creation after an unreal and scenic fashion."

THE SECRET OF POWER-KNOWLEDGE

To be sure, the epoch-making historical transition we are discussing here cannot be credited to one man. The breach of faith we speak of is not to be blamed wholly on Bacon. (Blame is beside the point in any case.) His thought is a single focus that illuminates a major cultural transformation. At most, Bacon, along with Descartes, only raised an epistemological edifice on a distrust for nature that stretches far back into the Judeo-Christian tradition. The Bacon who spurs mankind on to claim "the right over nature which belongs to it by divine bequest," who looks forward to the "dominion of the human race itself over the universe," only echoes the

God of Genesis, who made it Adam's prerogative to name the beasts and plants and subject them to his uses. Indeed, Bacon —especially the Bacon of the essays on classical fables—can often reveal a strong sensitivity to the criminal arrogance which comes with power. He often counsels moderation and restraint in our dealings with nature. But, as Paolo Rossi points out, his caution is directed primarily toward efforts that seek to dominate the world by what he takes to be external and miraculous means, rather than by means that work from within natural phenomena. The advice follows from the Baconian dictum that to command nature we must obey her. But domination remains the object; Bacon never deviates from his conviction that "the command over things natural— over bodies, medicine, mechanical powers, and infinite others of this kind—is the one proper and ultimate end of true natural philosophy."

This leads us to a baffling issue. How are we to account for the supreme confidence of Bacon and his disciples that the *novum organum* would lead uniquely to a natural philosophy of dominance? This is the theme most often and strenuously sounded in Bacon's writing—almost as if the claim required the service of his mightiest rhetoric to make it credible. As well it might, since Bacon himself was never able to produce any of the inventions his method promised. Nor is it at all clear that the New Philosophy, within the next two centuries, led to a single one of that "line and race of inventions" which Bacon—like Descartes—forecast. Almost without exception the progress of the mechanical arts throughout the seventeenth and eighteenth centuries owed nothing to the scientific research of the age. As David S. Landes has concluded, "if anything, the growth of scientific knowledge owed much to the concerns and achievements of technology; there was far less flow of ideas or methods the other way; and this was to continue to be the case well into the nineteenth century."

Yet, while contemporary scholarship can see the historical

lag between science and technology clearly enough, the new study of nature that was launched in Bacon's age did nevertheless enjoy the reputation of being intimately associated with invention and practical action. This was not only so among the Baconians who founded the Royal Society, dedicating it to "multiplying and beautifying . . . the mechanick arts"; the founders of other seventeenth-century scientific academies—in France and Berlin—took Bacon's promise of worldly power quite as seriously.

It would be easy enough to conclude that Bacon, Descartes, and their followers were simply lucky enough to be backing a good bet, a style of thought which has served to associate them with later scientific work that would indeed transform the face of nature. One might argue that the most the Baconians did to advance technology was to elevate the work of artisan and mechanic to a new cultural dignity so that it might be publicized and rewarded. And this is true enough. Bacon, like the Encyclopedists of eighteenth-century France, did much to upgrade the status of the craftsman. But he was also convinced that he was doing considerably more than performing the role of a publicist for the virtues of the workshop.

Joining the New Philosophy to technology was not, in Bacon's mind, a slipshod association. The link may be a subtle one, but it is hardly facile or fortuitous. Bacon was perfectly aware that innovation in the mechanical arts could be achieved without any assistance from his *novum organum*. In his writings he shows a clear appreciation of how much can be done by what we would call "craft invention"—the sort of pragmatic innovation that stems from (in Bacon's words) "casual discovery," "accident," or simple "animal instinct." The three inventions which Bacon credits with having changed the course of history—the magnet, the compass, and gunpowder—were products of just such craft invention. Recognizing this fact, Bacon goes on to predict that his *novum organum* will provide a different basis for invention, one that will lead to far richer and more wondrous results, in fact, "the effecting of all things possible." Yet in anticipating this vastly accelerated rate of innovation, Bacon is careful to qualify his promise and to do so in an especially interesting way. Without surrendering in the least his conviction that mighty improvements will be forthcoming from the *novum organum,* he emphasizes the need for an indefinitely long period of study during which much inapplicable knowledge will have to be collected and sorted out. The promised fruits sometimes seem to be very far off, since they are predicated upon man's capacity to "reach the remoter and more hidden parts of nature"; and for this "it is necessary that a more perfect use and application of the human mind and intellect be introduced."

> For first, the object of the natural history which I propose is. not so much to delight with variety of matter or to help with present use of experiments, as to give light to the discovery of causes and supply a suckling philosophy with its first food. For though it be true that I am principally in pursuit of works and the active department of the sciences, yet I wait for the harvest time, and do not attempt to mow the moss or to reap the green corn. For I well know that axioms once rightly discovered will carry whole troops of works along with them, and produce them, not here and there one, but in clusters. And that unseasonable and puerile hurry to snatch by way of earnest at the first works which come within reach, I utterly condemn and reject, as an Atalanta's apple that hinders the race.

The style is quaint; yet these might almost be the words of a contemporary scientist striving to explain to a budget-minded congressional committee (as Bacon was seeking to explain to a particularly tight-fisted monarch) the necessity of adequate "lead time" between research and development. The notion makes perfect sense to us today. But consider: Bacon was pleading for a *new* philosophy, untested and unproved, one that was not destined to achieve its "payoff" for generations to come. He could not even give a specific idea in his writing of what kinds of invention might be included in these "whole troops of works" he refers to. At points he sounds almost like King Lear, who loudly blusters

> I will do such things—
> What they are, yet I know not; but they shall be
> The terrors of the earth.

Yet, bravado notwithstanding, Bacon was right. The "harvest time" was to come. He was right too in his insistence on the lag between pure and applied science. We need not hold him guilty of either hedging or faking.

What is it, then, that accounts for his fervent conviction that some necessary connection exists between the new method of knowing and the promise of unprecedented worldly power? Why were Bacon and his followers so sure that their kind of knowledge would succeed prodigiously where the techniques of the alchemists and natural magicians had clearly failed? For they knew full well that not all who seek power find it.

Surely Bacon (and we can include Descartes here too) deserves more credit for sound intuition than dumb luck. Both men would seem to have happened upon a fateful insight— one that emerges if we look beyond their confused epistemology and attune ourselves to the sensibility that underlies it.

Once again, it is important to recall Michael Polanyi's contention that a purely impersonal knowledge is impossible to come by even in the exact sciences. But if an epistemology of total objectivity is unattainable, a *psychology* of objectivity is not. There is a way to *feel* and *behave* objectively, even if one cannot *know* objectively. Indeed, the capacity of people to depersonalize their conduct—and to do so in good conscience, even with pride—is the distinctive psychic disease of our age. We must return once again to the intimate link between the search for an epistemological objectivity and the psychology of alienation: that is, to idolatrous consciousness. It is no mere coincidence that this devouring sense of alienation from nature and one's fellow man—and from one's own essential self—becomes the endemic anguish of advanced industrial societies. The experience of being a cosmic absurdity, a creature obtruded into the universe without purpose, continuity, or kinship, is the psychic price we pay for scientific "enlightenment" and technological prowess. Only those who have broken off their silent inner dialogue with man and nature, only those who experience the world as dead, stupid, or alien and therefore without a claim to reverence, could ever turn upon their environment and their fellows with the cool and meticulously calculated rapacity of industrial society.

And here we have the secret of the New Philosophy, the insight that Bacon and his disciples dimly perceived through their often nebulous discussion of a *novum organum*. Essentially, theirs was the early search for a philosophy and an ethic of alienation. They had found the great truth: break faith with the environment, establish between yourself and it the alienative dichotomy called objectivity, and you will surely gain power. Then nothing—no sense of fellowship or personal intimacy or strong belonging—will bar your access to the delicate mysteries of man and nature. Nothing will inhibit your ability to manipulate and exploit. This is the same power we gain over people when we refuse to honor their claim to respect, to compassion, to love. They become for us mere things on which we exercise power. Between ourselves and them there is no commerce of the feelings, no exchange of sentiment or empathy. We know them only as a behavioral surface. And knowing them only in that way, we can then remark coolly how interesting it is that they make these sounds of protest, anguish, or despair; we can stand back and note this quaint behavior . . . the throb in the voice, the tear in the eye, the spasm of pain. But we make certain that their distress strikes no sympathetic chord in us—for we are only detached observers, and our project requires us to go no further than to record, to measure, to probe further, and to get on with the assigned job. The intimate relationship of such objectivity to the psychology of alienation could be made no clearer than it was by Clark L. Hull in describing his "suggested prophylaxis against anthropomorphic subjectivism":

> A device much used by the author has proved itself to be a far more effective prophylaxis. This is to regard, from time to time, the behaving organism as a completely self-manipulating robot, constructed of materials as unlike ourselves as may be.

No doubt this is an excellent device for dealing with "behaving organisms" not only under the researcher's eye in the laboratory, but under the bombsights of the military, under the guns of Murder Incorporated.

To be sure, it was Bacon's prayer that the New Philosophy should be applied "but for the benefit and use of life." He could scarcely have foreseen the assault upon humanity and the rape of the environment that would follow from an unrestricted application of the objective mode of consciousness to the whole of human experience. He would be horrified to see the *novum organum* become the license for the medical experimentation upon human beings that took place in the Nazi death camps (and which lingers on in our prisons and hospitals for the underprivileged) or for the juggling of megadeaths by our military strategists. And yet there are moments when even Bacon betrays a shocking, though inadvertent awareness of where the promised power of his method lies. Consider his weakness for the political realism of Machiavelli. Did he not recognize in this political context the cynical truth that power flows from a simple willingness to break faith, to harden the heart and abandon the fellowship of feelings? The Bacon who approves a Machiavellian manipulation of people for *raison d'état* is not far removed, psychologically speaking, from the Bacon who aspires to be "the instigator of man's dominion of the universe." Indeed, he is the Machiavelli of a cosmic power politics. In our relations with nature, as in our relations with men and women, the reward for destroying communion is power. In both cases, the method of destroying communion is the same: to suppress the person and to treat that which comes to hand objectively—like a mere thing lacking in sacred autonomy.

To accuse science of breaking faith between human beings and their environment may seem a harsh indictment. And yet, can any less dramatic—and demonic—conception of the scientific revolution do justice to the stupendous dynamism which has characterized western civilization over the last three centuries? Like no society before it, the modern west has played the conquering hero in its dealings with nature, attacking it with the sort of ferocity and wantonness that one only vents upon a foe little trusted and less to be pitied. But once we elevate such a psychic mode to the highest cultural dignity, identifying it as the only intellectually productive way of addressing the universe, all the profits of the Baconian investment are bound to be forthcoming in abundance. There will indeed be knowledge, power, dominion without limit. We are licensed to unravel all mysteries and to remake the world— including human nature itself. We need respect no obligations to nature—to beast or plant, mountain or forest, river or wilderness—because we may disregard the living address of the environment. Nature itself can claim no natural rights. It is simply the arena in which man plays out a Promethean role.

And too, as Bacon predicted, we arrive at a vast and proliferating research—a "knowledge explosion"—under the auspices, for the most part, of just such small and ordinary minds as he foretold us would be capable of utilizing his method. Objective knowing gives a new assembly line system of knowledge, one which relieves us of the necessity to integrate what we study into a moral or metaphysical context which will contribute existential value. We need no longer waste valuable research time and energy seeking for wisdom or depth, since these are qualities of the person. We are free to become specialists, and then, as impersonal researchers, we need only worry about being well informed (in our field), well bibliographied (in our field), and correct (in our field). By way of such microscopic professionalism, knowledge is indeed heaped up enormously on all sides, until at last we begin to worry that there will not be libraries or data-retrieval systems capacious enough to contain the abundance.

We may shake our heads wondering how our ancestors managed to survive for a day knowing so much less than we do. But there is a more pertinent question. How are *we* to create a sane life in the midst of such an expanding universe of disintegrated research? What our competitive and careerist knowledge industry has produced already hopelessly exceeds our ability to make graceful use of it. The abundance does not cohere. Like the physicist's particle zoo, it increases as the focus tightens; but no enduring patterns emerge. The sum total of such information contributes pitifully little to the quality of life as it is lived day by day; yet it is the duty of no profession to give it existential validity. Beyond the boundaries of his discipline, each expert plays dumb. It does not occur to us that it may be as irresponsible to leave unintegrated knowledge lying about as to produce babies and abandon them on the nearest doorstep.

Finally, we begin to resemble the sad hero of Ionesco's play *The New Tenant*, overwhelmed and immobilized by a mountainous conglomeration of intellectual furniture. So it becomes our desperate project to program this slag heap of data points into the computers. The machines will know it all! The idea that culture is an adventure of the human spirit, to be carried on in fellowship for the good of our souls, vanishes from sight. "Thinking machines" (or at least "memory tapes") which merely counterfeit the formal surface of a real idea (but never feel its depth or rich ambiguity, never sense its personal resonance) become the electronic stitchery of a cultural crazy quilt. And the thinking machines, of course, will be owned, programmed, and employed by the technocracy. They will not be *our* servants.

THE DESACRALIZATION OF NATURE

Let us be clear about one crucial point. There can be no question but that the worst vices to which the objective style of experience leads—callousness, authoritarian manipulation, simple indifference to the sensibilities of people and nature—are ancient and universal traits. People have since time out of mind fallen below the counsel of their saints, hardening their hearts for purposes of violence and exploitation. Mankind hardly required Bacon's *novum organum* to teach it such criminalities.

But Charles Gillispie goes to the heart of the matter when he portrays the history of science as the aggressive advance through culture of an "edge of objectivity." What is claimed for objectivity—and at last, as Bacon foretold, everything is—is claimed for science. To extend that claim is the common cause that binds together all the sciences and numerous would-be sciences, as well as all the modern scholarship, art, and philosophy which take their standard of intellectual respectability from the sciences. The scientific "act of knowing," as Gillispie tells us, "is an act of alienation." It is a forcing of experience out and away from the grip of the personal. As we have seen, what Baconian-Cartesian epistemology did was to bestow high philosophical status upon that act of alienation by insisting that it provided our *only* reliable access to reality. Far more directly than it encouraged callous behavior, this ennobling of the alienated psyche has progressively degraded every other form of awareness human beings possess. It has sapped our ability to defend the claims of the sacred in ourselves, our fellows, and our environment against the knife edge of objectivity. We may continue to cry up the dignity of man and the magnificence of nature, drawing rhetorically upon living truths of prehistoric origin. But we do so by virtue of the absurd in an alienated culture where such truths smack uncomfortably of the arcane and mystical. After all, as an enlightened, rational, scientific society, are we not beyond such primitive superstitions as the "pathetic fallacy"?

With Bacon, we are at the beginning of that most heroic and tragic of moral labors, the tradition of secular humanism. It is the tradition which tells us, "Yes, we shall live in the reality science has given us—for there is no other. *But* we shall retain all the good old human values. Indeed, our sense of humanity shall reach new heights!" Bacon, who still had a God he could address himself to publicly, was not quite the fully secularized humanist; but all the essential pathos of the tradition echoes through his fervent prayer:

> I humbly pray, that things human may not interfere
> with things divine, and that from the opening of the
> ways of sense and the increase of natural light there
> may arise in our minds no incredulity or darkness with
> regard to the divine mysteries; but rather that the understanding, being thereby purified and purged of fan-

cies and vanity, and yet not the less subject and entirely
submissive to the divine oracles, may give to faith that
which is faith's. Lastly, that knowledge being now dis-
charged of that venom which the serpent infused into
it, and which makes the mind of man to swell, we may
not be wise above measure and sobriety, but cultivate
truth in charity.

It is a glorious declaration, but by the most rigorous contemporary standards, sloppy philosophy. For, irony of ironies, once subject the universe to the *novum organum,* and
"things divine" crumble and vanish before the first breath of
an easy scientific skepticism. They become epistemological
embarrassments, the stuff of archaic superstition, the fraudu-
lent masks of ignorance or unjust privilege, nothing more.
Therefore—in the name of Reason—away with them one and
all! And on with the great business of research and development.

Imagine for a moment bringing Bacon's prayer to the laboratories and seminar tables of our universities and think
tanks, where the busy experts work out the latter-day implications of the master's New Philosophy. Imagine that we raise
the point: "Gentlemen, is it not time that we set aside an interval to consider the divine mysteries and the demands of
cultivating truth in charity?" Such quaint language would
surely be received as a bank teller receives an old and dis-
credited currency.

"Show me," demands the tough-minded skeptic. But he insists upon seeing with a dead man's eyes.

So we become a culture in which even the most great-
hearted of our humanist heroes cannot, upon agonized reflection, find in life itself—in *life!* . . . in the hot biological
lust to survive and enjoy—a project any less grotesquely absurd than the labor of Sisyphus taking his stone once again
up the hill.

THE LAST DITCH

Well then, says the conscience-stricken humanist, let us do as follows. Let us say that the objective mode of consciousness has its place—but that its place is not in the province of human affairs. Let us insist that a "science of human nature" must proceed from a radically different methodology. We shall draw a line—a sort of epistemological last ditch. On one side, we place the dead and stupid things of the world: the beasts and plants, the stars and chromosomes, the galaxies and the tiny stuff of the atom. Here will be the arena of objective scrutiny. On the other side of the line, we place people—for people are obviously different . . . special . . . a thing apart from all the rest of nature . . . a kind of magnificent freak. And with respect to people there must be a different mode of knowing, one that comprehends their vitality, their purposiveness, their sensibility. We must have a science of human nature that listens with the third ear and communes with the living mysteries of this unique phenomenon. This is Erich Fromm's strategy when he argues:

> . . . complete rational knowledge is possible only of *things*. Things can be dissected without being destroyed; they can be manipulated without damage to their nature; they can be reproduced. *Man is not a thing*. He cannot be dissected without being destroyed. He cannot be manipulated without being harmed. And he cannot be reproduced artificially. Life in its biological aspects is a miracle and a secret, and man in his human aspects in an unfathomable secret. We know our fellow man and ourselves in many ways, yet we do not know him or ourselves fully because we are not things.

The intention of the argument is undeniably noble. But it is apt to cut no ice with the hard-nosed behaviorist who will wonder why this particular conglomeration of molecules and atoms and electrochemical circuitry called the human being should indeed be regarded as different, special, unique. Is not the human being simply a rather complex bio-chemical-behavioral-feed-back system made up of many "nothing buts" not fully understood . . . *as yet?* We are led to a strange competition, then, between the tender-minded and the tough-minded—and it will surely be the *"more objective than thou"* tough-minded who do the better job of defending the claims of science. They move with the great momentum of the "edge of objectivity" and their argument is "let us have no failure of nerve."

But here is another possibility. Suppose we ask what justification there is for drawing the well-intentioned line that exempts the human being from the purview of the impersonal eye. The answer will be that the human observer experiences with people a transaction of the emotions, a sense of fellow feeling. Person calls out to person and we know that this individual before us is no mere thing to be charted and graphed turned into a statistical cipher and controlled from without. We know that this debases a person's living beauty. We *know* this, though we do not know it the way we ordinarily know the behavior of animal and plant. With respect to the plants and animals we can easily achieve objectivity, for what is objectivity but the measure of our will and capacity to alienate?

But now suppose this ability we have to find something of ourselves in people should be expanded, so that the same personal transaction occurred with animal and plant . . .

Suppose that ability began to reach out further still, discovering a reality of inventive pattern and communicable vitality even in what we once regarded as the dense, dead stuff of the world . . .

Suppose the whole of creation began to speak to us in the silent language of a deeply submerged kinship . . .

Suppose, like the child, the "superstitious" savage, the rhapsodic seer, we even felt urged to reply courteously to this address of the environment and to join in open conversation . . .

Suppose we discovered that the fallacy in the "pathetic fallacy" could be undone if, instead of reading human characteristics into nature, we realized that nature has read human characteristics into *us* . . .

Suppose, in brief, we came to understand in the depths of us what Blake means when he announces

I'll sing to you to this soft lute, and shew you all alive
The World, when every particle of dust breathes forth its joy.

Then would we not perhaps wonder with some sense of urgency what these dead man's eyes can see that is not more a blindness than a seeing?

CHAPTER 6

Fair Bait . . . Cruel Trap

A scientist should recognise in his philosophy—as he already recognises in his propaganda—that for the ultimate justification of his activity, it is necessary to look away from knowledge itself to a striving in man's nature [which is] not to be justified of science or reason, for it is in itself the justification of science, of reason, of art, of conduct.

Arthur Eddington

NATURE IN AN OBJECTIVE KEY

Francis Bacon might well· be thought of as the Moses of the history of science, the inspired seer who discerns in Canaan the vivid promise of milk and honey, but who surveys the promised land only from far off and indistinctly. Bacon adumbrates the revolution in consciousness from which the world of urban-industrialism takes its course; it fell to others

—to Galileo, Descartes, Newton—to perfect the single vision that would build that world. Compared to their sleek precision—especially in the application of mathematical technique—Bacon's attempts at methodology appear almost comically primitive. Bacon had little knowledge and less respect for mathematics, and given that bias, he failed to recognize that the secret of the depersonalizing *novum organum* he sought lay in the purely quantitative vision of nature which first appears in Galileo's new approach to terrestrial mechanics. For Galileo, measurement was all. In his science, the world was caught in a net of numbers. Whatever escaped must be regarded as non-science, the leftover realm of mind, of spirit, of "secondary qualities," the ghostly country that has progressively come to be regarded as less and less habitable by people of a practical nature.

Still, something of Bacon's global conception of the New Philosophy has survived among the mathematizers. There are those who continue to hope that, in time, everything—politics, ethics, all—can be trapped in the quantitative net . . . if only its mesh might be made sufficiently fine. The ambition lingers on in the two little words that forever qualify the behavioral scientist's ritualistic confession of ignorance: *as yet.* "We do not know enough about man, society, aspiration, 'peak experience,' creativity, human fulfillment to treat these matters scientifically . . . *as yet.*" But in time . . . when the net has been drawn tighter . . . with a bit more research . . . when some more refined system of measurement has been developed . . . when more data is in . . . *then* we shall know.

With the Newtonian synthesis, Bacon's objectivized nature was at last achieved; the world-picture was homogenized and qualitatively flattened. For the first time in the western tradition, the universe became in the most objective sense of the word a "universe": a cosmos uniform throughout its infinite extent, devoid of ethical nuance, of magic centers or charmed circles, of quintessential terrain. Henceforth, nature was seen to be spread out before the human observer like a value-neuter screen on which only the measurable behavior of things might be registered. And behind that screen, there was understood to be . . . nothing, no will, no animating purpose, no personality that might invite sensuous participation or answer the human desire to penetrate and commune.

Ordinarily, this Newtonian system is referred to as "mechanistic," with the machine metaphor understood to derive from the deterministic, clockwork precision of its astronomical movements. But the image cuts deeper, I think. The essence of a machine is that it acts to serve a function, never a purpose. Purpose is inherent and self-appointed; it is an indication of conscious willfulness, an expression of spiritual autonomy. This was exactly the aspect of Aristotelian science which the New Philosophy, borrowing upon the idolatrous psychology of Christianity, was most determined to destroy. Yet nature is evidently active; it is filled with motion, growth, and orderly change. What to make of this activity? The problem is nicely solved if we imagine that nature's action is that of a machine. A machine, being dead, cannot choose a purpose; it can only serve a function. In contrast to purpose, function is externally imposed by the machine's maker or user. A mechanistic nature, therefore, lacks vital intention. It becomes a tool in need of a job, presumably to be supplied by God; or eventually, in God's stead, by his earthly steward, man—the only purposeful agent left in sight. Nature perceived as machine is nature adrift, waiting to be put to use as man sees fit to use it.

One more point. The machine image objectivizes at a stroke whatever it touches by emphasizing its inert otherness from man, its non-communicability. In the magical worldview of the Old Gnosis, all things—animal, plant, mineral—radiate meanings; they are intelligible beings—or the natural faces such beings put on for us in the physical world. But for Newton, the celestial spheres comprise a machine; for Descartes, animals become machines; for Hobbes, society is a machine; for La Mettrie, the human body is a machine; eventually for Pavlov and Watson, human behavior is machine-like. So steadily, the natural world dies as it hardens into mechanistic imagery.

If these are the deeper psychological implications of mechanistic thought, then a disturbing conclusion follows. Since the advent of the quantum and the relativity theories at the turn of the twentieth century, it has become a familiar notion that Newtonian mechanism has been replaced by more humanistically acceptable conceptions of time, space, matter, causation. Some have given this "revolution" in modern physics such prominence that they seem nearly to suggest the entire history of science prior to Planck, Einstein, and Bohr can be written off as a defunct tradition—as if the authority of classical physics over a wide range of phenomena was not still respected by science; it does after all remain the physics of our local environment—of Euclidean space and common-sense time. Nevertheless, F. S. C. Northrup has insisted that "the old, rigid, cast-iron universe in which man seemed to be nothing but a mere cog in a vast cosmical machine, has evaporated. . . . No longer is nature to be conceived as a mere collision of individualistic, *laissez-faire* atoms, nor man merely as a collocation of such atoms, struggling for existence."

The statement typifies the hopes of many philosophers and scientists who have recognized the crushing inhumanity of western science and have grown desperate for an alternative worldview more hospitable to human aspiration. For such thinkers, the new physics has been greeted as, at last, their liberation from the death grip of the Newtonian world-machine, a rescue that arises, conveniently enough, from within science itself. Here is the line of thought which seeks to defend the freedom of the will by reference to Heisenberg's indeterminacy principle, and the philosophical virtues of paradox and ambiguity by reference to Bohr's principle of complementarity. Bohr himself once felt that the indeterminacy principle could be elaborated into a bulwark to protect the special status—the "irrationality"—of living organisms. During the nineteen-forties, there were, in fact, a number of physicists (most notably Max Delbrück and Erwin Schrödinger) who were sufficiently inspired by the breakdown of mechanism in their field to migrate into biology with the hope of proving that living things were governed by "other laws" than physical systems—a mysterious project indeed which has received less and less interest from the biologists as biochemistry has gone from strength to strength. Similarly, the humanist social scientist Floyd Matson has turned the new physics against behaviorist psychology and sociology, seeking to demonstrate that the behaviorist approach is invalidated by its antiquated devotion to the "broken image" of Newtonian mechanism.

All this is commendable for its humanistic intentions—and yet pathetic. For it vastly exaggerates the scale and wholly mistakes the character of this so-called revolution in modern science. It overlooks the psychological continuities that bind the old and new physics together; it fails to see the underlying sensibility to which mechanism only gave a surface expression. Mechanism was merely the first image on which single vision fastened in its effort to gain a purchase upon human consciousness. Once having served this function, the mechanistic model became quite dispensable. It could be retired without displacing the objective psychology it served to foster.

To be sure, over a certain range of phenomena in atomic physics and astronomy, the old machine metaphor has lost its serviceability. This has forced scientists working in those areas to revise some of their observational methods, to invent more ambiguous models and tentative paradigms, and to develop more sophisticated mathematical procedures for construing their experimental data. All of which has finished by making physics more inaccessible to the lay public than ever before—surely a dubious contribution to humanistic values. But the *psychology* of the enterprise has not changed; this is the string that holds all the scientific beads together from Galileo and Newton to the present day. In no sense does relativity (much less the quantum of action) imply a compromise of objective consciousness. One does not treat anti-sigma-minus-hyperons with any different sensibility than Newton treated the planets. The alienative dichotomy holds. And how sad it is to see so many intellectuals grasping at such straws, insisting that the advent of the linear accelerator and probability mathematics is, somehow, the salvation of the soul—as if it is only natural science that could legitimize a traditional human wisdom. Charles Gillispie has correctly observed that, in so far as there is any sort of "subjectivism" in modern physics, it is hardly a matter of "Einstein lapsing back into some Greek posture of humanism."

> It is all very well to say that there is no physics without a physicist. . . . But it would, after all, be more accurate to say "without an instrument", because for such purposes a physicist is an instrument. We are concerned, that is to say, not with a personal subjectivism, but with an instrumental subjectivism, the kind of which a computer is capable.

In short, when all the wishful thinking about the philosophical spin-off of the new physics has cleared away, the result is no gain for humanism. Worse still, when we turn to the life sciences, we find them pursuing a more crudely mechanistic mode of thought than ever. In biology, they persist in thinking of the cell as a "chemical factory," and of the action of enzymes as "cybernated feedback," and of DNA as "information transfer." If the interior of the atom has ceased to look like a steam engine, the chemistry of life has nonetheless been assimilated with gusto to the imagery of automated industrialism. "In science," as Joseph Needham, hardly the most boorish of our biologists, once said, " a man is a machine, or if he is not, then he is nothing at all."

The basic effect of Newtonian mechanism was to produce a nature that was felt to be dead, alien, and purely functional. This estranged relationship of scientist to nature has remained unchanged; it is still what our science most irreducibly is. Indeterminacy, complementarity, quantum mechanics, relativity . . . the tunes have been altered, but the mode of the music is the same always. We are still performing in the key of objective consciousness. It would remain so if we found angels at the end of our telescopes and then subjected them to spectrum analysis. It is single vision—the act of objectification—that defines science, not the imagery or technique by which, during any period of history, scientists may choose to express their objectivity. Our very assumption that physics is the most *basic* science and that its transformations effect all else is revealing. Why should physics be regarded as the field which provides the surest and purest foundation for our understanding of nature? Obviously, because its subject matter is most easily regarded as dead and alien stuff, that from which we feel the most remote, and therefore the reality single vision knows most reliably.

The point cannot be too strongly stated. It makes no automatic psychological difference that we exchange one theoretical model for another, or refine our methods of scientific measurement; the *quality* of our experience is the heart of the matter. And where evaluation and psychic participation are concerned, the scientific worldview remains as undimensioned today as in the age of Bacon and Newton. Single vision reigns supreme. Ours is still the universe Alexandre Koyré speaks of in his description of the Newtonian synthesis:

> . . . the world of science, the real world, is no more seen . . . as a finite and hierarchically ordered, therefore qualitatively and ontologically differentiated

whole, but as an open, indefinite, and even infinite universe, united not by its immanent structure but only by the identity of its fundamental contents and laws. . . .

This, in turn, implies the disappearence—or violent expulsion—from scientific thought of all considerations based on value, perfection, harmony, meaning, and aim, because these concepts, from now on *merely subjective,* cannot have a place in the new ontology. . . .

Modern science broke down the barriers that separated the heavens and the earth, and . . . united and unified the universe. . . . But . . . it did this by substituting for our world of quality and sense perception, the world in which we live and love and die, another world—the world of quantity, of reified geometry, a world in which, though there is a place for everything, there is no place for man.

GOD EXPERTLY EMBALMED

Such is the sense of nature our culture has come to take for granted and to which even the religious life of our society has adapted. It is a universe that has proved hospitable to only that fossilized form of Christianity which the Enlightenment called "natural religion" and which Blake shrewdly recognized as a euphemism for the total surrender of visionary experience. Newton, like so many of the early scientists, was an outspokenly pious man; professions of faith punctuate his great treatises. But in his science Newton could retain only the chilliest, most bloodlessly cerebral notion of the divine. In the famous "General Scholium" which he attached to his *Principia* to defend its religious intentions, God is allowed into nature only as a deduction from the order of things . . .

or else "how to keep the systems of the fixed stars by their gravity from collapsing?" He is the remote potentate who "governs all things, not as the soul of the world, but as Lord over all; and on account of his dominion he is wont to be called *Lord God pantocrator* or Universal Ruler." "We know him," concludes Newton, "only by his most wise and excellent contrivance of things . . . we reverence and adore him as his servants." Here is a God no longer experienced, but inferred by a none too solid logic from the design of nature. Of all the poetry in which the divine has ever been clothed, Newton could retain only the austere image of celestial monarchy, the most detached relationship possible between the sacred and the natural. But of course the Judeo-Christian tradition was well freighted with this diminished conception of God and gave Newton much support. Mainstream Christian orthodoxy, with its minimal investment in visionary experience, was more than willing to see its God become a functional postulate in a desacralized universe.

True, Deism has never been a robust faith; it exhausted its philosophical viability within a few generations of its initial appearance. Before the eighteenth century was out, Hume had driven his skeptical rapier through its heart. But natural religion was so anemic to begin with that it scarcely suffered for the wound. It survives today as an easy and shapeless orthodoxy among routine churchgoers. They may never have heard the word "Deism," but they continue to pay respects to that aloof "Somebody (or is it Something?) Up There," the managerial deity who stands well off behind the scientist's universe, careful never to intrude . . . a shy and shriveled divinity . . . an afterthought . . . a cliché. If God has at last died in our culture, he has not been buried. For the casually religious, he lingers on like a fond old relative who has been so expertly embalmed that we may prop him up in the far corner of the living room and pretend the old fellow is still with us. We have even taken pains to bend his fallen mouth into a benign and permissive smile . . . and that is a comfort. It makes him so much *easier* to live with. No more of the old hellfire and brimstone; no more of the terrible mystery and paradox that require the crucifixion of the intellect; no more dark nights of the soul. Is it any wonder that for many people, a dead and stuffed God seems preferable not only to no God at all, but to *any* God at all?

But there is a trouble about this religion of the minimal God. It is so tissue thin that even a fairly obtuse sensibility can hardly fail to discern the void beyond. And only to glimpse that nothingness wherein all things human become "nothing but" . . . "nothing but" . . . "nothing but" . . . is to taste the cosmic absurdity, the annihilating despair. The great question Nietzsche addressed to the scientists may not relate accurately to the still high-spirited age of Bacon or of Voltaire, but it applies emphatically to his own time and ours.

> Has there not been since the time of Copernicus an unbroken progress in the self-belittling of man and his *will* for belittling himself? Alas, his belief in his dignity, his uniqueness, his irreplaceableness in the scheme of existence, is gone. . . . Since Copernicus man seems to have fallen on to a steep plane—he rolls faster and faster away from the center—whither? into nothingness? *into the thrilling sensation of his own nothingness?* . . . *All* science . . . nowadays sets out to talk man out of his present opinion of himself, as though that opinion had been nothing but a bizarre piece of conceit. You might go as far as to say that science finds its peculiar pride, its peculiar bitter form of stoical ataraxia, in preserving man's *contempt for himself.* . . .

By now, the tougher natures among us have grown so accustomed to the reductionist pressure of science that a lament like this sounds perhaps quaintly old-fashioned, a shrill cry of post-Christian nostalgia. Whereas, how much *braver* it is to face the eclipse of God alone, unafraid, absurd. "I myself, like many scientists," announces Nobel laureate Francis Crick, "believe that the soul is imaginary and that what we call our minds is simply a way of talking about the functions of our brains." And he goes on: "Once one has become adjusted to the idea that we are here because we have evolved from simple chemical compounds by a process of natural selection, it is remarkable how many of the problems of the modern world take on a completely new light." Indeed they do. It is the funereal gleam by which we travel the wasteland, the light of dying stars.

Yet what is the alternative to humanist resignation? To forbid the quest for knowledge? Return to old superstition? Foster illusion? Deny the truth? Of course we must not grow contemptuous of the truth. But neither must we grow so contemptuous of our fellow human beings as to believe that the truth has been nowhere known or honored among them except in European society since the scientific revolution. To cast aside all the prescientific and non-scientific realities by which men and women have lived for so long is to settle for a truth that is little more than an operational superficiality; worse, a license for the making of well-informed fools.

THE VERIDICAL EXPERIENCE

Is there a way to avoid these extremes? I believe there is. Suppose we ask how the truth *becomes true* to us. What is the decisive, veridical experience that persuades us to accept any framework of discourse as meaningful and knowledge-yielding? For persuasion is the heart of the matter. What is true to me is what I am *persuaded* is true. Mind that I say "per-

suaded"—not brainwashed, intimidated, tricked, or duped
. . . but freely won over, while in full possession of my own
mind and critical faculties. Is there, then, a psychology of
persuasion which would account for our society's collective
decision to become a science-based culture?

If we would discover that psychology, we must be prepared
to see the truth as a multidimensional experience, an experience which resonates through the whole personality. Obviously, what people have considered true—the items we can
package up into a propositional inventory—has altered from
age to age, from culture to culture. But what of that? Trace
the experience deeper and the relativism of the matter is dispelled. We are, after all, more than the articulate intellect
and its logical apparatus; that is perhaps the last part of us to
go to work on the truth, applying it here and there, elaborating its implications once a context of meaning has already
been endorsed. What we are persuaded to call the truth is
that which engages us at many and more secret levels, until
we feel that the whole of our being has been warmed to life
and is now burningly *there,* alert, and animated. It is this
experience of truth—this bright response to a reality we sense
pressing in upon us along the many avenues of our awareness
—which is universal. Perhaps, then, if we could do justice
within ourselves to the reality others have been touched by,
we might even find *their* truth larger and more liberating
than our own, and so be persuaded to see things anew.

But once this transforming, veridical experience has entered
the lives of men and women, it is ironic what often follows.
The personality which received the truth whole now re-
shapes itself, even delimits itself, striving for an identity that
will best and most specially manifest its witness. Such a taking
on of roles is, it would seem, our innately human way of
celebrating the realization of truth. We adorn ourselves with
a new self, usually one that seeks to emphasize aspects of reality previously slighted. This may be the project of genera-

tions, each successive generation sharpening the identity pioneered by its forebears. So a culture works out its peculiar destiny, achieving style, if often at the expense of wholeness. Until, at last, it may lose touch entirely with dimensions of reality which initially inspired its distinctive identity. Then what a people call true will no longer be true as it was once experienced to be true. It will be the mere surface of the primordial experience: a collection of propositions, data, credos, dogmas, customs . . . at last institutionalized and enforced by authority. This is a diminishment of the personality; but it is important to realize that, initially, the whole person acted to create this half person—even as the whole and healthy actor might undertake to make himself over on the stage into a monomaniac, and then lose himself in the role.

In our personal lives, neurosis is such a playacting, the whole psyche seeking satisfaction by forcing itself into a lesser identity. Pico della Mirandola once called human beings, by their very nature, chameleons who are forever taking up one disguise after another. Perhaps there is no alternative to this human masquerade. But once any of our cultural roles becomes tyrannical and heavy with despair—once it forces us toward self-belittlement—it is time to excavate our inherited identity to find there the buried lineaments of the whole personality.

Those who feel—as I do—that culture based on single vision is dehumanizing, must sooner or later confront the question: why, then, did people enter so narrow a trap, and do so with a determination that still encourages them to make themselves at home in their captivity? We have already seen what a dark, idolatrous motif permeates the Judeo-Christian heritage. Some might, like myself, see in this movement the unfolding of a destiny whose nature yields to no purely secular explanation. Nonetheless, that destiny has had to wear an historical costume; or perhaps we should say, it has had to be baited with ideals that people could recognize, cherish, and covet. *What was this bait?* In the answer we give to this question there may lie our best hope of salvaging all that is most valuable in the scientific tradition. Though what we save may not be science as we now know it (let us be clear about that from the outset) but rather those qualities of the whole person to which single vision has had to appeal in order to gain its cultural supremacy.

If science had never been more than science, it would have had no significant future in our culture. Only those who attend to the varying relations any standard of knowledge assumes with the many dimensions of the personality—conscience, imagination, social self-interest—will be able to understand the spectacular course science has run over the past three hundred years—from a marginal curiosity, the hobby of a few amateur natural philosophers, to the prevailing Reality Principle of high industrial society, the legitimizing mystique of the technocracy. The achievement is the more remarkable when one recognizes that scientists, as a group, have been—at least until the Big Science of our own time— among the most unobtrusive members of society. Far from being pushy, they have been for the most part almost monkish in their desire for seclusion, peace, and anonymity. It has been propagandists like Bacon, Voltaire, Ernst Haeckel, Thomas Huxley, H. G. Wells—men not themselves primarily scientists—who have been most concerned to promote and popularize the worldview of science. The scientists themselves have frequently suffered the adulation of society like a curse; it has traditionally intruded itself upon their quiet search for knowledge.

But the modesty of individual scientists notwithstanding, the collective enterprise of science has been anything but humble and reclusive. From the age of Bacon forward, science has addressed itself to more than a professional audience. It has appealed to a broad spectrum of human aspirations, to the evaluative and aesthetic sensibilities, to man's taste for the dramatic, to the sense of daring, to the instinctive urge for freedom and dignity, and, yes, to our civilization's peculiarly demonic greed for power. Science has always had its cultural and social extensions; we turn it into a rarefied body of evolving intellectual constructs only by a ruthless simplification of the historical record. People have wanted more of science than a body of hypotheses and methods, data and theory; and consciously or not, even in spite of themselves, the scientists have provided them with more. They have provided a picture of nature and of nature's God; they have provided mankind with a place and a purpose within that picture; they have projected an ethical ideal for our culture to pursue. They have done all this, not as a mere by-product of their scientific activity, but as an inseparable aspect of their professional commitment. They have done it by what they have said and left unsaid; by what they have affirmed and failed to affirm; by what they have assumed and implied and denied. Most basically, they have done it by asserting their conception of what a reliable conception of nature is and how it is to be gained. All this has been the lure which has drawn mankind toward the culture of science and has influenced it to bestow the accolade of "truth" on the scientist's style of experience.

Let us spend the remainder of this chapter recounting the several ways in which science has gratified these wide-ranging aspirations.

"TO INTERROGATE NATURE WITH POWER": THE UTILITARIAN PROMISE

To begin with the most obvious point, consider the Baconian dictum that "knowledge is power." How far would the New Philosophy have carried without the promise of prodigious material benefit? "We shall become the masters and possessors of nature," Descartes announced, echoing Bacon. And, fortunately for the scientists, there was an important audience prepared to believe the prospectus and to identify the new style of natural philosophy with all the practical pursuits around them. When, therefore, we reach the *philosophes* of the Enlightenment, it was the most natural thing in the world for them to associate the Newtonian worldview with their own consuming passion for crafts, trades, and manufactures. Theoretical science and pragmatic invention, despite their wide separation from one another during that period, were allied in the minds of the *philosophes* as means of exploiting nature— and correctly so, for reasons we have mentioned in the previous chapter. In numerous gentleman's clubs and intellectual societies like the eighteenth-century Lunar Club of Birmingham, the scientists Joseph Priestley and Erasmus Darwin found no trouble in hobnobbing with industrialists like Josiah Wedgwood and Matthew Boulton. Here were men who shared a common Baconian worldview, and looked forward (in the master's words) to "a line and race of inventions that may in some degree subdue and overcome the necessities and miseries of humanity." Accordingly, when the bourgeois revolution which the *philosophes* had done so much to inspire came in France, one of the first projects of the Directory was to finance a new scientific and technical establishment in whose schools the first generation of academic research scientists appears. For precocious technocrats like Saint-Simon and his disciples, that establishment, in league with the industrial wealth of the society, looked like the only logical government of the new bourgeois nation.

This utilitarian aspect of science is such a salient feature of the history of science that its importance should really go without saying. If I emphasize the point here it is because there are still many scientists who pretend to a kind of purity which will excuse them from the responsibilities of power.

They invoke a "neutrality" which severs all connections with technology, and in so doing they falsify their own history.

Now, it may well be possible for individual research scientists to maintain such an aristocratic aloofness in the privacy of their own heads. But they purchase their purity by resort to an unbecoming historical amnesia; and turning a blind eye to the truth never buys real innocence. One need not even refer them to the outspoken utilitarianism of Bacon and Descartes; let them only read Newton's preface to the *Principia* to see how aware the great theoretician himself was of the technological implications of his thought. The object of the *Principia,* he announces, is to close the age-old schism between "rational" and "practical mechanics" by way of a new "universal mechanics." Presently, Newton observes, "artificers do not work with perfect accuracy." But "if any could work with perfect accuracy, he would be the most perfect mechanic of all, for the description of right lines and circles, upon which geometry is found, belongs to mechanics." And what is the secret of this "perfect accuracy" but to discover (as Newton did) the mathematical principles of natural philosophy?

From the earliest stages of the scientific revolution, the most consistent meaning assigned to truth in the sciences has been through and through operational. The purpose of observation, experiment, classification, and theory is, ultimately, to predict or anticipate; to connect an "if" with a "then"; to hold forth the promise that we may successfully manipulate natural forces, or, at least, adapt advantageously to events. Other worldviews have included the same intention; but never with such exclusiveness and centrality. It is of little consequence (and of no moral significance whatever) if the task of applying applicable knowledge is carried out by other hands. The power principle of scientific knowledge begins in the laboratory—indeed, in the cogitating brain of the scientist; it is baked into the conceptual framework of the purest research. Through the eighteenth century, this was no guilty secret, but the open pride of scientists. Science was—boastfully—no parasitic form of learning. For example, consider Sir Humphry Davy's contrast between primitive and civilized people, as he makes it in his *Discourse Introductory to a Course of Lectures on Chemistry* (1802). Primitive man, Davy concludes, is "unable to discover causes, and [is] quietly and passively submissive to the mercy of nature and the elements." But civilized man is "informed by science and the arts, and in control of powers which may be almost called creative; which have enabled him to modify and change the beings surrounding him, and by his experiments to interrogate nature with power, not simply as a scholar . . . but rather as a master, active with his own instruments." These are hardly the words of a man fastidiously seeking to disown the social repercussions of research. Rather, he eagerly claims them— for the greater glory of science.

This natural alliance between theory and praxis only became obscure during the middle and later nineteenth century as the sciences (especially in Germany) began to enter the university curriculum and yield to the spell of the ivory tower. Nineteenth-century research was richly productive, but much of it—even in medicine—far outstripped the capabilities of the then primitive industrial plant and the limited understanding of technicians, who were still little removed from being artisans and tinkerers. For a time much knowledge had to be "pure," because who was there to make use of it? So it became knowledge "for its own sake" . . . idle curiosity. Faraday, commissioned to study metal alloys, produced a host of them that finished up being locked away and forgotten in the vaults of the Royal Institution; the industrial needs and know-how of the day were incapable of assimilating such advanced, applied research. Similarly, one can only regard a discovery like Daniel Bernoulli's famous principle of the air foil—

achieved a century before Faraday's time—as "pure knowledge," because for the next one hundred and fifty years there
existed no aeronautical technology capable of exploiting the
idea for purposes of heavier-than-air flight. A principle of similar importance discovered in our own time would take how
long . . . ? three days . . . ? to be transformed into a better
ballistic missile.

Today, when the theoretical literature of science is well
monitored by sophisticated technicians whose whole training
has been aimed at digging application out of basic research,
one must strain to imagine a science distinct from technology,
except perhaps as part of a convenient division of intellectual
labor. There is actually only the single, ongoing, all-embrac-
ing process of Research and Development. And that process is
politically structured from start to finish. Scientists who blink
the fact are simply playing dumb, not only about their own
history, but about the sociological pattern in which they work,
like it or not.

Clearly, most are inclined to like it. More and more these
days, the developmental application of knowledge is carried
out by scientists wearing another hat: that of industrial con-
sultant. Moreover, when public moneys are being paid out,
the voice of pure science will always be heard intoning the old
song: "You never can tell how basic research will pay off
someday." There is nothing in the least misleading about the
assertion; it is only what history has demonstrated to be so
over and over again. Not because *all* knowledge is power; but
because science, from the study of the atomic nucleus to that
of the most distant quasar, is single-mindedly the pursuit of
that knowledge which *is* uniquely power—if only the power
to predict a pointer reading correctly. There are, of course,
other kinds of knowledge, those born of sensuous penetra-
tion, loving participation, ecstasy, transcendent aspiration.
But that way lies art, joy, wisdom, salvation—not power.

Science promised power as the means to all else. The promise was believed and at last realized, and so swept all before it. But we are left with no tolerance for these other varieties of knowledge, and so with no knowledge that can delimit power.

THE BOURGEOIS LIFESTYLE

It is hardly difficult to see why a style of thought so permeated by practicality should have managed to gain a sizable following during that era of turbulent social change which extends from the English Civil War to the French Revolution. It was the good fortune of science, not only that its worldview should have been so readily identified with praxis, but that there should have existed in Western Europe during the seventeenth and eighteenth centuries a restive class of practical-minded people who had begun to sense their own social importance. For these dynamic middle-class entrepreneurs, the New Philosophy conveniently became part of a bold liberal ideology, a weapon with which they might intimidate the parasitic clergy and aristocracy who had for so long smugly thwarted the bourgeois desire for full citizenly dignity.

To be sure, there were any number of clerics and aristocrats of Europe's *anciens régimes* who subscribed to the Newtonian worldview, priding themselves on their fashionably risqué "enlightenment." Nevertheless, the scientific sensibility belonged peculiarly to the bourgeois element in society. It endorsed their lifestyle—their secular energy, their penchant for utility and commercial gain—as it did that of no other class. Those who adopted their outlook were, to that extent, making concessions to an ideology that challenged the traditional virtues of the aristocratic "closed society."

Charles Gillispie has observed that, regardless of how willing scientists have always been to adapt to any political regime that comes to power, they have always, of necessity, been future-oriented in their outlook. "Neuter though [the scientific community] has been in politics, nevertheless the increasing orientation of all our modern sensibility to progress and the future pertains to science, though in what measure as cause and what as effect I should not like to try to say." For those social elements, then, which have been on the rise in modern times, which have felt no commitment to preserving the past but every incentive for shaping the future to meet their interests, the scientist, with his instinctive concern for novelty, discovery, innovation, became a natural ally.

Consider for a moment the figure of Benjamin Franklin, surely the prototype of the eighteenth-century bourgeois citizen. For centuries, since the rise of the medieval towns, the western world had known such crafty, self-reliant, self-made men. And for centuries they had been distinctly junior members of the political nation. But from the time of the English Civil War, that situation had begun to shift rapidly; a revolution that was as much a change of cultural consciousness as of political power was under way. So that by the time we reach Franklin, we find in the man's make-up something more than the traditional virtues of hard work, self-denial, and resourcefulness, something that now lent the man's presence on the historical stage a formidable dynamism. It was his mighty conviction that his lifestyle grounded him more authentically in the nature of things than that of any other class or estate, that he and his kind were peculiarly lords and masters of this Newtonian universe.

Franklin's gift for invention and disciplined rationality was no longer simply wealth-producing; it was *knowledge*-producing. It was an expression of the newfound human ability "to interrogate nature with power" in ways that revealed intoxicating truths about the world at large and the ways of God. The history of science remembers Franklin still for his signifi-

cant contribution to electrical theory. But—typically—it
omits the contribution's social and personal context. Yet that
context once bestowed upon science an inestimable dignity of
purpose and historical force. The familiar picture we preserve
of the dumpy, bespectacled Franklin flying his kite in a thun-
derstorm may seem comically quaint. But that unlikely figure
—precisely involved in that quaint task—is the very epitome
of a revolutionary class, rebelliously proud and invincibly self-
possessed as it makes up its appropriate worldview.

Franklin carried out his dangerous experiment, formulated
his results into an ingenious theory, pioneered the new frontier of electromagnetic research, (Priestley called his work
perhaps the most important since Newton), was accordingly
elected a Fellow of the Royal Society, and capped this phase
of his studies by inventing the lightning conductor. It was on
the shoulders of such men that science rode forward to take
possession of the modern world; it provided the universe in
which their struggle for liberation could claim the sanction of
nature and of nature's God. Turgot's epitaph for Franklin
nicely summarizes the revolutionary elan of the bourgeois
heroic age: "He snatched lightning from the heavens and
sceptres from kings."

THE EGALITARIAN ETHIC

We can trace this libertarian thrust of science even further—
down to the very epistemological foundations of the New
Philosophy. Here, as in so many other respects, it is Bacon and
Descartes who sound the leading theme.

We have noted how frequently Bacon compares his *novum
organum* to a tool or piece of machinery. Pressing this analogy
to its ultimate conclusion, Bacon was led to believe that his

method, once fully developed, could be appropriated by any-body and everybody. "The strength and excellency of the wit has but little to do in the matter," he tells us—and this aston-ishing assertion only follows logically from his premises. If method is, like a tool, a thing apart from its user, purged of all personality, then it must necessarily function for anyone who lays hands upon it. A truly objective method can be plugged into any mind and do its job. It is not an extension of the person, but an impersonal appurtenance, taken up and added on. Thus: "The course I propose for the discovery of sciences is such as leaves but little to the acuteness and strength of wits, but places all wits and understandings nearly on a level."

The qualifications "but little" and "nearly" seem to betray reservations on Bacon's part; but in fact they lead to nothing. Bacon never explores what qualities of mind or perception might shape scientific work besides his method. In fact, he goes on to campaign strongly against the importance in hu-man thought of any unspecifiable talents of imagination or fancy.

When we turn to Descartes, even these most meager reser-vations are gone. We are confronted with the categorical claim:

> . . . anyone who has learned this whole method per-fectly, however humble his abilities may be, will never-theless perceive that none of these ways is less open to him than to anyone else, and that there is nothing further of which he is ignorant because of any failure of ability or method.

Such became Descartes' great project: to formulate "rules so clear and simple that anyone who uses them carefully will never mistake the false for the true." It is a potent word, that "anyone"—perhaps more alarmingly democratic than

Descartes ever intended. Yet it follows from his conviction that the talent for gaining truth is no more than the proper application of that "good sense" which he takes to be "mankind's most equitably divided endowment." As he states at the outset of the *Discourse on Method,* disputes over the truth are "due not to differences in intelligence, but merely to the fact that we use different approaches and consider different things."

What we have here in the words of Bacon and Descartes is surely the highest and most unwarranted tribute that genius has ever paid to mediocrity. Still there can be no doubt that they meant what they say, extraordinary as the implications are. For if method alone is not the guarantor of truth, if other indefinable attributes intrude—gifts of insight, of vision, of erratic imagination—their entire project collapses. What, after all, would be the point of a well-wrought methodology if one finished by saying of it: "Do thus and so and (*provided* you are gifted with genius) significant knowledge will be forthcoming"? It would be rather like the famous recipe for stone soup, would it not? Start with a stone in boiling water . . . add everything else you can find in the kitchen that strikes your fancy . . . and *voila!* stone soup.

Now, in truth, the process of discovering knowledge—especially at the level of a Galileo, a Newton, a Darwin—requires indispensably the unpredictable flash of genius, the unaccountable spark of insight. As Thomas Kuhn has shown in his *The Structure of Scientific Revolutions,* it is precisely by such inspired leaps that the great "revolutions" occur in the several branches of science. And then, suddenly and amazingly, there is something—an idea, an image, a conjecture, a neat synthesis, a "paradigm" as Kuhn calls it —that captures the imagination and is accepted as knowledge. Often enough, it is a matter, as Yeats has put it, "of finding similarities among things thought different and differences among things thought similar." But how such perceptions occur is beyond routinization. Which means that methodology *is* the stone in stone soup, the most dispensable of all the ingredients. This is no less true of the so-called behavioral sciences, despite the fact that the learned journals of these disciplines brim over with the lucubrations of methodological specialists. It is all nonsense pure and simple. Who, except as an afterthought or as a pinch of incense on the professional altar, ever used another person's methodology to produce a significant idea of his own? The methodologies of a Max Weber or a Sigmund Freud yield brilliant insights only in the hands of a Weber or a Freud; in the hands of lesser talents, they yield what may be less worth having than the blunders of a great mind.

One might almost suspect that methodology is the preoccupation of mediocrity, the dullard's great hope of equaling the achievements of the gifted. *Almost* . . . were it not for such examples as we have at hand: Bacon and Descartes. No small minds these, and yet convinced that the process of knowing *could* be routinized and that knowledge *could* in this fashion grow by modest increments piled up by antlike armies of studious drudges. It is no better an idea for all their advocacy—though in their own time, it enjoyed the status of an unexplored and exciting new possibility filled with the drama of bold departure.

Clearly, science has profited enormously from the political implications inherent in the notion of impersonal method. If we take the idea at its face value, it places all people on a common noetic level. Knowledge becomes not a matter of inspiration or revelation; rather, it derives from the careful application of the right method. And this method—so Bacon and Descartes were convinced—may be readily acquired by any rational human being. Learn these thirty-four "Rules for the Direction of the Mind," Descartes tells us in an essay bearing that remarkable title, and you are well on the way to knowing all that can be known. Unhappily, Descartes worked out only eighteen rules in the unfinished treatise; nothing at all of the projected part three exists beyond the intriguing title "Concerning Problems Which Are Not Perfectly Understood." But no matter. If the enterprise in this instance remains incomplete, its spirit shines through clearly. It proclaims that the human race has not even begun to probe reality, that our predecessors have dallied away the generations engrossed by follies and errors, that the truth has yet to be discovered and now waits to be unveiled by anyone who trains himself in the use of a few simple rules.

Perhaps there is little science to be wrung from that assumption; but the seeds of a democratic politics lie hidden therein, a subversive belief in human equality founded upon the prospect of knowledge available to all on a non-privileged, non-classified basis. In such an unforeseen way, the Newtonian worldview became the stage on which the era of democratic revolution would be enacted. Whether that promised knowledge was forthcoming self-evidently in the "pure light of reason" or had to be pieced together out of empirical experiment, or whether perhaps it flowed from some combination of the two—on this point the Baconian and Cartesian traditions move off in rather different directions. But with respect to the root idea that the impersonal eye of method equalizes all people in their encounter with reality, the divergent traditions of rationalism and empiricism are united at their source and work in tandem to make the scientific revolution the forerunner of all the liberal and democratic revolutions that have followed.

In the long run, however, this facile association of scientific knowledge and egalitarian politics has run into serious contradictions. The proper ground on which to defend human equality is that of innate moral worth, not equivalence of intellect. That is, of course, the ground on which religious tradition since Amos and the Buddha has rested its plea for human fellowship; the ideal relates to a quality of soul, not an intelligence quotient—which is a statistical nonsense in any case. Intellect, especially the sort of intellect a technocratic society favors, is, like all human abilities, far from uniformly distributed. Where there is a social competition which selects such serviceable intellect for reward, we quickly arrive at a meritocracy which winnows out the disadvantaged, the rebellious, the slow starters, the possessors of eccentric or unmarketable talents. At which point there appear self-styled experts in "mental measurements" to report that there is no human equality after all, that the brains of the poor and the non-white are inherently deficient, and that we must adjust our educational and social ideals accordingly. It is a sad example of science (or at least an academic numbers game that is widely respected as science) undoing the very egalitarianism which was once a proud part of the scientific ethic.

A PASSION CALLED REASON

In dealing with these aspects of science—the practicality of its orientation, the assumed democracy of its method—we have stayed close to questions raised by the sociology of knowledge. Here we can see the claims of scientific single vision serving as an ideological weapon with which to beat back the entrenched privilege of aristocratic and clerical elites. Because, traditionally, the scientific worldview has been associated with the virtues of effort and invention, with the common man's aspiration for dignity, it has become as precious to socialist critics as to the bourgeois society they despise. Both the socialists and bourgeoisie have been allied in championing worldly enterprise, material progress, and the principle of equality. Thus the two most important social elements that urban-industrial society has inherited from the *ancien régime*—entrepreneur and worker—have found supportive values in science.

But the success of science does not derive solely from its compatibility with the self-interest of social classes on the rise. It would be an injustice to the scientific tradition if we did not acknowledge in it an authentically humanitarian appeal. I refer to the summons of the civilized dialogue.

It is scarcely a coincidence that Bacon's New Philosophy emerges from a period of unparalleled religious violence in western history. The war of the doctrines can still be heard in the background of Bacon's message; for example, when he declares that "the state of learning as it now is" can but produce "contention and barking disputations which are the end of the matter and all the issue they can yield." So he raises his voice in the midst of fanatical warfare and persecution, as if to ask: Is there no way for mankind to pursue the truth except with sword in hand? Must the battleground inevitably replace the dialogue?

Confronted with this great question, Bacon's contemporary Montaigne retired despairingly to a position of charitable agnosticism: better ignorance and reticence than bloody murder. But Bacon was the braver spirit. He insisted on breaking free of the impasse by reconstituting the cultural dialogue on new grounds. Again, his project is paralleled in intention by Descartes. Both men invite their audience to cast off those inherited convictions which admit of no consensus, and to build knowledge on the bedrock of what can reasonably be *proved* to be so. Since neither authority nor revelation provides a basis for dialogue—indeed, they seem only to serve for hotting up parochial loyalties and making murder legitimate— let them be laid aside, and let people begin again from scratch with a new, more civilized way of knowing.

The epistemological conundrums involved in this fresh approach to knowledge were not to be easily resolved. But before the seventeenth century was out, the New Philosophy had

achieved something better than a flawless theory of knowledge. It had, in Newton's work, a concrete example of what
was possible along the lines of its program. It had achieved
significant knowledge, as secure as numbers, demonstrable to
all who would look to see, and derived not from arcane
tradition or private revelation, but from observation and logical inference.

Here was the source of that intellectual clairvoyance and
humane good sense which flows down through the best minds
of the Enlightenment, the sweet reasonableness that stands
out so magnificently against the violence-prone obscurantism
of their times and of previous generations. Science was not
just the study of nature; it was readily identified as the brightest manifestation of rational conduct. For could not the
same dispassionate, Newtonian precision be extended to all of
life; to personal ethics and social policy as well as to sun, and
moon, and stars? The equation has by now become implicit
in all discussions of science. Science equals Reason; and Reason equals all good things. So, when the eighteenth-century
poet Mark Akenside set about writing a *Hymn to Science,*
before all else he praised science as the defense of civilized
good manners against all the vicious humbug of the world.
"Science," the poet implores,

> . . . first with thy resistless light,
> Dispense those phantoms from my sight,
> Those mimic shades of thee,
> The scholiast's learning, sophist's cant,
> The monk's philosophy.
>
> Oh! let thy pow'rful charms impart
> The patient head, the candid heart,
> Devoted to thy sway,
> Which no weak passions e'er mislead,
> Which still with dauntless steps proceed
> Where Reason points the way.

Put tempers, passions, in the scale,
Mark what degrees in each prevail,
And fix the doubtful sway.

That last, best effort of thy skill,
To form the life and rule the will,
Propitious Pow'r! impart;
Teach me to cool my passion's fires,
Make me the judge of my desires,
The master of my heart.

It is meager verse, as bloodless and stolid as much of the
culture of the English Enlightenment; but it nicely condenses
all those qualities we still commonly associate with "being
rational": candor, patience, emotional coolness, a keen eye for
windy nonsense . . . above all, unstinting self-control. (As
Alex Comfort has put it, what rationality means to most people is "the systematic avoidance of troublesome emotions.")
Here are the virtues—the safe and modest virtues—which
people of essential decency will always champion when they
have witnessed the high destructive passions at their work.
They are the virtues that promise the possibility of consider-
ate human relations, of respectful conversation and simple
courtesy. By the standards of such rationality, men and
women will hear one another out, weigh and assess views,
recognize one another's claim to a common humanity. Here
again, science becomes more than "pure science"; it assumes
a moral luster.

All that has ever challenged the worldview of science has
had, at last, to confront this ethical bastion erected in the defense of fellowship. One need not probe far below the surface
of even the most seemingly cold-blooded effort to scientize
the intellectual life in order to discover the moral fervor that
animates the project. Only consider the crusading zeal of the
logical positivists of the early twentieth century. A work like

A. J. Ayer's famous *Language, Truth and Logic* is, for all its chill precision, in reality an admirable manifesto in behalf of the civilized decencies. For some, indeed, science has offered nothing more important than its critical edge with which to hew down the obfuscators. So Ernest Renan concluded: "the main contribution of science will be to deliver us from superstitions rather than to reveal the ultimate truth."

It is along such lines, following the equation science= Reason=all good things, that Karl Popper, Joseph Needham, J. Bronowski, C. P. Snow, and Robert K. Merton have identified the scientific temperament as the secret of the democratic "open society." Karl Pearson, writing in 1892, put the argument as well and as vividly as it has ever been put since.

> The classification of facts and the formation of absolute judgements upon the basis of this classification— judgements independent of the idiosyncrasies of the individual mind—essentially sum up the aim and method of modern science. *The scientific man has above all things to strive at self-elimination in his judgements; to provide an argument which is as true for each individual mind as for his own.* The classification of facts, the recognition of their sequence and relative significance is the function of science, and the habit of forming a judgement upon these facts unbiased by personal feeling is characteristic of what may be termed the scientific frame of mind. The scientific method of examining facts is not peculiar to one class of phenomena and to one class of workers; *it is applicable to social as well as to physical problems,* and we must carefully guard ourselves against supposing that the scientific frame of mind is a peculiarity of the professional scientist.
>
> Now this frame of mind seems to me an essential of good citizenship. . . . Minds trained to scientific methods are less likely to be led by mere appeal to the passions or by blind emotional excitement to sanction

acts which in the end may lead to social disaster.
. . . Modern science, as training the mind to an exact
and impartial analysis of facts, is an education specially fitted to promote sound citizenship.

It is in passages like this that we begin to recognize how
much of a passion (if a denatured passion) this thing called
Reason is, and by how far it transcends a merely niggling
concern for neat intellectual habits or the accumulation of
knowledge for its own sake. *The appeal is ethical;* it addresses
the person with all the emotion (if none of the rhapsodic
power) of Hebrew prophecy. Paradoxically, it would have us
believe that impersonal knowing is the strongest defense of
personal right. After such fashion, love (which is what Pearson, Popper, and all the others are talking about) forswears
its proper language, and fellowship becomes, strangely, a matter of test tubes and bevatrons.

MYTHIC STATURE

It is in defense of the civilized dialogue that science has produced its heroes—and its martyrs. Whether we think of Voltaire's waspish debunking, or the high moral rhetoric of a
John Stuart Mill and Bertrand Russell, we are in the presence of people who have risked much to champion a conception of Reason they have felt was most perfectly expressed
by a steadfast commitment to science. But we can expand this
heroism beyond the exploits of particular social critics who
have appropriated the style and rhetoric of science, and, without exaggeration, give the pursuit of scientific knowledge an
epic dimension. Humble, reticent, and unassuming as individual scientists may often be, narrowly as they may conceive of
their professional duties, nevertheless there broods over them

a mythological identity of cosmic proportions. What was it Mary Shelley named her Dr. Frankenstein? "The Modern Prometheus." And here, too, we find one of the secrets of the triumph of science in our culture.

Myths make history. The mythic symbol taps unconscious reservoirs of energy in all of us, winning our assent and motivating action by its imaginative power. Perhaps nothing has more to do with determining what we will decide to regard as truth than the force of an empowered symbol superbly projected upon the cultural stage. Certainly science has enjoyed the subliminal persuasion of such an image from the earliest days of its history. I refer to the image of Newton, the archetypal scientist. More than an outstanding physical theorist, Newton became, in his own time, the supreme example of godlike intellect, comparable in Edmund Halley's seventeenth-century *Ode* to the prophet on whom the Lord had bestowed the tables of the law. Here was the mind that had achieved "reckonings divine." With Newton, Halley tells us, we are "admitted to the banquet of the gods," there to

> . . . contemplate the polities of heaven;
> and spelling out the secrets of the earth,
> Discern the changeless order of the world
> And all the aeons of its history.

The *Ode* concludes:

> Then ye who now on heavenly nectar fare,
> Come celebrate with me in song the name
> Of Newton, to the Muses dear; for he
> Unlocked the hidden treasures of Truth:
> So richly through his mind had Phoebus cast
> The radiance of his own divinity.
> Nearer the gods no mortal may approach.

Or consider James Thomson's panegyric for the dead Newton, no less unrestrained in lavishing its praise:

All-piercing sage! who sat not down and dreamed
Romantic schemes, defended by the din
Of specious words, and tyranny of names;
But bidding his amazing mind attend,
And with heroic patience years on years
Deep-searching, saw at last the system dawn
And shine, of all his race, on him alone.
. . . Nature herself
Stood all subdued by him, and open laid
Her every latent glory to his view . . .
O unprofuse magnificence divine!
O wisdom truly perfect! . . .
Did ever poet image aught so fair,
Dreaming in whispering groves by the hoarse brook?
Or prophet, to whose rapture heaven descends?

The scientist who fails to see the significance of such re-
sounding celebration scarcely understands the history of his
discipline. In the figure of Newton, the traditional imagery of
prophet, poet, sage, oracle, all merge to create a cultural
identity of superhuman dimensions. The great man's feat is
more than a contribution to knowledge; it is very nearly a
divine revelation. True, when we examine the biography of
Newton himself, it is a nondescript story, as colorless as the
private lives of most scientists. But by an achievement of the
intellect, Newton transcends his meager historical identity. He
becomes the scientist as cosmic adventurer, more daring by far
than any earthly explorer. Thus Thomson lauds Newton as one
who

. . . with awful wing pursued
The comet through the long elliptic curve,
As round innumerous worlds he wound his way . . .
The heavens are all his own, from the wide rule
Of whirling vortices and circling spheres
To their first great simplicity restored.

Perhaps Newton would have blushed for the praise. Modest men and women that they are, most scientists might cringe to have such extravagant sentiments heaped upon them. But no matter. Their supremacy within our culture borrows heavily upon a mythological perception which envisages them as the new Prometheus pitted against the hostile forces of nature. Blake, who hardly idolized Newton, has nevertheless given him that epic quality in his paintings: something of Apollo, something of Michelangelo's David . . . a gigantic protagonist who claims the universe for his theater. Surely more than a few of our scientists, even the most diffident of them, have felt the Faustian surge of this secret identity within them as they have yielded to the temptation of forbidden knowledge: life created in the test tube, the fury of the atom unchained, the mind of man duplicated and surpassed by the computer . . . J. Robert Oppenheimer, witnessing the first test of a nuclear weapon, confessed to tasting sin. But he and all his colleagues knew from the beginning what lay waiting at the end of the project. And which was the stronger flavor, the sin, or the satisfaction of having stolen fire from the gods? Our understanding of history becomes shallow when we lose sight of the spell that dramatic-mythic imagery can cast over the mind, even when it serves as demonic end.

IMAGINATIVE GRANDEUR

We have, in examining the psychology of idolatry, dealt with the contribution the Judeo-Christian tradition made to the growth of science. But there is another respect in which Christianity has served to midwife the scientific worldview.

If we think back to the cosmos to which Christan orthodoxy was bound until the time of Newton—the Aristotelian-

Ptolemaic world-system—it is impossible to avoid feeling how cramped this traditional cosmology seems in comparison to the universe the scientists have given us. To be sure, along the mystic fringe of western society—especially among the Hermetic and Christian cabbalist philosophers—the Aristotelian cosmos retained a symbolic resonance that provided unlimited room for imaginative elaboration. As we have mentioned, a transcendent symbol is inexhaustible; it can possess a *qualitative* infinity for those unburdened by single vision. But the idolatrous psychology of Christianity militated against just that symbolic openness; instead, it deadened and diminished everything it touched in the natural world. With the result that by the sixteenth century the Aristotelian world-system had degenerated into a stultifying arrangement of crystalline spheres, comfortable, well wrought, and secure, but scarcely a place where the mind could expand its imaginative energies. It had purchased its physical orderliness at the expense of grandeur, achieving, on the brink of the scientific revolution, an almost brittle refinement. Christian society found itself in possession of a neatly crafted little jewel case of heavenly bodies that threatened, by the very modesty of its scale, to compromise the magnificence of its creator.

This became one of the major liabilities of medieval Christian thought. By the sixteenth century, western culture was already beginning to feel the strain of this discrepancy between a theology of infinite divinity and a cosmology marked by claustrophobic smallness and cautiously finished order. It is hardly remarkable that a mind with the imaginative sweep of Giordano Bruno should begin to stifle within such a closeted cosmos. Bruno, the renegade Dominican who preached the infinity of the universe a century before Newton, described himself as one "who has swept the air, pierced the heavens, sped by the stars, and passed beyond the bounds of the world, who has annihilated the fantastic spheres with which foolish mathematicians and vulgar philosophers had closed us in." Bruno's soaring intuition of an infinite universe was no more than a cosmological extrapolation of the infinite Christian God. Yet so committed was the orthodoxy of his time to the lesser worldview of tradition that the Inquisition burned the man at the stake. Still the future lay with Bruno's visionary grandeur.

One need only compare the Aristotelian-Ptolemaic universe with the stupendous world-systems projected by other religious traditions—most notably by Hinduism, but even by many primitive religions—to realize how lacking the old Christian cosmology had grown in dramatic scope. It could no longer offer the mind either physical or metaphysical infinities to ponder. As late as the nineteenth century, the most orthodox Christian thought could not allow itself to envision a universe that spanned more than a paltry six thousand years since the creation. It was left to the geologists and astronomers to conceive cosmic time scales that stretched the imagination—and to do so against the bitter opposition of religious authority. What inspired vision has achieved in other cultures, the microscope, telescope, spectroscope, and carbon 14 dating have had to attempt in ours: the creation of a worldview than can evoke awe.

This is an incalculable advantage for science to have enjoyed in our culture. In the cosmological closet of traditional Christian thought, the scientists have been those who dared to cry out for room. They have won the attention of people because they have been prepared to think big; they have stood forth as giants among the theological pygmies. How much less dazzling their achievement would be had it been matched by a mainstream religion whose worldview was proportioned to the visionary magnitude of a Bruno or Blake, of the Hermetic philosophers, or of the Hindu and Jainist cosmologers. As it is, science and not the religious tradition has been the liberator of cosmological speculation in the west. Christianity has paid dearly for the small-mindedness of its inherited orthodoxies. It has had to stand by and watch an increasingly secularized science expand to fill the vacuum Christian theology left in the imaginative capacities of its society. Yet, ironically, during the age of Newton and for a century thereafter, the natural philosophers saw themselves as the true and devout celebrants of a nature now at last commensurate with the omnipotence of the Christian God. Here, for example, is the deeply pious conviction which sounds through Roger Cotes's eloquent preface to the second edition of the *Principia Mathematica.* How difficult it is to believe that a science which accumulates "knowledge for its own sake" and which lacks any theistic dimension has sprung from such sources.

> The gates are now set open, and by the passage Newton has revealed we may freely enter into the knowledge of the hidden secrets and wonders of natural things. . . . Therefore, we may now more nearly behold the beauties of nature, and entertain ourselves with the delightful contemplation; and, which is the best and most valuable fruit of philosophy, be thence incited the more profoundly to reverence and adore the great Maker and Lord of all. He must be blind who from the most wise and excellent contrivances of things cannot see the infinite Wisdom and Goodness of their Almighty Creator, and he must be mad and senseless who refuses to acknowledge them.

The human imagination possesses a wealth of energy and will expand itself magnificently. In the west, the idolatrous psychology of the Judeo-Christian tradition has thwarted that energy where it has sought to delve into the symbolic dimension of experience; nature, desacralized, can only rebuff such an adventure of the spirit like a wall of stone, forcing it into other channels. Lacking respect for the sacramental dimension of nature, our experience has become poor in quality. The alternative has been to seek a surrogate expression of the transcendent powers wholly in the extrapolation of objective quantity: size, variety, complexity of mechanism, vastness of space and time. Science has worked with the grain of this passionate need for physical infinities and has thereby profited enormously. Still, the depth dimension of nature, the sacramental consciousness which single vision forbids, remains to be explored. A science that turns from that exploration, insisting that it is more important to know much than to know deep, cannot help but to harden into a new prison of the imagination.

NEVER TWO CULTURES . . . ONLY ONE

Whenever scientists pretend that their calling is the pursuit of knowledge for its own sake, all that we discuss here—the rich background of moral strength and mythopoeic splendor —falls into shadow. And to that extent, the history of science loses touch with the whole human personality. The idea of "pure research" may have a comfortable aura of priestly detachment about it, as well as an air of unsullied innocence; but it has even less historical legitimacy than sociological validity. It was only because science engaged so broad a range of aspirations that it won our civilization body and soul to its conception of truth. Indeed, what we discuss here *is* the truth of science, for these are the factors that made ready our consciousness to perceive the world as the scientist perceives it and to say, "Yes, *this* is the *real* world." It would, then, be pointless to suggest that there is a *knowledge* left over after the ethical and cultural "excrescences" of science have been subtracted—and that it is this knowledge that scientists must pursue. Knowledge presupposes a standard of truth which will be its touchstone. And truth, as I have argued, depends upon a psychology of persuasion comprised of precisely those ethical and cultural "excrescences." The action of this psychology may sink to a subliminal level; but it is nevertheless there and makes all the difference.

Scientists who long for academic isolation and the license this grants them to pursue their careers without once looking beyond the narrowest professional assessment of their work, begin to live parasitically off the surface of their heritage. Worse still, they themselves cease to be whole persons; they become disembodied amnesiac intelligences, disclaiming responsibility to any other aspect of their nature than the intellect and its fascinations. Only then, when the full passion and heroism of the scientific enterprise has been rudely purged away, can one join with Charles Gillispie in his weary, elitist lament.

> [People] are not content to take science for what it is intellectually, a great creation, a description of how the physical world works, beautiful and admirable in itself, but empty of morals and lessons. They want more. They want reassurance about the existence of God from the design of nature and about His loving care from His continuing to repair its imperfections. . . . In short, they want science to give us a world we can fit, as Greek science did, and not just a world like any external object that we can first measure, and then destroy. . . . [The other elements of culture] are about man or God, personality or affairs. Science is about nature. It is about things.

And are we to pretend, then, that science did *not* make its way historically by addressing itself to man and God, personality and affairs? That it did not from its origin promise us "a world we can fit"?

More impossible still, are we to believe that science, being "about nature," has nothing to do with the "morals and lessons" of our civilization? That is an absurdity which permeates the entire discussion of the "two cultures." There has never been a culture whose vision of life and society was not deduced from its vision of nature. Voltaire follows from Newton; Spencer follows from Darwin; Sartre and Beckett follow from the whole scientific tradition as it finally enters its post-Christian phase. *And properly so.* Cosmology implicates value. That is the way culture works. It cannot be otherwise. There are never two cultures; only one—though that one culture may be schizoid. Scientists who ask that we go about our moral and spiritual business in a vacuum, leaving nature in their purely objective charge, ask the impossible. Even the effort to partition culture—science to one side, value to the other—produces in spite of itself a whole culture . . . though a psychically sick one. It is the culture of the wasteland.

Late in his life, the physicist Max Born complained that it was becoming "impossible to maintain the old ideal of the pursuit of knowledge for its own sake which my generation believed in." He was surely wrong in thinking that most scientists, still today, have any trouble shielding behind that professionally advantageous ideal. But he was even more in error to believe that the ideal was an "old" one. In fact, it was a latter-day trivialization of the full-blooded tradition of science, one which appeared in the universities of the late nineteenth century and which rendered science a thin and inhuman academic specialty.

And what a poor finish science so conceived makes for our modern Prometheus. Here is the culture hero to whom our society has, over three centuries, looked for moral progress, a just abundance, freedom, and spiritual well-being. For such was the promise all along. But now that we have delivered so much of our trust, our hope, and our resources into his hands, making ourselves as beholden to him as ever people were to the high priests of the temple . . . *now* he turns to us and announces:

"Sorry—you had me all wrong. As far as I am concerned, it has all been knowledge for its own sake, an absorbing game of the mind, you see. Nothing more. So please not to bother me with your non-intellectual needs. You must take your soul elsewhere for doctoring; you are getting in the way of my research."

One must insist, those who take this position are *not* defending the intellectual integrity of science. Rather, they are betraying the moral and mythic beauties which are properly an inseparable part of the scientific heritage.

But, so rebuffed, a despairing humanity will undoubtedly begin to consider taking its soul elsewhere, perhaps at the cost of sacrificing intellect wholly. Only it may then discover that, having fallen for the bait, it has sprung the trap and cannot easily free itself of its artificial environment and scientized culture.

And needless to say, trapped animals, should they grow desperate, will be quick to lose their nobility.

CHAPTER 7

Science *in Extremis:* Prospect of an Autopsy

> *Culture requires that we possess a complete concept of the world and of man; it is not for culture to stop, with science, at the point where the methods of absolute theoretic rigor happen to end. Life cannot wait until the sciences have explained the universe scientifically. We cannot put off living until we are ready.*
>
> *José Ortega y Gasset*

THE SLOW DEATH OF A REALITY PRINCIPLE

It is roughly a century since European art began to experience its first significant defections from the standards of painting and sculpture we inherit from the early Renaissance. Looking back now across a long succession of innovative movements and stylistic revolutions, most of us have little trouble recognizing that such aesthetic orthodoxies of the past as the representative convention, exact anatomy and optical

perspective, the casement-window canvas, along with the repertory of materials and subject matters we associate with "the
old masters"—that all this comprises, not "art" itself in any
absolute sense, but something like a *school* of art, one great
tradition among many. We acknowledge the excellence which
a Raphael or Rembrandt could achieve within the canons
of that school; but we have grown accustomed to the idea that
there are other aesthetic visions of equal validity. Indeed, innovation in the arts has become a convention in its own right
with us, a "tradition of the new." To such a degree that there
are critics to whom it seems to be intolerable that any two
painters should paint alike. We demand radical originality,
and often confuse it with quality.

Yet what a jolt it was to our great-grandparents to see the
certainties of the great academic tradition melt away before
their eyes. How distressing especially for the academicians
who were the guardians of a classic heritage embodying time-
honored techniques and standards whose perfection had
been the labor of genius. Suddenly they found art as they
understood it being rejected by upstarts who were unwilling
to let a single premise of the inherited wisdom stand un-
challenged, or so it seemed. Now, with a little hindsight, it is
not difficult to discern continuities where our predecessors
saw only ruthless disjunctures. To see, as well, that the
artistic revolutionaries of the past were, at their best, only
opening our minds to a more global conception of art which
demanded a deeper experience of light, color, and form.
Through their work, too, the art of our time has done much
to salvage the values of the primitive and childlike, the dream,
the immediate emotional response, the life of fantasy, and the
transcendent symbol.

In our own day, much the same sort of turning point has
been reached in the history of science. It is as if the aesthetic
ground pioneered by the artists now unfolds before us as a
new ontological awareness. We are at a moment when the

reality to which scientists address themselves comes more and more to be recognized as but one segment of a far broader spectrum. Science, for so long regarded as our single valid picture of the world, now emerges as, also, a school: a *school of consciousness,* beside which alternative realities take their place.

True, there have been many individuals and groups who have recognized as much over the past three centuries; but even within the religious community, these have been marginal elements. Mainstream Christianity, adamantly literalist in its confessions and burdened with its idolatrous sensibility, has blindly played into the unkind hands of its positivist critics. It has offered its visionary saints the minimal honors required, but has done nothing to help them in their task of cleansing the doors of perception. Long before our culture gave over to an austere scientific monotone, Christianity, with its rigidly cerebral theologizing and dogmatizing, was hard at work censoring the natural polyphony of consciousness. Under the pressure now of a triumphant scientific conception of nature, faith has ceased to be "the evidence of things unseen." It becomes instead the non-evidence of things held to be hopelessly unseeable, hence, an intellectual embarrassment.

But many of our youth, having tasted the desolation of spirit which comes of limiting vision to the impersonal gaze of a dead man's eyes and finding no sure footing on what Bertrand Russell once called "the firm foundation of unyielding despair," give attention once again to the Old Gnosis and defect from the dominant culture. Even among seemingly well-adjusted, middle-class adults, a subversive interest in psychedelic experimentation, non-verbal communication, sensory awareness, Gestalt therapy, and contemplative disciplines begins to spread through the Growth Centers of America, threatening to erode the official Reality Principle.

These are only fragile and scattered beginnings. They are

still the subterranean history of our time. How far they will carry toward liberating us from the orthodox worldview of the technocratic establishment is still doubtful. These days, so many gestures of rebellion are subtly denatured, adjusted, and converted into oaths of allegiance. In our society at large, little beyond submerged unease challenges the lingering authority of science and technique, that dull ache at the bottom of the soul we refer to when we speak (usually too glibly) of an "age of anxiety," an "age of longing." The disease is as yet largely unmentionable, like the cancer one would rather ignore than reveal for diagnosis. The political leadership, the experts and academicians, the publicists and opinion makers prefer for the most part to regard the condition of spiritual disintegration in which we live (if they admit there is a problem at all) as no worse than a minor ailment for which some routine wonder drug will soon be found. Modern man —so runs the by-now journalistic commonplace—is "in search of a soul." But this, like all the snags in the system, only attracts its quota of "problem-solvers," fair-haired young men with bright new techniques for filling "the meaning and purpose gap." Presidents summon together blue-ribbon committees on "national goals" and major corporations open up lunchtime "therapy tanks" for vaguely distraught employees. Specialists in "future shock" step forward to recommend strategies for adapting bedazzled millions to the mad pace of industrial progress. Always, always it is another dose of R & D, another appeal to expertise that will cure us.

Another point that helps to obscure the cultural crisis of our time. One need only glance beyond the boundaries of the high industrial heartland to see our science-based technics rolling across the globe like mighty Juggernaut, obliterating every alternative style of life. It is difficult not to be flattered by our billions of envious imitators. Though they revile the rich white west, we nonetheless know that we are the very incarnation of the "development" they long for. And if all the world wants what we have got, must we not then be *right?* Are we not the standard for all that progress and modernity mean?

But it is a pathetic self-deception to beguile the impotent and hungry with our power and opulence, and then to seek the validation of our existence by virtue of all that is most wretched in them . . . their dire need, their ignorance of where our standard of development leads, their desperate covetousness. Such easy self-congratulations have no proper place in a serious assessment of our condition. There are those of our fellows who still struggle to enter the twentieth century. Their search for human dignity sets them that task, perhaps as a necessary stage in cultural evolution. There are those of us who are now *in* the century (who have indeed *made* this century) and our task is another—possibly one which the underdeveloped will scarcely appreciate. They pin their highest hopes to science and technique, even as our ancestors did. Our job is to review the strange course that science and technique have traveled and the price we have paid for their cultural triumph. Here is the historical horizon to which we must rise.

We have reviewed the ideals for which the worldview of science has served as carrier over the past three centuries and by whose reflected glory it became our truth. Now we must consider the devolution of that tradition, which is destined, I think, to be the most important cultural event of our generation. For many, the decline and fall of scientific orthodoxy may seem—if it is conceivable at all—like a despicable reversion to barbarism, a betrayal of Reason that threatens a new dark age. But there is another way to view the matter. The barbarian may be at the gate because the empire has decayed from within. He may even come to voice well-justified grievances which, for the good of our souls, we dare not ignore.

If along the counter cultural fringes of our society, science now loses its ability to shape the consciousness of people, I believe this is for reasons that emerge from within science itself. It is due to serious failures and limitations that can be traced to the heart of the scientific enterprise, but which only the achievement of cultural supremacy could make vividly apparent. These might be called the negative potentialities of the scientific worldview, long hidden from sight but now unmistakably visible. Taken together, they explain why our unstinting commitment to single vision has led us not to the promised New Jerusalem but to the technocratic trap we find closing about us.

BIG SCIENCES: THE UNDOING OF THE HUMAN SCALE

The year that Rutherford died (1937) there disappeared forever the happy days of free scientific work which gave us such delight in our youth. Science has lost her freedom. She has become a productive force. She has become rich, but she has become enslaved and part of her is veiled in secrecy. I do not know whether Rutherford would continue to joke and laugh as he used to do.

Peter Kapitsa

Science, like all things human, has its history. Meaning, it too suffers the ironies of change, and probably in no respect more obviously than in its institutional development. Especially since the end of World War Two, science, as a pro-

fession, has become big, official, capital intensive and bureaucratic. Which is to say, its heroic age has ended. The day of
the great lone wolves, embattled heretics, and outsiders—the
Faradays, the Galileos, the Pasteurs toiling away in modest
laboratories and private garrets with makeshift equipment—
is at least two generations behind us; and not only gone, but
never to be recovered.

Bigness, thickly structured professionalism, and govern-
ment-corporation subvention have become indispensable to the
progress of both research and development. Science, being
objective, is cumulative; its knowledge detaches from the
knower (supposedly without loss) and piles up. Thus science
exhausts intellectual terrain as it races forward. This is what
"progress" means in the world of scientific research; this is
the peculiar pride of the discipline. Metaphysicians may still
dispute questions drawn from Plato or St. Thomas. Artists
may recompose still lives as old as Vermeer. But in science,
problems get solved; as Thomas Kuhn would put it, the
paradigms get filled in and the profession moves on to occupy
new ground. Each solution may, of course, raise new questions, so that the province of the unknown remains always
there to challenge study. But the new questions are *further
out;* they recede like an ever expanding frontier. Therefore,
it requires more intensive specialization, more teamwork,
more sophisticated equipment to catch hold of a piece of that
traveling frontier. So, as time goes on, there must be *more*
scientists, *more* money, *more* co-ordination of research, *more*
administrative superstructure, and, all together, *more* political
maneuvering within the scientific community, as well as between science and its society.

Just as the Church of the Renaissance popes was a far cry
from the Church of the martyrs in their catacombs, so the
science of what Norbert Wiener once called "the science
factories" is hardly that of Galileo in his workshop. It is a
very different institution, and of necessity a far less appealing

one. It has forfeited its human scale, and that is a grave loss. It means that science too joins in the ethos of impersonal giganticism, which is among the most oppressive features of our Kafkaesque modern world. When the layman views science today, he no longer finds there a community of self-actualizing men and women pursuing their chosen calling with style, daring, and simple passion. Such individuals may, of course, be there; but they are lost from sight within an establishment of baroque complexity, an acronymous labyrinth of official hierarchies and elite conferences, of bureaus and agencies filled with rich careers and mandarin status. Already the world of Big Science has seen instances of opportunistic lobbying that reach the level of major scandal. The infamous Mohole Project of the mid-sixties which wasted nearly a hundred million dollars in a futile attempt to drill a hole through the earth's crust is only the most notable example of how willing scientists can be to bamboozle their way aboard the federal gravy train. Mohole was sanctimoniously justified as "pure research" at every appropriation along the way, but finally collapsed without result in the midst of several highly suspect subcontracting concessions. The purposeful obfuscation and special pleading that have long surrounded the AEC's extravagent nuclear testing programs (overground and underground) and the unseemly competition of the universities for the federal funding of high-energy accelerators offer further melancholy examples of major scientific talent taking expensive advantage of the public gullibility.

Nor have the natural scientists been alone in their haste to gain official patronage. The several behavioral science professions have been every bit as eager (if less successful) to cut themselves in on the prestige of government sponsorship. They have long lobbied for a nicely endowed National Foundation for the Social Sciences to match the National Science Foundation. Meanwhile they have accepted the support of military and paramilitary agencies to finance high-cost, computerized research in counterinsurgency warfare or behavioral modeling. At times, their arguments have been as barefacedly nationalistic as that of any bomb physicist—as when Professor Kingsley Davis argued before Congress in 1967 that "the first nation which breaks through the barrier and manages to put social science on a footing at least as sound as that of the natural sciences, will be way ahead of every other nation in the world. I would like to see the United States be that nation. . . ."

Obviously, clever minds continue to enter Big Science; we know they must be clever because their colleagues tell us so, and all the colleagues reward one another grandly. But it is as Daniel Greenberg observes:

> With the mechanization of much scientific research, it is now possible to function and thrive in scientific research without the sense of inspiration and commitment that characterized the community in its penurious days. Science was once a calling; today it is still a calling for many but for many others, it is simply a living, and an especially comfortable one. . . .

Unavoidably, this routinizing and collectivization of research deprives us of the element of sympathetic personality in science—the clear perception of outstanding, often eccentric individuality. More and more those of us on the outside see Big Science (like Big Technics) as a featureless personnel—teams, groups, committees, staffs arranged around entrepreneurial leaders. But more important, such routinization selects a different breed of scientist, an organization man whose work is delicately geared to the technocratic imperatives: efficient group dynamics, submission to the powers, a proper respect for official channels and institutional procedures. As Michael Reagan observes, "today, team research might even

be said to *require* some unimaginative plodders," and therefore "some net loss in free-wheeling imagination, some tendency to shy away from the high risk projects because future
support might be endangered by failure to achieve positive
results."

Is there, in fact, anyone in our society who has a keener
awareness than the scientist and technician of how incom-
parably *productive* the technocratic style can be—or of how
richly rewarding "careerwise"? Of course the protest arises,
"But contemporary science and technology are inconceivable
without minute specialization, teamwork, sophisticated equipment, and much official patronage." Perhaps so. But *if* so,
then the last place we must expect to look for an alternative
to technocracy is among the scientists and technicians, for
whom technocratic forms of organization and finance have
become their professional life's blood.

Further, with the advent of Big Science and Big Technics,
there is the growing congestion of discovery and invention. So
much of everything . . . and too much to keep track of. In-
evitability hangs over every breakthrough; if it had not come
this year, then surely next. For with enough money and
brains applied to the task, are not "positive results" bound
to follow? So there is more and more the cloying sense that
innovation has become routine, the spectacular ordinary.
The excitement of the scientific enterprise cannot help but
to diminish with overstimulation. True, the public still gasps
and blinks at the achievements unveiled before it; it has little
else to expend its wonderment upon in the artificial environment. But even the admiration descends to cliché; the
words "miracle" and "marvel" come too readily to the lips.
One begins to *expect* the miraculous—an obvious contradiction. To such an extent that it takes a near disaster (like that
of Apollo 13) to remind us that the wizards are yet fallible.
Then—at the price of great risk—some touch of "human
interest" is lent to the well-oiled project. And, altogether, there

is too much limelighted posturing by the astronauts and the research teams and the Nobel prize laureates—all of them playing the same tiresome role over and again: the boyish modesty, the understatement, the winsome embarrassment at all the applause. While, on the other side, there are those of us who grow fatigued with endlessly applauding. One simply cannot send up a cheer for every last item that comes tumbling off the mass production conveyor belt.

It is just this sense one has of intellectual impaction within the world of science that has led several observers (Eugene Wigner, Alvin Weinberg, Bentley Glass, Kenneth Boulding) to speculate that scientific research may fast be approaching the point of diminishing returns in its hyper-productivity. Perhaps there is an absolute limit of research, an "entropy trap" as Boulding calls it, where the difficulties of communication and data retrieval monopolize all available energy. "It is quite easy to visualize a situation, perhaps in 100 years," Boulding remarks, "in which the stock of knowledge will be so large that the whole effort of the knowledge industry will have to be devoted to transmitting it from one generation to the next."

Already, Alvin Weinberg comments, it is nearly a full-time job for those at the top of their profession to keep up with the expansion of general theory in science. The standard journals can no longer process the glut; the use of semi-private mailing lists, informal newsletters, conference abstracts, preprint circuits increases by the year. By the time new knowledge has had the chance to be assimilated further down the hierarchy, it has often been undone or modified at the top. Accordingly, Weinberg has suggested the creation of "information centers" filled with "brokers" and "compacters of literature," whose role will be no more than to tally, file, and pass along the inflow of knowledge. There have been numerous proposals of the kind, a sure sign of overdevelopment.

Perhaps such conjectures about the limits of professional expansion—like the recurrent rumors one hears of entire fields of study such as high-energy physics being played out—are exaggerated. But the mass production character of Big Science is real enough and lies heavy as a pall over its public image. Never a week goes by but another ingenious astonishment is launched out of the research mills and across the front pages. The scene begins to smell of press-agentry and public relations. One cannot help but wonder, where does the genuine research and development leave off and the journalistic grandstanding begin?

EARTH-RAPE: THE UNDOING OF PROGRESS

Our ecological troubles are now common knowledge and hot politics; they require no detailed review here. What does need emphasis is the critical relationship between our environmental bad habits and the devolution of the scientific tradition.

It might seem unfair to lay the blame for impending environmental disaster at the doorstep of the scientists. Granted, the rape of the environment has not been carried out by scientists but by profiteering industrialists and myopic developers, with the eager support of a burgeoning population greedy to consume more than nature can provide and to waste more than nature can clear away. But to absolve the scientific community from complicity in the matter is quite simply to ignore that science has been the only natural philosophy the western world has known since the age of Newton. It is to ignore the key question: who provided us with the image of nature that invited the rape and with the sensibility that has licensed it? It is not, after all, the normal thing for people to ruin their environment. It is extraordinary and requires extraordinary incitement.

Let me repeat a quotation from J. Bronowski which I cited in the first chapter. Primitive people, he observes, "have failed in culture: in making a picture of the universe rich enough, subtle enough—one that they can work with and live by beyond the level of the stone age. They have failed because they did not create a mature view of nature, and of man too." Unquestionably, science has gotten us well beyond the stone age. But then the argument cannot work both ways. The scientific community cannot, with Bronowski, claim credit for our exponential economic and technical growth, and then beg off responsibility for what that impetuous growth has cost us in environmental stability. Nor can science, for all the good intentions that have motivated its labors, be excused for abetting the arrogance that still blinds so many to the values of alternative worldviews.

Because science has been linked (commendably) to a liberal political ethic in western society, it is easy to overlook how systematically the scientific community has managed to disparage such alternatives over the past two centuries. Until, at last, there is nowhere else our society has been able to look but to science for authoritative instruction about nature. To turn elsewhere has meant being written off as witlessly superstitious or inanely "Romantic." There are many subtle ways to enforce cultural orthodoxy; the scientists have done it by encouraging a smug airtight consensus around the power and plenty that flows from their kind of knowledge. What has fallen outside that consensus has been treated with cold neglect or crushing ridicule. For example, in one of the standard anthropology texts of the past generation, Alfred Kroeber without hesitation identifies the adoption of the scientific attitude as a prime criterion of cultural "progress." The alternative to science is "magic and superstition," and "in proportion as a culture disengages itself from reliance on these, it may be said to have registered an advance." Where deviation from scientific rationality occurs in our society, he observes, it is "chiefly among individuals whose social fortune is backward or who are psychotic, mentally deteriorated, or otherwise subnormal." Obviously, the views of "the most ignorant, warped and insane" among us are not to be taken seriously. "Or," Kroeber asks rhetorically, "are our discards, insane, and hypersuggestibles right and the rest of us wrong?"

It is just this stubborn prejudice in favor of single vision which has for so long closed our science off from that wise sense of natural harmony and wholeness, that knowledge of vital transaction between people and nature, which we now associate with the study of ecology. Surely the most remarkable fact about ecology is how late it arrives upon the scientific scene as a well-developed, publicly influential discipline. It was only in the very late nineteenth century that special studies of plant and animal ecology began to appear in biology, but without any great impact on science as a whole. No one, for example, has ever claimed for these fields the "revolutionary" importance granted to quantum theory, even though the ecological sensibility is a far sharper break with tradition. As for the more critical, comprehensive study of Human Ecology (which is the style of ecology that now commands so much public attention), this does not even emerge from the natural sciences at all. Rather, it traces back to a remarkable book published in 1864, *Man and Nature: Physical Geography as Modified by Human Action*. Its author, George Perkins Marsh, was not a scientist, but a diplomat and linguist; yet his work stands as the source of the modern conservation movement. His was the first significant study of how much damage human beings can do to their environment by "operations which, on a large scale, interfere with the spontaneous arrangements of the organic or the inorganic world," and the first prominent appeal to the industrial societies for "the restoration of disturbed harmonies" in nature. Closer to our own time, Human Ecology—both the name and the discipline—takes its origin from the writing of the off-beat sociologist Robert Ezra Park who gave the study its vogue during the nineteen-twenties and thirties. But after this brief, rather modish period of popularity, Human Ecology drifted to the margins of intellectual life, leaving little mark on the standard university curriculum. Only the recent panic reaction to the environmental crisis has ushered the ecologists, at last, into their proper, central place in the sciences.

When we examine the history of science prior to the comelately appearance of ecology to discover a single significant voice raised against our manhandling of the environment, the silence is embarrassing in the extreme. At what point before the present eleventh hour did our natural philosophers step forward in creditable numbers to support the simple compassion of conservationists and nature lovers? From Bacon and Descartes to the present day, the same unhealthy images of the scientific project have been repeated with dismal insistence. Either we have the picture of the human being standing apart from nature as isolated spectator; or we have the picture of mankind aggressively asserting itself against nature as (in Descartes' phrase) "lords and possessors." One can easily imagine the protest: the task of the scientist is to tell us how nature works, not how it is to be used well. But is science then to be pardoned on the grounds that it has systematically taught our society to regard knowledge as a thing apart from wisdom? Surely, where our ecological debacle is concerned, that is not a defense, but a confession of guilt.

As we observed in Chapter 4, the Judeo-Christian estrangement from nature was absorbed into the psychology of scientific knowledge, there to find a new epistemological dignity. Objective knowing is alienated knowing; and alienated knowing is, sooner or later, ecologically disastrous knowing. Before the earth could become an industrial garbage can it had first to become a research laboratory.

When Bacon first called upon mankind "to unite forces against the nature of things, to storm and occupy her castles and strongholds and extend the bounds of human empire," the ambition, though unbecoming, could be safely entertained. There was relatively little damage the human race could then do to its environment. The arrogance was as innocuous as it was exhilarating. But within the past few generations the scale of applied science has become global, and more than great enough to reveal the once negligible implications of the New Philosophy. Just as infinitesimal blemishes in a photograph may only become prominent when the picture is sufficiently enlarged, so the vastness of contemporary technical enterprise has magnified the innermost meaning of the scientific worldview and revealed its full ecological ignorance.

We deal now in a technology that alters the climates of entire continents and threatens to murder the flora and fauna of whole oceans. Compulsively optimistic technicians may continue to talk of finding a quick technological fix for every problem; but does it not grow clearer by the day that they are woefully out of tune with the environment they claim to understand? They promise to feed the hungry by way of Green Revolutions and the harvest of the seas. But the World Health Organization reports that what most immediately results from the saturation use of DDT as part of Green Revolution technique (monocultures dependent on chemical fertilizers and heavy pesticidal treatment) is the ruinous contamination of mothers' milk. Perhaps in societies where nursing is common and prolonged this might be regarded as a grisly form of population control imposed surreptitiously by the demands of progress, a sort of developmental sleight of hand which increases the crops and poisons the babies. Meanwhile, the rising levels of oil, pesticides, nitrate run-off, and methyl mercury in the lakes and oceans threaten to eliminate fish from the diet of an underfed world long before the seas will be harvested.

The importance of the massive environmental crisis for the future of our culture is that it forces upon all of us in urban-industrialized society a terrible, inescapable awareness of how intolerably high the price is of our Baconian power-knowledge. At the very least, all of us must suffer the immediate discomforts of "development blight" (quaint phrase!), the noise, the foul smells, the corrosive anguish of the eyes and throat, the devastation of amenities. For most people, ecological politicking still seems to reach no further than such issues, taken up piecemeal as necessity dictates and always with the hope that minor adjustments will serve—like building the airport or freeway somewhere else. But even this superficial sense of the problem can be enough to raise bothersome doubts about the meaning of industrial progress. For once real issues are joined and the easy ecological platitudes evaporate, are not the government and the corporate spokesmen quick to castigate the comfort-and-amenity-conscious citizenry for being Luddites and to warn them that the clock must not be turned back? Suddenly, it becomes a subversion of progress to assert the commonsensible principle that communities exist for the health and enjoyment of those who live in them, not for the convenience of those who drive through them, fly over them, or exploit their real estate for profit. After all, the argument runs, the factories, freeways, and airports must be built *somewhere,* must they not? The economy *depends* on them. And so it does. Given the lifestyle demanded by the artificial environment, the economy is bound to be anti-environmental.

As that realization sinks into the general awareness, the great western myth of progress and the science that is tied to it suffer severely skeptical examination. In what sense have we "progressed" if we now come to such a pass? By what right do we claim to possess a uniquely reliable knowledge of nature? Operational success has—supposedly—been the ultimate validation of scientific knowledge. Science is true, we have been told over and over again, because *"it works."* But now we discover that the scientific worldview does *not* work. Not if our outlook is wholistic. Not if we consider the long run—which, in the case of industrial society, seems to be about two centuries. More and more it looks as if the future is not destined to be an endless escalator of improvement. Rather, we may yet take our place in folk-memory as the Age of the Great Sacrilege, which was smitten from on high for its wanton ways. And children will cringe to hear how vile in the sight of God was our existence.

Currently, the most ecologically involved young people in our society appear to be learning more about their proper place in nature from American Indian lore, Zen, and Tantra than from western science. Science seems at best only able to furnish them with so many microscopic details that only assume meaning when assimilated to a primordial wisdom. This is a startling fact of our time; we will return to it in a later chapter, where I will argue that what we call ecology is only a rough translation into our scientific vernacular of these borrowed sensibilities. Surely it is a strange kind of progress, then, which brings us to the point where, under pressure of dire emergency, urban-industrial society must look beyond its own science to such primitive and exotic traditions for a life-enhancing natural philosophy.

TECHNOCRACY: THE UNDOING OF THE OPEN SOCIETY

"Democracy," Joseph Needham has said, "might . . . almost in a sense be termed that practice of which science is the theory." We saw in the previous chapter how this assumed connection between science and liberal values has served to associate science with both the bourgeois and socialist currents of revolution in the modern world—and so to place it in a position of peculiar ideological importance. The formula is a simple one; it has been quoted at length from Karl Pearson in the last chapter. Science is pre-eminently the practice of Reason; Reason is the exclusive province of critical intelligence and civilized dialogue; critical intelligence and civilized dialogue are the essential ingredients of the open society. Conversely (again to quote Needham), "the subjective and the irrational are anti-democratic; they are the instruments of tyranny." So we arrive at the curious conclusion—but a convenient one for the scientists—that those who busy themselves engendering fetuses in test tubes or tabulating pulsars are *somehow* the guardians par excellence of the democratic ideal.

The argument—including its crude dichotomy between rational and irrational psyches—remains the stock-in-trade of modern political liberalism, even though twentieth-century history does little to support its logic. On more than one occasion in the past few generations we have seen science and technique adapt themselves to the most illiberal regimes. Nazi anti-Semitism made Germany inhospitable for Jewish scientists; but scientists as such made a poorer show of resistance to Hitler than the Jehovah's Witnesses. Joseph Harberer has concluded that "the National Socialists' attack on traditional science and its institutions was met with near total acquiescence on the part of the German community of science"— and with a few remarkable examples of willing collaboration at the highest levels of the profession.

> In contrast to noteworthy instances of open and determined resistance to National Socialism from religious, literary, military, economic, and political individuals and leaders, German scientists, including their leaders, showed no significant resistance to the advent and implementation of National Socialist policies.

Instead, they worked on at a commendably high rate of intellectual productivity, given the wartime pressures. Similarly, if heart surgery is any measure, the sciences seem unimpeded in their progress in South Africa. The Soviet Union, having once lapsed into Lysenkoism, has learned its lesson: best let the scientists go their own way if the society is to gain the full benefit of their brains. Left to their research and rewarded handsomely, they are "safe" personnel within the system. But difficult artists and writers still waste away in Siberian prison camps while the laboratories hum with activity. Can anyone any longer seriously assume that the number of particles that physicists add to the nuclear inventory is a criterion of their society's liberalism?

This is precisely the assumption that is now being aggressively questioned by many young scientists in America, Japan, and Europe. Their protest—sometimes carrying to the point of outright defection—is being made against a background of unprecedentedly prolific research. On this score they could have little to complain of. Rather, their argument is that productive research has no necessary relationship to social health and freedom. Quite the contrary. They recognize that their careers—proficient in research and personally rewarding—have been smoothly assimilated to a sociological pattern that is increasingly undemocratic. In fact, what they rebel against is the technocracy, the working alliance of scientific expertise and social elitism. They refuse to play the court wizard.

Here, for example, is how Dr. James Shapiro and his colleagues put their case for dissent in the natural sciences after creating the first "naked gene" at Harvard in 1969. (Shapiro was soon afterwards to resign his career in biology.)

> In and of itself our work is morally neutral; it can lead either to benefits or dangers to mankind. But we are working in the United States in the year 1969. The

basic control over scientific work and its further development is in the hands of a few people at the head
of large private institutions and at the top of government bureaucracies. These people have consistently
exploited science for harmful purposes in order to increase their own power. . . . What we are advocating
is that scientists, together with other people, should
actively work for radical political changes in this country. . . . If our arguments mean that "the progress of
science itself may be interrupted," that is an unfortunate consequence we will have to accept.

We have already discussed in Chapter 2 how science assumes a new sociological character within the artificial environment. It need only be emphasized here how, in contrast
to its earlier identity as a force for revolutionary change,
science now becomes the ballast of the status quo. It must be
"secured"—meaning placed on the payroll—if the powers
that be are to keep the artificial environment functioning and
maintain the appearance of unassailable competence. "Even
in a secular age," W. H. Armytage has observed, "knowledge
monopolized tends to become arcane, elevating its holders into
a priesthood." At least a few perceptive minds recognized
this elitist potentiality in science long ago. In the early days
of the French Revolution, Filippo Buonarroti reported a widespread popular concern "that men, devoting themselves to
the sciences, would imperceptibly form for themselves out of
their acquirements, real or supposed claims to distinctions,
to superiority, and to exemption from the common burden"
and might then indulge "in disastrous enterprises against the
rights of simple and less informed persons."

As obvious as this technocratic potentiality has been to
many people since Huxley wrote his *Brave New World,* it is
remarkable how obtuse scientists have remained on the issue
—if not downright eager to collaborate with power. Money

and privilege work wonders in dissolving an intelligent political skepticism. This is especially distressing when the social sciences volunteer their services so willingly to the state. Daniel Moynihan is all too typical in his readiness to see "the emergence of social science coupled with and based upon a system of social accounting that will give government an enlarged capacity to comprehend, predict, and direct social events." He is a happier man than I am if he knows of any government of any major country in the world that has proved itself worthy of holding such power. Certainly the examples we have of state-sponsored social science are as dismally compromised as anything one can charge the natural sciences with, and represent a far more dangerous drift toward technocratic management.

There has been, for example, Project Cambridge at the Massachusetts Institute of Technology, funded to the tune of seven and a half million dollars by the Department of Defense. Project Cambridge is an expensive computerized exercise in complex behavioral modeling which promises to find out how societies *really* work by at last getting all the thousands of variables under secure, quantitative control. A dubious possibility to say the least, but it is only by making such grandiose promises that science shores up its profitable mystique. The military's interest in the project is in gaining scientifically impeccable policy projections for, say, the prevention of peasant violence in Bolivia, or the invasion of Cuba, or the selection of a winning political faction in Thailand, etc. Which is exactly what our foreign policy needs, is it not? Quantitatively elegant alibis for criminal incompetence.

Whatever the role of Reason may still be in defending the open society, it should by now be abundantly clear how easily the rationality of contemporary science passes over into a mere instrumental expertise within the technocratic hierarchy.

QUANTIFIABLE MAN: THE UNDOING OF THE
POLITICAL COMMUNITY

But let us press the point still further. Science, we say,
participates in the technocracy because it, like all else, has
been caught up in the evolution of industrial society. It too
yields to the imperatives of the artificial environment. In
spite of itself . . . ? Due to circumstances beyond its control . . . ? If so, then one might hope that principled dissent
within the scientific community would correct the situation.
Clearly, such dissent is to be encouraged, if science is not to
lose touch completely with the moral stature that initially
dignified its pursuit.

Yet there is a deeper question. Does scientific objectivity,
even at its principled best, have anything of value to contribute to the preservation of democracy? Or is there perhaps
hidden in the scientific ideal itself a sensibility that vitiates
the open society?

To argue, as I will, that the latter is the case is to take
issue with many thinkers whose democratic commitment I
share: Needham, Popper, Bronowski, Snow, Merton . . .
What can I say but that I believe they have chosen poorly
in selecting science as the bulwark of the open society? What
has misled them is the facile identification of several social
virtues (which they package up as Reason) with a specific,
and now highly specialized intellectual activity (scientific research). I have already spoken of the imposing tradition
behind this identification. But traditions have a way of turning back upon themselves; they may be one thing in the
seed, and another in the full flowering. That is what it means
to read history with an eye for dialectical transformations.

Turn back to the passage cited from Karl Pearson (pages

208–9). What is the assumption that underlies his argument? It is that political debate can be made very nearly as factual as laboratory experimentation. Then, presumably, the dispassionate and purely analytical consciousness of the professional scientist can be brought profitably to bear on social issues. (We may overlook here the important point made by Polanyi, Kuhn, and Ziman: that even scientific debate brings into play its politics and passions, its irreducible element of personal pride and commitment. Still and all, disputes in science are rarely as messy and ungentlemanly as those in society at large. Matters of justice are never involved.)

Yet anyone who has even the slightest experience of politics knows how foolish Pearson's assumption is. The factual element in serious social conflict is almost always the most marginal aspect. Hard fact and well-honed logic *may* strip away lies, inconsistencies, phony cover stories; they can be invaluable critical instruments. But logical argument deals with the surface not the substance of politics. The very nature of politics is that people *don't* heed fact and logic. It does no good to say they should; they willfully don't. Why? Because the great issues derive from the stormy clash of incommensurable values, backed by the hunger for justice or selfish advantage. Ethical rhetoric and not statistics is the language of politics; action not analysis is its culmination, and its resolutions can never be neatly rounded out. Frustration, imprecision, and impermanence are of the essence of political life. Necessarily so, because people consciously engage in politics with *more* of themselves than scientists feel professionally obliged to take with them into research. As Aristotle recognized long ago, the political animal is political with very nearly the whole of his being; his zealous will to power, his secret resentments, his twisted ego drives, his noblest aspirations . . . and perhaps least of all with his weighing and measuring intellect. That is why Aristotle wisely gives so much range to tact, to finesse, to sloppy compromise in the polis, knowing that here, as in all ethical discussion, there can be no exact accountings or neat classifications. Rather, we are in the always murky province of moral prudence, where the sage, the statesman, the novelist—those with a shrewd Balzacian eye for the paradox of life and with an awareness of its tragic irreconcilabilities —are apt to be more at home than the physicist. To bemoan the messiness of politics is not just a folly; it betrays a dangerous impatience with basic human realities. It is like becoming disturbed that people do not fall in love sensibly— and so deciding to computerize the problem.

The position from which Pearson speaks confuses the impersonality of scientific objectivity with the simple virtue of unselfishness. There is a sense in which both involve a denial of self; but the psychological mode is very different in each case. Objectivity involves a breaking off of personal contact between observer and observed; there is an act of psychic contraction back and away from what is studied for the sake of a sharp, undistracted focus. In contrast, moral unselfishness means to identify with the other, to reach out and embrace and feel with. Far from being a contraction of the self, here we have expansion, a profoundly personal activity of the soul. At its warmest and most complete, this expansive relationship of self to other becomes love, and issues forth gracefully in compassion, sacrifice, magnanimity. And *these,* not any sort of rational calibration or intellectual precision, are the secret of peace and joyous community. These alone provide a balance to the murdering furies of the political arena. The problem, as Gandhi recognized, is not to purge politics of its emotional turbulence, but to *enrich* its emotional content by devising ways for love and fellowship to apply successfully.

Science has profited greatly from its claim to hold the secret of civilized dialogue. Certainly both Bacon and Descartes conceived of the New Philosophy as a method of settling disputes without sacrifice of the human decencies. But when all is said and done, what Bacon gave us was a way of deciding questions which turn on matters of empirical fact; what

Descartes gave us was a way of deciding questions which turn on matters of mathematical logic. Scientific questions are peculiarly those that yield to one or the other (or both) of these approaches; that is why science is, as John Ziman puts it, "the consensible discipline." Issues of justice seldom yield to either.

But that realization need not lead to despair. Recall that Bacon and Descartes had a contemporary who was no less passionately concerned to keep people from one another's throats. This was George Fox. His appeal to the Inner Light and the sense of the meeting has won little attention from academic philosophy, since Fox does indeed lead us into mystical terrain. Nonetheless, it is the Quaker tradition which has offered more to the ideal of civilized dialogue than science. In its effort to "speak truth to power," it has faced up squarely to the terrible angularities of moral conflict. What is it that Reason is supposed to mean? Honesty, generosity, openness, mutual respect, restraint, tolerance . . . Which of these great qualities has the Society of Friends not displayed with more consistency and intensity than any other well-defined group in our society? On what question of equality, freedom, peace, and charity do the Quakers fail to have a cleaner, more precocious historical record than our scientists, mathematicians, and logicians?

Whatever this Inner Light is that has provided the Friends with such singular moral clarity, I doubt that anyone would associate it with scientific rationality. Yet would the open society be safer in any other hands?

But all this is not to say that it is impossible to imagine a politics in which the objectivity of the scientist might reign supreme. If the intellectual virtues of the laboratory are irrelevant to political life (and they are), one might yet attempt to devise a new politics that *is* suitable to the laboratory . . . and then *impose* it upon social reality. A politics of means, techniques, and measurements. A politics in which no substantive discussion of justice or value, sanity or goodness ever arose—or rather, in which all such issues might be quantified and solved by formula. In brief, a politics in which nothing remained but the administrative adjustment of people to specifiable standards of conduct and interaction. As Hannah Arendt has observed, "The trouble with modern theories of behaviorism is not that they are wrong but that they could become true, that they actually are the best conceptualizations of certain obvious trends in modern society."

There exists a well-developed intellectual tradition which has aspired to such a quantified, objectified politics. One can trace it down from Bacon's New Atlantis and from Hobbes, through the seventeenth-century statistician William Petty, through Saint-Simon and the Positivists, through Bentham and the Utilitarians, even to a marked degree through the Marxist aspiration for a *scientific* socialism, through Veblen's social engineers and J. B. Watson's behaviorists, down at last to the systems analysts of our own day. Auguste Comte may serve at the spokesman for this family of terrible systematizers.

> We shall find that there is no chance of order and agreement but in subjecting social phenomena, like all others, to invariable natural laws, which shall, as a whole, prescribe for each period, with entire certainty, the limits and character of political action: in other words introducing into the study of social phenomena the same positive spirit which has regenerated every other branch of human speculation.

Here we have the intellectual genealogy of the technocracy, a formidable tradition, characterized at every point along the way by an infatuation with the stern exactitudes of mathematics and physics, a distaste for the unruliness of human ways, a mania for system, centralization, control. Here, if anywhere, is the direct translation of scientific objectivity into the political arena. The thrust of the effort is clear enough. It is toward the programmed society, the republic of automatons, toward human community subjugated to the Cartesian co-ordinates.

If Reason means searching dialogue and fair-mindedness, then the human race needed no scientific revolution to teach it the importance of these virtues to its political life. Socrates learned as much from his mysterious voices, as did Fox from his Inner Light. No end of saints and seers have celebrated those humane qualities—and, even more important for our politics, the warm-blooded beauty of compassion. In so far as scientists and philosophers of science speak for those qualities, they join a tradition far older than science. The *distinctive* contribution of science to social affairs has been the grotesque model of a politics reduced to quantity and formula and, accordingly, of life robotized. That vision of society never existed before the advent of science. In this connection, the appeal to Reason comes to mean something very different. The image of totally quantified man is one of the oldest obsessions of the scientific imagination. It is born of the fear of vital spontaneity and a hostility toward the mysteries of the human heart. More than industrial necessity binds science to the technocracy.

THE REDUCTIONIST ASSAULT: THE UNDOING OF THE MYSTERIES

> *And as for admiration in the sense of wonderment, the behavior we admire is the behavior we cannot yet explain. Science naturally seeks a fuller explanation of that behavior; its goal is the destruction of mystery.*
>
> *B. F. Skinner*

Quantifiable man is only one expression of scientific reductionism, an aspect of its style which has lost science the
allegiance of many sensitive souls, and which now even begins
to alienate many younger members of the profession. This
is especially the case in contemporary biology where the latest
work in genetic engineering comes more and more to resemble
the fantasies of Hieronymus Bosch. But adjustive psychiatry and the behavioral sciences have suffered their many defections too—and for the same reason.

Again, let us begin by noting the irony. We have observed
how the initial effect of the scientific revolution was to vastly
enhance the stature of man and the magnificence of nature.
The dominant tone in the work of the early scientists is
exuberant celebration. They exalt human understanding and
glorify God's handiwork. That tone (though purged of its
theological resonance) still lingers on today. But there has
been mixed with it since the beginning a darker motif: the
compulsive need to disenchant whatever was mysterious, im-
material, transcendent: in a word, *to reduce* . . . to reduce
all things to the terms that objective consciousness might
master.

Reductionism flows from many diverse sources: from an
overweening desire to dominate, from the hasty effort to find
simple, comprehensive explanations, from a commendable desire to deflate the pretentious obscurantism of religious authority; but above all from a sense of human estrangement
from nature which could only increase inordinately as western
society's commitment to single vision grew ever more exclusive. In effect, reductionism is what we experience whenever
sacramental consciousness is crowded out by idolatry, by the
effort to turn what is alive into a mere thing.

Undeniably, there are aspects of reductionism that merit
appreciation. Where critical intelligence undertakes to debunk
the mystifications that protect sheer ignorance or special
privilege, it does invaluable service. But the debunking spirit

of science has reached well beyond that. It has taken on the character of a nihilistic campaign against the legitimate mysteries of man and nature. Indeed, our cultural heritage has been so ruthlessly debunked that the very concept of mystery has become hopelessly trivialized. The root of the word "mystery" is the Greek verb *mueîv*: to close the eyes and lips willingly as in the presence of what commands only enraptured attention. This is mystery as a sacred rite in which only the initiated will find knowledge; mystery as the experience of a transcendent symbol. A far cry, this, from having the wool pulled over one's eyes.

But for western intellect, all mysteries have become mere puzzles or dirty secrets—and we tear them apart with a fury of curiosity, only to find they are "nothing but" . . . "nothing but" . . . "nothing but". . . . Goethe's Faust characterizes the reductionist investigator neatly:

> He digs for riches with greedy hands
> And revels to turn up a worm.

Reductionism is no recent vice of the scientific mind. It has been there since the earliest dawn of the scientific revolution. It has been there since Galileo boldly read the human observer out of nature by concluding that the "primary" qualities of reality (*real* reality) are its objective measurables; and so nothing more, nothing personal and ethically intuitive need enter into our examination of nature. It permeates Hobbes's quest for a social mechanics, and Descartes' conviction that animals are nothing but a species of clever machine, and so too the human organism. It is reflected in Spinoza's effort to reduce ethics to geometry (an effort which fortunately weakens in so many marvelous ways) and in the efforts of his Dutch contemporary Jan DeWitt to reduce politics to mathematics.

A history of reductionist thought would have to include the

eighteenth-century fascination with clockwork automata, the forerunners of all later attempts to devise a mechanical replica of the organism and its conduct. The reductionist tendency culminates in the behavioral approach to psychology and sociology, where the living reality of the person and society is replaced by so many one-dimensional, statistical counterfeits.

All this has not failed to arouse a deep anxiety in our culture generally. Blake's mythic image of Urizen, tyrannically subjecting the universe to "Satan's mathematical holiness," is a classic depiction of the reductionist menace. Just as Georg Büchner's Woyzeck, the simpleton who becomes the unwitting object of callous scientific scrutiny, epitomizes the human laboratory specimen. A popular mythology of "mad doctors" haunts the history of nineteenth- and twentieth-century science: Dr. Frankenstein, Dr. Moreau, Dr. Cyclops, Dr. Caligari, Dr. Strangelove . . . cold-blooded manipulators and makers of monsters. Easy enough to write off this literary tradition as fictitious exaggeration. But to do so would be a sad mistake; the myth of the mad doctor refuses to be dispelled. It survives because it embodies a profound, popular realization of the moral ambiguity of science, a legitimate fear that the scientist does not exist primarily to serve the human good, but to pursue a fleshless ideal called "knowledge for its own sake," in the presence of which even one's fellow humans are reduced to mere experimental material. And, of course, these mad doctors are not simply literary inventions. They have emerged from the science fiction and bad dreams of our society to move among us. Have we not known in our time Nazi physicians who could treat imprisoned men and women as laboratory specimens in their ghoulish search for knowledge . . . "for its own sake"?

Along other lines, reductionism of a proudly militant stripe has worked its way into the official ideology of many collectivist societies, where a strange, self-cannibalizing human-

ism gnaws at its own flesh. Here we have societies brought
into being by revolutions of the highest idealism, but in the
name of a worldview that cynically insists on translating all
ideals into crude material fact. Thus Pavlov's degraded image
of man becomes the fulfillment of Marx's moral vision and
society is harshly manipulated into productive obedience "for
its own good" by leaders who understand nothing more about
the good than Dostoyevsky's Grand Inquisitor. In the Marxist
countries, reductionism easily takes on a crusading zeal, for
it draws upon red-hot moral energies initially driven into
fiercely anti-religious channels. What can this at last produce
but a grotesque new religion of science for which materialism
is dogma? As Michael Polanyi has put it, in his *Tacit Dimension,* describing especially the old Bolshevism:

> Scientific skepticism and moral perfectionism join
> forces then in a movement denouncing any appeal to
> moral ideals as futile and dishonest. . . . Marxism
> embodies the boundless moral aspirations of modern
> man in a theory which protects his ideals from skepti-
> cal doubt by denying the reality of moral-motives in
> public life. . . . Thus originated a world-embracing
> idea, in which moral doubt is frenzied by moral fury,
> and moral fury is armed by scientific nihilism.

And there we have the tragic paradox of modern history:
how nihilsm can come to be an ethical imperative in the
struggle for a justice and dignity long denied.

But we need not look abroad to Nazi or Communist
societies to find science beset by well-rationalized reductionism. There are more than enough research zealots in the contemporary west pursuing "knowledge for its own sake" with
a maniacal energy that sets personal curiosity and careerist
advantage above every humanistic consideration. Their work
undeniably produces what their profession values as "results"; but at what a cost in simple humanity. The question

grows more troubling with each passing year: how much of what yesterday's science fiction regarded as unspeakably dreadful has become today's award-winning research? For those who care to sample the reductionist temperament as it makes its way through the current research of the natural and behavioral sciences, I attach a small appendix at the close of this section. It does not make pretty reading.

Abraham Maslow once wisely observed that if behavioral scientists would pay attention to the whole human situation before them in their research, they would see that the predictability they seek is sharply offensive to their subjects. And *that* is a supremely significant finding, is it not? "When I *can* predict what a person will do," Maslow states, "somehow he feels that it implies a lack of respect for him . . . as if he were no more than a thing. He tends to feel dominated, controlled, outwitted. I have observed instances of a person deliberately upsetting the predictions simply to reaffirm his unpredictability and therefore autonomy and self-governance."

Maslow's observation goes far, I think, toward explaining the often willful zaniness of the disaffiliated young in their dress, their dance, their theater and festivity. Like all self-respecting human beings, they too come to the point (but far sooner than their parents) where they must *will* unpredictability, randomness, chaos . . . *against* the oversystematized social order, *against* the technocratic manipulators. In our time such Dadaist gestures of madness have become for many the last resort in saving sanity.

Of course there is much science which is free of any reductionist intention. I do not dispute that for a moment. But reductionism—the turning of people and nature into mere, worthless things—is *also* part of science. It is part of the *mainstream* of science. It has been there from the outset. It continues in force today and has even increased its scope through the biological and behavioral sciences. If the scientific community still can find no way to exile this degrading nonsense from the profession (if, indeed, it shows no special interest in so doing except at the dissenting fringe) this is for one very definite reason. *In principle, there is no way for science to do so without seeming to violate its own most basic values.* Reductionism is quite simply inseparable from single vision. It is born from the act of objectification; it is implied by the assumption that knowledge must be the power to predict and control; it is embedded in the unfortunate notion that knowledge is to be sought for its *own* sake—as a thing apart from compassion, humanity, wisdom, beauty. From such ill-considered premises mad doctors take their course. And, of course, the technocracy, with its zeal to organize, control, and engineer acquiescence, is more than willing to have them aboard and the madder the better.

Those who begin to desert scientific culture in disgust at its incorrigible reductionism are correct to believe that the scientific community is incapable of eradicating the vice. Ethical resolutions and passionate appeals to principle can have little effect. They will always seem to compromise the "freedom of inquiry" and "intellectual adventure" scientists have been taught to prize above all else. (See the remarks of Professor S. E. Luria in the appendix that follows.) Most scientists will find it simpler (and more advantageous to their careers) to resort to Pilate's strategy and wash their hands, vaguely laying the blame for any "misuse" of knowledge on the technicians, the state, the public, on everyone in general . . . and no one in particular. Do not discussions of social responsibility in science always finish, after much ritualistic soul-searching, in such quandaries? In any event, a timid cry for prudence will never drown out the bravado of "the quest for truth."

The antidote for reductionism is not negative ethical restraint imposed externally. That is bound to taste of privation or despotic intervention. Rather, it is a wholly new science, transformed from the psychic ground up, that will lead us to recognize with an inescapable cogency what single vision will never see: that reductionism is an ugly lie and that those who extend its province degrade the truth. If our powers of perception could but recover a portion of their original brilliance—that "visionary gleam" of which Wordsworth sang—we should then see that, to one degree or another, all things are enveloped with a magic which it is gratifying (but how weak a word that is!) beyond all else to witness. The well-focused eye may see sharply what it sees, but it studies a lesser reality than the enraptured gaze.

But this is to speak of a kind of knowledge our science knows nothing of, a knowledge that produces no "data points." Reach here for hard fact, and you come away . . . empty-handed. Like the hands of St. Francis, held open to the birds . . . empty, yet full.

ESOTERICISM: THE UNDOING OF SHARED CULTURE

Newtonian physics was once discussed over coffee in gentlemen's clubs. Benjamin Franklin, a jack-of-all-trades, used Leyden jars and a kite to do spare-time research in electrical energy. Goethe took time out from his lyric poetry to discover the intermaxillary bone. Faraday never had more than a smattering of higher mathematics; he got his grounding in science from free lectures at the Royal Institution, and in turn passed on his own far-reaching research by way of public demonstrations which required no more elaborate equipment than can be found in any high school laboratory. The Victorian debate over Darwin's theory enlisted politicians, publicists, novelists, poets, clergymen; the great biologist's writings can still be perused and pondered by laymen without loss of fine points.

Science has never been simple; but it has in the past been generally accessible to the basically educated. In the societies where it flourished, it moved along the arteries of a common body of knowledge. If its ideas—Newton's *Principia,* Lavoisier's chemistry—were demanding (as no doubt they were to the first generations confronted by them) there were yet decades if not centuries during which the paradigms of its research could sink in and be assimilated. The pace of discovery was moderate, the fields of research few and broad; above all, scientific thought was linked to intellectual models and images the layman could grasp. Even if the thought of scientists might tend to unsettle traditional culture, it was at least in touch with that culture.

Increasingly in the twentieth century this has ceased to be so. Both science and technology have taken on a very different intellectual character. They move toward esotericism and professional exclusiveness. As for the well-defined conceptual models . . . they dissolve into mathematical shadows, statistical generalizations or biochemical complexities which translation into ordinary language more distorts than clarifies. The result is that the public appreciation of science grows ever more vicarious. It is, in fact, for the most part restricted to explanations of what new knowledge will allow us to *do* with nature. Thus, what most people "know" about the chemical obscurities of molecular biology is that it may lead to test-tube babies. The rest is a matter of journalistic popularizations that are usually—as the experts are the first to protest—a poor approximation of firsthand knowledge; never quite subtle enough, never quite up-to-date enough. Does anyone have even the remotest conviction that a sound undergraduate curriculum in science, plus constant reading in good popular science journals, would produce laymen who could do more, at best, than barely follow simplified explanations of current research in the ten thousand branches of contemporary science and technology? Even so, attentively listening to experts is not participating in dialogue; it is just "keeping up" with the latest.

Worst of all, when we inquire after the moral and metaphysical *meaning* of scientific thought, once the most critical measure of how integrated science was with the common culture, we find we have entered an intellectual vacuum. Few scientists are prepared to discuss such cloudy subjects at all; they deftly fall back on a dusty vocabulary of evasions and platitudes. (How often have I been told by scientists, whose whole knowledge of religion is a Sunday school banality about "Mr. Somebody Upstairs," that, no, they see no reason why science and religion cannot be "compatible." Compatible!) Or, as we have seen Charles Gillispie do, they will insist that science must not be assigned *any* meaning at all. True, science is the exhaustive study of mankind, nature, society, mind, matter, heaven and earth; but, really—we are told— it is all a self-contained, self-justifying intellectual fascination . . . an unscrambling of tricky puzzles . . . an elegant artifact of the mind, and not the proper subject matter for metaphysical speculation. Even the possibility that meaninglessness itself has meaning—that it leads to the existentialist abyss—eludes most scientists. Few of them seem to recognize that the black absurdities of Samuel Beckett are played out on a stage they have designed.

Erwin Schrödinger once observed that

> . . . a theoretical science . . . where the initiated continue musing to each other in terms that are, at best, understood by a small group of close fellow-travellers, will necessarily be cut off from the rest of mankind; in the long run it is bound to atrophy and ossify, however virulently esoteric chat may continue within its joyfully isolated groups of experts.

Those who make up such "joyfully isolated groups" may live in a dizzy state of professional excitement. But those who are not part of this expanding universe of expertise live on the margins of contemporary culture. They know that technology saves their lives; they know that (somehow) science validates technology. But they must watch these grandly consequential activities like spectators at an incomprehensible performance; perhaps like untutored peasants witnessing the mystery of the Catholic mass. Science, John Ziman tells us, is "public knowledge." But that public has indeed become a select group: specialists writing for fellow specialists.

There is obviously no blaming the scientific community for these developments—not once we grant the premises from which research proceeds. Science is the captive of its objective ideal. Its impersonal purpose is to produce knowledge, to accumulate fact, to refine its methods of inquiry and observation, to render its body of theory ever more abstract. The task is to increase what is known, not to deepen the personality of the knower. That is why science (and all forms of intellectuality that pattern themselves on the natural sciences) allows for, indeed encourages, such a degree of specialization. As with mass production technology, "efficiency" comes to mean atomizing the project, restricting the focus of attention, and then driving one's labors on to a fever pitch of intensity. The result is a "culture" which is a collage of specialized bodies of knowledge. What was in previous ages the very essence of culture—searching conversation between generally educated people—becomes a lost art . . . and not even a respected one. For by the specialist standards of our days, the polymathic gentlemen Dr. Johnson gathered about him at his club or the eager disputants Socrates collected in the agora simply did not know what they were talking about. Amateurs and dilettantes all.

So far has the specialization of scientific knowledge gone that it is all but impossible to say that there any longer exists such an animal as a "scientist." Rather, there are the many specialists: physicists, chemists, geologists, biologists . . . and each of these, in turn, break down into their several subdivisions. Just as nobody any longer studies "the humanities" (one studies Shakespeare . . . the tragedies . . . the *late* tragedies) so nobody, not even undergraduate students, studies "science." One selects a specialty—and makes a career of it. The only sensible usage of the word "science" today is in reference to an administrative satrapy of a university—though perhaps one can credit a few philosophers and historians of science with having a decent overview of the field as a whole. Surely it is reasonable to ask, what holds all this researching together? But the unhappy answer is: nothing . . . nothing except a demonic commitment to expand single vision in all directions.

And here is an effect of scientific progress that has received far too little attention. In a world of experts, what becomes of the imaginative energies of ordinary people? Where everything—*everything*—has been staked out as somebody's specialized field of knowledge, what is the thinking of ordinary people worth? Precisely zero. For what do they know about anything that some expert does not know better? There are even experts on *their* sex life, *their* dreams, *their* relations with *their* children, *their* voting habits, *their* morals and manners, *their* tastes, *their* needs.

Once, when the human race was, by our standards, overeyes in ignorance, the imaginative energies of people could be exercised in filling unknown times and places with free speculation. The result may perhaps have been gross superstition; but more often delightful fantasy and wise mythology. Science and scholarship have not of course eliminated the unknown. But they have made it inaccessible to most of us by parceling it out among the specialists. No, we do not know all there is to know as yet about DNA, or the origin of the universe, or the function of REM sleep, or value theory, or the history of Bosnia-Herzegovina. But when we do know more, it will be experts who know it. For concerning these unknowns, the layman may not even have command of the vocabulary for responsible speculation.

Yet the imaginative energies to which we owe so much of the world's myth and folklore remain within us, hedged in on all sides by the authority of superior knowledge. And life becomes gray indeed if they cannot be exercised, since, to an important degree, we come to know ourselves and to orient ourselves morally and metaphysically through the projection of freely imaginative contents. Traditionally, such projections have brought much wisdom up with them out of the depths of the psyche. A proper appreciation of alchemy, astrology, or the Tarot would have to recognize in the lore of these subjects the simultaneous and integrated projection of free fantasy and living wisdom. We still recognize as much in literary masterworks like Dante's *Divine Comedy.* For us, the cosmology of the poem is all wrong; and yet, clearly, this is beside the point. Dante's world-system is uniquely embroidered with wisdom, with cogent metaphysical insight, with visionary power. It is truer than it is false . . . though that is indeed a strange turn of phrase. Perhaps what I mean is, though any schoolchild could now refute Dante's cosmology, yet Dante's vision claims more of the veridical experience.

To a degree, the literature of science fiction has tried to provide an outlet for the free imagination. It is no coincidence that science fiction rose to prominence in the time of Jules Verne, precisely as advanced scientific thought began to grow esoteric. From the age of Newton until well into the nineteenth century, science had always been able to enter freely and directly into a commonly shared culture. It did not have to be translated into fictitious narrative. Rather, science itself became the subject of moral and metaphysical brainstorming. For us, this has become an impossibility—as witness the obscure banalities that come of trying to turn the principle of indeterminacy into a defense of the freedom of the will. It is science fiction which, at its best, seeks to preserve the popular, speculative excitement of science, to find drama, moral instruction, and meaning in the universe science has given us. It invents accessible and didactic fictions to make up for the impenetrable, highly specialized research of contemporary science. But when all is said and done, science fiction *is* fiction, and purports to be no more. It is simply another deferential and derivative way of talking about science as it is. It finishes by leaving science still in charge of the culture and does nothing to diminish the advance of esotericism in scientific thought.

It is my own conviction that as the baffling subtleties of contemporary science drift further away from the understanding of the lay citizen, the resulting spiritual strain will be much greater than most people can live with gracefully. One cannot go on indefinitely acknowledging that that which makes one's world go round and mediates all reliable knowledge of reality is hopelessly beyond one's comprehension, and therefore one's control. Or rather one cannot go on indefinitely this way without being eaten alive by self-loathing —not in our society at least, where, thanks in large measure to the scientific tradition itself, the ideal of equal and democratic participation in one's culture is highly prized. So much so that even the technocrats must spend much of their energy counterfeiting the forms of participation, even while they violate its spirit.

For reasons I have already mentioned, I think there is little chance that improved popular education in science or the institution of countervailing expertise can offset the esotericism of scientific culture—let alone repeal the other elements we have discussed that now play their part in the devolution of science. An intellectual enterprise grounded in depersonalized specialization and aimed at the boundless proliferation of knowledge for its own sake is inherently non-participative. It deserves its place in the world, but its place is not at the top. It cannot sustain a democratic culture; it cannot generate a shared reality—other than the alienated existence of the artificial environment. The boast of science is precisely that it alone is progressive and cumulative. And that is the dilemma. Science progresses by expertise and accumulates objective fact by rejection of personal and qualitative experience. Perhaps one prefers such a style of life and thought. Well and good. But one cannot have it both ways. Objectivity is alienation; and for alienation, one pays a price . . . a dear price.

Doubtless in centuries past, the higher theology of the Catholic Church eluded most of its ordinary parishioners—and perhaps still does. At least the Church was able to offer its flock an active ritual life at the core of which resided an authentic sacramental experience. Science offers us nothing remotely resembling such opportunities for popular sacramental participation—and indeed works to degrade sacramental consciousness. But even the Church, despite its ritual and sacrament, was constantly faced with an undergrowth of superstition and heresy that tended to fill the schism between official theology and the human need to express one's imaginative energy.

The same phenomenon now takes place within our scientized culture. This is precisely what happened in Germany under the Nazis and what continues in force in the Communist societies. There, ideologies of the most patently superstitious variety have filled the gap between popular understanding and the state's commitment to scientific and technical progress. Outside the Nazi and Communist societies, no such enforced ideological conformity has been possible. Instead, we have made do with a sort of residual ideology made up of the free-floating worldview of the Enlightenment: the easy assumption that all good liberal values can be automatically guaranteed by the headlong advance of science and technology. It is this assumption that now steadily crumbles away beneath us for all the reasons discussed in this chapter. Big Science and Big Technics, richly subsidized as part of the apparatus of domination, race on ever more productively; but everything that once joined them to a participative culture withers away. So now we see a recrudescence of mystical religion, primitive lore and ritual, occultism, disciplines of meditation . . . a determination, by no means restricted to the young, to open out consciousness beyond the limits of scientific expertise. This is far from being the mere fad the mass media pretend it is; but I have no doubt that the citadels of academic and scientific respectability will so regard it. Until perhaps someday the custodians of Reason-with-a-capital-R-for-repression look out of the window and discover the surrounding population up in arms against them. Though I would prefer to see the population besiege those grim bastions of the orthodox consciousness with love feasts and gladness, until they come tumbling down and their occupants join in the celebration. For the new natural philosophy will need to find place for the old science as well.

We are in for an interlude during which an increasing number of people in urban-industrial society will take their bearings in life from the I Ching and the signs of the zodiac, from yoga and strange contemporary versions of shamanic tradition. The quest for a communal reality assumes the shape of a massive salvage operation, reaching out in many unlikely directions. I think this is the great adventure of our age and far more humanly valuable than the "race for space." It is the reclamation and renewal of the Old Gnosis. For those who respond to the call, what happens within the world of science, though still consequential in public policy, will have less and less existential meaning. The scientists and their many imitators will become for them an arcane priesthood carrying on obscure professional ceremonies and exchanging their "public knowledge" within the inner sanctum of the state temple.

If this weaning away from the dominant culture becomes sufficiently widespread, the result is bound to be a highly unstable social order. Unstable because the commanding mystique of the technocracy will be dissipated. There will simply be too many people about (and who knows? some of them even in the corridors of power) living by alternative realities. Then perhaps, if the bomb holds off and the environment endures, we will be ready to make the transition to a truly postindustrial society. But that will be a revolutionary transition; no doubt of that.

The Reductionist Assault

I use the word "reductionism" here broadly to designate that peculiar sensibility which degrades what it studies by depriving its subject of charm, autonomy, dignity, mystery. As Kathleen Raine puts it, the style of mind which would have us "see in the pearl nothing but a disease of the oyster."

Abraham Maslow has characterized reductionist intellect as a "cognitive pathology" usually born of fear, rather like a kind of exorcism needed by the chronically distrustful to drive off the menacing spirits they sense about them in the world. Doubtless in our culture, reductionism traces back to the Judeo-Christian mania for desacralizing nature. It is mixed, too, with a compulsively masculine drive to demonstrate toughness, expel sentiment, and to get things under heavy-handed control. The result is a dismal conviction that knowledge can only be that which disenchants and cheapens both knower and known.

So habitual has this type of knowing become for many scientists and scholars that they seem oblivious to the collective effect of their individual research in depreciating our experience of the world. Or perhaps they accept that depreciation as an epistemological necessity and are hardened to it as the price of intellectual progress; they simply know no other way to know. Others obviously take a strange joy in being tough-mindedly irreverent toward what was traditionally held sacred. But most frightening of all are those who are convinced that the degradation of life is actually good for what ails us. This last is the argument of B. F. Skinner in his book *Beyond Freedom and Dignity.*

There has been, throughout its historical career, an impish streak in science, a desire to shock by an unblushing show of impiety. It can be found as far back as Hobbes, with his brash, aggressive materialism. It is there in Galileo too, both in the rapier wit of his polemics and in his basic assumption of a purely mathematical reality. As E. A. Burtt observes of Galileo's vision of nature: "Man begins to appear for the first time in the history of thought as an irrelevant spectator and insignificant effect of the great mathematical system which is the substance of reality."

Three centuries ago, against a backdrop of oppressively smug religious dogmatism, there may have been a refreshing profanity about these reductionist gestures—and certainly a breathtaking courage. Yet seen from another angle, even at their best they call to mind the prankishness of little boys pissing against the church wall or shouting out nauseating and naughty remarks to see how many passers-by they can "turn green." It is a great satisfaction to see arrogant authority taken down a peg: a bit of boyish mischief may serve that end admirably. But once everything in heaven and earth has been debunked twice over and skepticism has settled into a general condition of anomie, we are well past the point of diminishing returns. It is time to ask whether there remains anything in our lives that can be affirmed as being of more than arbitrary and purely sentimental value.

The following is a brief but representative survey of reductionist intellect at work on the frontiers of knowledge. All of it is respectable research by reputable scientists.

1. The Automatization of Personality: Behavioral research claims to be nearer than ever to its long-sought goal of a fully engineered human psychology. "I believe," says Professor James V. McConnell of the University of Michigan, "that the day has come when we can combine sensory deprivation with drugs, hypnosis and astute manipulation of reward and punishment to gain absolute control over an individual's behavior. It should be possible then to achieve a very rapid and highly effective type of positive brainwashing that would allow us to make dramatic changes in a person's behavior and personality." Like many behaviorists, Professor McConnell has only the best of intentions at heart. His purpose is "to learn how to force people to love one another, to force them to want to be behave properly." By which he means "psychological force." "Punishment," he insists, "must be used as precisely and as dispassionately as a surgeon's scalpel." (James V. McConnell, "Criminals Can Be Brainwashed—Now," *Psychology Today*, April 1970.)

B. F. Skinner reveals the fateful continuity that connects this search for "a technology of behavior" with the single vision of the natural sciences. "Physics," he observes, "did not advance by looking more closely at the jubilance of a falling body, or biology by looking at the nature of vital spirits, and we do not need to try to discover what personalities, states of mind, feelings, traits of character, plans, purposes, intentions, or the other perquisites of autonomous man really are in order to get on with a scientific analysis of behavior." (*Beyond Freedom and Dignity,* New York, A. A. Knopf, 1971, p. 15.)

2. Therapy by Terror: H. J. Eysenck, a leading British behaviorist, observes that "psychology, as the behaviorist views it, is a purely objective experimental branch of natural science. Its theoretical goal is the prediction and control of behavior." Aversion therapy (or reinforcement therapy) is the psychiatric extension of that theoretical goal. It is now a well-established technique, especially in Great Britain, where it has been used on institutionalized patients to obliterate drug addiction or sexually deviant behavior (on a voluntary basis, of course). The procedure is a crudely simple application of Pavlovian conditioning to human beings on the principle that if one gets rid of the symptoms, one gets rid of the neurosis.

One case Eysenck reports with admiration is that of a handbag fetishist. The man was injected with apomorphine and then shown a collection of handbags just before he began vomiting with nausea produced by the drug. He was given this treatment on a two-hourly schedule day and night for one week, during which he was denied food and was kept awake round the clock with amphetamines. Treatment was suspended for eight days, and then resumed for another nine. "By that time he was showing strong aversion to the fetish objects." (See H. J. Eysenck and S. Rachman, *The Causes and Cures of Neuroses,* London, Routledge and Kegan Paul, 1965).

Dope addicts have been treated with a curare-like drug that produces paralysis and agonizing suffocation. The doctor then whispers to the immobilized patient frightful accounts of the dangers of narcotics. The procedure may be repeated many times over until the terrifying reflex is ingrained. (See I. G. Thompson and N. H. Rathod, "Aversion Therapy for Heroin Dependence," *Lancet* (London), Vol. XVII, August 1968, p. 382.) In the treatment of male homosexuals, a special apparatus can be fitted to the penis to register any forbidden quivers when the patient is shown erotic pictures.

Possibly the aversion therapists will in time even find an application for experiments like those in the "arousal of fear" reported from the Claremont Graduate School in California in 1970. Here, men and women were seated before a conveyor belt laden with razors, pistols, tarantulas, scorpions, snakes, and rats. And then, as this unsettling collection was rolled close up to them, the subjects' pulse, galvanic skin responses, and screams were recorded with minute statistical precision. Tarantulas proved to be the most effective horrors. (See *Behavior Today,* Vol. I, No. 12, August 3, 1970, p. 4.)

3. Physical Control of the Mind: It is now possible to fit both animals and humans with remote-controlled, microminiaturized, electronic stimulators wired directly into selected areas of the brain. These "stimoceivers" can then be activated by radio signals which, in turn, may be computer-controlled by a predesigned program. "Cats, monkeys, or human beings can be induced to flex a limb, or reject food, or to feel emotional excitements under the influence of electrical impulses reaching the depths of their brains through radio waves purposefully sent by an investigator." So reports Dr. José M. R. Delgado of Yale University, one of the most enthusiastic proponents of ESB (electrical stimulation of the brain). "ESB," he continues, "could possibly become a master control of human behavior by means of man-made plans and instruments."

Dr. Delgado has electronically induced angry bulls to become timid, mother monkeys to reject their young, and cats to fight for no good reason. He has found an orgasmic "pleasure center" in the brain that makes animals and people marvelously euphoric when stimulated—again, for no good reason. Rats have exhausted themselves very nearly to death by continually sparking their own pleasure center. So too, human subjects have shown a fascination with prolonged stimulation of these portions of the brain. Dr. Delgado has wired them up and given them a portable apparatus with a button to push . . . and they have pushed it and pushed it. Surely the commercial possibilities of such a gadget are limitless.

Dr. Delgado also employs ESB to make patients or experimental subjects friendly, even loving. In one case, after the doctor had stimulated a female subject's pleasure center (electronically) "she started giggling and making funny comments, stating that she enjoyed the sensation 'very much.' Repetition of these stimulations made the patient more communicative and flirtatious, and she ended by openly expressing her desire to marry the therapist." Dr. Delgado looks forward to the day when the result of his research will be a "psychocivilization" adorned by a population "happier, less destructive, and better balanced than present man." (See José M. R. Delgado, *Physical Control of the Brain: Toward a Psychocivilized Society,* New York, Harper and Row, 1969.)

Along slightly different lines of brain manipulation, Professor Francis Crick, co-discoverer of the structure of DNA, has suggested the possibility of human split-brain experimentation. "If, for long periods of time, one could prevent the two brains from communicating with one another, one could perhaps convince one brain that it was in the same body as another brain—in other words, one could make two people where there was only one before." This might be "disturbing," Professor Crick admits, but it is "an area of research that is likely to lead to interesting consequences." (Francis Crick, *Of Molecules and Men,* University of Washington Press, 1966, pp. 87–89.)

As the techniques of physically manipulating the brain increase, the reality of emotion and the autonomy of the person seem to grow progressively more illusory. Professor John Taylor of Kings College, London, has concluded that "the mind appears now to be a near-powerless 'epiphenomenon' of the physical brain." He is working toward a "relational theory" of the mind which allows feelings and thoughts to be "given purely in terms of the physical states of the brain and [which] leads to a breakdown of the completely subjective nature of mental states." In Professor Taylor's theory, "free will would be purely an illusion" created by the "spontaneous effects" of the "convergence of tens of thousands of neurons in the cortex and lower brain structures." He enthusiastically predicts the use of brain manipulation as a way of rehabilitating criminals and thus eliminating the use of imprisonment: "cure of such social deviants must be regarded as one of the priorities of applied brain research." (John Taylor, "The Shadow of the Mind," *New Scientist* [London] September 30, 1971.)

4. Artificial Intelligence and Mechanistic Counterfeiting: The more objectified the study of behavior grows, the more remote it becomes (at least for many scientists) as a form of experience known from within. Until it finally becomes quite sensible to speak of machines that "see" or "remember," "think" or "create" —as well as people, or even better. Thus Professor I. J. Good predicts the UIM, the ultra intelligent machine. "When we have the very intelligent machine we can educate it in the theory of machine intelligence. It will then design a much better machine, even if it needs to be creative to do so. This process can be repeated until we have an ultraintelligent machine and we shall have an intelligence explosion that will nullify Lukasiewicz's ignorance explosion. (By this he means that knowledge is expanding so fast that the fraction of it that any man can know is tending rapidly to zero.) The UIM will enable us to solve any practically soluble problem and we shall perhaps achieve world peace, the elixir of life, the piecemeal conversion of people into UIP's (ultraintelligent people), or the conversion of the world's population into a *single* UIP." (I. J. Good, "Machine Intelligence," *Impact* (published by UNESCO), Winter 1971.)

Within recent years, I have come across glowing reports of computer machines that have "consciences," that "teach" and "learn," that "compose music," and that "feel" and "hurt," even machines that do or will soon do architecture. Nicholas Negroponte and Leon Groisser head the Architecture Machine Project at MIT, which hopes to produce machines that will design better buildings than people can. See their article in *Architectural Forum,* October 1970. Certainly their computers could not produce a more impersonal, machine-tooled architecture than our cities are now being cursed with.

The prospectus for artificial intelligence machines is limitlessly optimistic. It includes their use as a superintelligent governing apparatus to run a total national economy and to plan military strategy. (See Ian Benson, "Machines That Mimic Thought," *New Scientist* [London], September 2, 1971—which is a highly perceptive critique of the claims made for the machines, and especially of the misuse of anthropomorphic terms.) Richard Landers looks forward to the day when our closest friends will be "conversation machines" . . . so much better than real people. "When the day comes that conversation machines are developed, I strongly believe that many will prefer them to humans as telephone partners—particularly the machines that are 'tunable' to one's personality." (*Man's Place in the Dybosphere,* Englewood Cliffs, New Jersey, Prentice-Hall, 1966.)

5. Brain Extraction and Transplantation: However outmoded mechanistic imagery has become in advanced physics, it goes from strength to strength in the life sciences, especially in medicine, where "spare parts surgery" is now the most glamorous field of endeavor. Regardless of its promise and its good intentions, this form of surgery becomes worrisomely reductionist when it begins to infringe upon the integrity of the personality and to involve forms of experimentation that are nearly ghoulish.

For example, Dr. Robert White of Cleveland Metropolitan Hospital has pioneered a surgical technique for isolating the living brains of monkeys. The procedure involves burning and paring away the skull while the brain is fed from an artificial blood supply. Dr. White then administers stimuli to prove that the isolated brain remains "conscious." The procedure is potentially applicable to human beings. (Dr. R. J. White, "Experimental Transplantation of the Brain," in F. T. Rapoport and J. Dausset, eds., *Human Transplantation,* New York, Grune and Stratton, 1968.) With respect to any suffering the monkeys suffer in the course of the experiment, Dr. White explains, "I believe that the inclusion of lower animals in our ethical system is philosophically meaningless and operationally impossible . . ." (See his justification of his research in his exchange of views with Catherine Roberts in *The American Scholar,* Summer 1971.)

Professor David Hume of the Medical College of Virginia may yet go Dr. White one better. He proposes the preservation of the whole disembodied head, which might then be transplanted, eyes, ears, nose, taste buds, and brain intact—provided a healthy, freshly decapitated body happens to be conveniently available. (Report in the *Times* [London] September 16, 1970).

In the Soviet Union two-headed dogs and other anatomical curiosities have already been assembled by such transplantation. Their maker, the leading Russian surgeon Dr. Vladimir Demikhov, has come up with a proposal that "human vegetables" might one day serve as living organ banks. These would be human beings who had lost intelligent life, but upon whose surviving bodies various spare parts could then be grafted and kept vital until needed. (Report by Anthony Tucker in *The Guardian* [London] January 20, 1968.)

6. The Nihilism of the New Biology: The message of science, Nobel prize biologist Jacques Monod insists, is that man "is alone in the universe's unfeeling immensity, out of which he emerged only by chance." The new biology, he feels, has decisively demonstrated this truth by proving that "chance *alone* is at the source of every innovation, of all creation in the biosphere. Pure chance, absolutely free but blind, at the very root of the stupendous edifice of evolution: this central concept of modern biology is no longer a hypothesis among others, possible or at least conceivable. It is today the *sole* hypothesis, the only one that squares with observed and tested fact." (*Chance and Necessity,* New York, A. A. Knopf, 1971, p. 112.)

It is this nihilistic framework which raises severe doubts about the purposes to which the powers of our new medical science, especially genetic engineering, will be put. There is clearly no discipline of the sacred to control even the simple experimental inquisitiveness of the men and women involved in the research. Molecular biology opens up the possibility of a nearly limitless range of genetic hybrids, including man-animal chimeras. Why should we not assume that the most outlandish monstrosities will be attempted—just to see if they can be pulled off? Professor Joshua Lederberg, the Nobel laureate in genetics, has speculated that biological technicians might soon invent animals with assorted human limbs and organs—and vice versa. "Before long," he predicts, "we are bound to hear of tests of the effects of dosage of the human twenty-first chromosome on the development of the brain of a mouse or the gorilla." (Lederberg quoted by Gerald Leach in *The Observer* [London] April 5, 1970, p. 25 and in Leach's book *The Biocrats,* London, Jonathan Cape, 1970.) Francis

Crick has made the same prediction of man-animal hybrids (British Broadcasting Corporation Radio Four lecture, February 19, 1969).

Professor S. E. Luria of the Massachusetts Institute of Technology is already seriously concerned that "in principle, Huxley's made-to-order human being has become feasible much sooner than he anticipated." He asks, "When does a 'repaired' or 'manufactured' man stop being a man (whatever that means) and become a robot, an object, an industrial product?" If even a Nobel prize-winning biologist cannot answer that question, I rather feel that we would be well advised to spend the next century or so pondering the matter before we blunder further into the genetic quagmire. But Professor Luria believes such a "moratorium on science" would be "the least rational and least effective approach" since it would inhibit "freedom of inquiry" and "intellectual adventure." (See S. E. Luria, "Modern Biology: A Terrifying Power," *The Nation,* October 20, 1969.)

Other possibilities in the near future of biological research include the "cloning" of an individual gene pool so that an indefinite number of carbon copies of that individual might then be mass produced. Dr. J. B. Gurdon of Oxford has already achieved this result with toads. By extending this procedure to humans, "we could," Professor A. Buzzati-Traverso believes, "achieve a kind of immortality." (See A. Buzzati-Traverso, "Biological Engineering and New Moral Responsibilities," *Society for Social Responsibility in Science Newsletter,* No. 184, December 1967. On the new biology generally, see Gordon Rattray Taylor, *The Biological Time-Bomb,* New York, World, 1968.)

These new techniques of genetic engineering—especially eugenic nuclear transplantation—taken together with the rapidly developing expertise in extrauterine fertilization and gestation (the "test-tube baby" research of experimenters like Dr. R. G. Edwards at Cambridge University) have encouraged some biologists to predict the day, not far off, when medical science will be able to achieve a physical and intellectual "quality control" of the human population. As one obstetrician has put it, "the business of obstetrics is to produce *optimum* babies." This may be a commendable way to think about industrial merchandise, but it is no way to think about people. Leon R. Kass is quite right to remind us that "increasing control over the product is purchased by the increasing depersonalization of the process. The complete depersonalization of procreation (possible with the development of an artificial placenta) shall be, in itself, seriously dehumanizing, no matter how optimum the product." (See Leon R. Kass, "The New Biology: What Price Relieving Man's Estate?" *Science,* November 19, 1971.)

The inventory of such bizarre efforts to control, to manipulate, to systematize and counterfeit could be increased indefinitely without departing a step from the contemporary scientific mainstream. I have not included any detailed description of the animal experimentation that stands behind much biological and behavioral research, the endless torment, maiming, confinement, and harassment of beasts that is not urgently (or often even remotely) related to a humanly useful end, but only to the satisfaction of idle and unfeeling curiosity. I realize how cranky it sounds to make an appeal for compassionate treatment of these animals; but their sufferings are nevertheless a measure of how far the reductionist thrust of science degrades us and cheapens life. One need only check through the "animal psychology" section of the *Psychological Abstracts* to gain some impression of what transpires in this clinical chamber of horrors. There one will find countless efforts to induce "experimental psychosis" by starvation and ingenious frustrations; efforts to measure "pain endurance" by severe electric shock over prolonged intervals; efforts to terrify, disorient, and panic by convulsion-producing drugs, intense noise, or vertigo; efforts to test this or that foolish hypothesis that finish by killing, crippling, or emotionally destroying. We are assured that such sadistic ventures yield all sorts of interesting "findings." For example, they teach us that uttering "high-pitched vocalizations" is an "index of fear" in white rats threatened with electric shock, that dogs with severed spines seem to have a heightened "pain perception" and lose their sexual interests, that rhesus monkeys raised from birth in total isolation for periods of up to two years tend to be "emotionally disturbed," that guinea pigs systematically terrified whenever they attempt to eat begin to salivate profusely. (For a review of recent animal experiments, see James Wellard, "Drunken Dogs and Crazy Cats," *New Society* [London], August 27, 1970. On the ethics of animal experimentation, see the excellent essays by Catherine Roberts in *The Scientific Conscience*, New York, Braziller, 1967.)

Most scientists have come to accept such ludicrously trivial "results" as justification enough for inflicting experimental miseries on "lower" animals. But the callous reductionism that turns these poor beasts into laboratory raw material is really no different from that which degrades the human subject to the status of a mere specimen whose every mystery, personal and social, must be undone—as if knowledge had to be the antithesis of all uniqueness, spontaneity, autonomy, plasticity. Yet in the absence of these qualities, what has any creature left that will pass for dignity? What, in fact, *does* "dignity" mean to the world of science? Does it mean anything at all?

In a perceptive critique of contemporary research, Leon R. Kass of the National Academy of Sciences, has put the issue with strength and precision.

> . . . there is nothing novel about reductionism, hedonism, and relativism; these are doctrines with which Socrates contended. What is new is that these doctrines seem to be vindicated by scientific advance. . . . Here, perhaps, is the most pernicious result of technological progress—more dehumanizing than any actual manipulation or technique present or future. We are witnessing the erosion, perhaps the final erosion, of the idea of man as something splendid or divine, and its replacement with a view that sees man no less than nature, as simply more raw material for manipulation and homogenization. [*Science,* November 19, 1971.]

PART THREE

A POLITICS OF ETERNITY

How the Romantic artists, dissenting from single vision, re-discovered the meaning of the transcendent symbols and thereby returned western culture to the Old Gnosis, and what part the ideal of rhapsodic intellect must play in our journey to the visionary commonwealth.

"What relation have the politics of time to the politics of eternity?"
"I think," said Lavelle, "that Heaven and Earth must be a unity, and that men are often Heaven-inspired, and that ideas descend on us from a divine world, and they must finally make a conquest of Earth and draw us into a conscious unity with the Heavens. If the universe is a spiritual being, everything finally must be in harmony with it, the wild creatures, the elements even, undergo a transfiguration, fierce things become gentle, and . . ."
"The shark becoming vegetarian," interrupted Leroy. "O Lavelle, Lavelle, you are the imperialist of idealism."

George Russell (A.E.), *The Interpreters*

CHAPTER 8

Romantic Perversity

> *What were the scenery of this*
> *beautiful universe which we in-*
> *habit; what were our consolations*
> *on this side of the grave—and*
> *what were our aspirations beyond*
> *it, if poetry did not ascend to*
> *bring life and fire from those*
> *eternal regions where the owl-*
> *winged faculty of calculation dare*
> *not ever soar?*

> *Percy Shelley*

THE ROMANTIC COUNTERPOINT

I cannot recall that I have ever heard the word "Romantic" applied approvingly to a contemporary work of art or thought. The adjective, well exercised in abusive criticism, drips contempt or condescension: a diagnosis of emotional indigestion. Moonstruck lovers and Byronic seizures, great cloudy symbols and Faustian ardor no longer appeal to more sophisticated tastes—primarily, I suspect, because few of us, once past adolescence, dare make ourselves as vulnerable as the Romantic sensibility demands. We have not the courage to risk the folly of strong feeling, much less the innocence.

I want here to salvage something of the Romantic spirit, but hardly to make an apology for the movement as a whole. In my eyes too the Romantics, even the best of them, committed inanities without precedent in the cultural history of the west; when they failed, they failed crushingly. Has any movement in the arts ever produced so much genius flawed by so much banality? Yet there lay within Romantic art a sense of life—of the vastness and splendor of life—that redeems (at least for me) the puerile histrionics. Romanticism is the struggle to save the reality of experience from evaporating into theoretical abstraction or disintegrating into the chaos of bare, empirical fact. It is a critical counterpoint to the imperial advance of science we reviewed in the previous section. There are many more facets to Romanticism than this chapter and the next will discuss, but this, I think, is the special legacy the movement leaves behind: that by more than a century it forewarned of excesses in our scientized culture that only now arise as issues of political concern. Certainly it is by way of their critique of single vision that the Romantics become most our contemporaries.

To discuss Romanticism in this respect is to take up one of the lost causes of modern history. It is clear enough that both scientific thought and industrialism rolled on undeterred by the reservations of Blake and Goethe, Wordsworth and Shelley. The very sense many readers may have that the word "critique" is out of place in this setting, that art (especially Romantic art) cannot be taken seriously as any sort of thought, that music, painting, and poetry are unrelated to knowledge and therefore improper vehicles for philosophic criticism—this is in itself a measure of how decisively the disciplined prose of science has scattered its poetic opposition. But then, the Romantics, in their challenge to science and industrialism, were too far in advance of their times to be widely understood to their full cultural depth. In the Romantic period itself, neither science nor industrialization had traveled more than the first few steps along the path they were to follow. Much still lay untouched by the objective mode of consciousness. Psychology, the study of man and society (with the possible exception of Adam Smith's economics), even a deal of biology had yet to be clearly staked out as fields of scientific study. Moreover, nothing remotely resembling the technocratic ideal existed, except as the brainchild of rather cranky ideologues like Saint-Simon and Bentham.

And yet—what shrewd premonitions these Romantics had. They were the first to gaze into the abyss of nature disenchanted, the first to discover in the scientist's worldview that sense of cosmic abandonment which has become the obsession of contemporary existentialism. The Romantics' gesture of despair was perhaps more theatrical, their analysis of the disease less meticulous than that of Sartre or Beckett. But their *Weltschmerz* was nonetheless a real anguish and drove not a few delicate spirits toward the same suicidal nihilism. With Keats, they had seen how

> . . . all charms fly
> At the mere touch of cold philosophy.

Similarly, long before the demonic possibilities of science had become clear for all to see, it was a Romantic novelist who foresaw the career of Dr. Frankenstein—and so gave us the richest (and darkest) literary myth the culture of science has produced. Above all, in the Romantics' loathing for system, abstraction, routine, in their passion for free self-fulfillment, we hear that cry of the heart that sounds again whenever the world of industrial necessity proves to be "too much with us."

If science is the peculiar intellectual achievement of western

man and science-based industrialism the west's peculiar contribution to the world, then, by the same token, the Romantic
critique is of peculiar relevance to our historical horizon.
Far from being merely one more among many cultural
styles, Romanticism is the first significant antitoxin generated
within the body of our society to meet the infectious spread
of single vision. It holds that uniquely paradigmatic place
in the ancestry of the counter culture. Which is why, in
our day, the disaffiliated young instinctively drift back to the
Romantic pattern, to the same fascination for drugs and
dreams, childhood and wildness, the occult and magical. In
the critique of science, there are, I think, richer traditions
of thought and art to draw upon than Romanticism; we
are beginning to learn of these from other cultures, other
ages. But Romanticism is uniquely our own in the modern
western world; and surely it takes its course from a fiercer
struggle with the forces of secularization and single vision
than any other society has experienced. Something of its spirit
will doubtless always live on in the west as a wellspring of
inspiration. Whatever we must leave behind of the Romantic
style, we can scarcely afford to abandon its steady determination to integrate science into a greater vision of reality, to
heal and make whole the dissociated mind of its culture.

It was wholeness the Romantics craved. But the prevailing
cultural style they inherited—the hard-edged cerebral elegance
of the Enlightenment—insisted on less than the whole both
as a matter of taste and of principle. It wanted no more
and would tolerate no more of life than sound logic, good
prose, and exact numbers might accommodate. Its nobility
and excitement lay in its irreverent wit; but its "sovereign
rights of criticism" (as Peter Gay has called the ideal of the
era) were purchased at high expense to the non-intellective
aspects of personality. This was the heyday of lexicographers
and encyclopedists, verbal systematizers and data processors
determined to bestow on all things a clarity and practical

order equal to Newton's laws of motion. "Figurative speech,"
Locke pontificated in his "Essay Concerning Human Understanding," "serves but to insinuate wrong ideas, move the
passions, and thereby mislead the judgement." Therefore,
he prescribed a set of "remedies" for the "imperfections and
abuses" of words, which would perhaps do much to improve
the precision of inter-office memoranda, but would make
poetry impossible. But then poetry in the wake of the Newtonian synthesis had come to seem rather less valuable than
good, crisp conversation. The Enlightenment belonged to an
intelligentsia which believed devoutly in the omnicompetence
of *bon sens* and the well-turned phrase; and for whatever
deviated from disciplined discourse, it had a word, a dirty
word: *enthusiasm*—by which it meant a swinish disregard
for civilized custom.

Rebelliously then, the Romantics fell in love with enthusiasm. "Enthusiasm is the All in All!" Blake insisted un-
ashamedly. "Enthusiastic Admiration is the First Principle of
Knowledge & its last." That was the battle cry of a new
Reality Principle, as none knew better than Blake. Just as
none knew with more painful conviction than he that it was
the survival of religious sensibility which was at stake in the
confrontation with single vision. The Romantics could be
fierce and perverse in their fascinations; they immersed themselves with perilous mindlessness in the ineffable, the irrational, the paradoxical. Theirs was an art of cloud and storm
and dizzy high passion. But the perversity of their taste was
compensatory, an appetite for varieties of experience which
scientific rationality rigidly excluded.

There were few important figures in the Romantic movement who wished simply to erase the achievements of Reason
from the human repertory—as if that were even conceivable.
Rather, the Romantics accepted Reason as properly part of
the full spectrum of mind. But *only* a part, one color among
many. Thus, for Blake, Reason was "the bound or outward

circumference of Energy"—the articulate exterior of intellectual passion. For Wordsworth, "Reason in its most exalted mood," became identical with imagination; but on its own and functioning below the level of imagination, it degenerated into

> . . . that false secondary power by which
> In weakness we multiply distinctions, then
> Deem our puny boundaries are things
> That we perceive and not that we have made.

Shelley, a lifelong enthusiast for science, argued the point this way in his *A Defense of Poetry* (the title alone is revealing; why should he have felt poetry needed a defense?):

> We have more scientific and economical knowledge than can be accommodated to the just distribution of the produce which it multiplies. . . . We want the creative faculty to imagine that which we know; we want the generous impulse to act that which we imagine; we want the poetry of life: our calculations have outrun conception; we have eaten more than we can digest. The cultivation of those sciences which have enlarged the limits of the empire of man over the external world has, for want of the poetical faculty, proportionally circumscribed those of the internal world; and man, having enslaved the elements, remains himself a slave. . . . The cultivation of poetry is never more to be desired than at periods when, from an excess of the selfish and calculating principle, the accumulation of the materials of external life exceed the quantity of the power of assimilating them to the internal laws of human nature.

Calculation and poetry . . . external and internal . . . head and heart: Romanticism was born of these tearing polarities now aggravated to the extreme by the dynamism of science. But where to find a principle of synthesis that would make peace between the warring factions of the personality? The western tradition flowed so strongly and broadly into the culture of science that it gave the Romantics no purchase for their critique. As we have seen, orthodox Christianity yielded with little protest to the Newtonian worldview and its "natural religion." How was one to get back behind this mighty alliance of Newton and Christ? Above all, how was one to break free of the idolatrous psychology which, thanks to Christianity, lay so heavily upon the mainstream of western culture? What the Romantics desperately needed was a native mystical discipline: meaning, a mature and comprehensive study of mind in all its keys and registers. As we shall see, Blake and Goethe (like Rimbaud, the terrible child of late Romanticism) tried to salvage that discipline from the quasi-Christian Hermetic tradition. Orthodox Christianity, however, was no use at all. Its history included a scattered contingent of ecstatic saints, celebrated yet marginal figures whose discontinuous biographies do not add up to a tradition —or even to a school of thought. Again we return to the critical fact in the evolution of western consciousness. Mainstream Christianity had sacrificed the rhapsodic for the theological, the mythic for the literal. It had become religion of the word, not the experience. It was without a discipline of the visionary powers.

There were some Romantics who tried to make good this deficiency by conjuring up a sentimental medievalism and with it a Christianity of vaguely mysterious atmospheres. But that way, finally and at best, lay scholarship or historical fiction—not psychotherapy. Others, more fruitfully, cast off their Christian allegiance altogether in favor of more heretical attachments; either to the still superficially known mysticism of Islam and the Hindus, or more often to Europe's own buried paganism. The Romantics tried on many exotic costumes; but they assumed their greatest authority when they stayed close to home and grew intensely personal, attending to the nature immediately before their eyes and the artistic impulse within.

Even when it came to vocabulary, the Romantics had to raise themselves by their own poetic bootstraps. From the mainstream of their culture they inherited no framework of psychological thought that handled with any grace and complexity that dark side of the mind which exists still for most westerners only by way of negative definition as "the unconscious." How were the Romantics to give voice to their turbulence of spirit? Something cried out for rescue within them like a suffocating being. What was its name? Passion . . . feeling . . . the heart . . . poetic genius . . . inspiration . . . intuition . . . sensation . . . sympathy . . . ? For that matter, what was its negation to be called? Reason . . . intellect . . . the calculating faculty . . . logic . . . ? Poets do not work by committee; they are not the people to agree upon a standard terminology, least of all to invent a scientized jargon. The personality was divided against itself, deeply and grievously divided; the Romantics knew that. For them, as for all wise psychologists, psychic warfare was the first fact of life. When it came to naming the contestants, the poets selected many labels. But one word shines bright as a beacon through the storm clouds of Romantic rhetoric —a word much degraded in the course of the seventeenth and eighteenth centuries. It is peculiarly an artist's concept: *imagination.*

Imagination was the imperiled quality of mind the Romantics undertook to defend. Blake, as usual, put the matter most dramatically; for him imagination was no less than the "divine body" of Jesus and its persecution another crucifixion of the savior:

The idiot Reasoner laughs at the Man of Imagination
And from laughter proceeds to murder by undervaluing
   calumny.
. . . those combin'd by Satan's Tyranny . . . are Shapeless
   Rocks . . .
Retaining only Satan's Mathematic Holiness, Length, Bredth,
   and Highth,
Calling the Human Imagination, which is the Divine Vision
   and Fruition
In which Man liveth eternally, madness and blasphemy against
Its own Qualities, which are the Servants of Humanity . . .

THE DEFENSE OF IMAGINATION

> *God forbid that we should give
> out a dream of our own imagina-
> tion for a pattern of the world.*
>
> *Francis Bacon*

On the face of it, the Romantics' attempt to deny science
its claim to imagination would seem to be a non-starter.
In the twentieth century we have come to see in science a
supreme exercise of the imagination; we see its history studded
with dazzlingly imaginative feats. Was not Copernicus able
to imagine the massy earth into motion; Galileo to imagine
away the very atmosphere that inhibits uniform acceleration
due to gravity; Newton to imagine the first universal laws
of nature; Darwin to imagine the grand scheme of natural
selection out of the most scattered hints and scraps of evidence; Einstein to imagine his way beyond absolute motion
and simultaneity . . . ? Clearly the scientist, in his cogita-

tional realm of ideal gases and perfectly elastic bodies, of infinitesimal genes, quarks, and quanta, of curved space and
the expanding universe, must think constantly against the
grain of common sense and obvious appearance. Where but
in imagination does he find the lineaments of theory? Yet
once grant that science is a labor of the imagination, and it is
only one small step to the conclusion that science and art are
in essence one. What are we left to think, then, but that the
Romantic artists could not recognize imagination when it
stared them full in the face. And if that is so, then Blake's
"mental war" with Newton evaporates into a steamy misconception . . . on *Blake's* part of course.

That is a convenient solution, but it is wholly wrong. Far
from being confused about imagination, the Romantics *alone*
knew what it was. In fact, the Romantics invented imagination as the psychological concept we know today and can
now plainly see at work in the scientific mind. Neither the
scientists nor the philosophers most associated with the worldview of science were able to realize the action of imagination
within themselves until the Romantic poets had first reclaimed the experience from obscurity, pondered it, and
named it. Or rather, the scientists, having no interest in the
"merely subjective," were unable to experience imagination
as we experience it today, as an activity of the mind that is
positive, pleasurable, and welcomely indispensable to the creation of knowledge. The issue is a tangled one and involves
much sorting out if the achievement of the Romantics is to be
properly understood.

We now tend to take the importance of imagination so
much for granted that it may be difficult to believe our ancestors could ever have overlooked its value and centrality.
Yet it is so. One need only turn back to Bacon and Descartes
to find astonishing examples of anti-imaginary prejudice at
the very dawn of the scientific revolution. All the more re-
vealingly, we find that prejudice at work in two of the most

brilliantly imaginative minds in our culture. Recall that for both Bacon and Descartes, the great task was to devise a method of impersonal knowing wholly untainted by whim or fancy. As we have seen, both men insisted that such objectivity required the most strenuous self-policing and mental purgation—to the point of demanding a machine-like routinization of thought. Thus Descartes warns that "Whether awake or asleep, we ought never to allow ourselves to be persuaded of the truth of anything unless on the evidence of our reason. And it must be noted that I say of our *reason,* and not of our imagination or our senses."

Now, what Descartes means by imagination is very different from our understanding of the word; and this is precisely because he writes prior to Romanticism, at a time when the concept was still undeveloped. He means that image-making faculty in the mind which merely combines the data of the senses into coherent wholes and images them forth. Still for another century after Descartes, imagination was taken to be such a mental assembly shop—until at last Coleridge and the Romantics gave the name "fancy" to this lesser activity, reserving imagination for another, far more creative function. But Descartes is unaware of that distinction; so he subordinates imagination to Reason. Throughout his writing, he knows imagination *only* as that disconcertingly wayward faculty which, if once let off the leash, conjures up all manner of fictions—especially when it runs riot in dreams. Such playful misbehavior troubled Descartes as greatly as it did Bacon, for both men were determined to have only certain, reliable knowledge. Descartes knew that by virtue of imagination, we invent dragons and unicorns—and there are none such. In contrast, Reason accurately reflects the "real" world of extension and motion, because Reason is a mathematician, uniquely in touch with the objective, geometrical reality. To us, Descartes' mathematical reconstruction of nature might seem a prodigious feat of imagination. But that is not how Descartes

felt the matter. For him, the world Out There *is* mathematical—nothing more. "Give me extension and motion and I will
construct the world," announces Descartes. Whatever is left
over is treacherously subjective, a lesser and untrustworthy
reality.

With Bacon, the rejection of imagination is even stronger;
it reaches out unabashedly to degrade the art of poetry.
"Whosoever shall entertain high and vaporous imaginations,"
said Bacon, "instead of a laborious and sober inquiry of truth,
shall beget hopes and beliefs of strange and impossible
shapes." The man who "allows his imagination free play"
attempts "to interpret the whole of nature after the pattern
of the little he knows." At that point "his philosophy passes
into the realms of fancy or dreaming and consigns him to the
category of the poet." And the trouble with poetry? It is,
says Bacon, one of "the diseases or corruptions of theory"—
for it is "unrestrained by laws" and "extremely licentious"; it
indulges in "unnatural mixtures" and "feigns" unrealities.
That is why poetry only enjoys "high esteem in the most
ignorant ages and among the most barbarous people, whilst
other kinds of learning were utterly excluded." In short, poetry is pre-eminently the activity of weak-minded primitives.
The contrast with Romantic values could not be more
marked.

Bacon's notorious distaste, not only for poetry, but for theoretical generalization in science, follows from his abiding distrust of the native powers of the mind. It unsettled him to feel
how the mind yields to the irrepressible habit of acting personally upon experience. This is exactly where the Romantics
found the glory of imagination and celebrated its energy. Not
so Bacon. "The human understanding," he laments, "is like
a false mirror that, receiving rays irregularly, distorts and
discolors the nature of things by mingling its own nature with
it." Later, Goethe would shrewdly recognize that "everything
factual is *already* theory"; but for Bacon the best defense

against the abuses of theory seemed to lie in the raw facts of a stubborn empiricism. Bacon is not completely without an appreciation of theory; but his uneasiness with imaginative energy again and again prejudices him toward caution, restraint, almost toward mediocrity. Hence the famous warning: "The understanding must not be supplied with wings, but rather hung with weights, to keep it from leaping and flying"—precisely the remark to make Bacon, in Blake's view, an ally of Satan.

Again, my interest here is not in the epistemology of Bacon and Descartes, which may very well be flawed by many contradictions. But that is, I think, an academic question. What concerns me is the underlying psychology of their project, the *feel* of their ideas. For from it flows that distrust of imagination which settles over all aspects of European thought for the next century and a half (and which continues to haunt the sciences and would-be sciences of our own time in their pursuit of a perfect objectivity).

Imagination, enthusiasm, poetic fantasy; in the course of the seventeenth and eighteenth centuries all these dynamic aspects of mind were to grow ever more suspect to that cult of Reason, which, as we have seen, enlisted science as its chief weapon in the struggle against bigotry, fanaticism, and humbug. But, at the same time, this principled rejection of strong feeling and imaginative energy led to the conviction that Reason ought, ideally, to be a state of mental passivity, a mere calibrator of extension and motion, or only so much wax to the stamp of experience. So, at the extreme, we have Locke's notion of the mind as a *tabula rasa*. And, not far removed in spirit, we have David Hartley and the eighteenth-century associationist school of psychology with its quaint theory that thinking is nothing more than a switchboard-like activity which exhausts itself in random connections of sensory particulars.

To take only one striking example of where this depreciation of imaginative energy leads. Confronted with a mighty concept like "infinity," Locke was forced to account for its existence in a ludicrous way. Since in his view the mind is bound to the senses and cannot create independently of them, it must therefore arrive at the idea of infinity additively. It simply combines one plus one plus one . . . until perhaps it exhausts itself and recognizes that this tabulation could go on indefinitely. Thus infinity is not a whole and autonomous concept, but a by-product of simple, empirical addition. The image Locke seems to summon to the mind is that of milestones or fence posts disappearing into the distance and so escaping enumeration. Infinity is just too many to count and eternity too much time to keep track of. It is against the backdrop of such petty-minded and pedestrian philosophy that one must read lines like these by Blake, where infinity and eternity are whole, intuitive, and apocalyptic concepts:

> To see a World in a Grain of Sand
> And a Heaven in a Wild Flower,
> Hold Infinity in the palm of your hand
> And Eternity in an hour.

This is a sharp slap at Locke in defense of a quality of experience that the Romantics took to be essential to art, namely, the capacity of the mind to create ideas that vastly outstrip or wholly transcend sense data and its logical arrangements.

Even when the philosophy of the pre-Romantic period had to admit the participation of mind in the act of knowing (for how to avoid the irrepressible truth?) it did so reluctantly, as if it were accepting a necessary evil. Hume, brooding over the inescapable fact that the mind supplies the "connections between distinct existences," was led to a sullen skepticism. Did not such subjective intervention defeat hopelessly man's ability to know the objective truth? At last, in Kant's major critique we arrive at an ingeniously ambiguous and supremely influential philosophy of knowledge. Rather in the spirit of intelligent resignation, Kant admits the activism of the mind as a necessary element in knowledge. There is still held to be an objective reality, but it is inaccessibly Out There beyond the act of knowing. We contact it only as it is "synthesized" by the mind, like some raw material being strained and filtered. This synthesizing agency of the mind is conceived of as once and for all given in form and process; it is an unalterable cognitive machinery whose basic patterns are tied forever to classical physics—as if these Newtonian patterns were not originally the products of creative imagination and might not therefore yield place to new modes of awareness. But once admit the possibility that the patterns are mutable and Kant's program for a "transcendental idealism" becomes a perhaps endless search for the total potentialities of mind. Then everything—and especially the sufficiency of science—is called into question.

Kant's hope was to install science securely between two impenetrable territories: Out There, the "thing in itself" forever beyond reach of the mind; and In Here, the transcendent self which imperceptibly synthesizes the objective and subjective. It is the remarkable feature of Kant's scheme that it carries us to the very brink of the unconscious, where epistemology merges with psychology, but then refuses to cross over. We are introduced to the pregnant idea that there is a mental dynamics that shapes experience below the threshold of awareness. Yet once Kant has raised that much to a conscious level of discourse, he denies us the power to modify those dynamics . . . and perhaps free ourselves from their influence. But this is in fact what we do every night in our much-censored dreams. Then all the categories of experience are playfully thrown into chaos—which is possibly why our dreams are so severely censored. But Kant, like most western epistemologists, pays no great attention to dreams.

The Romantics did, however. They attended to dreams,

hallucinations, suicidal depressions, narcotic reveries, morbid fantasies, ecstasies, epiphanies, demonic seizures, panic, mània, frenzy . . . to the full variety of consciousness. In time, this passion to explore the most forbidden reaches of the mind was to become blatantly antinomian. With Rimbaud and the French symbolists, it yielded to a self-annihilating desire for the "total derangement of the senses." Debauchery, criminality, and the martyrdom of public execration were deliberately pursued in the quest for extreme states of experience. Somewhere behind this lurid phase of Romanticism there lurks a psychological need similar to that underlying the techniques of the Left-handed Tantra, but (as usual in the west) the improvisations are without tradition or discipline. From such risky experiments it is only a short step to the inane perversities of the Decadents and the kitsch Satanism of an Aleister Crowley. Yet, from this brave exploration of the personality, the Romantics established beyond question that there exists a power within the mind which transforms—perhaps astonishingly—the reality in which we reside. Expand the consciousness and the shape of the Kantian categories is bound to alter. This uncanny power of mind is "imagination" as the Romantics knew it. In Kant we have a vivid realization of the mind's participation in the act of knowing. But that participation is routinized; it is imagination fossilized, embedded forever in the Newtonian worldview. What Kant does not allow for, nor any of the epistemologists of the cult of Reason, is the role of genius, which is to revolutionize thought by imaginative daring. Yet it is only by virtue of imaginative daring that modern science has been able to redesign the framework of classical physics and to project new conceptions of time, space, and causation. Only in relationship to imagination does the idea of genius take on meaning. And genius, like imagination, is a Romantic discovery.

By now, most philosophers of science have learned to make

a generous place for imagination. Breakthroughs are now widely understood to be of the essence of scientific thought— to the extent that theoretical work often carries far more glamour with it than experimentation. This much of the Romantic ideal of imagination has been generally appropriated and can easily now be read into the history of science, thus giving us (for example, in the studies of Thomas Kuhn) the concept of scientific "revolutions." But this raises an all-important question. Why then did not the Romantics themselves read imagination into science? Why did they not see science as also a child of this imaginative energy they had discovered—as much so as art? Why did science remain for them more a rival than an ally?

To answer that question we must dig yet deeper into the Romantic concept of imagination, for we are far from having exhausted its full meaning. What we have discussed so far is that form of imagination which allows the mind to play with data and hypotheses, to repattern them in ever more comprehensive ways, to try out hunches and different perspectives, and so to speculate fruitfully. This is the theory-making intellect, and this the Romantics did recognize in science as we do today; they too (by and large) could admire the speculative daring of Newton. For them, as for us, imagination included intellectual originality. But there was *more* to the imagination; and this something more they did not find in science because it was not there. It is not easy to find a separate name for this elusive quality since the Romantics tended to assimilate it to imagination. But Wordsworth more than once calls it *"visionary power"*—and perhaps this is as good a label as any for that mysterious ingredient which lends Romanticism its special passion and perversity. Here is the quality of experience Rimbaud and the French symbolists placed far above science and Reason. For Rimbaud, the authentic poetic powers were those of the *voyant*, the seer; the essence of creativity was illumination. From this viewpoint, the proper affinity of art is in no sense with science, but with those traditions science has worked to exile from cultural respectability: alchemy, magic, the sacramental vision of nature. Sudden ecstasy, an awareness of the heavens and earth swept by awesome presences, the mind on fire with rhapsodic declaration: this is more than—and other than—intellectual innovation. It is the recovery of the Old Gnosis, for so long banished from western culture.

In the chapter that follows, we will see how the Romantic poets—Blake, Wordsworth, and Goethe—came to grips with visionary power. But before we finish here, let me add an anecdote which points up the irony of the reality games human beings play.

In the history of science, Descartes is remembered primarily as the foremost propagandist of the mathematical analysis of nature. The Cartesian co-ordinates would make a suitable emblem for the scientific revolution. Ever since their invention, the highest expression of objectivity in science has been quantification; the purest sciences have been those that speak the language of number most fluently.

But how did Descartes happen upon this momentous insight? The story we have from Descartes himself is that in November of 1619, an angel descended upon him in three dream-visions and revealed the possibilities of a marvelous new mathematical science. This, Descartes decided, was surely the angel of truth, and with its inspiration he devised the analytical geometry. If the tale is true, then we may take it that the most pregnant idea in the history of science was itself a product of visionary power, and that the father of modern mathematics took his inspiration from a source as old as the oldest oracles. And yet, never in all his philosophy of knowledge does Descartes give serious thought to dreams or visions in the life of the mind. Instead, he cleaves to impersonal method and radical doubt—as if the angel's one message were the last word.

And here perhaps we have the fateful assumption which has made science what it is, and our culture the captive audience of the scientist's single vision: that the angel of truth can speak but once and then only as a mathematician.

CHAPTER 9

Mind on Fire: Notes on Three Old Poets

Unless the eye catch fire
The God will not be seen
Unless the ear catch fire
The God will not be heard
Unless the tongue catch fire
The God will not be named
Unless the heart catch fire
The God will not be loved
Unless the mind catch fire
The God will not be known

BLAKE: THE FOURFOLD VISION

Blake against Newton. Fourfold against single vision. "Abstract Philosophy warring in enmity against Imagination (which is the Divine Body of the Lord Jesus, blessed for ever)." But Blake insists single vision is not to be rejected; it is to be embraced within the fourfold whole: the naturalistic within the sacred, Newton's science within Blake's Imagination.

The Atoms of Democritus
And Newton's Particles of Light

> Are sands upon the Red sea shore
> Where Israel's tents do shine so bright.

Newton's particles are there; so too the atoms of analytical science—*but* as sand grains in the visionary landscape. Single vision *dis*-integrates the landscape, reduces it to bits and pieces, discovers how it works, but not what it *means*. The action of the parts blocks out the meaning of the whole.

Again, in the letter to Thomas Butts (November 1802) Blake returns to Newton's "particles bright/the jewels of Light," recounts a vision. In it he has seen "each was a Man/Human-form'd"; and how all the world's particles assumed the shape of One Man:

> The Jewels of Light,
> Heavenly Men beaming bright
> Appear'd as One Man
> Who Complacent began
> My limbs to infold
> In his beams of bright gold . . .

One Man: Blake's "Divine Humanity": the cosmos human-shaped and human-faced. The cabbalistic Adam Kadmon. Man is nature as microcosm; nature is man as macrocosm. As above, so below. The secret of the universe lies in the alchemist's homunculus: how the elemental stuff of nature shall be made magically alive and transmitted into a human meaning. "Everything is Human, mighty! sublime!/In every bosom a Universe expands as wings . . ."

Blake (drawing on Boehme) makes the Hermetic wisdom his reply to Newton. Newton's study is true science, *but* exclusively the science of the fallen state: of "generation," of "vegetation," of the mythical realm called Ulro. Ulro is for Blake the death-in-life of the cosmos: "in Satan's bosom, a vast unfathomable Abyss"; "a self-devouring monstrous Human Death . . . a frozen bulk subject to decay and death." But Ulro is no more to be rejected than to be obsessively studied. It is to be *redeemed* from its fallenness, reclaimed for the spirit. How? By a revolution of perception; by the "Divine Arts of Imagination" which reveal "the real and eternal World of which this Vegetable Universe is but a faint shadow."

Newton's universe is matter, motion, force, law: alien, "petrific," "a wondrous void." Blake's universe is a universe of Beings, mythic presences that merge, multiply, are fluidly transformed: a *dramatis personae* of dream-beings. (The prophetic books are presented as dreams; there is much of Blake's dream texture in Joyce's *Finnegans Wake*—the same symbolic plasticity and ambiguity.)

The principal Beings are the Zoas; they are the key to Blake. Fourfold vision is peace and right order restored among the four Zoas: "Four Mighty Ones are in every Man: a Perfect Unity/Cannot Exist but from the Universal Brotherhood of Eden,/The Universal Man . . ." The Zoas are Blake's peculiar psychology of mythic entities. In the prophetic books, they are bitterly at war; they torment, oppress, cheat, deceive.

Their battlefield is Albion, the universal man, the human soul. Albion divided and at war is "generation," "vegetation," "Ulro." Albion integrated and risen is "Eternity," "Jerusalem." "Beulah" is the threshold of Eternity: the locus of metaphysical harmony.

There is a place where Contrarieties are equally True:
This place is called Beulah . . . Created around Eternity,
    appearing
To the Inhabitants of Eden around them on all sides.

Who are the Zoas?

Urizen, "cold and scientific," the Zoa of Reason.

Luvah, "pitying and weeping," the Zoa of Energy, Passion, Feeling.

Los, "fierce prophetic boy," the Zoa of Prophetic Power.

Tharmas, "Parent power," the Zoa of Spirit.

Take them one at a time.

1. *Urizen.*

By far Blake's most compelling image, a masterful creation. Urizen, from the Greek ὁρίζειν: to limit, bound, restrict; also "Your Reason." Urizen is single vision: functional logicality, that which divides up, limits, draws lines—the dominant Zoa of scientized culture, the Zoa that rules modern society. His sign is "the Starry Wheels": law, logic, inexorable order: the world-machine.

Urizen embodies Blake's full horror of the scientific cosmos, which is a "soul-shudd'ring vacuum" fashioned conceptually by a demon intelligence:

> Lo, a shadow of horror is risen
> In Eternity! Unknown, unprolific,
> Self-enclos'd, all-repelling: what Demon
> Hath form'd this abominable void,
> This soul-shudd'ring vacuum? Some said
> "It is Urizen."

It is *Your Reason.*

Yet Urizen is after all a Zoa, a god of the creation. As the rational power, he was in Eternity "the Prince of Light," a figure of majestic beauty. But in the fallen state, in isolation and stern dominion ("petrifying all the Human Imagination into rock & sand") he becomes Satan, "Newton's Pantocrator."

(Urizen, as Satan, is also the "tyger, tyger burning bright":
the god of brute, unfeeling power, antithesis of the lamb of
God.)

In the most famous of Blake's drawings, Urizen is the bearded
demigod, the ancient of days, creator of the fallen world,
reaching down to measure off space with giant calipers.

> Time on times he divided & measur'd
> Space by space in his ninefold darkness,
> Unseen, unknown . . .

Here, Blake's nicely balanced ambiguity. The image is among
his most dramatically impressive (certainly his most often reproduced). Yet it is (for Blake) also an image of horror, of
force without vision, "the idiot Reasoner."

Again, Urizen is "the great Work master": the demiurgos:
the God of wrath and jealousy: giver of moral laws. For
Blake, this was the Biblical Elohim, the demon-god of fallen
mankind: Newton's heavenly watchmaker, god of "natural
religion" and of the churches: "Nobodaddy"—"my vision's
greatest enemy." But, shrewdly, Blake sees: "Man must &
will have Some Religion: if he has not the Religion of Jesus,
he will have the Religion of Satan"—meaning the worship of
science: idolatry.

Under the despotism of Urizen, the life of the senses decays,
"vegetates." We fall to the empirical lie.

> We are led to Believe a Lie
> When we see with, not through the Eye
> Which was Born in a Night to perish in a Night
> When the Soul Slept in Beams of Light.

"Our infinite senses" shrink and grow opaque. The extreme
limit of this opacity, this materialization and objectification of

sense life, Blake calls "Satan." Psychically and morally, the
shrinkage is experienced as "Selfhood": the alienated identity
"shut in narrow doleful form." Philosophically, the shrinkage is experienced as the "truth" of the scientific worldview:
the world as seen by a dead man's eyes.

The Visions of Eternity, by reason of narrowed perceptions,
Are become weak Visions of Time & Space, fix'd into furrows
 of death . . .
The Eye of Man, a little narrow orb, clos'd up & dark,
Scarcely beholding the Great Light, conversing with the
 ground:
The Ear, a little shell, in small volutions shutting out
True Harmonies & comprehending great as very small . . .

To such diminished consciousness, nature becomes Blake's
Vala, the "Shadowy Female" (the veil: the delusion: physi-
cally Out There but lacking moral and poetic significance:
Maya, who deludes by claiming to be the totality).

No breaking Urizen's tyranny, then, but by cleansing "the
doors of perception":

Let the Human Organs be kept in their perfect integrity,
At will Contracting into Worms or Expanding into Gods,
And then, behold! what are these Ulro Visions . . .

"If the doors of perception were cleansed every thing would
appear to man as it is, infinite."

But . . . Urizen is also the Zoa of physical power. That is his
trump card. Urizen is builder of the "dark Satanic mills,"
architect of vast geometric structures, imperial cities: master
of the "Mundane Shell," genius of the machines: "the Loom
of Locke . . . the Waterwheels of Newton . . . cruel Works of
many Wheels, wheel without wheel, with cogs tyrannic . . ."

This is Urizen-Satan's spell over mankind: "To Mortals thy Mills seem everything."

Alienated Reason brings vast technical power—even though alienated Reason is

> An Abstract objecting power that Negatives everything.
> This is the Spectre of Man, the Holy Reason,
> And in its Holiness is closed the Abomination of Desolation.

And yet Urizen dares to teach, can *only* teach that the Spectre ("the Reasoning Power") is the *whole* person:

> "Lo, I am God," says Urizen. *"The Spectre is the Man.*
> The rest is only delusion & fancy."

But of course, "the Spectre is in every Man insane, brutish, deform'd . . ." That is why (here is Blake's great insight) Urizen's will to power is grounded *wholly in despair!* He sits among his vast works "folded in dark despair," knowing nothing of purpose, value, meaning . . . except to build more, subdue more; knowing nothing of Eternity, but only of time's bondage and the absurdity of mortality.

> . . . he stood in the Human Brain,
> And all its golden porches grew pale with his sickening light,
> No more Exulting, for he saw Eternal Death beneath.
> Pale, he beheld futurity: pale, he beheld the Abyss . . .

> Stern Urizen beheld . . .
>   if perchance with iron power
> He might avert his own despair.

No living motivation here: only the frenzy of desperation, the fever pitch of anxiety: the panicky flight from meaninglessness: keeping busy, conquering, achieving . . . on the brink of the void. As in Beckett's *Godot:* the only purpose left is to pass the time . . . any mad project will do . . . keep your mind off it . . . think up a game . . . make up a task . . . something spectacular . . . rockets to the moon. Camus missed a nice irony: Sisyphus finishes by inventing himself ingenious machines to roll the rock. "Progress": the mechanization of absurdity.

The regime of Urizen-Satan is despair, despair, *despair.* Where Urizen appears in Blake's work, the word is on every page. Single vision is despair: clever-minded despair. Blake has the matter by the throat: what Marx and all the later ideologues failed to see: once endorse scientific-industrial values, and the struggle for justice is pitched on the edge of Urizen's wasteland.

2. *Luvah.*
Energy: love: the full, free emotive power of the soul: spontaneous vitality. But Luvah is the least well drawn of the Zoas, a poor and elusive sketch. Why? Because Urizen far overbears him. The age belongs to Urizen. Urizen has driven out Luvah: Reason has imprisoned feeling, made it unconscious, irrational, bad, black, guilty, the underdog, the outcast, the nigger, the female.

Luvah was cast into the Furnaces of affliction & sealed.

He cries:

They have surrounded me with walls of iron & brass
. . . I suffer affliction
Because I love, for I was love, but hatred awakes in me . . .
The hand of Urizen is upon me . . .
O Urizen, my enemy, I weep for thy stern ambition,
But weep in vain.

Even for Blake, the life of free, natural impulse must have been hard to conceive. "Jesus was all virtue, and acted from impulse, not from rules." But in Urizen's world, we all become strangers to our native vitality. Hence, the thin delineation of Luvah. Blake's best treatment of Energy is in *The Marriage of Heaven and Hell*, where we find: "Energy is the only life, and is from the Body; and Reason is the bound or outward circumference of Energy. Energy is Eternal Delight."

As in Blake's magnificent painting "Glad Day": the joy of innocent play: mortality, the body, and the earth freely enjoyed: the Great Affirmation. Adam before the fall. Luvah is that total, spontaneous knowledge which was Adam's "knowledge" of Eve: a knowing so complete it can be carnally savored.

But this is what the ascetic workmaster Urizen cannot tolerate: exuberance, the life of the free emotions. He appears at the end of the *Marriage* as the jealous, gloomy "starry king": the law-giver god who persecutes "the sons of joy" and "promulgates his ten commands."

See how shrewdly Blake links Biblical law with Newton's universal laws of nature. He sees the psychic continuity: God as moral policeman carries over into God as cosmic technocrat: order, control, discipline, system, ascetic rigor: the maniacal asceticism of "intellectual respectability."

Luvah is weakly drawn. But not so his negative alter ego, Orc, "the demon red" (from Orcus: hell; from ὀρχίς: testicles). As Satan is to Urizen, so Orc is to Luvah: the fallen aspect of once-divine beauty. Orc is Energy turned hideous with restriction: the chained beast of thwarted desire, howling, howling. (Hence the terrible saying: "Sooner murder an infant in its cradle than nurse unacted desires.") Set free, Orc is mayhem, devastation, the bloodbath of revolutionary terror. He is the "lover of wild rebellion" . . .

The firey joy that Urizen perverted to ten commands . . .
That stony law I stamp to dust . . .

(Even so, Blake puts into his mouth the great line:

For everything that lives is holy, life delights in life;
Because the soul of sweet delight can never be defil'd.

But this was in 1793 in the poem *America,* before the revolution in France had run to mass butchery. In the later poems, Orc grows more ferocious, remains bound and raging in the deeps.)

Blake foreshadows both Nietzsche and Freud: cool head outlaws hot blood; Urizen drives the passions into dungeons of unreason. Science increases the pressure upon sensual joy: empiricism becomes *empiricide,* the murder of experience, Science *uses* the senses but does not *enjoy* them; finally buries them under theory, abstraction, mathematical generalization. At the foundations of Urizen's palace, Luvah-Orc lies writhing, burning for vengeance.

"Damn braces: Bless relaxes." "He who desires but acts not, breeds pestilence." Blake saw: there is no cure for civilization's discontents by way of repression. So the image of wild Orc enchained is Blake's symbol of war: "Energy enslav'd." The last resort of embattled vitality is blind, indiscriminate destruction.

Easy at this point to mistake Blake for Wilhelm Reich or D. H. Lawrence. But Energy, while "from the body," participates in Eternity. With Blake, *everything* moves toward Eternity. Heaven and Hell, Reason and Impulse are to be married, but *within* the fourfold vision of the prophetic books. There are two Zoas more, and they take us well beyond sexual liberation. Blake could strike the Rabelaisian note . . . but only in passing. Sex belongs to the garments of the soul.

3. *Los.*

The Eternal Prophet. From Sol, the alchemical sun; but also from "loss," for Los is the fallen alter ego of Urthona, the perfected prophetic genius. In Eternity, Los and his consort Enitharmon are united as the one figure Urthona, the androgyne. The secret meaning of prophecy lies, for Blake, in this androgynous origin.

It is when Los and Enitharmon part in bitterness ("She drave the Females all away from Los, And Los drave the Males from her away") that Urizen—masculine discipline and abstraction—rises triumphant over Ulro. His supremacy is the sign of "their divisions & shrinkings." As Los warns:

> . . . for One must be All
> And comprehend within himself all things both small & great.

Yet the rupture takes place: the masculine and feminine souls part company in dominance and submission. This is Blake's version of yin and yang falling out of harmonious balance. Thus Los, wounded and diminished, is Prophesy reduced in power—but nonetheless struggling on heroically against single vision. He is the embattled poet in this world of generation. Los's cry, Blake's own:

> I must Create a System or be enslav'd by another Man's,
> I will not Reason & Compare: my business is to Create.

Los is ever the strenuous workman. Creation is a sweaty labor for him; hammer and anvil, looms and furnaces. Like Blake, his genius is born of the fiery forge with bellows and tongs. Los and Enitharmon are, though divided and weakened, nonetheless the enduring creative forces of human culture. Between them, they raise up the strange city called Golgonooza, the fallen paradise: the best of civilization under conditions of alienation. Golgonooza holds out against Urizen and Orc, between Eden and Ulro, between Beulah and Generation. Blake acknowledged: though we are fallen, yet there is Milton, Shakespeare, Michelangelo . . . the saving remnant that reminds and draws us on.

The polarity of Urizen-Satan and Luvah-Orc is mirrored in the split between Los and Enitharmon. Los is "the Sublime," gravitating toward Urizen, Enitharmon is "the Pathos," gravitating toward Luvah.

> . . . no more the Masculine mingles
> With the Feminine, but the Sublime is shut out from the
>   Pathos
> In howling torment, to build stone walls of separation,
>   compelling
> The Pathos to weave curtains of hiding secresy from the
>   torment.

Los's weakness is suppression of the feminine. He ejects Enitharmon from himself and seeks to dominate her. Enitharmon resists ("be thou assured I never will be thy slave"). She goes into hiding ("I will Create secret places"). She grows furtive, devious, vengeful.

Two Wills they had, Two Intellects, & not as in times of old.

From this follows the sexual delusion: masculine and feminine become sexual roles rather than attributes of the integrated soul. Sexual union becomes a corporeal counterfeit of psychic unity. Man and woman then seek to appropriate one another's psyche through sexual love, physically and externally: "terrified at each other's beauty, Envying each other, yet desiring in all-devouring Love." Blake can accept sex at that level, as a *beginning*. But he also sees the divine correspondence—as in the Tantric symbolism of Shakti and Shiva. (He realized too that the role playing can make a mess of sex rela-

tions. He is precociously good on the issue of women's liberation—as in his *Daughters of Albion.*)
So Los declares:

> . . . Sexes must vanish & cease
> To be when Albion arises from his dread repose . . .

Importantly, Los forges the chains of both Orc and Urizen.
What does Blake mean by this? It is another image of the split
between Los and Enitharmon. Prophesy ("poetic genius") is
the struggle to integrate divided mind. For Blake, the integration is a constant labor, often failing. Los can never rest; the
task of holding Urizen and Orc at bay goes on forever. Surely
Los is autobiographical: Blake himself toiling fitfully at the
marriage of heaven and hell, suffering within himself the
great western dissociation:

> the laborer of ages in the Valleys of Despair . . .
> he kept the Divine Vision in time of trouble . . .

So we have the Zoas of Reason and Energy—and the Zoa of
Prophesy, which is "the true man." And when Prophesy
achieves masculine-feminine wholeness, if only for a moment
. . . what then? Then the quality of perception alters, "Creating Space, Creating Time, according to the wonders Divine
of Human Imagination . . ."

A new reality where the *meanings* of things predominate;
where the transcendent correspondences shine through. It is
the world turned inside out by visionary power: a world of
bright symbolic presences.

> Mental Things are alone Real; what is call'd Corpo-
> real, Nobody knows of its Dwelling Place: it is in
> Fallacy, & its Existence an Imposture. . . . I assert
> for My Self that I do not behold the outward Creation

& that to me it is hindrance & not Action; it is as the Dirt upon my feet, No part of Me. "What," it will be Question'd, "When the Sun rises, do you not see a round disk of fire somewhat like a Guinea?" O no, no, I see an Innumerable company of the Heavenly host crying "Holy, Holy, Holy is the Lord God Almighty." I question not my Corporeal or Vegetative Eye any more than I would Question a Window concerning a Sight. I look thro' it & not with it.

And he means it. He *means* it!

Los: "the magician of perception" (Kathleen Raine)

As above, so below.

4. Finally, *Tharmas.*
The most subtle image. He is the alchemist's *deus absconditus,* awaiting redemption: the spiritual essence of nature—the *chrysosperm*—trapped in matter. Matter is personified in his temptress-consort Enion, the watery principle in which spirit first contemplates its reflection, and then, Narcissus-like, falls.

The Neoplatonic-Hermetic myth: light fallen into darkness, the subtle and gross joined in forced marriage. *But* Enion is *not* for Blake a figure of evil and contempt; Blake could not be so world-denying. Rather, she is pitiful: a lonely and guilt-stricken woman bordering on non-entity, wanting Tharmas, loving him, yet afraid of his spiritual potency.

Their troubled love affair is the alchemical master myth of Blake's prophetic books, leading at last to their reconciliation and apotheosis—and to some of Blake's loveliest lyric passages.

Thus Enion:

"The clouds fall off from my wet brow, the dust from my cold limbs

Into the sea of Tharmas. Soon renew'd, a Golden Moth,
I shall cast off my death clothes & Embrace Tharmas again."
Joy thrill'd thro' all the Furious forms of Tharmas humanizing.
Mild he embrac'd her whom he sought; he rais'd her thro'
    the heavens,
Sounding his trumpet to awake the dead, on high he soar'd
Over the ruin'd worlds, the smoking tomb of the Eternal
    Prophet.
The Eternal Man arose.

The love feast and "chemical marriage" of Tharmas-Enion:
this is what imagination, at its highest power, perceives. The
Zoas unify in this master symbol. Blake is talking about more
than psychic transformations. Jung would not do justice
here. For with Blake, perception *makes* reality. At the heart
of the fourfold vision we have the universe as the stage on
which the sacrificial drama is eternally played out: "Visionary forms dramatic"—amid which the human soul performs
its peculiar role as witness and celebrant.

Here was what Newton's science could not, would not see
behind the veil of appearances: the descent, passion, and resurrection of spirit, the redemption of inert nature, nature
sanctified. For the whole meaning of science is to "vegetate
the Divine Vision," to block out the transcendent correspondences in favor of power-knowledge.

The science of Ulro is—*uniquely and willfully*—love-drunk
on the "delusions of Vala": necrophilia.

Against Newton's sleep, the conclusion of *Jerusalem* raises up
its Hermetic paean of joy: the ancient science for which everything, *everything* was live and holy. "And every Man
stood Fourfold; each Four Faces had." And the vision was of
unity:

All Human Forms identified, even Tree, Metal, Earth &
    Stone: all

Human Forms identified, living, going forth & returning
    wearied
Into the Planetary lives of Years, Months, Days & Hours;
    reposing,
And then Awaking into his Bosom in the Life of Immortality.

What at last, is the "sickness of Albion," *our* sickness? That
we cannot perceive the sacrificial drama in which we are *in
spirit* participants. Albion cannot see that natural history is
the projection at large of his own spiritual history. "He has
lost part of his soul; and conversely, the phenomenal world,
emptied of spiritual life, has become a desert." (Kathleen
Raine)

Blake's prophetic epics are a troubling literature. For all
their power—and there are passages as great as anything in
the shorter lyrics—they are too often impossibly bookish.
(Here again Blake reminds of Joyce.) Blake takes his symbolic vocabulary from formidable sources: the Gnostic and
Hermetic philosophers, Boehme, Paracelsus, Thomas Taylor,
Swedenborg, the Bible, and all this overlaid with the Christianity of the English "Everlasting Gospel" tradition—an intoxicating brew, but often murky in the extreme. There is a
deadening amount of haze and allusive congestion—and
much that is bound always to hide in the obscurity of the initial inspiration.

Blake says he took the poems down from "immediate dictation . . . without premeditation & even against my will."
"Spiritual Mystery and Real Vision" was what he wanted,
not well-wrought allegory—the obvious vice of this type of
literature. A watertight system would have been a surrender
to Urizen, prophetic power yielding to neat intellectual equa-
tions. But often still he gropes his way out of the mythological
density by resorting to flat prosaic statements of abstract
metaphysics:

What is Above is Within, for everything in Eternity is
    translucent:
The Circumference is Within, Without is formed the Selfish
    Center,
And the Circumference still expands going forward to
    Eternity . . .

These are deep sayings; but it is not Blake at his poetic best.
And there is much of this.

The weakness relates to Blake's greatest problem. He worked
from esoteric tradition because he could nowhere else entrust
his vision. The world he lived in—both human and natural—
had become for him a void, an unreality: too fallen and corrupted to take into his art. He could take nothing for what it
simply and immediately was. He was like a man with X-ray
eyesight. *He never saw the world before his eyes. He never
wanted to.* His gaze burned right through the "Mundane
Shell" to the visionary dimension beyond it; as he put it,
"melting apparent surfaces away, and displaying the infinite
which was hid." Blake's vision was only for "the Permanent
Realities of Every Thing which we see reflected in the Vegetable Glass of Nature."

There is not a single piece of autonomous, physical nature in
Blake: no poetic still lives or landscapes. Everything natural
and social is subordinated to its transcendent correspondence.
The tyger is not for a moment nature's tyger, but a symbol.
The sunflower is not nature's sunflower, but a symbol. The
London Blake walked through was, though not wholly, a symbolic London—and the chimney sweeps he writes of have more
metaphysical echoes than flesh and blood to them. Even the
stars could not be for Blake the beautiful sight they simply
are to the eyes, but became (uniquely for him of all poets) a
negative image: they belong to Urizen as the symbol of frigid,
regimented Rationality.

Sad to say: Blake did not love nature. It remained for him the Shadowy Female, the seductive Vala. "Satan's Wife. The Goddess Nature." "Natural Objects," he confesses in his notes on Wordsworth, "always did & now do weaken, deaden & obliterate Imagination in me." And elsewhere: "Nature Teaches nothing of Spiritual Life but only Natural Life." Love of nature, Blake felt, had to be purchased at the cost of divine love: "Everything is atheism which assumes the reality of the natural and unspiritual world." Finally, at his Gnostic darkest: "Nature is the work of the Devil."

Blake's anti-naturalism cuts him off sharply from the other Romantics. But why the hostility? Because nature had become, since Newton, the province of the single-visioned scientists. They laid claim to "saving the appearances" and Blake (mistakenly) surrendered to the claim—then reacted against the loss by bitterly abandoning all poetic interest in "natural objects." They survive as symbols to him, but as nothing in their own right.

Blake was too naïvely, too crudely the disciple of Berkeley. "Mental Things are alone Real." Accepting that the world was "really" in the mind, he could not then make much of the fact that it is also "really" in the senses and there to be enjoyed.

To be sure, in the *Marriage*, Blake pleads for "an improvement of sensual enjoyment." The *notion* is there; Blake is nothing if not rich and various. But the idea never makes its way into his poetry. He discusses it, but does not *express* it.

What he failed to grasp is that the scientist's sense-world (Ulro) is *not* the sense-world *as it really is*. It *claims* to be "empirical," but is in fact a materialist-theoretical model designed for the sake of power-knowledge. It corresponds to nature as a map does to a landscape: as a useful reduction of reality. It is painters and poets who *really* look at the world

—and look at it, and look at it, until they lovingly gaze it into their art; no explaining, no theorizing, no generalizing, no analyzing . . . only the pure pleasure of seeing (or hearing, or smelling, or feeling). The "Newtonian Phantasm" *is* exactly that: a phantasm, a gray ghost of the immediate sensory environment.

So to grow drunk on the sensory delights of nature—birdsong, flowersmell, skycolor, herbtaste—is as much a way of undermining "Satan's Mathematic Holiness" as to pierce through to the visionary correspondences. Here was an element of Hermeticism which Blake lost along the way. For alchemy is a science of just those "secondary qualities" that Galileo, Descartes, Locke had banished: the feel and odor, hue and texture of the world's sensible stuff.

But then, Blake could not do the whole job. His task was to save the other aspect of Hermetic science: the transcendent symbolism.

I rest not from my great task!
To open the Eternal Worlds, to open the immortal Eyes
Of man inwards into the Worlds of thought, into Eternity
Ever expanding in the Bosom of God, the Human Imagination.

*   *   *

WORDSWORTH: "NATURE AND THE LANGUAGE OF THE SENSE"

With all the madcap perversity of genius, Blake attacked Wordsworth as an *atheist!* And with not the least charitable restraint to his accusation. Thus—from Blake's notes on

Wordsworth's *Poems:* "I see in Woodsworth the Natural Man rising up against the Spiritual Man Continually, & then he is No Poet but a Heathen Philosopher at Enmity against all true Poetry or Inspiration." More fiercely still, in Blake's *Milton* (with Wordsworth the obvious target):

These are the destroyers of Jerusalem, these are the murderers
Of Jesus . . .
Who pretend to Poetry that they may destroy Imagination
By imitation of Nature's Images drawn from Remembrance.

(Blake even complained that reading Wordsworth gave him a "bowel complaint"; and yet concluded, with magnificent inconsistency, that Wordsworth was "the greatest poet of his age.")

Out of his one weakness, Blake attacked Wordsworth's supreme qualities, his sacramental vision of nature, his childlike joy in the life of the senses. For Blake, "outward creation" had no spiritual authenticity except as a collection of metaphysical symbols; in Wordsworth, we find no need of symbols, but only the direct acceptance of nature for what it is purely and immediately in the senses. Blake's eye had to pierce nature as if it were a delusive veil; Wordsworth could let the natural aspect rest easy in his eye and there become the simple wonder it is.

Both these are ways and means of transcendence. Both transcend single vision. But Blake beneath his Gnostic burden sweats at the job; he must climb home to heaven hand over hand, hauling himself free of the "vegetable universe." Wordsworth relaxes into the visionary mood, moves submissively (with "a feminine softness") along the grain of things, finding himself already at home *within* the "outward creation." He is not afraid to enjoy Vala's beauties; he does not close out the "pure organic pleasure," but delicately unfolds its secret.

> I held unconscious intercourse with beauty
> Old as creation, drinking in a pure
> Organic pleasure from the silver wreaths
> Of curling mist, or from the level plain
> Of waters colored by impending clouds . . .
>
> To every natural form, rock, fruit, or flower,
> Even the loose stones that cover the highway,
> I gave a moral life: I saw them feel,
> Or linked them to some feeling: the great mass
> Lay bedded in a quickening soul, and all
> That I beheld respired with inward meaning.

Wordsworth's tone: always one of stillness, of pregnant calm. But beneath the placid surface, there is a revolutionary current strongly running. Not political revolution (which Wordsworth embraced in youth, rebuffed with age) but a revolution of perception—in fact, that very apocalypse-promising "improvement of sensual enjoyment" Blake himself demanded.

In Wordsworth, in all the Romantic nature lovers, the secret idolatry of Judeo-Christian tradition finds its most militant opposition. The natural objects cease to be idols; they are resurrected and pulse with life. Their "inward meaning" returns. They glow, they breathe, they speak. ("my mind hath looked/Upon the speaking face of earth . . .) Wordsworth talks to mountains . . . to trees, seas, clouds, birds, stones, stars—*person to person*. It is no poetic convention but true conversation.

Here is indeed natural philosophy—but nothing of our science. For Wordsworth does not probe, prod, dissect ("We *murder* to dissect"). No research, no theory. He but attends and converses. And *then* it happens: the *power* breaks through . . . "gleams like the flashing of a shield."

> . . . and I would stand,
> If the night blackened with a coming storm,
> Beneath some rock, listening to notes that are
> The ghostly language of the ancient earth
> Or make their dim abode in distant winds.
> *Thence did I drink the visionary power* . . .

A "wise passiveness" does the trick. There is much here of the Tao: the illuminated commonplace.

> . . . in life's everyday appearances
> I seemed about this time to gain clear sight
> Of a new world . . .
> Whence spiritual dignity originates.

Wait, watch, be still, be open: even the humblest objects may allow "fit discourse with the spiritual world."

"The spiritual world." Yet the spirit must always be a palpable, sensible presence: seen, touched, smelled, heard, tasted. Wordsworth is pre-eminently the psychologist of the visionary senses. A mystic sentiency. His "visitings of imaginative power" emerge invariably, necessarily, from

> an ennobling interchange
> Of action from without and from within;
> The excellence, pure function, and best power
> Both of the object seen, and eye that sees,

and their sign is "aching joy," "sensations sweet felt in the blood," "dizzy raptures," "bliss ineffable": an *erotic* knowledge.

> Wonder not
> If high the transport, great the joy I felt
> Communing in this sort through earth and heaven
> With every form of creature.

Wordsworth has been criticized (especially in his own time by Shelley) for the asexuality of his poetry. But the charge misfires. Wordsworth's eroticism is pregenital, diffused throughout his senses—especially through his vision and hearing. (At least his metaphors are always of raptures seen or heard.) His poetry reports orgasms of perception—an infantile delight in the world-discovering, world-caressing eye and ear. He could even find "a grandeur in the beatings of the heart." We have little poetry in the language that is sensually richer than his.

Wordsworth's ecstasies of the sense are real; so too the natural world that excites them. He never lets us doubt for a moment the reality of sense-life or its objects. His study of nature is through and through empirical. And yet (here is where the prophetic lightning strikes) nature lovingly embraced by the senses becomes suddenly "a new world"—in fact, "the spiritual world." Magically . . . it becomes more than it is . . . *no!* it becomes all that it *really* is, but is rarely seen to be.

And *then,* Wordsworth tells us, we pass gracefully beyond, "the bodily eye," "the fleshly ear." But "beyond" is only reached *"through." The spirit is in the thing* and must be, can *only* be, palpably known therein. Again: this is Adam's "knowledge" of Eve: the person *in* the flesh.

Blake protested: "Wordsworth must know that what he Writes Valuable is Not to be found in Nature." But Wordsworth's reply would be: the vision can be found *noplace else but* in the mind's marriage to living nature.

> To every Form of being is assigned . . .
> An *active* Principle:
>   . . . it subsists
> In all things, in all natures . . .

> Spirit that knows no insulated spot,
> No chasm, no solitude; from link to link
> It circulates, the Soul of all the worlds,
>   . . . and yet is reverenced least
> And least respected in the human Mind,
> Its most apparent home.

The idea is elusive, paradoxical. We are dealing with a quality of awareness, *not* a methodological procedure. What sense will ever be made of Wordsworth at this point by those who have not caught at least a glimmer of the sacramental vision? For Wordsworth, visionary power works solely through the "faculties of sense"; it is "creator and receiver both"

> Working *but in alliance* with the works
> Which it beholds.

So we must conceive of a moment when nature, senses, and mind all merge to become a charm-locked unity . . . a more, a something-other than the sum of these parts we can analyze out of the whole. They become a unique entity. Wordsworth calls the experience a sort of marriage: a "great consummation" for which his poetry is "the spousal verse." In that instant of "blended might," the Kantian dichotomy, a secondary abstraction, evaporates, allowing Wordsworth to marvel

> How exquisitely the individual Mind
> . . . to the external World
> Is fitted:—and how exquisitely, too—
> Theme this but little heard of among men—
> The external World is fitted to the Mind;
> And the creation (by no lower name
> Can it be called) which they with blended might
> Accomplish:—this is our high argument.

The refutation of Kant is head-on, unmistakable. Question: Why is Kant's authority among the philosophers so much greater? Indeed, why is Wordsworth not even brought into court? Answer: Because Wordsworth works from *experience;* Kant works from logic. Wordsworth requires the roaring wilderness for his "high argument"; Kant reduces conveniently to print on the page and perches nicely on the seminar table. Alienated intellect will always prefer fastidious abstractions, tricky arguments; it works from secondary levels of the personality. Word-game philosophy.

These, then, are the great moments, "when the light of sense/ Goes out, but with a flash that has revealed/The invisible world." For these moments (and "Such moments are scattered everywhere") Wordsworth possessed the strange gift of eidetic memory. Years later, he could reconstruct the experience in vivid detail, enjoying

> An active power to fasten images
> Upon his brain; and on their pictured lines
> Intensely brooded, even till they acquired
> The liveliness of dreams.

Wordsworth called it "the power of a peculiar eye."

But—the obvious question—what is it such a "peculiar eye" *sees?* Wordsworth gives no answer. He knows better than to give an answer. His art is one of eloquent and utterly honest evasion. Master of language, he knew the limits of his medium. The power of his poetry, building through the great passages into a mounting wave of rhetoric, conveys the authority of the experience. Yet, when the wave peaks and breaks, the experience is left secret. We learn only that he has known "the latent qualities and essences of things"; "the types and symbols of Eternity"; "the shock of awful consciousness"; "authentic tidings of invisible things"; "the mysteries of being"; a "presence" . . . or, in one of his supreme passages (from *Tintern Abbey*), he leaves it at a tense and pregnant "something."

> And I have felt
> A presence that disturbs me with the joy
> Of elevated thoughts; a sense sublime
> Of something far more deeply interfused,
> Whose dwelling is the light of setting suns,
> And the round ocean and the living air,
> And the blue sky, and in the mind of man:
> A motion and a spirit, that impels
> All thinking things, all objects of all thought,
> And rolls through all things. Therefore am I still
> A lover of the meadows and the woods,
> And mountains; and of all that we behold
> From this green earth; of all the mighty world
> Of eye and ear—both what they half create,
> And what perceive; well pleased to recognize
> In nature and the language of the sense
> The anchor of my purest thoughts, the nurse,
> The guide, the guardian of my heart, and soul
> Of all my moral being.

(Who else could get away with that "something" . . . ? That anti-poetic, totally artless "something"? It is not a word; it is a helpless gasp, a catch in the breath. The rolling wave of the verse crests in the hush before that "something," breaks in the astonished silence. —Of course, of course: couldn't our analytical philosophers take such a shambling incoherence apart at the seams in nothing flat? For what does it all *prove? But where are we to believe such poetry comes from?* Do people just "make it up"? Out of *nothing?*)

Wordsworth, of all poets, most often confesses the "sad incompetence of human speech." He could not, like Blake, reach for a piece of mythic tradition to express "the spiritual presences of absent things." The furthest he goes is, in several places, to liken his vision—but darkly—to the presence of *mind* in nature. As at the close of *The Prelude*, where he stands in flooding sunrise at the summit of Mount Snowdon:

> There I beheld the emblem of a mind
> That feeds upon infinity, that broods
> Over the dark abyss, intent to hear
> Its voice issuing forth to silent light
> In one continuous stream; a mind sustained
> By recognitions of transcendent power . . .

This could, no doubt, be theologized into deism . . . pantheism . . . panentheism . . . what have you. But it is *not* theology. It does not argue or deduce or seek to prove. It is living experience, rhapsodically reported—utterly vulnerable to critical analysis. Just that. No elaborations or clarifications. Wordsworth has found mind-likeness in nature. He invites us to share the vision. Open up. Accept. Enjoy. *Our loss if we refuse.*

An old cliché: that art and science both begin in wonder, and are at one in their pursuit of beauty. How convenient to think so. But this is a treacherous superficiality. Wordsworth was not the polemicist Blake was; he never takes severe issue with the scientists. Yet he knew the difference. In the preface to *Lyrical Ballads* he shrewdly observes that the key philosophical distinction is *not* between poetry and prose, but between "Poetry and Matter of Fact, or Science." The difference is the primacy in poetry (and absence in science) of Imagination-as-visionary-power.

Because science objectifies. Its beauty is that of the behavioral surface: uniform relationships, predictive regularity . . . depersonalized order—which is surely a real and legitimate beauty. The beauty of the puzzle cunningly solved, of the machine broken down to its working parts. So James Watson called the DNA double helix "an idea too pretty not to be true." But such aesthetic tastes have not prevented the new biology from taking the most fiercely reductionist course any science has ever followed. "Living beings are chemical machines," says Jacques Monod—cleverly synthesized nothing-buts that now invite strange fantasies of molecular engineering. How should it be otherwise? Objectified order is dead order. It does not *speak*. Charles Gillispie, discussing Leonardo, draws the distinction with a fine, clean edge:

> For Leonardo da Vinci, as for many a Renaissance humanist, there was a whole world in man. In his eyes science and art were both illumination—the reality of the great world suffusing the consciousness of the little in the act of perception. *This was not to be, of course.* The two modes of grasping nature are different, the one particular and concrete, the other general and abstract. [*The Edge of Objectivity*]

Or again, as Henri Poincaré once put it:

> If nature were not beautiful, it would not be worth knowing . . . I am not speaking, of course, of the beauty of qualities and appearances. I am far from despising this, *but it has nothing to do with science.* What I mean is that more intimate beauty which comes from the harmonious order of its parts, and which a pure intelligence can grasp. [*Science and Method*]

But Wordsworth's beauty is the experience of a speaking *presence*, "carried alive into the heart by passion." Cloud, flower, mountain, sea . . . let them be unruly forms, anarchic motions . . . things just happening . . . just *being there*. The sheer impact of their phenomenological address to the person is enough. Wordsworth's poetry begins *and ends* in the clair-voyant sense of an empowered *presence* in nature.

Presence before order. Where this priority is lost, it is always at the expense of visionary art.

Here is precisely why art—visionary art—does not "get be-yond" initial wonder. Because there is nowhere more impor-tant to be. Such art rests in the spell of the sacred. It does not lead to research. It is content to celebrate its revelations over and again. It does not seek progress or accumulation, but repetition . . . or rather, stasis: the still point, where we balance "Like angels stopped upon the wing by sound/Of harmony from Heaven's remotest spheres." For who would want to turn off and move on . . . to *other* things?

Yes, there *are* other things worth doing. But not *just* as worth doing. Not by a long way. Either we know that, or there can be no discipline of the sacred to guide curiosity and learning. Wordsworth is gentle in his critique, but he makes it clear that, compared to knowledge of the sacramental re-ality, science is a strictly "secondary power"

> By which we multiply distinctions, then
> Deem that our puny boundaries are things
> That we perceive and not that we have made.

First things first, he insists. *First,* knowledge of "the spiritual presences". *Then* (perhaps) research and analysis. But— only *afterwards:*

> Science then
> Shall be a precious visitant; and then,
> And only then, be worthy of her name:
> For then her heart shall kindle; her dull eye,

> Dull and inanimate, no more shall hang
> Chained to its object in brute slavery.

Judged by mainstream Christian standards, Wordsworth's nature worship is heresy of the first water. Fearing as much, he makes an apology in Book Two of *The Prelude.*

> If this be error, and another faith
> Find easier access to the pious mind,
> Yet were I grossly destitute of all
> Those human sentiments that make this earth
> So dear, if I should fail with grateful voice
> To speak to you, ye mountains, and ye lakes
> And sounding cataracts, ye mists and winds . . .

At first glance, Wordsworth's sacramental vision of nature looks like the old paganism reborn. (Blake bluntly called him a "pagan.") But where are the bridges that connect Wordsworth back across the Christian centuries to the pagan worship? They are not there. Take Wordsworth at his word: he did not borrow his vision from some manner of historical influence, but found it in his own "underconsciousness." It was an "awful Power" that "rose from the mind's abyss." That is what gives his work its authority: he is not imitating, but recreating.

Coleridge said what his age needed (and our age still) was a "Reconciliation from this Enmity with Nature." Wordsworth possessed the singular gift that answered the need: the vibrant retention of "infant sensibility, great birthright of our being." His poetry is an archaeology of consciousness, burrowing back through time . . . back to childhood and to that reality "apparelled in celestial light" which the child alone knows in full splendor.

One poem—the *Intimations of Immortality from Recollections of Early Childhood*—throws a new and startling light across the entire history of human culture—but especially over modern adulthood's "Reality Principle." One simple, explosively subversive idea: *"Heaven lies about us in our infancy."*

Wordsworth is ambiguous. He sometimes thinks adult recollection (*if vivid*) can salvage philosophical gold from raw childhood wonder. At other times, there is the sense of an unmitigated loss that comes with age. (Wordsworth seems to have lost his capacity for trancelike rapture at the age of thirty.) In any case, by the going standards of adulthood, we clearly sacrifice more than we gain in "growing up." Worst of all, we lose (beyond even feeble recollection) "the visionary gleam." We lose all sense that the child is (by nature)

> Mighty Prophet! Seer blest!
> On whom those truths do rest,
> Which we are toiling all our lives to find,
> In darkness lost . . .

Blake knew as much, and Rousseau. Wordsworth was only more obsessed with this devastating insight. Further back still —a century before the Romantics—beautiful, neglected Thomas Traherne knew it best of all:

> How wise was I
> In infancy!
> I then saw in the clearest Light;
> But corrupt Custom is a second Night.

Endlessly celebrating "sweet infancy," working a theme so marvelously mad, so radically original that it earned him two hundred years of unrelieved obscurity, Traherne realized before all the others that "the first impressions are immortal all." He traced the fact to the child's "dumness"—to perception unburdened by language and its empiricidal abstractions. Before the words take over: a different universe: Eden reborn with every child.

> And evry Stone, and Evry Star a Tongue,
> And evry Gale of Wind a Curious Song.
> The Heavens were an Orakle, and spake
> *Divinity* . . .

A century later, Wordsworth and the Romantics rediscover independently the same buried garden of childish delights. Another example of a subjectivity so deep it has become interpersonal . . . universal. And following the Romantics: Freud, Wilhelm Reich, the offbeat psychiatrists (especially the Gestaltists), and the libertarian educators:

> . . . every child, before family indoctrination passes a certain point and primary school indoctrination begins, is, germinally at least, an artist, a visionary, and a revolutionary. [David Cooper]

But, as Wordsworth knew, this fragile sensibility goes down before

> The tendency, too potent in itself,
> Of use and custom to bow down the soul
> Under a growing weight of vulgar sense,
> And substitute a universe of death
> For that which moves with light and life informed,
> Actual, divine, and true.

"*A universe of death.*" The world that is "too much with us." Pre-eminently, the world of single vision—as Coleridge observed in a letter to Wordsworth: "the philosophy of mechanism . . . in everything that is most worthy of the human

Intellect strikes *Death*." The world as seen through a dead man's eyes. Blake's Ulro.

And, like Blake, Wordsworth knew: to transcend Ulro risks the charge of madness, perhaps risks madness itself. Wordsworth suffered the accusation. He was, in his youth, reclusive and much bemused . . . "so that spells seemed on me when I was alone." Even at school, or in the midst of cities, he was "a dreamer in the wood," eidetically recollecting the wilderness of the Lake Country.

> Some called it madness—so indeed it was,
> If child-like fruitfulness in passing joy,
> If steady moods of thoughtfulness matured
> To inspiration, sort with such a name;
> If prophecy be madness; if things viewed
> By poets in old time, and higher up
> By the first men, earth's first inhabitants,
> May in these tutored days no more be seen
> With undisordered sight.

"Undisordered sight": gift of the child, the poet, the mystic, the primitive. From such unlikely types, Romanticism drew its new standard of sanity . . . with all the perversity of desperation.

I have said Wordsworth had "no need of symbols." A better way to put it: he needed only *one* symbol—if by "symbol" we understand a magical object. And this was the whole natural world—as it reveals itself to what Wordsworth called "higher minds," by which he meant those

> By sensible impressions not enthralled,
> But by their quickening impulse made more prompt
> To hold fit converse with the spiritual world . . .
> For they are Powers; and hence the highest bliss
> That flesh can know is theirs—the consciousness

Of Whom they are, habitually infused
Through every image and through every thought,
And all affections by communion raised
From earth to heaven, from human to divine.

What more? What more?

*　　*　　*

GOETHE: THE SENSUOUS IMAGINATION

In Goethe, the best of Blake and Wordsworth meet: Blake's
transcendent symbolism drawn from the esoteric tradition
(Gnosticism, Christian cabbalism, the Hermetica), Wordsworth's sacramental vision of nature. Only Blake, among the
Romantics, matches Goethe's urgent concern for the modern
crisis of consciousness. Both marked out Newton as their
prime antagonist. But Goethe brought a greater philosophical
subtlety to the encounter—and a greater care to salvage the
science of nature from militant reductionism.

Three related aspects of Goethe's natural philosophy: (1)
contemplative non-intervention; (2) the primacy of the
qualitative; (3) organic dialectics. The first two have to do
with method; the last with worldview.

1. Contemplative Non-intervention.
From *Faust:*

> Mystery-filled in the light of day,
> Nature won't have her veils stripped away.
> Hide or show: it's hers to choose.
> She'll not be forced with rack or screws.

Goethe in his nature studies used microscope and prism—
but always reluctantly. He was uneasy with the instruments,
fearing they would distort the phenomena, do violence to the
immediate reality of nature . . . or rather to the senses that
have been formed in and by and for nature to gaze upon her
in her "natural" scale and appearance.

The instruments betokened for Goethe man's increasingly
alienated stance over against nature—and the aggressiveness
that follows therefrom. "It is," he remarked, "a calamity that
the use of the experiment has severed nature from man, so
that he is content to understand nature merely through what
artificial instruments reveal, and by so doing even restricts her
achievements." For what can such manipulative procedures
ever "prove"—except the possibilities of manipulation?
which, as Bacon long ago promised, are tantalizingly great.

(Goethe would not even wear spectacles willingly, believing
that eyesight is integral to the personality, a part of one's
peculiar destiny, and not to be artificially standardized.)

"The human being himself," Goethe insisted, "to the extent
that he makes sound use of his senses, is the most exact
physical apparatus that can exist." An idea that could easily
reach a fussy, foolish extreme—for nature composes some of
her loveliest poems for microscope and telescope. But Goethe's
suspicion of the instruments, of experimental constraints generally, is far from cranky; it leads to significant philosophical
questions.

Does modern experimentation "discover" or "manufacture"
the effects it studies? Eddington raises the issue (in his *Philosophy of Physical Science*), asking if advanced experimental
equipment does not tell us how nature can be *made* to behave, rather than how she cares to act.

A tricky point. Perhaps the equipment is *already* a carrier of
assumptions, for its job is exactly to isolate and focus—mean-

ing, *to screen out*. On what basis? True, the equipment helps collect facts. But as Goethe knew: "everything factual is already theory." Thus we find nothing but an objectified nature because that is all we look for: a universe whose only "meaning" is that of predictive regularity. The rest is "contamination", "experimental error" . . . mere "side effects." "In natural science the object of investigation is not nature as such, but nature exposed to man's mode of enquiry." (Werner Heisenberg)

Goethe, rejecting domineering analysis, preferred a radically different approach: "passive attentiveness" . . . with a sharp eye for the unique moment, the astonishing insight which finally crowns perhaps years of watchful waiting and which no amount of research could ever piece together. Nature (he knew) invites and rewards curiosity, but not aggressive probing. The trick is to get into the swing, the flow of the phenomena . . . gradually, patiently, receptively . . . even as we get to know-by-loving and love-by-knowing another person. Such knowledge does indeed seem to come "of itself," in startling quantum jumps: *Gestalten*. "One instance," said Goethe, "is often worth a thousand, bearing all within itself."

What happens in that unique moment? The discovery of what Goethe called the *"Ur-phänomen."* (How we could use an English equivalent of that dark, throaty German *Ur-* . . . meaning ancient, primordial, basic, elemental, archetypal. *Urphänomen*—call it the "deep down phenomenon.") The "open secret" which nature co-operates with her respectful students to bring to light . . . like Wordsworth's "great consummation" that gracefully fits mind to universe. All these nature lovers are born Taoists.

For Goethe the deep down phenomenon always revealed an instance of organic dialectics . . . form in metamorphosis (more of this below). Contra-Kant, Goethe felt the human mind exists in nature to complete nature's forms, to discover her "ideal in the real" . . . as if the mind were an organ of sensuous perception . . . an inner eye that "sees" underlying ideas.

Does this not rank Goethe, then, among the founders of both Gestalt psychology and phenomenology? He did not much philosophize on his method; but (unlike most phenomenologists, who drown us in endless, abstruse, theoretical preliminaries) he did put the technique to work in studies of anatomy, botany, and the color spectrum.

Important here: the fruitful notion that knower must blend unobtrusively with known . . . rather than manhandle his subject. Obviously, this means getting in close, working with the grain, trusting, merging . . . like the fish in the water.

> By contemplation of an ever-creative nature, we might make ourselves worthy of participating intellectually in her productions. Had not I myself ceaselessly pressed forward to the archetype, though at first unconsciously, from an inner urge; had I not even succeeded in evolving a method in harmony with Nature?

(Compare with Bacon's sense that nature, deceitful and hostile, must be ambushed and coerced into giving up its secrets.)

The wisdom of Goethe's approach has been abundantly demonstrated in the new humanistic social sciences, where participative involvement now replaces objective neutrality. Also in ethology, where at last we study the animals in their environmental field on their own terms . . . only to discover they are far smarter, more dignified, more communicative than we ever guessed. Yet this is only the "method" our "primitive" ancestors used as they meditated on the ways of the beasts.

A deep question: how far can such contemplative non-intervention carry us in the understanding of nature? To what levels of reality? How much can we de-objectify (recover from the alienative dichotomy)? Theodor Schwenk's studies of water and fluid forms take us beyond the plants and animals: an attractive new prospect. (See his *Sensitive Chaos*.)

Abraham Maslow has recommended the I-Thou relationship generally as a new "paradigm for science." He calls it "fusion knowledge," a "caring objectivity":

> . . . if you love something or someone enough at the level of Being, then you can enjoy its actualization of itself, which means that you will not want to interfere with it, since you will love it as it is in itself. . . . if you love something the way it is . . . you may then see it (or him) [or her] as it is in its own nature, untouched, unspoiled, i.e., *objectively*. The greater your Being-Love of the person, the less your need to be blind. [Maslow, *The Psychology of Science*]

Goethe, all the way.

But the approach implies *limits*—demands respect for those limits: a discipline of the sacred . . . patience, forbearance, perhaps renunciation.

The ability to allow nature its mysteries . . . because mystery is truth's dancing partner . . . because a respect for mystery may go deeper than our knowledge ever can . . . and because our knowledge, where it pretends to replace mystery, may only be an arrogant caricature of truth. So Goethe's "respect for the unfathomable." Beyond the *Urphänomen*, he said, lies "the realm of the Mothers." Probe further, and you only bring back manipulative tricks: levers, buttons, and switches.

Does the brainwasher who can expertly maneuver your behavior (via electrodes, chemicals, behavior therapy) *really* "know" what you're all about? Or does he "know" you less and less, *precisely as* he becomes more proficient?

Obviously there is no formal way to draw the implied limit. We must be guided by the spirit, not the letter. But the rough rule of thumb, the *feel* of Goethe's studies throughout: nature is neither machine nor dead carcass; treat her always as you would a beloved friend. For so she is . . . if we only knew.

2. The Primacy of the Qualitative.

> Trust to what the senses show.
> There's nothing false in what they know
> If Understanding stays awake.
> Joy and freshness in your vision couple.
> Roam free afield, stay sure and supple.
> See what riches are yours to take.
> [Goethe, *Vermächtnis*]

Goethe kept his natural philosophy innocent of mathematics, of all reductive abstractions. (He once called mathematics "a scientific coffin.") His sensory data were never measurements taken, but qualities savored. He worked from the qualities —*always* from the qualities: color, texture, above all *form* . . . the sweet nourishment of the senses. Artist's soul food. His eye for form and color was almost voluptuous; it caressed what it studied and felt its way in deep.

Goethe called it his "exact sensory imagination" (*exakte sinnliche Phantasia*)—an intuitive power within the senses which can alone midwife the *Urphänomen*.

The idea is much like Wordsworth's "language of the sense," which (paradoxically) transcends the "bodily eye" *only* by working *through* it, toward a deeper sensory participation. And like Wordsworth's "great argument," the idea is a direct rejection of Kant. Deliberately so on Goethe's part. For Goethe, like Wordsworth, enjoyed "the power of a peculiar eye."

Hence, Goethe's impassioned attack on Newton's theory of light and color. Charles Gillispie has called Goethe's own color theory "the painful spectacle of a great man making a fool of himself." Very nearly. But *why* did Goethe—untrained in optical research and mathematics—decide to run the risk?

Because he astutely saw in Newton's *Opticks,* in the exclusiveness of that ingenious study, an early example of what would become the dismal scientific rule: empiricide—the subordination of qualitative experience to quantitative generalization— to the extent that "empiricism" finishes as no more than a checking of measurements . . . often no more than a reading of meters.

So Newton had objectified the study of light and color. He had made the spectrum a matter of variable refraction (eventually to be measured out as wavelengths), had atomized light into theoretical corpuscles. A brilliant achievement. But what had become of the *feel* of vision: the evocative aesthetic action of light and color in the eye . . . the living experience? Where was the sense of beauty in Newton's research? Where were the rich emotional and symbolic associations—the very *meaning* of color?

Shelved. Crowded out. Become suddenly less real . . . merely subjective . . . uninteresting from the *scientific* point of view. Dissipated among the colorless, unobservable particles of light.

Goethe bridled at the loss . . . and rebelled. He would, he said, "rescue the attractive study of colors from the atomistic restriction and isolation in which it has been banished, in order to restore it to the general dynamic flow of life and action which the present age loves to recognize in nature."

For who were these "mathematical opticians" to pretend they alone know the truth about color?

> . . . they no longer continue to ask if there are in this world painters, dyers, someone who observes the atmosphere and the colorful world with the freedom of a true physicist, or a pretty girl, adorning herself to suit her complexion.

The attack on Newton is much too shrill, totally out of keeping with Goethe's usual Olympian calm. But he *would* not see the colors abandoned to objective consciousness. He loved them too much—as an artist, poet, visionary philosopher . . . as a child loves them. For they *are* a sensuous joy and a superb symbolic vocabulary. But *only* if they survive *fundamentally* as *qualities* of experience.

Consider how Newton studied light. By hiding away in a dark room, trapping a single ray of sunshine in his prism— and then (in cold blood) committing measurements upon it. But what sort of way was this (Goethe asked) to seek an understanding of light, something so simple and universal . . . it fills the wide air and bathes the earth . . . and *that* is its natural habitat. (Again the question: does the experiment "discover" or "manufacture" its effects?)

Goethe's mocking response: the poem *Murky Law* (where "your teacher"=Newton).

> Friends, leave behind that darkened room
> Where light of day is much abused,
> And, bent low by crooked thought and gloom,
> Our sight is anguished and confused.
> The superstitious gullible

Have been with us quite long enough;
Your teacher has but filled you full
With spectral, mad, delusive stuff.

An eye that seeks the broad daylight
Becomes itself a heavenly blue;
In the Sirocco's late twilight
Pure fire-red the sun's last hue.
There nature gives away her glory
Gladly to whole hearts and eyes.
And there we'll ground *our* color theory
Upon a truth that never dies.

In no respect does Goethe's alchemical background shine through more brightly than in his defense of the qualities. For alchemy, being a science of *meanings,* is the science of qualities: a visionary complex wherein art, science, religion mingle and no one level of consciousness is expanded at the expense of the others. (What a strange notion that must seem to the research specialist!)

Goethe referred to his alchemy as "my mystical-cabbalistical chemistry." R. D. Gray observes: "The degree to which alchemy had established control over Goethe's interests in early manhood can scarcely be overemphasized. . . . Almost the whole of his scientific work might well be described as a more logical development of traditional alchemical ideas." (See his *Goethe the Alchemist.*)

"What is the hardest thing of all?" asked Goethe—and answered: "What seems the easiest to you: to use your eyes to see what lies in front of them."

Strange remark. And yet . . . was there ever a culture that granted less *reality* to the sensory life than does the scientific west? Have we not been persuaded ever since Galileo-Descartes-Locke that sense qualities are "secondary" . . . merely subjective? Does not physics (which is, after all, the *basic* science) teach us that real reality is brittle atomic bits, ghostly oscillations, vibrations, matter waves . . . "unobservables" that theoretical intellect cunningly deduces from indirect observation? Even time and space are not what experience makes of them, but weird mathematical enigmas.

> . . . neither the immediate sense perceptions, like red, blue, bitter, sweet, resonant . . . nor the consciousness itself of which they are part, appear as such in the objective picture of Nature; they have here formal representatives of a totally different kind, namely, electromagnetic vibrations, frequencies, chemical reactions . . . and the physiological function of the central nervous system. [Erwin Schrödinger, *What Is Life?*]

I once asked a theoretical physicist in what sense he—in this most basic of all sciences—ever "sees" nature. In this wise, he said:

1. Somewhere in the world there is a cloud chamber.
2. A camera takes pictures of events in this chamber.
3. Hired student assistants routinely "scan" the photographic plates, hunting for certain hen-scratches thereon.
4. Their results are measured up and often run through a computer to digest the results.
5. The computer produces a print-out.
6. A senior experimentalist looks over some selected plates and the print-out, decides what's what, and tells a junior member of the team.
7. The junior member writes up a report.
8. The report is published.
9. The report is abstracted.
10. My friend has an assistant who surveys the current literature and abstracts the abstracts.

11. My friend reads the abstracts of abstracts, and proceeds to do basic research.

Empiricism . . .

Goethe catches the paradox of it all in his epigram: "Empiricist: Who would deny you've chosen the surest road of
all? But yet you grope like a blind man along that best paved
road."

Undeniably, it is a prodigious feat on the scientist's part to
"think away" the qualitative display of nature. And of course
it was necessary to read the qualities out of primary nature if
scientific man was to gain the state of objectivity (alienation) which power-knowledge demanded. But Goethe and the
Romantics were more concerned for what was lost than
gained.

Move through the chemist's periodic table. What is the difference there between the elements? Their atomic number: a
purely quantitative shift. But we do not *experience* the elements or their compounds as a matter of more-or-less. (e.g.,
gold as merely something more of whatever oxygen is.) No
more than we experience red as being something more or less
of what blue is.

Our senses (and here is one of the deep mysteries) grasp the
differences as qualitatively spaced and segregated: differences
radically of kind, not of degree. And this too is a *reality:*
what Goethe called "the *true* illusion." There is surely a
troubling gap here.

> . . . quantum mechanics implies all the properties of
> copper sulphate; but it would be difficult indeed to
> deduce the blue color of copper sulphate from quantum
> mechanics. And yet copper sulphate *is* blue, and
> insofar as science is a description of the world, our
> science is imperfect if it ignores the blueness of copper

sulphate. [Alvin M. Weinberg, *Reflections on Big Science*]

The trouble with qualities: they will not be added and subtracted. Quantities can be counted (which is objective); qualities must be evaluated (which is subjective). Of course, qualities can be reduced to quantifiable causes; that is what Newton did with color. But then they are no longer qualities. We do not *see* wavelengths; we deduce them.

> The difference between Goethe's and Newton's color theories rests mainly on the fact that Newton considered light and colors "indirect phenomena," whereas Goethe considered them *addressed,* i.e. "direct phenomena." [Adolf Portmann, *New Paths in Biology*]

"Addressed" . . . like something laid out, played out before us . . . a presentation. Perhaps (so alchemy insisted) a message, subjective but universal: a script of qualities, there to be read. Newton and his heirs translated the script into another language, killing the poetry. Goethe the alchemist preferred to read the original . . . and was led inevitably to other meanings.

3. Organic Dialectics.

> Joyously, so long ago,
> My eager mind did strive
> To study and discover
> Nature in her works alive:
> She, the everlasting Oneness
> In the manyness divined.
> Big minuteness, tiny bigness,
> All according to its kind,
> Ever changing, ever constant

Near and far, far and near,
Shaping and reshaping . . .
Why but to wonder am I here!
[Goethe, *Parabase*]

"Goethe's sense of nature was an awareness of one pervasive pattern of process, of formation and transformation, which was equally evident to him by introspection and by observation. His entire life was devoted to the clarification of this sense of . . . unity in process . . ." (L. L. Whyte)

"Unity in process"—the study which Goethe invented and named morphology: a remarkable new vision of nature—and Romanticism's most characteristic contribution to science. For morphology requires the Romantic relish for organic aesthetics, for fluid, never-quite-complete, creative shapings . . . as if one were watching nature sculpture itself *from within,* flowing through invisible, projective patterns . . . striving toward a higher end.

Morphology holds a permanent place in biology, thanks to Goethe's *Metamorphosis of Plants.* And without the Romantic fascination with organic form and flux, no Darwinian breakthrough. Evolutionary theory builds on the morphological eye for unity in process. Goethe himself had no doubt whatever about evolution via adaptation to the environment:

> . . . we shall eventually regard the whole animal
> kingdom once more as an element in which one species
> is supported on and by means of another, if not
> actually orginating one from another.

But Goethe paired environmental selection with the *internal factors* of evolution: life striving against the odds to realize its archetypal form, its *Urphänomen.* Goethe's conception of evolution, merging internal thrust with external pressure, destiny with selectivity, was more sophisticated than Darwin's

. . . but (seemingly) less "objective" because involving the notion of inner purposive tendency: *Bildungstrieb*.

(Darwin objectified evolution by simply reading Malthus and the rigors of cutthroat capitalist competition into the "mechanism" of selection—a classic example of scientific "neutrality" adapting itself naively to the social ethos of the day.)

But for Goethe, morphology reached beyond botany. It was the key to a universal process, which included the inorganic as well. Morphological dynamism was nature herself. It was the moving signature of the cosmos.

The meaning of that signature? *Polarity and synthesis*—the energy behind all formative tendency: the divine rhythm. As in Blake: the strife and reconciliation of Los and Enitharmon.

Goethe's major scientific speculations—in botany and color theory—grow from his vision of polarity moving toward an "intensified" union of opposites: a "higher third." The paradox-logic of synthesized contraries which flows so richly down through Hegel, the post-Kantians, Marx, Freud.

Polarity and synthesis: the master image of Goethe's natural philosophy. Thus the plant (the ideal plant: the *Urpflanz*) is seen as an infinite series of variations on one basic form (the leaf) driven forward by the polarity of expansion and contraction . . . expansion and contraction up through seven cycles from cotyledons to flowering fruit. And back to seed again.

Very late in life, Goethe switched his botanical morphology over to another polarity, which opposed the vertical to the spiral tendencies in plant growth. But the basic idea is the same:

> When we see that the vertical system is definitely male
> and the spiral definitely female, we will be able to

conceive of all vegetation as androgynous from the root up. In the course of the transformations of growth, the two systems are separated, in obvious contrast to one another, and take opposing courses, to be reunited on a higher level.

In Goethe's color theory, the polarized tension is between dark and light: "Darkness and light have eternally opposed each other, one alien to the other . . ."

> We see on the one side light, brightness; on the other darkness, obscurity: we bring the semi-transparent medium between the two, and from these contrasts and this medium the colors develop themselves . . . directly tending again to a point of union.

The "point of union" here is the "intensification" of the spectrum to a pure red (*Purpur*) which is the "true reconciliation" of all color contrasts: "the acme of the phenomenon."

Further: Goethe was impressed by the polar character of magnetism and electricity—a fascination that works its way through German *Naturphilosophie* into Faraday's (non-mathematical) research on the electromagnetic field, the first break within science from strictly mechanistic models. (See L. Pearce Williams, *The Origins of Field Theory*.)

From the *Color Theory:*

> To divide the united, to unite the divided, is the life of nature; this is the eternal systole and diastole, the eternal contraction and expansion, the inspiration and expiration of the world in which we live and move.

To see all nature as a rhythm of opposites, a vital pulsation ("I compare the earth and her atmosphere to a great living being perpetually inhaling and exhaling") moving toward higher organic unity . . . this again is Goethe the alchemist speaking.

For alchemy is grounded in such an organic dialectics. Goethe's *Urpflanz* is the Hermetic androgyne, union of the masculine and feminine powers, the yin and yang. His color theory is modeled on the three major stages of the alchemist's Great Work: the blackening of the *prima materia* (the *nigrido*), the whitening (the *albedo*), and finally, surmounting the black and white, the reddening (the *rubedo*), which is embodiment of spirit.

Both the *Urpflanz* and the colors "climb up the spiritual ladder" to the point of maximum "intensification" (Goethe's *Steigerung*—the alchemical term).

But all this—for Goethe as for Blake and Wordsworth—belongs to the "eyes of the spirit." ("The observer does not see a pure phenomenon with his eyes, but more with his soul.") The natural object becomes, like the alchemist's Great Work, a mandala-like focus for meditation: studied *into* and *through* . . . until the senses are themselves "intensified" by the object . . . so the transcendent correspondences emerge . . . and, at the highest stage, the harmony of the Whole: "the open secret."

> Science of nature has one goal:
> To find both manyness and Whole.
> Nothing "inside" or "Out There,"
> The "outer" world is all "In Here."
> This mystery grasp without delay,
> This secret always on display.
> The true illusion celebrate,
> Be joyful in the serious game!
> No living thing lives separate:
> One and Many are the same.
>   [Goethe, *Epirrhema*]

More than any artist before or since, Goethe made the heroic effort to integrate science with traditional wisdom. He sought a disciplined nature study which might yet be artistically and morally "useful": a science of the whole person, the base for a unified culture.

Goethe's model was alchemy, but an alchemy purged of its musty bookishness and distracting metaphorical confusion, and returned once again to the simple contemplation of living nature. A revitalized alchemy, free of the dust and clutter that fill old Faust's study at the opening of the play. Goethe returned alchemy to fresh air and sunlight, the better to see the sacramental vision: the splendor of the chemical marriage, always there in the background of his art and thought. And what is natural philosophy without that?

Goethe tried. But orthodox science is after all no natural philosophy; only a "productive research" in pursuit of "hard results." As Charles Gillispie observes (disdainfully): in Goethe's nature "everything blends into everything . . . not to be embraced by measurement but to be penetrated by sympathy."

The sensuous imagination yields joy and poetry; it discovers meaning . . . but little power. And that little is only what comes of moving with the grain. Which requires much trust, much love. As it turns out, *too* much for the likes of most of us moderns.

So Goethe's lament for the age:

> Woe, woe!
> You have shattered it,
> This lovely world,
> With mighty fists.
> It reels, it collapses!
> A demigod has smashed it
> Utterly!

CHAPTER 10

Uncaging Skylarks: The Meaning
of Transcendent Symbols

Ah, no wings of the body could compare
To wings of the spirit!
It is in each of us inborn:
That feeling which arises and ascends
When in the blue heaven overhead
The lark calls out in thrilling song.

Goethe

THE POPULAR HISTORY OF AVIATION

The musical accompaniment is by Richard Strauss: *Also Sprach Zarathustra*. Over it, a portentous voice announces, "From the beginning of time, man has dreamed of one supreme adventure: to traverse the heavens with the grace of a bird."

And now, a bird appears before us, neatly sailing the wind. From below, a man gazes up, his face filled with fascination and longing. He is shaggy, covered in animal hides . . . a stereotypic caveman. But he has fashioned himself a pair of outsized wings. He ties them on and steps to the edge of a dizzy precipice. And then, as his troglodytic colleagues stand by in awed amazement, as the music rises to a trumpeting crescendo, the original aviator spreads his wings and soars away into the sun . . . only to be transformed in midair into a Boeing 707, the *true* "wings of man."

It is a television commercial for a prominent American airline, a slick, pretentious spot announcement that finishes by reminding how all of us can now enjoy the "supreme adventure" for as little as $214 Los Angeles to Atlanta round trip, Mondays through Thursdays, economy fare.

I watch . . . and ponder the wealth of artistic and religious symbolism that lies hidden beneath this popular, potted history of aviation. Classic images of flight and ascendance fill my thoughts . . . the skylark of the Romantic poets . . . Geruda, the divine vulture, the vehicle of the yogis . . . St. Bonaventura's ascent of the mind to God . . . the Taoist holy men who rode the wind in carriages drawn by flying dragons . . . the prophet Elijah in his chariot of fire . . the Vedic priest scaling his tall pillar, crying from its summit with arms outspread, "We have come to the heaven, to the gods; we have become immortal." I think of the angels pinioned with flame, the furies, genies, and wing-footed gods . . . and behind all these, shining through from the dawn of human consciousness, reflected in a thousand mythical images, the shamanic vision-flight, the ecstasy with wings.

All this passes through my mind, the real but subterranean meaning of flight, buried now beneath a glamourous technology of jet planes and moon rockets, lost, totally lost from the common awareness; and I grow sad to see a noble imagery debased to the level of so poor a counterfeit.

True, there are always the sensitive few, among the artists especially, who can tell the original from the counterfeit; and maybe a few more who have, by way of the drug trip, recaptured something of the primordial meaning of being "high." But for the rest, I think this television commercial —like so many of the clichés on which advertising and the popular arts draw—summarizes the conventional wisdom. It does more than volumes of scholarship to express the central credo of urban-industrial society: the conviction that only now, under our auspices, do all the best ancestral dreams come true as tangible realities. For us, it goes without question that the aspiration of flight had no significant place in culture until Leonardo da Vinci first looked at a bird and proclaimed it "an instrument working according to mathematical law which it is within the power of man to reproduce." How did Leonardo make flight a realistic proposition? By embedding it in a machine. The machine may not have worked, but it was at least a "practical" step away from mere wishful thinking toward the day when, after generations of experiment with balloons and gliders, industrial technology could finally provide the power and know-how to make heavier-than-air flight a reality. Only then could the "supreme adventure" become available to millions.

THE "REAL THING"

But what has become of that adventure as a matter of living experience? Now that millions are convinced that they possess in fact this ideal that a thousand generations before us could only entertain in dreams, what does it amount to? The question is worth a moment's reflection, because here, I believe, we find an important cause of that chronic despair so characteristic of our culture, that nagging sense of malaise amid world-beating achievement.

All of us who have passed through a major air terminal have been able to see on the thousand tired and anxious faces around us what it means to play the jet-propelled Icarus. The faces of nervous tourists scrambling to locate lost luggage, change money, catch up with the latest rescheduling, clear through customs, find ground transport . . . the faces of jet-fatigued executives routinely shuttling across the globe with heads full of money and worry . . . one struggles among them through congested waiting rooms to find a strong drink or some fresh air . . . never enough places to sit and the air conditioning perpetually overloaded. One waits in traffic queues three miles long to creep into the airport, and, once there, must line up again to check in baggage, obtain information, buy insurance, get a fast snack, load up with duty-free merchandise. The planes are invariably late departing or arriving; one makes haste only to spend hours waiting among impatient babies and bored adults.

As for the flight itself, is it not universally regarded as so many hours of cramped tedium? Hence the many distractions . . . music by stereophonic earphones, movies, cocktails, magazines, perhaps (for the sagging junior executives on board) stewardesses decked out like harem girls. Rather as if the object were to screen out the entire sensation of flying by turning the plane into a cinema or night club. What is it we say of a successful flight? "Never knew we were in the air."

In the summer of 1971 a man and woman, strangers to one another when they boarded a BOAC jet en route from New York to Australia, are reported to have unsettled a few hundred fellow passengers by having sex in their seat about midway in the trip. An understanding airline spokesman afterwards explained to the press that such antics were not uncommon, because people did after all get bored on these long-distance flights. The obvious remedy, then, is to introduce supersonic transport that will get the tiresome business over with even more quickly.

All this is not meant as a tirade against air transport,

but only as an ironic comment on the "supreme adventure" of traversing the heavens as you and I have come to know it. Back in the 1930s, the poet Antoine de Saint-Exupéry could still salvage a bit of high romance from flying the mail routes in a primitive craft open to the elements and equipped with a single risky engine. Today we fly five times faster and ten times higher, but the only romance we may find is that of the BOAC passengers resorting to the oldest amusement of all. Clearly, if air transport is the fulfillment of primeval aspiration, then our ancestors vastly overrated the experience. They expected towering exhilaration; but we know better. After the novelty wears off, it turns out to be a trouble and a bore. *Another* trouble and bore . . . like so many other inconveniencing conveniences of modern life.

Yet how *could* so great and ancient a dream turn out to be so trivial? We are forced to conclude, with a kind of routine disillusionment, that only ignorance of the real thing in all its tedious detail allowed our ancestors to enjoy their dreams. To preserve the dream one must forgo the reality; to possess the reality one must forfeit the dream. Either we resign ourselves to that dismal conclusion, or we must recognize that somewhere along the line we have lost touch with the traditional aspiration. We have made it real—materially, historically real—but at the expense of some other, greater reality . . . something that eludes us for all our power and cunning.

THE SECULARIZATION OF SYMBOLS

What we think we see in the airplane—the contemporary realization of an archaic dream—we easily read into countless other technical and scientific achievements. I emphasize flight in this chapter only because it is a particularly dramatic and characteristic achievement of industrial society, as well as being a widely shared experience. It makes for a nice focus. But the example can be multiplied. What was the alchemist's search for the secret of transmuting metals? A fantasy precursor of our nuclear physics. The age-old quest for immortality? A vain hope prefiguring genetic engineering and transplant surgery. Divine omniscience? A dream that now yields place to the ultraintelligence machines we are promised by the computer technicians. The superhuman strength with which our ancestors endowed their gods? A helpless longing for the power our engines and dynamos, especially our globe-shattering weaponry, make real. (What names do we choose for our mightiest technics? Zeus, Titan, Poseidon, Thor, Saturn, Atlas, Apollo . . .)

Most important of all—because it wraps all the rest together in a single ideological package—we cling to the revolutionary conviction bequeathed to us by the French *philosophes* that the heavenly city has ceased to be "pie in the sky" and has become a *real* historical project, a state of ultimate well-being to be tangibly embodied on earth in the near future. This passion to secularize so many human aspirations is the special pride of our culture. It is what makes us feel uniquely progressive and realistic.

One would not think that anybody even casually familiar with the fascination of the Romantic poets for images of flight and ascendance could mistake their poetry for a premature longing for air travel. (Does not Shelley tell his skylark outright, "Bird thou never wert"?) Yet if there is—"obviously"—another way to understand such images (flight, immortality, omnipotence, the heavenly city), how little effect it has on the popular mind and the course of affairs. As symbols of what besides technological possibilities do they hold any influence over our lives? If there is a second way of flying, what is it? Is it worth caring about? Has it any connection with historical so-called realities? Clearly the conventional wisdom thinks it has not.

Our way with symbols is to treat them as *mere* symbols—"ciphers," as I have called them in an earlier chapter. We technologize them, psychologize them, find a word or thing to decode and replace them—a facile exercise that turns the symbol into a little verbal puzzle. So we say the poet's skylark equals . . . what? We can find a dozen phrases to balance off the equation: creative ecstasy, *joie de vivre*, beatitude, spiritual fulfillment . . . One is as good as the next. But Shelley himself does not hesitate to confess to his lark, "what thou art we know not." Because he knew that the poem's job is to project symbols in their full power, not to decode them. He knew that behind a poetic symbol there lies, not another word that takes its place, but an *experience* to which that symbol uniquely attaches. Poetic diction uses language to set the skylark free, not to trap it in a cage of verbal interpretation. "A rose is a rose is a rose" —meaning (I think) that for what the rose, shrewdly chosen and precisely used as a symbol, so exquisitely expresses there are no "other words." Poetry, one might say, is the therapeutic subversion of language by language; it is language doctoring its own worst disease of literalism with the medicine of symbolic play.

I have suggested that the strength of Romanticism lay primarily in its defense of that special facet of imagination which Wordsworth called "visionary power." Imagination as visionary power is the ability to *feel* one's way through the surfaces of experience, to enter that symbolic dimension of life where things become a live and speaking presence. This is the respect in which Romanticism stands as a turning point in the history of western consciousness—though obviously its influence has for most of the past century and a half been limited to the arts and the more mystical schools of philosophy and psychology. Here is where Romanticism becomes more than an aesthetic style and impinges upon the buried religious tradition I have called the Old Gnosis. By way of their fascination with primitive and pagan worship, Hermeticism, cabbalism, and nature mysticism generally, the Romantics make clear their kinship with that great and ancient spiritual current.

In our own day, the Romantic sensibility has been joined by a wealth of new cultural discovery that vastly strengthens its hold on the Old Gnosis: the insights of eastern religion, the non-reductive study of primitive myth and ritual, the sympathetic investigation of occult traditions like those of the Sufis, alchemists, and Gnostics. All these begin to emerge from the dungeons where single vision had locked them away as superstition and heresy. We may yet learn to read the symbols again in that original tongue which has for so long been a dead language for us.

But before we press further with our discussion of the transcendent symbolism, let me emphasize once again, as I did in Chapter 4, that I am not interested here with symbolism as it occupies logicians or analytical philosophers. It should be clear by now that I am speaking of symbols in the sense in which a skylark or a mountain or a ritual can be a symbol. It is the symbol as sacrament, not as logical cipher that concerns me. My meaning is that of Coleridge:

> A symbol is characterized . . . above all by the translucence of the Eternal through and in the Temporal. It always partakes of the Reality which it renders intelligible; and while it enunciates the whole, abides itself as a living part in that Unity of which it is representative.

THE VISION-FLIGHT: EXPERIENCE AND SYMBOL

> *The Divine Being Himself cannot be expressed. All that can be expressed are His symbols.*
>
> *Gershom Scholem*

There is a remarkable passage in Carlos Casteneda's *Teachings of Don Juan*. At one point in the narrative, Casteneda, a young anthropologist acting as apprentice to the Yaqui sorcerer Don Juan, has fed on "devil's weed" (the *Datura* plant) and has experienced the vivid sensation of flight while in a state of trance.

But "did I *really* fly?" he asks afterwards. "Did my body fly? Did I take off like a bird?" The old sorcerer wearily shrugs off the question. "You always ask me questions I cannot answer. . . . Birds fly like birds and a man who has taken the devil's weed flies as such."

The apprentice persists, because, as he tells Don Juan, "you and I are differently oriented." Where was his body while he flew? "In the bushes." So then if the apprentice had brought friends with him, they would not have seen him fly, would they? "That depends on the man," the old man answers. If the friends knew the power of the devil's weed, they would have seen the apprentice fly. But, asks Casteneda, suppose he tied himself to a rock with a heavy chain; would he then still fly? "Don Juan looked at me incredulously. 'If you tie yourself to a rock,' he said, 'I'm afraid you will have to fly holding the rock with its heavy chain.'" And there the discussion ends.

Modern philosophy gives us a convenient rule of thumb for dealing with such a tangle of cross purposes. We revert to Descartes and simply slice the discussion down the middle. We say there is an objective realm and a subjective realm. (Freud's Reality Principle again.) The apprentice is talking about objective behavior. The sorcerer is talking about subjective feeling. The apprentice is talking about *real* flying. The sorcerer is talking about the *illusion* of flying. Reality is objective and happens "outside." Illusion is subjective and happens "inside." In this case, the illusion is a mental reflection (a hallucination) of real flying. So it is unreal.

How utterly sensible. But why does the old sorcerer not see it that way? Why does he not agree that his flying is an illusion of flight and therefore unreal? It is not because he cannot distinguish between the way a bird flies and the way a person flies. That is as obvious to him as it is to us. He is neither feebleminded nor mad. What he sticks at is the ontological priority of the distinction: which is more real than which? "Did I *really* fly?" It is the prejudicial adverb that makes the trouble. The dispute between the two men leads us back to Plato's cave, where all significant philosophical controversy must return sooner or later. Which reality is the substance and which the shadow? The old sorcerer is at the same disadvantage as the sun-stunned philosopher who must explain daylight to those who have lived all their life in darkness.

For Don Juan, the real experience of flying belongs to an old and formidable tradition. He brings us back to the shamanic vision-flight, one of those supreme symbols of human culture which has been elaborated into thousands of religious and artistic expressions, embedded in the foundations of language, driven like a taproot into the bottommost stratum of our consciousness. Because we are used to dealing with *mere* symbols (ciphers), we ask automatically: what is the vision-flight a symbol of? But there is no answer, except to say that this symbol belongs uniquely to an ubiquitous experience of enraptured awe which is to be *lived*—whether suffered or enjoyed—but not in any sense "explained." The experience is transcendent. The symbol is as close as we can come to expressing its reality. All discussion of whether the symbol means to say "I flew," "I felt *as if* I was flying," "I did something that was a kind of flying," "Metaphorically speaking, I flew," etc., is totally beside the point. The symbol *means* the experience. The experience is non-verbal bedrock; the symbol lies next against it as its universally compelling expression. No words can delve below the bedrock; no words can impose themselves between the bedrock and the symbol without distorting meaning. We can only work away from experience and symbol by way of abstraction or metaphorical extension.

Experience and symbol taken together are what we might call a *root meaning:* an irreducible sense of significance, a foundation the mind rests and builds upon. For thought must begin somewhere, with some rudimentary material. These are the root meanings. The task of human culture is the elaboration of root meanings in the form of ritual or art, philosophy or myth, science or technology—and especially in the form of language generally, by way of progressively more attenuated metaphors drawn from the original symbol. Root meanings cannot be explained or analyzed; rather they are what we use among ourselves to explain—to give meaning to—lesser levels of experience. They are the diamond that cuts all else.

In the case of flight, all language that associates height, levity, loftiness, climbing, or elevation with the qualities of superiority, dignity, privileged status, worthiness, etc., is an extrapolation from the original symbol of the shamanic vision-flight. Hence the "highness" of kings, the majesty of mountains, the prestige of being "upper" class. Conversely, lowliness comes to betoken inferiority, sinfulness, ignobleness, etc. We are drawn "upwards" to God, and "fall," "slide," or "plummet" into hell; we "climb" to social heights and are dragged "down" into the gutter. The same symbolism can be extended into other forms of expression: music, architecture, dance also have their soaring and falling gestures. The dancer's *jeté*, the singer's high note, the Gothic vault fly with the mind like the poet's lark. The symbolism is universal and hardly arbitrary; the same root meaning lies behind all these elaborations, mined out of a primordial experience.

A great symbol—like that of the vision-flight—is a prodigious human invention. It is the substance from which human understanding is fashioned. As imagination stretches form and language away from root meanings toward ever more distant associations, the power of thought grows potentially richer and more subtle. I say "potentially," because there is always the risk that root meanings will be lost amid their multitudinous and increasingly remote reflections. That is Casteneda's problem in the encounter with Don Juan. Casteneda lives amid abundant reflections of the vision-flight, but, like most of us in the modern west, he has grown hopelessly away from the root meaning. So when Don Juan takes him back to the source, he fails to recognize it for what it is, and asks, "Did I *really* fly?" When we become so estranged from the meaning of symbols, language loses touch with experience and goes into business on its own, becoming a collection of perplexing abstractions. And then all sorts of absurdities and pseudo-problems ensue. For example, the root meaning of the vision-flight associates divinity and the skies. But when the experience that underlies the root meaning is lost, we are left with an absurdly literal proposition which seems to locate God in physical space above the clouds. Then, when the Russian cosmonauts fail to find the old gentleman there, village atheism holds itself vindicated.

Few pagan or primitive peoples, grasping intuitively as

they do the true ontological status of myth and symbol, would ever be so foolish. Their reality is polyphonic: it has overtones and counterpoints and resonances—which is exactly what we, with our two-value, objective-subjective sensibility, are inclined to call "superstition." Only Christians, especially Protestant Christians, have ever been so far gone with the disease of literalism as to produce a monstrosity like Biblical fundamentalism. The irony is, of course, that the fundamentalist and the scientific skeptic share the same single visioned consciousness. They stand or fall together by the same Reality Principle.

THE LAW OF GRAVITY

> *God keep me . . . from supposing Up and Down to be the same thing as all experimentalists must suppose.*
>
> *William Blake*

Let us consider another, rather more complex transformation of vision-flight symbolism—in this case one that has played a critically important part in shaping basic scientific thought. The argument is a circuitous one, but by the time we reach the end of it, we shall see how single vision borrows from the traditional symbolism of human culture, but then loses the root meanings of things.

From the shamanic vision-flight we inherit the religious and mythic connotations that cling so stubbornly to all thinking about rising and falling, up and down, light and heavy. The vision-flight asserts levity as the prime orientation of the soul. The notion of gravity—"weighed-downness"—comes into existence as a companion idea, almost by negative definition. Gravity is the shadow side of levity; in the shaman's experience, it becomes symbolic of what one feels when the soul drifts from the sense of buoyancy that keeps it close to the sacred. Gravity in any other sense is not a fundamental preoccupation at this cultural stage. That is why—and the fact is remarkable—gravity traditionally played no important part in human thought prior to late Greek speculation. There is simply no body of folklore or mythology dealing with the creation of a force or substance we would recognize as physical gravitation. And yet gravity is such a (seemingly) basic, simple, inescapable notion. Why did no one "discover" it until so late in history? Because—so the conventional wisdom reasons—people did not always enjoy a *realistic* relationship to nature. Before the modern western era, they had not paid rational attention to the world around them, but had distracted themselves with speculations about angels and devils, animistic figments and mere secondary qualities.

And in some respects the conventional wisdom is not far wrong. The intellectual slot we reserve for the physics of gravitation is taken up in non-scientific cultures by the spiritual experience of "fallenness," the loss of visionary levity. The concept is moralized and mythologized. From such a viewpoint, to take on weight is not primarily a physical fact; it is first of all a symbol of having descended from a normal and proper condition of grace. Thus, in cabbalistic philosophy, the quintessential body of Adam Kadmon, the primal human being, is weightless, just as the crystalline spheres of Ptolemaic astronomy—being in a state of original and eternal perfection—are without weight. Gravity becomes an important and isolated concept only after weightiness (fallenness) begins to seem like an irresistible fact of life needing to be accounted for. This happens as the sense of levity ceases to be a readily

accessible, normal experience and becomes more and more
exotically mystical—or perhaps evaporates from the mind altogether. Only then does gravity remain as a thought-provok-
ing "something" that demands explanation.

It was not until the time of the later Greek philosophers that
the transcendent symbolism of lightness and weight gave way
to a more strictly scientific discussion of two physical forces
of nature called "gravity" and "levity." In Greek and medieval European science these forces were still faintly embued
with the sort of animism that Galileo and Newton would later
eliminate. There was still the sense that ascension moved an
element or object closer to divine perfection, and that things
strove or willed to rise and fall depending on their degree
of worthiness. This way of thought was, however, well on its
way to becoming a mere convention, no longer deeply felt as
part of a comprehensive religious worldview. The ideas had
become *explanations,* not experiences. It is significant that
as this happened, gravity was upgraded to the point of becoming coequal to levity in Greek and medieval natural
philosophy. The sense of a levitational norm had weakened
as the symbolic significance of the concepts faded.

But it was not until the age of Newton that gravity finally
exiled levity entirely from the scientific mind and became a
domineering concern of natural philosophy on which much
thought had to be expended. Indeed, the universal law of
gravity holds a special place as the master concept that in-
augurated the scientific revolution—as if the first thing
modern science had to do was to destroy the symbol of the
vision-flight. Bacon very nearly says as much in the *Novum
Organum* as part of his open warfare on imagination. "The
understanding," he insists, "must not be supplied with wings,
but rather hung with weights to keep it from leaping and
flying." To mistake these for mere metaphors is to miss the very
role symbols play in the creation of language and the molding
of the psyche. A society that decides it must keep its thinking

"down to earth" is a society that begins taking the phenomenon of gravity seriously.

Significantly, this new concentration on gravity as a basic and universal fact of nature corresponded to the growing obsession with human fallenness in the religious thought of the sixteenth and seventeenth centuries. As the sense of human degradation before God increased and as the soul took on an impossible weight of sin, the problem of gravity began to tease the mind. Up to this point in history, we have been dealing with perceptions of morality and nature derived from an ancient symbolism that united the experience of weight to the experience of ungodliness. But now something of supreme importance happened; the two lines of thought—spiritual and natural—parted company to become separate realms of discourse. The scientists took up the discussion of gravity as if it were without a spiritual meaning; they cut the natural phenomenon away from its primordial religious connection. They demythologized it. They could simply no longer feel gravity in their understanding as symbolically related to an experience of transcendent significance. What is ironic, of course, is that their very loss of this dimension of experience was itself a sign of ultimate fallenness. They—and their society generally —were losing their capacity to perceive the universe about them as a repository of spiritual meanings. In the new science, there was to be no trace of sacredness left in nature. What is this if not the very state of cosmic abandonment that provides the basis for Protestant Christianity?

Essentially, gravity finds its place in the human understanding as the experience of fallenness, the loss of spiritual buoyancy. That is its root meaning. But the single vision of the scientific style required that this experience, being "merely subjective," being part of a failing mode of consciousness, must be eliminated. With Newton's speculations on gravity, we are at the beginning of a natural philosophy grounded in alienation, the measure of alienation being the degree to which the symbols used by a culture to achieve understanding have been emptied of their transcendent energy. Of course, from the standard scientific viewpoint, this is the whole value of Newton's thought. He at last objectifies and secularizes the phenomenon of gravitation. He "liberates" all thinking about up and down, rising and falling in nature, from its mythic and religious connotations. That, says the conventional wisdom, is what makes his approach "realistic."

"OCCULT PROPERTIES"

But to objectify gravity was to separate it from the experience that had always provided its meaning. As the scientist's derivative conception of fallenness, gravity could no longer be attached symbolically to a religious significance. This made scientific discussion of gravity strangely abstract—even for Newton himself, and he became much troubled. Yes, he could express gravity mathematically as a behavior of things in nature. But he could not help wondering if this thing he had now so ingeniously measured must not have *some* sort of substantial reality to it, something solider than mathematics. What *was* gravity besides an algebraic equation?

Newton finally contented himself that it was a "force" that acted at a distance. But this only took him into deeper waters. Instead of giving him the sort of tangible, material thing his science seemed to require, it gave him another deracinated abstraction. For the kind of ultimate cosmic force Newton invoked was also a symbol. As Durkheim recognized, all the strange, elusive, but seemingly indispensable "forces of nature" that haunt western scientific theory trace back to the original religious experience of *mana*, the sacred power. "The idea of force is of religious origin," Durkheim reminds us. "It is from religion that it has been borrowed, first by philosophy, then by the sciences." No primitive people acquainted with *mana* would have any difficulty grasping the idea of a force that acts magically at a distance; though of course they would translate the idea into a religious experience, an action of the divine. That would carry the idea of force back to its root meaning.

But Newton's fellow scientists, being objective in their approach to nature, could no more find the root meaning of force than they could of gravity. The notion therefore looked suspiciously meaningless. Was such a force there at all? If so, what was its cause? And how could it possibly act at a distance? Newton was hard pressed by such questions—but when it came to the "suchness" of gravity, he had no answers. His critics, even those who accepted his mathematics, accused him of inventing "occult properties." A major part of Roger Cotes's preface to the second edition of the *Principia* is spent fighting off these charges of obscurantism. Newton bridled at the challenge, but finished by giving up the problem. A "force" of gravity must exist, because how else to explain the behavior of the objectified universe? But, he confessed, "the cause of gravity is what I do not pretend to know, and therefore would take no time to consider it." On this point, said Newton in a famous remark, "I frame no hypotheses." Gravity was simply left as a measurable behavior of things.

In effect, this was to leave the key concepts of "gravity" and "force" suspended in a vacuum of abstraction. The only experiences that could restore their original meaning to these words lay on a transcendent level which was no longer in the repertory of western consciousness. So the terms finish as mere words tenuously linked to mathematical formulations. The same might be said of that other, even more critical term in the Newtonian synthesis, "law"—the most obviously metaphorical borrowing in science and probably the most important notion involved in launching the scientific revolution. It too traces back, even more obviously, to origins in religious experience. But as all these concepts have been drawn away from their root meaning by the demands of objectivity, they have come to seem more and more dispensable—like many another substantive noun in science. Unitl at last they are so much excess linguistic baggage loosely attached to the *real* thing—which is the mathematical description of behavior.

THE NEWTONIAN PHANTASM

Let us make one final observation about the idea of gravity as it comes down to us from the scientific revolution. As we have seen, objectivity demanded that Newton strip his scientific vocabulary of its symbolic resonance; one was no longer to talk about nature in animistic or visionary ways, lending transcendent meanings to natural phenomena. But the result was not, as one might expect, to make nature more physically real. True, from Newton onwards, there is a growing ethos of what we call "materialism" in western culture, carried mainly by the scientific tradition. But—paradoxically—that materialism is remarkably abstract; it is more an idea than an experience. We find more and more people thinking about matter and its attributes, but—as our discussion of the Romantic poets has suggested—with very little enrichment of sensory experience.

For example, Newton never once discusses the physical sensation of gravitational pull. He never explores gravity as a feeling—something that tugs at the body, shaping its movements, sculpturing its structure, grafting it into the natural continuum. There is no sensory awareness to his theory, only linguistic and mathematical conceptualization. Nor has physics since Newton paid any greater attention to the living experience of gravity on the organism and within the organism. It has not seen this in the least as an interesting line of inquiry.

Instead, Newton treated gravity as a relationship *between* bodies; it is a force acting at a distance that affects only the hypothetical mass-points of bodies. It does not physically permeate them. In short, the idea has been totally alienated—turned out and away from human participation. It is Out There, in the universe . . . an objectified something. As we observed in Chapter 3, single vision is as anti-organic as it is anti-symbolic. It has done nothing to deepen the quality of our sensory experience. Only now, three centuries after Newton, do we learn from our astronauts that gravity is as much in the body as oxygen is in the lungs and bloodstream. When it is subtracted, the organism deteriorates.

This astonishing neglect of the organic phenomenology of geotaxis happens not because there is nothing there of importance to learn. Modern dance (especially the work of Martha Graham) and Structural Integration therapy (the work of Ida Rolf) have made extensive explorations of gravitational dynamics within the body. Along these lines, we arrive at a deep physical knowledge of gravity that scientific empiricism has wholly ignored. But then Newton was a scientist—a *good* scientist; and science diets on abstractions. What he wanted was a quantifiable, conceptual model and only that. So in his work, we are left with a word, "gravity," no longer understood to be a symbol but only a cipher, no longer related to visionary or organic experience, no longer accompanied by its once dominant counterpart, levity. To this word Newton then attached various mathematical generalizations in order to describe the behavior of mass-points influenced by a mysterious force. In this way, he achieved an operationally efficient conception of gravitational phenomena. But his thought no longer had any conscious connection with experience or with symbol. We are a long way from root meaning. Perhaps we can now begin to see how revolutionary this scientific revolution was.

Thus the paradox of physics, the "basic" science on which all others build. The more determined the physicists become to be hardheadedly empirical, materialistic, mechanistic— "realistic" in every tough-minded sense of the word—the more cluttered their science becomes with mathematical abstractions, statistical generalizations, and purely theoretical, disposable models. Blake referred to the scientist's nature as a "Newtonian Phantasm." Why does it become so? Because scientists (like their culture as a whole) can no longer consciously relate symbol to transcendent experience. Nor have they that openness to the sense life which will allow them to perceive a symbolic presence in the nature they study. For such a sensibility, even so basic a symbol as the vision-flight, which undergirds all thought about gravity and levity, comes at last to seem "unreal" . . . "merely subjective." And since it is held to be unreal, it cannot be used to help us find meaning, because only what is *felt* to be real by people can be meaningful to them. So we are forced to search for meaning and reality elsewhere: in something conceived of as external and independent of mere subjectivity, something that is fact and not fantasy.

But once this inside/outside dichotomy has gained control of our experience, once we forget that a root meaning derives from an experience which is *at once subjective and universal,* the project becomes futile. Science and sound logic construe the traditional symbols as so many "propositions" about an "objective reality" and then proceed to "prove" them "meaningless." We are left to conclude that the entire human past was inhabited by simpletons and madmen hopelessly out of touch with the Reality Principle. Yes, they generated much interesting culture, but they were mistaken about its *real* meaning, which is to be found in class interest, Oedipal drives, tribal cohesion, legitimization of authority, etc., and which only our psychology and social anthropology can understand. Yes, they invented language—but having no linguistic sophistication or logical precision, they clearly did not know what they were talking about.

Meanwhile, as this self-congratulatory ethnocentrism makes a shambles of human culture, inevitably a philosophy and literature of despair grows up which has but one sad message to deliver. "Very well: if the Old Gnosis is meaningless, then life is meaningless."

After this fashion, the ontological priorities are inverted; we stand the world on its head as we secularize the cultural repertory. Or, as Blake put it:

The Visions of Eternity, by reason of narrowed perceptions,
Are become weak Visions of Time & Space, fix'd into furrows
    of death . . .

The shamanic vision-flight becomes an illusion; the airplane becomes the real thing. Then what is the old sorcerer who works by another priority of things to say when his apprentice asks, "But did I *really* fly?"

A symbol torn away from the transcendent experience that generated it is a morbid thing. It has died as surely as the body dies once the heart is torn out. The world we build from such cadaverous symbols is the world of the dead—Blake's Ulro. The symbols are still with us; they must be as long as there is human culture—language, art, thought, all are crafted of symbols. But dead symbols are counterfeits, in the same way that a well-embalmed corpse counterfeits a live body. And just as a corpse becomes more grotesque the more it is painted to imitate life, so a defunct symbol only grows ghastlier the more desperately we labor to disguise its death with the pretense of life.

This, I think, is what it means, most basically, to charge science with being reductionistic. It is the effort to make up a reality out of morbid symbols, symbols from which, in the name of objectivity, all sacramental vitality has been drained away. This ghoulish project cannot be *blamed* on science. That would be to mistake symptom for cause. The symbols have died in our culture as a whole. The activity we call science is what passes for natural philosophy in a culture that has collectively lost its sense of transcendent symbolism. It is our peculiar, crippled effort to understand nature as best we can by way of the lifeless symbols we inherit.

SEEING AND "SEEING"

The myths, rituals, linguistic metaphors, and artistic motifs with which the vision-flight adorns itself are of human making. But where experience chooses a bird or a mountain height as its symbol, it takes to itself a part of nature already there. The skylark is a symbol of the vision-flight, but in its own right as an object perceived, it is also an occasion for the experience which generates the symbol. The living bird can assume a transparency to the imagination, as if it were a "found poem." The poet who appropriates the skylark has borrowed his symbol from nature and incorporated it in the human cultural inventory. Was this perhaps how people learned the art of symbolic transformations, by discerning in the objects of nature around them that transparency which allows an object to act as the window for deeper meanings? "All spiritual facts," said Emerson, "are represented by natural symbols."

Here is a special magic which imagination works. It does not only project symbols, but *finds* them in the world. For the world is indeed filled with natural symbols that can assume an absolute transparency. Where the visionary powers

are robust, such symbols can appear anywhere and everywhere, in every pebble, shell and leaf; they can illuminate
the humblest objects. So Wordsworth tells how, as his visionary imagination strengthened:

> . . . then and there my mind had exercised
> Upon the vulgar forms of present things,
> The actual world of our familiar days,
> Yet higher power . . .

For those who have the eyes to see ("the spiritual eye," as
Goethe called it) all nature can become a script of root
meaning wherein everything is simultaneously ordinary and
sacred, at once itself and yet invitingly transparent. Where
this happens we have that magical or sacramental vision of
nature which is the antithesis of single vision.

"There may be," Goethe said, "a difference between seeing
and seeing; so that the eyes of the spirit have to work in
perpetual connection with those of the body." How effortless
this second way of "seeing" can be for the well-developed
imagination is nicely expressed by Don Juan, who, at one
point, tries to explain to his apprentice about the visionary
ambiguities of the world he sees about him:

> "Once you learn, you can *see* every single thing in
> the world in a different way."
> "Then, don Juan, you don't see the world in the
> usual way any more."
> "I see both ways. When I want to *look* at the world
> I see it the way you do. Then when I want to *see*
> it, I look at it the way I know and I perceive it in a
> different way."
> "But . . . what's the advantage of learning to see?"
> "You can tell things apart. You can see them for
> what they really are."

For the pagan and primitive peoples whom Jews and Christians alike have always reviled as idolaters, the moving air, the fire on the hearth, the rhythm of the seasons, the bird on the wing, the markings and movements of beasts, the streaming waters, the circling stars . . . all these, and the works of man's own hand are alive with an intelligible presence. They are symbolic doorways that invite the imagination through to high experience. Nothing in heaven and earth is without its transcendent correspondence. In Goethe's words, "Nature speaks to other senses—to known, misunderstood, and unknown senses. So speaks she with herself and to us in a thousand modes. To the attentive observer she is nowhere dead or silent." Similarly, Kathleen Raine has remarked that as we probe the symbols of nature more and more deeply, "we are asked to make increasingly animistic assumptions about the world."

But there has occurred in our culture—peculiarly—a strange and tragic process: a *densification* of the symbols, by which they lose their subtle nature. They survive for us, if at all, by hardening into purely secular things, historical projects, objective formulations. They are real for us *only* at that level. We are indeed like the prisoners in Plato's cave, transfixed by the shadows we see, sealed off from the sunlight. Even to mention the notion of transcendent correspondence would perhaps sound mystical in the most outlandish sense to the great majority of people in our society. Yet it is only to speak of what has been in other cultures a daily commonplace—and within our culture as well for an exceptional few. For the Blakes, Wordsworths, Goethes, and those who share their powers, it has been as natural as breathing to read the meanings of the world's symbolic script; one just does not see anything as a "nothing but," but rather as a "both/and." Which does not for a moment deny the reality of the natural object "in itself" or of any human artifact or project. Instead, the other "seeing" recognizes that it is in the nature of a thing "in itself" to be a symbolic presence.

The plant was, for Goethe, as real a thing as it is for any botanist; but also, it was the unfolding saraband of its growth, fertilization, flowering, and decay—a choreography of symbolic gestures. Its reality was on both these levels—indeed, the two realities were locked together hierarchically. To encounter the world in this way is to abolish the alienative dichotomy so that the distinction "In Here," "Out There" no longer obtains. That dichotomy cannot sensibly cope with the question, "where do we find the plant's symbolic meaning?" For what is "Out There" only acquires its naturally transcendent meaning when it has entered "In Here." Nothing can be a whole reality until it enters and mingles with what we call "subjectivity." This need not be an explosive psychic upheaval, an annihilating revelation that wipes out the personality and absorbs all things into "the godhead"—though this is the way the more dramatic mystics often describe the experience of a root meaning. But it is especially remarkable how in artists like Goethe and Wordsworth the experience is one of great calm and normality that seems only like a homecoming of the spirit. And in such a surrender to quiet rapture there is, I find, more conviction than in strenuous ecstasies.

Because our orthodox consciousness has become objectified (alienated) to the point of freakishness, there is much misunderstanding of what it means to "overcome the subject/object dichotomy." The usual academic reading of the experience takes it to be some sensational obliteration of identity—the dazzling effect many people seek in the psychedelic drugs. But sensitive reflection might best reclaim the experience from our "normal" state of alienation by small exercises in self-awareness which show up how meaningless the alienative dichotomy is. For example, Owen Barfield, in his *Saving the*

Appearances, asks us simply to consider where a rainbow is. In Here? Out There? The answer also tells us where the transcendent symbolism of natural objects is.

TECHNOLOGY AND MAGIC

It may well be that the richest symbols in human culture come down to us from an early generation of supremely gifted visionaries, shamanic geniuses touched by unique powers. Perhaps in the early evolution of consciousness mankind passed through a singular interval when the mind took fire as it never would again and the symbolic raw materials of culture were, like the phenomenon of human speech itself, generated all at once. Myth and occult tradition have more to tell us about this state of our development than science or scholarship ever will; for at least the myths are touched with a wonder that does justice to the event.

Clearly the great symbols have been with us for a very long while. Within recorded history, the major cultural activity has not been that of adding to the basic symbolic repertory, but of re-enacting the disciplines of visionary power and elaborating their contents. Exploring the richness of the symbols or lending them a new ethnic relevance: these are the foremost tasks of cultural life. For a great symbol is an inexhaustible potentiality. It is superabundant and all but cries out for endless restatement. It is there to be reworked; it needs incessant renewal.

So it is entirely right and natural that the symbol of the vision-flight should, in time, be projected in the shape of an airplane. Technology is also an art of symbolic transformations; its inventions unfold from consciousness as so many material embodiments of transcendent symbols. This deserves emphasis, since it might seem that what we have discussed so far dictates an anti-technological conclusion. It decidedly does point to a lesser status for technology; but let us be clear that technology draws upon the symbols as legitimately as any art or ritual. In fact, in a healthy culture, invention would properly be indistinguishable from art and ritual; technological progress would be simultaneously a deepening of religious consciousness.

There is no space here to recount a history of invention within the magical worldview. If I pause to mention the point, it is mainly to ease the fears of those who have come to believe that only the scientific worldview puts us usefully in touch with reality. This opinion is so prominent a feature of the conventional wisdom that, as we noted at the outset of this book, it can leave us baffled how mankind ever survived before there was an artificial environment.

Take only one example of magical technology. If the advent of urban-industrialism deserves to be considered one of the two or three major cultural transitions in human history, the invention of agriculture surely rivals it in importance. The industrial revolution, obviously enough, had been carried over the past two centuries by the scientific worldview. But how was the agricultural revolution transacted? Did perhaps some intellectual mutation suddenly occur among our neolithic ancestors which inspired them to take a "realistic" view of the plants and to suspend their superstitious ways long enough to undertake a few agrarian experiments? That is often the way the achievement appears in studies of prehistory: an unaccountable outbreak of rationality . . . or else a lucky accident.

But that will not do. Culture is a whole, and within a culture of myth, magic, and ritual one does not find isolated instances of scientific mentality. Agriculture was invented by people living within a magical worldview and *by virtue of* that worldview. Most likely it was (at least through the horticultural stage) an invention of women, who perceived in the fecundity of seed and soil an image of their own sexuality. From that initial poetic insight the technics of cultivation burgeoned into a splendid variety of sexual-spiritual symbols. The new agrarian cultures saw the earth as a mothering womb, the seed and rain as sperm, the crops as a bearing of offspring. The furrows in the soil were the female's vulva, the digging stick and plow were the male's phallus. The coming together of earth and seed, furrow and plow was a marriage. One celebrated this marriage and blessed the bride with sacrifices to ensure her fertility. What was born from that marriage was, like humanity, mortal. The autumn and winter were the death of the Corn God. Then the vegetation went underground as if into a grave. The womb had become a tomb. The earth and sky grew sad and barren. Now the land was a widow mourning for her dead consort, her divine child; one must join with her in her mourning. She was searching for her lost love through the netherworld. She found his corpse and nursed it; one helped her in her nursing with ritual festivities. He warmed to life and in the spring the goddess and her spouse mated again and brought forth. Tammuz and Ishtar . . . Isis and Osiris . . . Attis and Cybele . . .

Such are the familiar motifs that come down to us in a hundred variations as part of the oldest agrarian myth and ritual. *This* is how agriculture was understood and in no other way. In this form farming know-how was transmitted to every part of the globe. This was technology, but it was at the same time religion. It was true invention, but it was shot through with spiritual meaning. In this yearly death and resurrection of nature, in this fruitful union of earth and heaven, there was more than an economic payoff; there was a transcendent symbolism which served to feed the soul as much as the belly. Here was nature teaching the whole human personality its destiny by way of this cosmic display of deathless fertility. And on that symbolism a wealth of human culture was founded: myth, drama, metaphysical speculation, cultic rite, dance, painting, song, sculpture, architecture . . . It would be no exaggeration to say that more human energy went into these cultural elaborations of the symbolism than into agricultural labor itself. This was no alienated technics pursued single-mindedly for the sake of exploiting nature. It was a means of salvation; it was intrinsically an act of worship.

But it was *also* an economic means. And as such it *worked*. It prodigiously enriched the material existence of neolithic society. Which is the point I stress here: that technical progress of the highest order has taken place over and again within the magical worldview. The visionary imagination finds a utilitarian responsiveness in nature; it does not leave people helpless and wretched. To see the earth as Mother Earth is no superstitious mistake but a brilliant and beneficial insight. If we fail to appreciate any longer the vision of reality that belongs inseparably to that insight, it is not because we have grown smarter, but because we have grown very stupid about the meaning of symbols.

A similar account could be given of the magical worldview underlying the technics of hunting, metallurgy, weaving, brewing, mining, pottery. Mircea Eliade has written extensively on the sexual-religious symbolism that inspired primitive technology; he has shown how the lore of the metallurgist was so rich in religious overtones that it was even able to survive, in the form of alchemy, as a nature mysticism detached wholly from its technical origins. The Hellenistic mystery cults were much the same phenomenon: agrarian symbolism moved off the land, separated from its technology, and transformed into religious rite. In none of these techniques was the symbolism simply laid on as poetic decoration. Rather, the symbols directly translated the deepest perceptions of their culture. One finds very few societies like our own where a tool is nothing but a tool, instead of a richly symbolized and highly decorated cult object, and where work is not a sacred endeavor.

This much, however, is indisputably true. Where people find their way in the world by magic, their technology evolves far more slowly than we are used to. It is the project of many generations to work out the technology of a transcendent symbolism; much energy must be devoted to the rites and meditations attending. Sacred ways and objects are not manhandled by those who know their special status. This does not mean magical technologies never change. Agriculture did replace hunting among the neolithic societies; and all the basic handicrafts were invented and expanded within the sacramental vision of nature. We even have the more recent example of the Cheyenne Indians in the course of the eighteenth and nineteenth centuries moving into the Great Plains and revolutionizing their hunting technics by use of the horse and rifle; but without casting away the ancestral religion. Such changes do, however, take time, since in cultures that preserve a magical worldview no technique can ever be *just* a technique, or and artifact *just* an artifact. Everything must be much ritualized; there must be occasion to come together with one's fellows and celebrate the mysteries. One spends much time talking to rivers and beasts and trees.

How bizarre such a ritual regulation of technics must seem to us; and what a waste of time. V. Gordon Childe voices the conventional wisdom in his mocking account of primitive man making a tool for himself. (But how many of us who now suffer the agonies of a runaway technology will find much humor left in such easy sarcasm?)

> To make a D-scraper, collect a flint nodule (1) at full moon, (2) after fasting all day, (3) address him politely with "words of power", (4) . . . strike him

thus with a hammerstone, (5) smeared with the blood
of a sacrificed mouse.

No doubt about it: any culture that wishes to plunge itself
headlong into total psychic alienation and ecological disaster
had best begin by treating the Old Gnosis with uncompromising contempt.

THE ECLIPSE OF MEANING

> *Every natural Body is a kind of*
> *Black Lanthorne, it carries this*
> *Candle within it, but the Light*
> *appears not, it is Ecclips'd with*
> *the Grossnesse of the matter. The*
> *Effects of this Light are apparent*
> *in all things; but the Light it self*
> *is denyed, or else not followed.*
>
> *Thomas Vaughan*

No question, then, but the symbols must also find their
technological expression. Things go wrong only when a culture cuts the symbols away from their transcendent correspondence and so allows them to densify; then our sense
of reality diminishes. But in what sense "diminishes"? With
what justification may a densified symbol be regarded as the
expression of an inferior reality?

I have said that the root meaning of a symbol derives
from the experience that underlies it. That experience is
still there in a machine or historical project; the experience
of the vision-flight stands behind the image of airplane or

rocket. But once the symbol has been densified, the experience meets the resistance of a thickened medium and is
deprived of power. Only then do we begin to think of the
experience as being uniquely *in* this material object; the object comes to be "the real thing." As a result, we may still
feel an exhilaration, but we do not know what it is we are
actually responding to. In the case of flight, we think it is
the machine itself, its design and power . . . or perhaps the
physical sensation of overcoming gravity and moving through
the air. No other conception of flight seems real. The image
of the plane fails to carry us in full consciousness back to the
root meaning.

It is just for this reason that the airplane and rocket so
rapidly give out as engaging sources of experience. In themselves, they have too little emotional substance; they are
soon exhausted. Why else should air travel so early in its
history become a bore that must be offset by trivial in-flight
amusements? Why else should the Project Apollo moon shots,
after the first few landings, have dropped so remarkably in
the television ratings? When I was a child, people still used
to rush to the window to see a plane pass overhead; children
stopped playing to look up and follow it out of sight. Today,
as I write these words in the west end of London, a jet liner
packed with weary tourists roars over my roof every ninety
seconds . . . and I keep wax earplugs handy to muffle the
unwelcome noise. No one on the street bothers to look up
as the planes pass over. The image is too familiar and conveys nothing beyond itself. It has been depleted.

Here we arrive at the heart of the matter. A symbol that
has become dense carries no enduring *meaning* into life.
It has become only a ponderous and opaque object before the
senses; it cannot transcend itself. *Meaning* is the measure of
difference between live and morbid symbols: "meaning" not
of course in the trivial sense in which formal logic might
use the term, but as we use it traditionally when we ask

after the meaning of life itself. And for life there is no sense of meaning when the root meaning of the symbols has been lost. A culture that has only densified symbols to live by darkens with despair; it begins to brood over the meaninglessness of life, the absurdity of existence. More and more its psychotherapists find that what their patients suffer from is the existential void they feel at the bottom of their lives. The malaise of a Chekhov play settles upon daily life: the slow death of the soul. And no amount of Promethean history making or humanist bravado drives off this secret despondency for more than a little time.

Let us be honest enough to confront our culture in its entirety and ask: is it merely coincidence that, in the midst of so much technological mastery and economic abundance, our art and thought continue to project a nihilistic imagery unparalleled in human history? Are we to believe there is not a connection between these facts?

It is not that our technological achievements are all worthless, though even the greatest of them have often been overdone and oversold. It is rather that they are *meaningless* in the absence of a transcendent correspondence. They leave ungratified that dimension of the self which reaches out into the world for enduring purpose, undying value. That need is not some unfortunate psychic liability left over from the infancy of the race which we ought now to outgrow. It is, rather, the emotional reflection in mankind of that intentional thrust we can find in the most basic organic stuff, in the purposeful action of the protein matter that toils away in every cell of our being. How can we help but to be creatures in search of value and meaning? Not the tiniest microparticle of us but throbs with a lively need to work out its destiny. At the level of mind, that need becomes like an organ of sense, as eager to know its proper object as the eye to know light, the flesh to know touch. And that object is the reality of transcendent symbols.

Rhapsodic Intellect

Receive this stone which is not a
stone, a precious thing which has
no value, a thing of many shapes
which has no shape, this unknown
which is known to all.

Zosimos the Panopolitan

TO KNOW AND TO KNOW

There is a moment in Tolstoy's *The Death of Ivan Ilyich*
when the dying Ivan wanders back in memory to an episode
in his early education. He recalls a lesson in logic . . . the
familiar textbook syllogism that begins "All men are mortal."

"All men are mortal" . . . he knew it then, as a boy: an
indisputable fact. And here on his deathbed, he confronts
the fact again. "All men are mortal." But now there is a
special light that plays over the words, gravely changing their
character. It is as if Ivan has for the first time come to
know his mortality. And yet he has always known it, as a
matter of simple deduction from the premise. He has always
known it . . . but never known it, not as he knows it

here and now. There is nothing he can add to the fact;
he cannot increase its "information content." Nothing about
the fact has changed . . . and yet everything about it has
changed. Ivan has at last learned what these four words
really *mean*. He cannot say anything more or different than
when he was a schoolboy in his logic class; yet what he
knows now carries the weight of increased *meaning*. Ivan does
not know more; he knows deeper.

But where is this increased meaning to be found? No
longer in the words, but in the whole man who hears and
speaks them. It is in *the feel of the words* as they pass
through his mind and in the power they have acquired to
change his life. The words are the same, but now when Ivan
ponders them, there is a *resonance* that was not there before.
The meaning is in the resonance. And the resonance swells
within him until it rocks the foundations of his life.

There are ways of knowing and ways of knowing. Tolstoy's Ivan Ilyich is a study in existential knowledge, knowledge that possesses the resonance of personal crisis. The
knowledge of transcendent symbols has much the same character. It too must have its resonance: the resonance of root
meaning. In both cases, we are carried beyond verbal surfaces. In both cases, knowledge is deepened and personalized
by the impact of urgent experience, but without increase of
information. So we are left knowing more than we can say
—unless perhaps we have the gift of rhapsodic declaration.
We are in the position of the Zen master who began as a
novice knowing that mountains are only mountains, rivers
only rivers, and finished as a sage knowing that mountains
are only mountains, rivers only rivers . . . ah, but finished
knowing it *wisely*. How to talk about such things?

I have argued that the alternative to the idolatrous reality
we inherit from "single vision and Newton's sleep" is the
reclamation of transcendent symbols. This is to appeal for a
richer kind of knowledge, yet nothing that distinguishes itself

by yielding additional data about the world. That is the dilemma of the symbols. They fill our lives, our art, our language; but those who do not attend to the resonance of symbols will invariably move along the surface of experience, mistaking the densified derivative for its transcendent original. Failing to see the vital difference, they will insist that one tell them what *more* there is to know than they already know. Single vision, we must remember, deals in the same repertory of symbols as do religion, ritual, art. It covers much the same *quantity* of cultural space, but without qualitative depth. Its habit is always to interpret the symbol down and away from its transcendent source, to densify it into articulate fact, empirical object, and then to say, "See! *Here* we have the real meaning of the thing."

The Old Gnosis has, over the past century or more, been run through any number of ingeniously reductive "interpretations." Its economic, psychological, sociological meanings have all been filtered out for study. And of course these secular accretions are also there to be examined. They are part of the human story. But not all. There is that which remains behind when the accretions have been peeled away from the symbols. *Root* meaning. The gold amid the dross. God's portion.

RESONANCE AND LITERALISM

The peculiar degeneration of consciousness from which we suffer—the diminishing awareness of symbolic resonance—is especially a crisis of language. In our culture, almost uniquely, we have inverted the hierarchical relationship between rhapsodic declaration and literal prose, between matters of myth and matters of fact. Rhapsody and myth—the prime linguistic carriers of symbolic resonance—have long since ceased to be regarded as sources of knowledge. Whatever else Christianity borrowed from Judaism, it left behind the lyric spirit of prophecy, preferring desiccated theological discourse. It worked that weakness for literalism well into the grain of western consciousness until, in the modern period, most of our keenest minds had come passionately to believe, like Dickens' Mr. Gradgrind, that "in this life, we want nothing but Facts, sir; nothing but Facts." What else could follow from this but a culture whose realities are restricted to flat, functional prose, unambiguous quantities, and Baconian inductions. As a result, the one-dimensional language of the logician, scholar, and critic—and eventually of the technician and scientist—has been promoted to a position of omnipotence among us. Has there ever been such a culture of explainers and clarifiers, expounders and logic choppers?

Think how fanatically verbal our education is, our *good* education that strives for "excellence" by force-feeding children with reading-writing-and-arithmetic from the earliest possible age, and never ceases exercising that narrow range of skills from nursery school to graduate school. Lecture, textbook, recitation, examination, note taking, research, criticism, debate, discussion . . . from Dick and Jane to the seminar table and learned journal. If there is more to the human anatomy than the reading eye, the logical ear, and the articulating voice box, our schools know nothing of it. God help the painters and dancers, the musicians and contemplatives among our students! When we educate, it is invariably on the assumption that the meanings of things can be exhausted by making good, clear, logical talk about them. Where there should be the resonance of experience, we demand more language. Or better still: numbers. For modern mathematics has achieved the special status of a language devoid even of those last quavers of resonance that cling stubbornly to words: ambiguity, emotional shading, etymological echoes. To suggest in any of our academies that there are things words and numbers cannot and ought not try to cope with is to commit an anti-intellectual outrage. Like Ivan Ilyich, we are the prisoners of literal surfaces. For Ivan, it came as an astonishment and terror to realize that the logical premise "all men are mortal" had an experience attached to it. Besides the word "death," there was also . . . *death*. So too the symbols demand experience of us. They must be received with the openness of our total being. And when they take hold, they strike us dumb.

To live fully is to live resonantly. Language isolated from its non-verbal resonances can adequately express only the monotones of life: simple information, unambiguous operations. Yet the major effort of analytical and positivist philosophy over the past several generations has not been to amplify resonance, but to imperiously drive all meaning into just such monotonous linguistic formulations . . . and then to shoot on sight whatever refuses to be herded into this intellectual concentration camp. As if language had become the private property of logicians, technicians, and scientists, and henceforth all communication must be modeled on the hard-edged exactitudes of laboratory research—without even allowance for the contribution that intuition, hunches, word-play, metaphor, and rule-of-thumb make to all worthwhile research.

Here we have another ironic example of how Christian religious psychology has paved the way for the skeptical positivism that was to be religion's deadliest opposition. The literalist mentality has never been more at home than in Christianity, where it has systematically reduced religion to abstract discussions of Belief and Doctrine. "A God to whom human words cannot point," Harvey Cox has said, "is not the God of the Bible." Sad to say. For where religion invests so exclusively in discursive theology, insisting that the word divorced from vision and conduct can embody the spirit, the effect is to scotch the resonant meaning of language. So we have those grotesque idiocies of Christian history that have made religion stink in the nostrils of so many decent people: the official catechism learned by rote, wars fought over articles of faith, the judgment of people by the creeds they mouth, the persecution of heretical professions.

All this comes of unloading upon ordinary language a burden it cannot bear. The proper question to ask of any people's religion is, "What have they experienced and how may we share in this experience?" Christianity has single-mindedly pressed another question: "What do they say they believe and how does it square with our creed?"

I vividly recall my own mind-murdering struggles with the Catholic catechism in childhood. Question and answer, question and answer . . . a jackbooted parade of lifeless verbal formulas, every one of them to be recited letter perfect, every one of them to be literally believed under threat of corporal punishment. Dogma and doctrine were marched through my brain like storm troops flattening every natural barrier childish inquisitiveness might raise. It was open warfare on young imagination. Can there be any question what damage has been done to the visionary powers in our culture by generation after generation of such ruthless creed-mongering? For the good of my soul, I was being programmed like a human computer with data points of the true faith. Among all my so-called religious instructors, there was not one, I think, who knew that even Saint Thomas laid aside his theology once the supreme vision had settled upon him, saying, "All that I have written seems to me like straw compared with what has now been revealed to me."

Understandable enough that the rebellious positivist should despise the authoritarian folly of dogmatic theology to the point of dismissing all religious discourse as "meaningless." It was my own reaction to the inanity of Christian literalism. But this only repeats the dogmatist's error. It overlooks that the meaning of visionary and metaphysical parlance is in the resonance of its symbolism. That is where its power lies to shape conscience and consciousness without resort to inculcation. In his conviction that language without resonance is the full measure of reality, the positivist is really the secret blood brother of the dogmatic theologian. The one nails his literalism to creed and scripture, the other to empirical verification. The one dismisses whatever lacks doctrinal authority, the other whatever lacks empirical fact. Between them, as between two millstones, the symbols have been ground to dust. And from those little literal bits we have pieced together the language of operational efficiency and single vision.

DREAM MEANINGS

I spoke in an earlier chapter of dreams, and of how they suffer the dream-thieving habits of orthodox consciousness. Yet, insofar as we retain them, dreams are the most vivid, continuing acquaintance we have with symbolic resonance. That is their special charm and enjoyment. Our dreams are symbols in endless transformation. Whatever falls under their spell ceases to be a "nothing but"; it becomes "both/ and," entering into that infinite play of visual and verbal ambiguities which stream of consciousness writing and surrealist painting have salvaged for the contemporary arts.

A sphere appears in my dream . . . and becomes a ball, a familiar childhood toy I had forgotten. At once the dream begins to heap up associations around this ball. It plays exuberantly with the word "ball" . . . with every possible rhyme, pun, slang connotation, homonym. Suddenly, there are elegant people dancing on and around the ball; it has become

a fancy-dress ball . . . where people are having a ball . . .
balling the jack . . . drinking highballs . . . getting drunk
to the eyeballs . . . Balls: a man's balls . . . to have balls
. . . to be on the ball. Ball: to ball a woman . . . to ball
up the job . . . to bawl like a baby. Ball: bald. Ball:
fall . . . as hair falls . . . leaving you bald as a billiard ball.
People named Ball: John Ball . . . George Ball . . . Lucille
Ball. Ball: Baltimore . . . the Baltimore & Ohio . . . high-
balling down the line . . . And the dream plays too with
the form of the ball, until it reflects every sort of round,
rolling, bouncing thing . . . globes, planets, wheels, balloons,
bubbles, circles, eggs, oranges, coins, fireballs, goof balls, golf
balls, footballs . . . a baseball which is "the old apple"
. . . forbidden fruit . . .

Out of this chaos of imagery and wordplay, the dreaming
mind rapidly improvises a strange dramatic coherence all its
own, a totally original story in which everything echoes everything else and each thing rapidly slides off toward secondary
and lateral associations. And perhaps, if this is one of those
rare numinous dreams that can haunt the memory for years,
there will be a ball that begins to glow and swell until it
becomes a splendid, shimmering globe, bright as the sun,
transparent as glass . . . a celestial orb . . . a crystalline
sphere . . . the Hermetic world-egg. This too figures in the
dream, even though I may know nothing of Ptolemaic astronomy or alchemical lore. Nevertheless, by way of the
dream, I am delving to the root meaning which has made
the sphere "somehow" the uniquely right symbol of perfection
for people everywhere.

What is the meaning of the sphere that appears in my
dream? *All* of this is the meaning. Everything in the dream
is at once the resonant meaning of that one image. It is not,
as practical waking logic requires, some one thing connected
unequivocally with cause or effect or strict deductive proce-

dure. It is simultaneously scores of seemingly incompatible possibilities, personal and transpersonal, trivial and profound, woven together into one crazy quilt texture of meanings.

No one in our time has exploited this quality of mind more brilliantly than James Joyce. In the pursuit of resonant meaning, he worked language more mercilessly than any poet ever has. I think not always with the happiest results. His dream epic *Finnegans Wake* is too often a torment of language where what is needed is the advantage of cinematic montage. Lacking that necessary dimension, the book too often strains at the limits, until it smothers itself in scholarly puns. Joyce's weakness was his pedantry. Nevertheless, the mode of consciousness Joyce explored through all his works —and I sometimes think most subtly and successfully in his short stories—was meant to be the salvation of transcendent symbolism. For Joyce the sacred had always to be rooted in the profane, the universal in the vulgar particulars of life. Nothing in his world lacked magic, no matter how commonplace. One city could be the universe; one man all men; one woman all women; one night of dreams the history of the world. It is all right here, Joyce is telling us, right under foot, on the pavements, in the shop windows, in the hills and rivers, the small talk and gossip, the men and women around us. And it has always been that near by. All we have ever needed is the eyes to see, the ears to hear.

Joyce required no moon rockets to write the Odyssey of modern man. Leopold Bloom wandering the streets of Dublin was enough of an adventure for him to build on. And in an old vaudeville ditty about the drunken hod-carrier Tim Finnegan who breaks his neck and then rises from the dead when his friends slosh whisky over his coffin, Joyce could uncover the living symbol of death and resurrection. What a way this is to see the world. Not a bit of it wasted, not the least scrap or crumb. For Joyce, every garbage head held epiphanies.

"THE FIRST TILL LAST ALSHEMIST"

If one had to locate so extraordinary a talent in our culture, perhaps it would be more accurate to think of Joyce neither as poet nor philosopher, but as an alchemist of the spoken word. Joyce called himself "the first till last alshemist," and that, I think, is his tradition. For alchemy was also a study in dream logic. Its object too was the experience of resonant meaning: a science of the transcendent symbols.

At the core of the alchemical vision there stood the Great Work, a sacramental experience whose symbol was Oneness. As in Goethe's natural philosophy, the guiding image was the union of opposites. The Great Work may or may not have been performed as a laboratory project; for many alchemists, the use of apparatus seems to have been unnecessary. In either case, the essential activity was meditative not manipulative. Where experiments were actually carried out, their function was to act as a mandala-like focus for contemplation. Even the apparatus used had a symbolic purpose. Thus the althanor and mercury bath were seen as the womb or the grave or an egg in its nest: images of death and resurrection.

In the alchemical imagination, everything brought under study experienced such symbolic transformations, often passing through several levels of metaphor. Here was, par excellence, a poetry of nature. The polarities of the universe were, for example, symbolically embodied in the sulphur and quicksilver. In turn, these chemicals became the lion and the dragon, the King and the Queen, the sun and the moon, and innumerable variations of the dark—light, male—female antinomies. The union of opposites which produced the master symbol of Oneness was known as the chemical marriage of the King and Queen, or as the androgynous Mercurius. The lion and dragon unified became the winged griffin. The Oneness of nature was also symbolized in the sun, and the sun in its turn as gold, which became to all other metals what the sun was to all the planets, their spiritual suzerain.

The ever-elusive "philosopher's stone," which drew forth the gold of the soul, wore a hundred symbolic costumes depicting the many subtle stages of spiritual regeneration. The stone might be the eagle, the white dove, the *elixir vitae,* the staff of Hermes (the caduceus), the chrysosperm, the salamander that lives in the fire, the lily of five petals . . . and, in Christian Hermeticism, the grail or Christ himself.

For all of these there were further symbolic elaborations —metaphors of metaphors of metaphors which reached out like poetic vines in all directions to embrace beast and plant, the heavenly spheres, the colors of the spectrum, geometrical forms, the metals and minerals of the earth, and countless allusions from Jewish, Christian, or Islamic scripture. In true alchemy, the body itself became the symbolic althanor of the Great Work and, as in the cakra yoga, its every part assumed a transcendent correspondence. The purification alchemy sought was as much of body as of soul. The ubiquitous genital symbolism of alchemical lore (the phallus associated with tree of life, rod of Moses, staff of Mercury; the vulva associated with crucible or mystic rose, the uterus with the bain-marie) was no unconscious sublimation of eroticism in the Freudian sense. It was deliberate and unashamed. The sexual images were overtly the vestments of sacramental mysteries, as they are in Tantric Buddhism.

To be sure, alchemy had its own vices. As time went on and as the symbolic vocabularies of great alchemical adepts were collated into later systems, the metaphorical congestion became overpowering, a potent brew that easily intoxicated and clouded the vision. There are many alchemical texts where the lore has piled up into a hopeless poetic palimpsest.

Moreover, European alchemy suffered from the same vice of literalism that dogged mainstream Christianity. Essentially, Hermeticism was a surviving strain of nature mysticism which sought to preserve the sacramental vision of the universe that Christianity had excluded as idolatry. But many of the lesser minds that were drawn to alchemy imported the Christian weakness for literal meaning and were only after the "vulgar gold"; for these, physical transmutations were, like the Christian miracles, an evidence of true belief. The more robust mystical powers of Sufism tended to save Islamic alchemy from such confusion and cheapening. But for penetrating European minds, like Boehme and Blake, Goethe and Rimbaud the root meanings that had generated the symbols were never obscured.

"As above, so below." This was the simple visionary formula that illuminated the symbolic proliferation. The thrust of alchemy was to transmute every element of common experience into a potential epiphany, to unite heaven with earth, time with eternity and so to dissolve the alienative psychology of Christian orthodoxy which had made the sacred *super*-natural. Here was the very antithesis of objective detachment, a meditative discipline that worked to assimilate all things to their transcendent correspondence and finally to the master symbol of Oneness. For the mature alchemist, everything in nature, in the works of man, in his own body, served to remind of his place in the natural continuum. The whole universe became for him—as for Blake, Wordsworth, Goethe, Joyce—a magical object. This was why every alchemist began the Great Work (in thought or in deed) with a *materia prima* composed of the world's vilest, most cast-off stuff: dung, urine, carrion, decomposing vegetation, the proverbial witch's brew of bizarre and disgusting ingredients. But it was precisely from this organic dross that he would make his philosopher's stone. The Work began in putrefaction, in the darkness and corruption of the life cycle, under the symbols of the skull and the carrion crow, of lusterless lead and brooding Saturn. And so it would proceed, in prayer and concentration, for weeks, months, even years, often through hundreds of painstaking distillations . . . until the red tincture of life and light, the spiritual Mercury, emerged to redeem the world's mortality. "For everything that lives is holy."

It is the constant theme of Hermetic literature how the philosopher's stone hides in the waste and offal of the world —especially there, where it can best bear witness to the universality of the divine. It might be in the dust at one's feet. The early Greek alchemist Zosimos called the stone "a precious thing which has no value . . . an unknown thing which is known to all." And the sixteenth-century tract the *Gloria Mundi* tells how the stone is

> familiar to all men, both young and old, is found in the country, in the village, in the town, in all things created by God; yet it is despised by all. Rich and poor handle it every day. It is cast into the street by servant maids. Children play with it. Yet no one prizes it, though next to the human soul, it is the most beautiful and the most precious thing upon earth, and has the power to pull down kings and princes. Nevertheless, it is esteemed the vilest and meanest of earthly things.

I suspect that our science inherits much of its fascination for the common stuff of the world from the Hermetical tradition. But it only finds that stuff, when finely studied, *interesting*—not symbolically resonant.

If Goethe had had his way (and if the alchemical tradition had survived into our own time) he would have returned Hermeticism to the more immediate contemplation of living nature. It was in the plants and animals, minerals and open skies that Goethe found his transcendent symbolism. As for

Joyce, his genius was for finding the symbols amid the rubble of the metropolis, tarnished on the surface but bright as ever inside. Who knows how far this awareness of symbolic resonance might not have carried into modern science itself if the Hermetic sensibility had not been obliterated? Philip Rawson has observed that to the Tantric adept, "the table of elements or the abstract form of molecular structures and particle physics amount to revelations of the actions of Devata and can be welcomed as such." Surely no alchemist would have been surprised to learn that the secret of life does have after all to do with the sacred sign of the double helix— the caduceus borne by Hermes.

I think any effort to revive alchemy in our time—except as Joyce did in the form of art, or as Norman Brown has done in the vertiginous wordplay of *Love's Body*—would be little better than a pedantic curiosity. The tradition has been decisively ruptured, and as with all spiritual disciplines, once the direct master-to-apprentice line of transmission has been severed, there is little chance of recovering the real thing. I am not, in any case, suggesting a return to this particular version of the Old Gnosis. Rather, I offer alchemy as an example of perception and intellection that had not yet been torn away from the symbolic sensibility of our dream life. The result was a natural philosophy which insisted on the paramount place of meaning, purpose, and poetic splendor in its investigations. What can one do but lament how this wisdom, once so creatively part of our culture, was destroyed by the intolerance of single vision? That Hermeticism should ever have been written off as superstition is a measure of how gross the sensibilities of "enlightened" minds can become. The common notion that alchemy was some manner of proto-science that did not "work," a failed magic that could not change lead into gold, betrays the degeneration our consciousness has suffered. How far we wander every day from the self we are each night in our dreams.

For of course alchemy *did* work in the way that matters most. But when we seek, by our nuclear physics, to transmute the elements in some "realistic," "practical" way, what happens? We finish with the hydrogen bomb as the crowning proof of how maniacally our science "works."

There have been efforts—notably by Jung—to salvage Hermeticism by psychologizing it. This has helped restore some of the tradition's dignity, though at the cost of narrowing its metaphysical range. In effect, Jung's studies of alchemy only provide another set of symbolic correspondences in which to express the vision. A mystical psychology is no more the final interpretation of alchemy than was the old mystical anatomy in which the adepts phrased themselves. Some Jungians, however, tend to treat their inventory of psychic symbols as *the* meaning of the tradition. But the alchemists were talking about the unconscious mind in exactly the way they were talking about metals and planets. Their symbols are not projections of psychic processes in any sense that makes them "merely subjective." The symbols must always transcend the In Here–Out There dichotomy or their root meaning will be lost. As Titus Burckhardt has observed:

> It is . . . quite vain to wish to describe psychologically the real essence of alchemy or the secret of "the chemical marriage". The more one strives to dispense with symbols and to replace them with scientific concepts of one sort or another, the more rapidly does that spiritual presence vanish which is the very heart of the matter, and which can only be transmitted by symbols, whose nature is conceptually inexhaustible.

There is, however, one thing we might yet glean from Hermeticism, especially with the help that artists like Goethe, Blake, and Joyce give us: the spirit of rhapsodic intellect.

I mean by this a ready awareness of resonance which never lets an idea or action, an image or natural object stray from its transcendent correspondence. Such an intellect loses none of its precision, need sacrifice none of its analytic edge. But it remembers always and first of all where the language in our heads came from. It remembers the visionary origins of culture when all things were, as they still might be, symbolic doorways opening into the reality that gives meaning.

ONENESS: "OBJECTIVELY ANALYZED . . . SUBJECTIVELY PENETRATED"

The demise of alchemy marked the end in the western world of natural philosophy grounded in a sacramental vision of nature. Remnants or faint echoes of Hermeticism survived into the Romantic movement to bolster its resistance to single vision; but only a few Romantics were much studied in the tradition. Others—like Wordsworth and Novalis—worked up their nature mysticism almost wholly from spontaneous inspiration. But the supreme goal of alchemy and of the Old Gnosis generally—the ideal expressed in the many variations upon the symbol of Oneness—did not vanish with the tradition. Like all the archaic symbols, it was appropriated into the era of single vision stripped bare of its resonance. It became the fundamental principle of modern science: the uniformity of nature.

The transition this great symbol has undergone is worth special attention, for here we have another striking example of how a transcendent symbol is densified and thereby deprived of meaning. In this case, since we are dealing with the master concept both of the Old Gnosis and of modern science, the degeneration of the symbol brings us face to face with the most critical moral and ecological issues of the day.

From Newton's demonstration of universal law down to the dramatic discovery by the molecular biologists of the chemical uniformity of all living things and the regularities of their genetic code, the passion of modern science has been to unify the variety of phenomena. Scientists may spend much time at piecemeal, highly specialized research, at the laborious collection of fact, at the dog work of checking and rechecking results. But the great achievement in science—unanimously honored by every laboratory drudge and Baconian lint-picker —is a theory that orchestrates all the scattered findings and serves as the paradigm for generations of research to come.

Thus the high excitement that has attended biochemistry over the past generation stems from its success at dovetailing biology into basic physical theory. "The ultimate aim of the modern movement in biology," Francis Crick has stated categorically, "is to explain *all* biology in terms of physics and chemistry"—a goal which most molecular biologists would now consider achieved at the molecular and cellular level in all but the fine points. So now many scientists, like Crick, look to new frontiers. They anticipate the extension of the physical-chemical-biological continuum to higher orders of complexity, to problems of growth and organic co-ordination, and finally to the intellective processes of the human brain itself. At which point behavioral psychology and artificial intelligence research would doubtless bid to take over with their rigorously objective explanations of language, thought, value, and culture. At the same time, science works to extend the continuum historically, back toward the origins of life, (mainly along the lines of A. I. Oparin's theory) into the prebiotic stage of chemical evolution, and from there to connect with the theories of contemporary cosmogony. Once linked together, these major areas of research would comprise an unbroken physical continuity leading across cosmic time from the inorganic to the organic, and at last to mind and culture. This would give us a modern great chain of being, forged entirely from reductive, analytical explanations.

Now, there is a problem about this physical continuum that has led some highly reputable scientists (though I think not many—sad to say) to doubt that the chain can ever be joined without seriously lowering our standards of what it means to "explain" or "understand" nature. The problem is the classic reductionist dilemma and is worth a deal of discussion in its own right. But I have no wish to take up that question here. Rather, I want to emphasize how scientific reductionism is swayed by an age-old zeal to find unity in nature—even at the expense of agonizing distortion. Reductionism cheapens the great chain of being. It flattens the natural hierarchies and manhandles wholistic and intentional processes; it is, for all the talent that its research requires, hasty and small-minded science. But it is nonetheless another expression of mankind's perennial love affair with the supreme symbol of Oneness—though in this case that love, in its insensitive aggressiveness, approaches an act of rape.

> The sense of being at one with nature—we all have it at times . . . [J. Bronowski has said] as a strangled, unformed and unfounded experience. But science is a base for it which constantly renews the experience and gives it a coherent meaning.

"Unformed and unfounded experience . . ." Is that indeed how we are to understand the towering images of unity that come down to us since time out of mind? As a mere hunch . . . a lucky guess? As an unproven hypothesis awaiting the advent of scientific method to become "coherent"? Here is a classic example of the ontological priorities being stood on their head. Think of the heritage of living insight from which the human race learned its love songs of the unitary vision. Merely to list the variations on that theme would fill a book. Lao Tzu teaching how "the great Tao flows everywhere" . . . the Vedic wisdom which can say of all things the eyes may light upon *"tat tvam asi"*—that's *you!* . . . the Avatamsaka Sutra that transfigures the universe into the Buddha's sacred body of light . . . the mighty Hermetic Uroborus inscribed "One Is All" . . . the *Wakan-Tanka* of the American Indians, whose presence made every object holy, as much the stone as man . . . Blake summoning us "To see a world in a grain of sand" . . . Dylan Thomas discovering that "The force that through the green fuse drives the flower drives my red blood" . . .

No, we are not dealing here with a hypothesis, or with "strangled, unformed and unfounded experience." We are confronted with absolute conviction expressed with a rhapsodic power that sets the mind afire. We are dealing with an insight that has been *lived* as only the truth can be lived. We are dealing with *knowledge*. Here are the voices of people who have *known* unity with all the force of a veridical experience. It is from them that our science inherits the concept of cosmos, the meaningful whole. The visionary knowledge of Oneness is the symbolic original; the uniformity of nature which our science now labors so awkwardly to piece together like a collage of experimental findings and mathematical generalizations is the derivative.

Is it not clear what has happened to the knowledge of Oneness as it has passed into single vision? We have here once more a symbol that has been densified into a fact of the physical universe. Once the expression of a transcendent experience which dictated the ideal of human brotherhood and demanded a sensitive solidarity with nature, Oneness has become for us a piece of information about the constitution of matter or an inferential principle passed on to us by physicists, chemists, biologists. Dimly, somewhere behind the fact and the principle, we may still catch a glimmer of the transcendent correspondence, feel its dramatic pull upon our imagination . . . but we finish with objective cognition, not with experience. Certainly Oneness is true at the physical level; the symbols translate with validity on every level of reality. *But Oneness as we know it is not an experience.* It does not ravish the heart and impose a loyalty. It does not open us to an irresistible ethical demand. In what sense do we know that all things are one? In just the same way we know that acceleration due to gravity is thirty-two feet per-second-per-second. We know it at second hand and on good authority —as Ivan Ilyich in his boyhood knew that "all men are mortal." We know it . . . and yet we do not know it at all. For there is no resonance to our knowing.

"Goethe," Charles Gillispie observes, "asserted the biological continuum, the stream of life."

> Now, the continuum is by no means always the wrong side. Who studies to perceive the unity of nature necessarily adopts it. . . . But the mathematical expression of the continuum was geometry, as in Einstein, as in the Newtonian void, as in Descartes, and ultimately back in Platonic mathematical realism. This is rational. It is objective, or may be. . . . Goethe's nature is not objectively analyzed. It is subjectively penetrated. His is the continuum, not of geometry, but of sentience, not to say sentimentality.

"Objectively analyzed . . . subjectively penetrated." There we have precisely the difference, the world of difference, between the two ways of knowing a symbol. What our science forgets (or even denies) is that the continuum "subjectively penetrated" is indeed knowledge of the One: a knowledge primeval and universal, the basis of intellectual enterprise, artistic creation, and moral passion. And that is what distinguishes *really* knowing from *merely* knowing.

ECOLOGY AND THE USES OF MYSTICISM

The psychic distance that separates the scientist's objectified uniformity of nature from the Oneness of the Old Gnosis is immense. It is the distance separating St. Francis from Albert Camus' Stranger. Existentially speaking, it is all the difference between the life of one who is at home in the universe and the life of one who feels himself to be a cosmic freak.

Universal law, the mathematical continuum, the physical continuity of life . . . none of these do justice to the symbolic resonance of the chemical marriage. But there is a better place to listen for that resonance in the contemporary world. The science we call ecology is the nearest approach that objective consciousness makes to the sacramental vision of nature which underlies the symbol of Oneness. In fact, the ecologists at times fall so much under the spell of the Old Gnosis that they very nearly wander over that frontier of the mind which divides respectable science from nature mysticism.

Ecology has been called "the subversive science"—and with good reason. Its sensibility—wholistic, receptive, trustful, largely non-tampering, deeply grounded in aesthetic intuition—is a radical deviation from traditional science. Ecology does not systematize by mathematical generalization or materialist reductionism, but by the almost sensuous intuiting of natural harmonies on the largest scale. Its patterns are not those of numbers, but of unity in process; its psychology borrows from Gestalt and is an awakening awareness of wholes greater than the sum of their parts. In spirit, the discipline is contemplative and therapeutic, a concernful listening with the third ear. Lynn White, Jr., has appropriately nominated St. Francis as the patron saint of ecology; I would be inclined to name the Hermetic philosophers and Romantic poets as its founding fathers. And from somewhere further back still, the vision of the Tao feeds into the study.

Moreover, like all the healing arts, ecology is through and through judgmental in character. It cannot be value-neuter. Perhaps this is its most marked contrast with the other sciences. The patterns ecologists study include man in body, mind, and deed, and therefore they prescribe a standard of health. What violates the natural harmony must be condemned; what enhances it, be endorsed. For the ecologist, being right means living right; the virtues of prudence, gentleness, mutual aid flow gracefully from his study. Ecology is the closest our science has yet come to an integrative wisdom. It, and not physics, deserves to become the *basic* science of the future.

It is all to the good—gloriously so—that our science should be enriched by this new sensibility. But this *is* a departure from scientific tradition, and it comes late in the day. How great a departure may be gauged by Otis D. Duncan's undisguised ambivalence in his article on human ecology in the latest edition of the *Encyclopaedia Britannica*. (1971)

> The holistic emphasis implied by the very idea of human ecology has been a continual threat to the unity of the discipline. Comprehensive treaties on the subject typically have represented expressions of social philosophy rather than empirically grounded statements of scientific theory. Indeed, numerous commentators have put forth the view that human ecology must remain primarily a philosophic viewpoint rather than aspire to the status of a systematic discipline.

In other words, the more life-saving wisdom ecology offers us, the less right it has to "aspire" to the lofty "status" of a true science. The scientific community properly makes haste to embrace the ecologists as their spokesmen in the environmental crisis. But, in truth, this is rather like the Catholic Church, at a late stage, canonizing a Joan of Arc, whom its previous custodians had burned at the stake for witchcraft.

Still, better late than never.

Yet there is a deeper issue here—one which even our keenest ecologists have yet to confront. And when they do, will they be able to keep their discipline on the safe side of scientific respectability? Potentially, there is heresy hidden within this new ecological sensibility that now spreads through the industrial world, though perhaps only those who come to ecology already dubious about the sufficiency of the scientific vision of nature can as yet recognize that fact.

Let me illustrate what I mean. The point I am after emerges clearly in the following highly imaginative reading of primitive ritual. The passage comes from the landscape architect and city planner Ian McHarg and nicely reveals the ecological insight he brings to all his work.

> Among the Iroquois the bear was highly esteemed. . . . When the hunted bear was confronted, the kill was preceded by a long monologue in which the needs of the hunter were fully explained and assurances were given that the killing was motivated by need, and not the wish to dishonor. Now if you would wish to develop an attitude to prey that would ensure stability in a hunting society, then such views are the guarantee. . . . The hunter who believes that all matter and actions are sacramental and consequential will bring deference and understanding to his relations with the environment. He will achieve a steady state with his environment—he will live in harmony with nature and survive because of it.

McHarg's sensitive interpretation is welcome relief from the ethnocentrism that would have us think our prescientific ancestors were not quite wholly and competently human. Here we have the sort of sympathetic insight that is now making anthropological activists of so many young people, influencing them toward a "neolithic conservatism" (Paul Goodman's phrase) that seeks to revive the primitive folkways.

But read the passage again, and notice: McHarg's appreciation of what he calls "the pantheist view" (the transcendent experience of Oneness) is entirely functional. His conclusion is that the sensibility he describes just happened, by a stroke of luck, to be serviceable; it worked to produce a ritually regulated ecosystem. Now, he argues, industrial society must invent a similarly successful expedient for dealing with its environment. But when McHarg takes up discussion of that prospect, he begins by asking "where else can we turn for an accurate model of the world and ourselves but to science?"

And here is the crux of the matter. *Is this purely functionalist analysis of the perennial nature mysticism sufficient?* Or do we not see here once again a transcendent symbol in the process of densification? Ecology stands at a critical crossroads. Is it, too, to become another anthropocentric technique of efficient manipulation, a matter of enlightened self-interest and expert, long-range resource budgeting? Or will it meet the nature mystics on their own terms and so recognize that we are to embrace nature as if indeed it were a beloved person in whom, as in ourselves, something sacred dwells?

The counsel of ecology is caution. But *why* should we be cautious? Only because our own poor hides are at stake? That is one answer. And by the terms of that answer, nature remains objectivized, if more expediently exploited. But there is another possibility. We must deal cautiously with nature because caution is an expression of love, and our love is invited— in no merely metaphorical sense.

Sooner or later (in fact, the time is now) ecology will have to come to grips with the sensibility of that Iroquois hunter— with the vision of all the nature mystics—by way of something more than a reductionist functionalism. It will have to confront in all honesty the paramount fact that modern science in its profoundist ecological insight is indebted to religious traditions reaching back to shamanic origins. For the experience of nature's Oneness burned bright in human awareness long before Newton found the numbers with which to caricature that great truth.

Ecology already hovers on the threshold of heresy. Will it be brave enough to step across and, in so doing, revolutionize the sciences as a whole? If that step is to be taken, it will not be a matter of further research, but of transformed consciousness. Kathleen Raine, in a single line of poetry, gives us the razor's edge of the issue neatly honed: "It is not birds that speak, but men learn silence."

For many of our cultural drop-outs who have already learned that silence—which is the symbolic resonance—ecology represents a last tenuous connection with the scientific mainstream. It is the one science that seems capable of assimilating moral principle and visionary experience, and so of becoming a science of the whole person. But there is no guarantee ecology will reach out to embrace these other dimensions of the mind. It could finish—at least in its professionally respectable version—as no more than a sophisticated systems approach to the conservation of natural resources. The question remains open: which will ecology be, the last of the old sciences or the first of the new?

A SCIENCE OF RHAPSODIC INTELLECT

This book has had much to say that is severely critical of the scientific worldview. Because science dominates the reality game of high industrial society, I am convinced that a hard critique of its psychology now has everything to do with restoring our cultural health. If we fail to alter that game radically, neither sanity nor democracy has much chance of holding out against the technocratic imperatives of the artificial environment. For that matter, science itself is not likely to survive as more than a caricature of its finest aspirations unless it joins in the adventure of expanding consciousness—though this is sure to cost it most of the privileges it now enjoys as the brain trust of the technocracy.

There have been many wise prescriptions offered for the ills of our single-visioned science. Abraham Maslow has called for an "hierarchical integration" of many modes of knowing, including those we are learning from the Zen and Taoist traditions. Lewis Mumford has long been advocating a science based on "an organic world-picture," rather than mechanistic models. Lancelot Law Whyte has sought to unite art, ethics, and natural philosophy within a "science of form" whose genealogy traces back to Goethe. Thomas Blackburn has employed the concept of complementarity as a model for integrating sensuous experience, intuition, and objectivity. Arthur Koestler has become a major public voice for those biologists and psychologists who dissent from reductionist and behavioral methods, demanding a new emphasis on wholes and systems. My views share a large common ground with all these thinkers. The essence of their critique and mine is that science is far too narrowly grounded in the personality. It closes out too much experience and in this way drastically distorts what it studies. As a result, it has become a highly productive research machinery; but what it pours forth does not add up to a life-enhancing natural philosophy.

But I believe science has more to do than live down its reductionist and mechanist vices; it must also purge itself of the idolatrous sensibility it inherits from its Judeo-Christian background. No change of scientific mind will go far enough that does not return us to the sacramental vision of nature.

On this point, my own thinking echoes that of Seyyed Hossein Nasr. Like him, I believe our science must once more learn to contemplate nature "not as an independent domain of reality but as a mirror reflecting a higher reality, a vast panorama of symbols which speak to man and have meaning for him." In brief, the task is to create a science of rhapsodic intellect.

Perhaps this is too much to ask of a tightly organized profession seemingly in the flood tide of success and bedazzled by its capacity to proliferate "hard results." Single vision is so far removed from the participative and multidimensional consciousness which rhapsodic intellect requires. And yet, in another sense, rhapsodic intellect begins as close to home as the symbols that guide the scientific mind in its downward course through time and matter. If only the scientists might recapture for us and for themselves the root meaning of those symbols and realize the debt they owe to the visionary powers from which the symbols stem. Even in the barest mathematical formulations of science the symbols linger on, waiting to be warmed into life. The numbers have not always been so bereft of resonance as modern philosophy has labored to make them. They too were once objects of contemplation. Within the Pythagorean tradition—which is doubtless a comparatively late version of the old number magic—every act of calculation served as an expression of partial harmonies within the One.

A reductionist mathematics, eager to get on with its manipulative measurements, sees more utility in atomizing the One and then counting up its parts into discrete and meaningless agglomerations: heaps of things here and there in the void. "The atoms of Democritus and Newton's particles of light . . ." But that is not the only way to experience number. There is also an *internal* counting which preserves the sense that all things are parts of the whole, that the many is a playful flux within the One. For such a sense of number, every equation is a balancing out of polarities, a making of one out of two. As for the geometric forms: they have never lost their charm for the artist, and probably not for the mathematician either. It is unlikely that any amount of utilitarian objectivizing will ever wholly dispel the symbolic resonance that arises from that strange tension between shaping line and unshaped space, between bounded and boundless. The forms and numbers need lose none of their usefulness for remaining in touch with their old mysteries. Though of course meditation takes time from calibration; it slows down the research and is nothing that can be run off by a computer.

But all this is only to observe once again the paradox that makes transcendent and densified symbols both identical and yet antithetical—like the positive and negative versions of the same photograph. Which should warn us that a science of rhapsodic intellect can never be achieved on the cheap by simply tacking an afterthought on the business as usual of non-stop research. Nor can it be done by processing young scientists through an additional course of study in Taoist nature mysticism. It is a matter of changing the fundamental sensibility of scientific thought—and doing so even if we must drastically revise the professional character of science and its place in our culture. There is no doubt in my mind that such a revision would follow. Rhapsodic intellect would slacken the pace and scale of research to a degree that would be intolerable by current professional standards. It would subordinate much research to those contemplative encounters with nature that deepen, but do not increase knowledge. And it would surely end some lines of research entirely out of repugnance for their reductionism, insensitivity, and social risk.

What place would science then occupy in our culture? Stephen Toulmin has compared scientific thought to the activity of map making, suggesting that the relationship of theory to nature is much like that of a map to a landscape. I find this a fruitful analogy to ponder—though like all analogies it has its limits. Like a map, a sound body of scientific knowledge helps us to plot short-run successful journeys through those parts of the world that have been charted. It is an ingenious utilitarian device which allows us somewhat greater certainty in our prediction and adaptation. Without question, this is a precious human skill, and a fascination in its own right. But just as no map can ever be more than a selective approximation of its terrian, so no theory can be more than a schematic representation of nature. That does not make it a "mere" model, for there is always some point of real contact between the theory and the portion of nature it relates to. But that point of contact is no more than a point, and it can be devilishly difficult to say precisely what its character is, beyond saying that it orders the world for more successful manipulation.

Scientific knowledge, like a map, ignores a great deal for the very sake of such utility. That is the basis of its selectivity. We forfeit the whole value of a map if we forget that it is *not* the landscape itself or anything remotely like an exhaustive depiction of it. If we do forget, we grow rigid as a robot obeying a computer program; we lose the intelligent plasticity and intuitive judgment that every wayfarer must preserve. We may then know the map in fine detail, but our knowledge will be purely academic, inexperienced, shallow. To that extent, it may finally become disastrously impractical, thus defeating the original purpose of the map. As every wise explorer in history has known, not even the best map can replace the advice of a native guide, who may not even know what a map is. But the guide knows the pitfalls, shortcuts, and hidden resources of the country. He knows where the dangerous beasts are and the fever spots. He knows how to listen for the secret messages of the land and how best to live there.

When we insist on making scientific expertise the arbiter of all knowledge, it is exactly like believing that cartographers know more about the terrain than the natives who live there, or the artists who have come to paint its beauties, or the priests who tend its holy places. And that is (to borrow a phrase from Bentham) folly on stilts. It leads to the absurd arrogance of the book-learned sociologist who insists that, on the basis of his behavioral models, he knows more about slums and ghettos than the people who live in them. Or the sort of systems analysis that includes every kind of expertise, but never the experience of the people on the receiving end of the planning. Or the sort of psychotherapy that assumes the doctors know more about alcoholism or drug addiction or psychosis than those who have lived through the terrors. Or the sort of astrophysics that finds it sufficient to know everything about the stars except why they were once regarded as divine.

When scientists think about nature or society or people, they are really thinking about a vast collection of contrived schemes and models which are indispensable to the research their profession respects as worthwhile. The artificiality of these schemes is extreme and the gaps between them will always be large enough to let whole worlds of experience fall through. To believe that all the schemes will one day be pieced together into a perfect replica of reality is like attempting to construct a "perfect" map that leaves nothing out. If that could be done, it would provide a map as big and miscellaneous as its terrain—and therefore wholly impractical. But the very justification for the scientist's highly abstracted way of viewing the world is its selective, well-defined utility. Even the intellectual fascination of working out the puzzles of theory is related to utility as its validating touchstone. What comes of the enterprise is, after some fashion, supposed to "work"—if only to help sharpen the pure researcher's ability to anticipate the outcome of his next experiment.

Our culture has become extremely good at this style of thinking over the past three centuries. We have polished it into a superb skill—in the natural sciences at least. (The behavioral sciences are a dubious project rather like making maps of imaginary landscapes that change by the hour and are recreated afresh by their inhabitants in the light of what every new map reveals.) The pride we take in this skill is legitimate. But it is a restrictively specialized vision of reality. Discussion among scientists is like discussion of the advanced problems of map making in a cartography seminar. The cartographers are talking about their maps and not landscapes. That is why what they say frequently becomes so paradoxical when translated into ordinary language. When they forget the difference between map and landscape—and when they permit or persuade us to forget that difference—all sorts of liabilities ensue. The risk then is that we may drift hopelessly out of touch with the landscape itself, so much so that whatever progress we continue making in the techniques of cartography is only an expedition deeper into learned stupidity. At which point, it would be better to close down the science for the sake of regaining the sense we were born with.

Worse still, we are in danger of letting ourselves be mystified by experts whose rarefied knowledge now seems vastly beyond our reach. And that is the beginning of technocratic politics. In effect, the artificial environment gives us a map to live in, instead of a landscape—and so a world peculiarly beholden to the skills of mapmakers.

But worst of all, to mistake maps for landscapes is to degrade every other way of knowing the world's terrain into some sort of illusion, and in this way to close off the richest sources of joy and enlightenment in the personality. Then we forget that to map a forest means less than to write poems about it; to map a village means less than to visit among its people; to map a sacred grove means less than to worship there. Making maps may be absorbing and useful; it may take enormous intellectual talent and great training; but it is the most marginal way of knowing the landscape.

Does it lower the status of science to view it in this way?

Obviously it does. But then science has been lionized out of all proportion by the necessities of urban-industrial life and by the political opportunism of the technocracy. Science never deserved to stand on the cultural pinnacle it now so gracelessly occupies; it will find itself a more becoming human activity once it steps down from that summit. As a human skill it is as worth pursuing as any; but its product, unless integrated into an ideal of rhapsodic intellect, has nothing to do with what gives life meaning.

What chance is there that such a transformation of sensibilities will take place within the scientific community? I think not much. Rhapsodic intellect would mean a revolution of consciousness, and true revolutions never happen from within the palace—especially when the living inside is so easy. If the sacramental vision of nature is ever restored to science as a discipline of the sacred, the job will be done from outside the profession—by mavericks and dissenters who have sacrificed the mandarin privileges of their profession for the sake of staying close to the Old Gnosis. In the technocratic society, a natural philosopher pays a heavy price for believing that wisdom counts for more than expertise. Big Science passes over such poor investments in favor of high-yield research specialists. But already there is a sizable contingent of adventurous science drop-outs young and old willing to keep company and mingle sensibilities with artists, nature mystics, far-out philosophers, and assorted cultural subversives. It is an alliance that will surely bear fruit in time.

Our science (like our technics) is maniacal because it bears the cultural burden of finding meaning for its society where meaning cannot possibly be found: in a reality of densified symbols. The task is an exercise in futility. For a densified symbol is precisely one that has been alienated from its root meaning. It is only good for power-knowledge. Nevertheless, science continues to thrust its way fanatically into ever denser regions of being, hoping to strike through to some ultimate truth that will vindicate its quest . . . the secret of life concocted in a test tube . . . the origin of the universe . . . the mechanisms of intelligence . . . But all it finds are reductionist caricatures, nihilist know-how.

If the Reality Principle of the modern world is ever transformed, the change will happen, perversely and heretically, at the fringes of our culture and work its way in toward the center. The scientists, the guardians of single vision in urban-industrial society and the intellectual linchpin of the technocracy, may be among the last to hear the news.

CHAPTER 12

The Visionary Commonwealth

Whenever historical destiny had brought a group together in a common fold, there was room for the growth of a genuine community; and there was no need of an altar to the city deity in the midst when the citizens knew they were united round—and by—the Nameless.

Martin Buber

THE STORY SO FAR

My argument has been that single vision, the ruling sensibility of the scientific worldview, has become the boundary condition of human consciousness within urban-industrial culture, the reigning Reality Principle, the whole meaning of sanity. On that Reality Principle and on the artificial environment which is its social expression, the technocracy has been raised as a benevolent despotism of elitist expertise. Whatever else we must do to supplant the technocracy, we must, indispensably, throw off the psychic style from which it draws its strength. This is necessary not only if democracy is to be preserved, but also if we are to be healed of the death-in-life of alienation, which is the psychic price of single vision.

Our politics has become deeply psychological, a confrontation of sanities. But if our psychology is not itself to be debased by scientific objectification, then it must follow where liberated consciousness leads it; into the province of the dream, the myth, the visionary rapture, the sacramental sense of reality, the transcendent symbol. Psychology, we must remember, is the study of the soul, therefore the discipline closest to the religious life. An authentic psychology discards none of the insights gained from spiritual disciplines. It does not turn them into a scholarly boneyard for reductive "interpretations," or regard them as an exotic and antiquated mysticism. Rather, it works to reclaim them as the basis for a rhapsodic intellect which will be with us always as a normal part of our common life.

And suppose the reality we live by should experience such a revolution . . . what sort of political program would follow from that?

Nothing less, I think, than that we should undertake to repeal urban-industrialism as the world's dominant style of life. We should do this, not in a spirit of grim sacrifice, but in the conviction that the reality we want most to reside in lies beyond the artificial environment. And so we should move freely and in delight toward the true postindustrialism: a world awakened from its sick infatuation with power, growth, efficiency, progress as if from a nightmare.

One reflects for a moment on how prodigious a task this is . . . on the burgeoning megalopolises eating their way voraciously as cancers across the world landscape . . . on the proliferating mills and factories, dynamos and highways, mines and agrindustrial combines . . . on the accelerating techniques of communication and transport . . . on the torrential flow of research and development . . . on the tightening global networks of finance and trade . . . on the disciplined, if disgruntled millions moving obediently through the intricate patterns of production and consumption. One reflects on the scale and pace and monomania of all this which comprises urban-industrial society, and how unthinkable it seems that this vast apparatus should ever give way to another cultural form, that we should even see it slow down in its expansion or diminish in its scope.

Unthinkable, yes. Almost as unthinkable as it would have been only four generations ago to imagine that we could have created the monster in the first place. But it was of our making. And it is yet ours to unmake and replace.

DEURBANIZATION

As the final illustrations for his book *The City in History*, Lewis Mumford selected two pictures that represent alternative futures. One was a sketch by a group of Japanese city planners of a perfected artificial environment, a constructivist assemblage of plastic and metal domes piped and wired into a central command-and-control module. It is a city-sized machine for living, with not a thing in sight that is not man-contrived. Mumford might have found any number of important minds at work on equally morbid fascinations. Buckminster Fuller, Paolo Soleri, Constantinos Doxiadis are only the more famous exponents of these Buck Rogers vistas of the future. Nor is this merely the stuff of academic fantasy. Had the RAND Corporation's plans for a nationwide civil defense shelter system been steamrollered into official policy in the early sixties, we might now be approaching just such a totally controlled, hermetically sealed, wholly inorganic environment.

Over against this prospect, Mumford placed an old Chinese scroll painting of the Spring Festival: a garden filled with sunlight and wildlife and people, all resting easy in the Tao. It is of course no blueprint for Utopia, only an image. But such images are the very foundation of intelligent praxis. They suggest the feel of what we are searching for. In this case, a graceful symbiosis of people and nature, an organic community.

To my own way of thinking, this latter image of the post-industrial future does not rule out the survival of cities or of selective industrial production. It is emphatically not an anti-technological choice; it is rather a matter of keeping first things first. The city and industry are not in the picture, but they could be somewhere just behind it, contributing to it. The important thing is that they should exist in a supporting role and be strictly subordinated to the general pattern of life. They should be options and possibilities, the storehouses of certain skills and resources, but not the dominant mode.

To call for the de-urbanization of the world is only to recognize the historical truth that city life has never suited more than a strict minority of mankind—mainly merchants and intellectuals. Of course intellectuals tend to make much of the city because it is congenial to their temperament and necessary to their role in the world. They relish the fast turn-over of new ideas, the intensive interaction of contrasting tastes and values. But the city is, at best and even on its modest, premodern scale, hectic and wearing. It burns up its human material rapidly and therefore has not been to the liking of many. That is why, until the latter nineteenth century, cities were few and small by our standards. And yet, though small, they were often far more culturally fruitful than the contemporary megalopolis. Athens of the Golden Age and Renaissance Florence, for example, were about the size of Lubbock, Texas, or smaller. We now tend to think of cities as necessarily immense, and the bigger the more truly citylike—as if more people in the city meant more people sharing the spirit and benefits of the city, a foolish non sequitur, rather like assuming the more people in church on Sunday, the more true Christians in the world.

As anyone who loves city life knows, size kills cities and replaces them with cadaverous "urban areas" full of people who loathe the city and appreciate none of its essential values. In *The Secular City,* a sadly misguided encomium on "technopolitan culture," Harvey Cox has praised the supercity as "an ingenious device for vastly enlarging the range of human communication and widening the scope of individual choice" —which rather suggests that every dormitory suburb and decaying slurb in America enjoys the lively ethos of New York's Greenwich Village, or Chicago's Near North Side, or Berkeley's Telegraph Avenue. But there are not more than a few dozen inner-city neighborhoods in the entire United States where something remotely like real city life can be found, and most of these are smothering under pressure of the hypertrophic urbanism around them. When cities swell into urban areas, it is their fat that increases, not their creative heart and vital organs. The essence of city living was never size or density, anonymity or mobility; those are the liabilities of the city. But they are as much as most urbanized Americans will ever know of city life.

What do cities mean to most people now living in them? Crime, dirt, congestion, expense, hustle, danger, noise, aggravation, high blood pressure, unwanted violations of privacy in the midst of terrifying isolation, trouble, trouble, trouble. Why then do people live there? Because it is where the work or the welfare are . . . or are most likely to be. Because the towns and villages they or their parents left behind are now even more dismal and depressed places to live, the futureless remnants of a destroyed American past. They, like the millions who have flocked to the city since industrialization began, were driven by necessity or drawn by the lure of high wages. Where would they rather be? In a suburban lotusland where life is (so the realtors tell them) clean, quiet, neighborly, lawful, leisurely, private, sane, and where the kids can grow up straight and safe. So as soon as they can afford to flee, they flee. Though seldom far. They wind up somewhere further out in the sprawling conurbation, where they continue to suffer most of the disadvantages of the city (plus worse commuting problems) with none of the benefits. The suburb is simply a failed effort to escape the city on the part of people who remain economically tied to the city. Yet the suburbs grow and grow.

Everywhere in the world today cities are stuffed with people who are not citified and have no wish to be. That is why all urban problems become steadily more intractable. Cities are not buildings, freeways, cultural centers, or real estate. Cities are essentially people. And people who hate cities have no interest in saving them. Why should they? The city is their cage, not their home. That is the one fact most city planners and city politicians in both the developed and underdeveloped countries choose to ignore in their desperate effort to move with the tide of history and somehow make megalopolis work. But one cannot build cities out of people who are anti-city.

Nor should we try. The real solution to the urban problem is massive de-urbanization. We must find ways out of the city for those who want to leave. Well-developed rural and village life, autonomous small towns must become a live option, a necessary kind of variety. And I am not referring to villages and towns that are characterless metropolitan satellites. Ideally, as in ancient Attica, the country roundabout should be regionally integrated with the opportunities of an accessible, humanly scaled polis. The gates of Athens respired rural dwellers in and out of the city in a regular rhythm; that was one of the secrets of its vitality. However it is to be done, it is imperative that the cities should be scaled down and thinned out, and the choice of living free of them be vastly increased. We must come to see that enforced, wholesale, and rapid urbanization has been an irrational obsession of the industrial ethos. We must recognize that the continuation of this freakish historical departure has nothing to do with population pressures or the necessities of a high living standard. Rather, we are the victims of a cultural style—a passion for megatechnics and artificiality—which only the urban area can embody in its full, diseased magnitude. We have defined the city as progress, rural and village ways as backward, and we have shaped our economy to suit this distorted conception of historical necessity. How such a bizarre vision of reality has made its way in the world has been the subject of this book.

To be sure, we could design an economy in which every inch of field and forest, every ounce of natural resources was subjugated to the appetite of the metropolis. And then indeed it would seem that there was no open space left on the face of the earth where a town or hamlet or family farm might stand, and that urban concentration was absolutely imperative. That is precisely what we are in the way of doing as we expand the artificial environment to encompass the globe. But, as this chapter will suggest, the economy of the artificial environment is a fabric of waste, extravagance, compulsive consumption, and purely technogenic necessities. The pressure which we tend to interpret wholly as population pressure is largely the product of a sick lifestyle. One should be able to say this without being misunderstood as meaning that population creates no problems in its own right.

AN ECONOMICS OF PERMANENCE

As for the selective reduction of industrialism, this requires a searching discussion of the meaning of work. Heavy industrial plant does save labor, and to reduce its presence drastically would mean doing a deal more work in other ways. The great question is: how much work does industrialism save that we really need to have done at all; and how much more does it do that we would rather have done on a handicraft or intermediate technologies basis—for the sake of conserving other values?

We have become so accustomed to the dreary notion that work must be exploitative, alienated drudgery, that it seems almost futile to raise that question now in public discussion. For most people, work is a bore and a burden; it is done for other people's profit and to other people's specifications. It is done for money, rarely for love. So of course everyone rushes to unload their labor on to the machines and the big systems. These in turn justify their existence by grinding out the swanky garbage which the official economics tallies up into a statistical mystery called "the standard of living." And the void that is left behind when the machines have taken over the drudgery that no one ever wanted to do in the first place is called "leisure"—a vacuum rapidly filled with cheerless, obsessive getting and spending, with idiocies like pre-packaged tourism (the chance to make an international nuisance of oneself), or with pure boredom.

But where work becomes a personal project and is done in community, its character is wholly transformed. It can even become, as it was for the Christian monks and has been for most primitive peoples, a form of prayer. Work can be the chance to innovate, fraternize, and serve. Its tools and patterns can be filled with transcendent symbolism. It can be a fulfilling expression of the personality. But we are a long, long way from that.

Just as we are a long way from realizing, as Lewis Mumford has for so long cogently argued, that the true object of political economy is plenitude, not plenty. An economics that does not, like the "biotechnics" of the living organism, balance itself by the standard of enoughness is bound to be maniacal. It has lost sight of the existential values which commodity values only exist to further. These vices of our economic thought have of late been criticized by many wise heads and there is no point in repeating the arguments here. Even some very square economists, under pressure of the environmental crisis, have come round to seeing the validity of what E. F. Schumacher has called "an economics of permanence." Which means, for the developed societies, zero growth—if not an extended interval of overall anti-growth within a new ordering of priorities. "Anti-growth" is surely an odd way to have to express a positive value. But the conventional wisdom forces us toward paradox. I suspect that a major effort to expand public mass transport in the cities while rapidly phasing out the automobile would, on balance, show up as a loss of "growth." So too, if people began to give up on tourism, thus forcing the airlines to cut back on new orders, that would also show up as a reduction of growth. But meanwhile life would have become saner, the air cleaner, the streets safer, the world quieter . . . and everybody's cost of living would have been lowered . .

Robin Clarke has proposed it as a "golden law" that the technology of the future "will have to be valid for all men for all time." And that is surely what our guideline must be: an economics which uses neither people nor nature as its proletariat. From the vantage point of the artificial environment, of course, such a discriminate leveling down of super-

industry in favor of humanly scaled, labor-intensive alternatives looks like a retreat to rags and ruin. One nearly despairs
of the possibility that our entrenched economics of alienation,
greed, and anti-sociability will ever lose its authority over
people's minds. But there is one way forward: the creation
of flesh-and-blood examples of low-consumption, high-quality
alternatives to the mainstream pattern of life. This we can see
happening already on the counter cultural fringes. And nothing—no amount of argument or research—will take the place
of such living proof. What people must see is that ecologically
sane, socially responsible living is *good* living; that simplicity,
thrift, and reciprocity make for an existence that is free
and more self-respecting.

Currently, many well-intentioned ecological propagandists
are busy wrapping zero-growth economics in the hair shirt of
dismal privation, as if a healthy relationship with nature must
mean grim, puritanical self-denial. This is not only politically
futile as a stance in public debate, but it is simply untrue.
Economy of means and simplicity of life—voluntarily chosen
—have always been the secret of fulfillment; while acquisitiveness and extravagance are a despairing waste of life. That
ought to be a platitude. In our situation, it is a heresy.

"WHY TRIBE?"

At least in outline, it is already becoming clear what sort of
society people seek once they have broken the spell of the
urban-industrial Reality Principle. We can see the postindustrial alternative emerging in a thousand fragile experiments
throughout America and Western Europe on the part of the
young and the no longer young: communes rural and urban;
voluntary primitivism; organic homesteading; extended fami-

lies; free schools; free clinics; handicraft co-operatives; community development coops; Gandhian ashrams; neighborhood rap centers; labor gift exchanges . . . the entire range of social improvisations one finds reflected in publications like the *Whole Earth Catalog* and *The Mother Earth News*. Here is the new society piecing itself inventively together within the interstices of the old.

Almost without exception, these experiments blend into the tradition of anarchist socialism. There is nothing doctrinaire about the matter; probably few of those involved have ever read Kropotkin or Malatesta. They have no need to. Their anarchism is the healthiest kind: a natural, rebelliously personal response to the distortions of urban-industrial life and the technocracy, as spontaneous as the need to breathe free after airless captivity. It is remarkable that even those young militants, both black and white, who loudly, if vaguely, lay claim to being Marxists, Leninists, Trotskyites, Maoists—I suppose mainly for the shock value of running up the banner —are more naturally anarchist than anything else, even if they will not admit it. They spare little thought for the problems of industrial discipline that occupied Marx, Engels, Lenin; less still for the national unity or the military necessities of the people's army. And for the judgments of scientific expertise they have no use whatever. Their politics runs to workers' control and community home rule, seemingly without any awareness of how antagonistic the tradition of "scientific socialism" has always been to such decentralist ideals. Even the current militant infatuation with guerrilla insurgency belongs in spirit to Makhno's black flag, not Trotsky's red army. Here and there one happens upon old-style apparatchiks still young in years; but in truth there is no public left in the west for authoritarian, top-down radicalism. It simply would not hold together from midnight to dawn. There is not the willingness to depersonalize, or the patience with external discipline.

No question but that the ingrained radical resistance to bossism and elitist privilege has much to do with the anarchist ethos of contemporary dissent. But though anarchism is, outstandingly, the politics of ruggedly independent people, of mavericks and boat-rockers, there is something more to these experiments. When Gary Snyder (in *Earth House Hold*) raised the question "Why tribe?" he thought the answer had much to do with the advent of a new organic awareness which links people once more to the great tradition of the hunters and gatherers, the essential society in which mankind lived a hundred times longer than in the cities. Doubtless this is so. Communitarianism is the political expression of ecological intelligence. Anarchism has always been, uniquely, a politics swayed by organic sensibility; it is born of a concern for the health of cellular structure in society and a confidence in spontaneous self-regulation.

If Darwin patterned his biology (unconsciously) on the image of cutthroat capitalism and *Realpolitik,* Kropotkin took his model of nature from the peasant and tribal communes of the Siberian frontier. There he discovered among people the same mutual aid and organic co-ordination he was later to discern in nature generally. From Kropotkin, who found more collaboration than contest in the progress of life, we inherit a sort of neo-Taoist naturalism and communalism that has ramified through the political thought of people like Patrick Geddes, Lewis Mumford, Herbert Read, and Alex Comfort. Along other lines, the same organicist sensibility flows down through Wilhelm Reich's psychiatric yoga into the Gestalt anarchism of Frederick Perls and Paul Goodman, here with a special new emphasis on the liberation of the total organism. I suspect this bright sense of organic harmony can be tracked back to the sacramental vision of nature that was so prominent a feature of Romanticism.

But there is one more overtone that must be added to anarchist politics—I think the most important. Ours is becoming—against all the odds—an age of self-discovery and personal integration: the process Jung called "individuation." The old Romantic lust for uninhibited personal development is with us again—but now no longer confined to a few artist-rebels. As this quest for the whole and authentic personality digs deeper into the psyche, it inevitably finds its way back to the rich religious disciplines of self-realization, since there is no improving on these. For those who embark on this inner journey, anarchism becomes a natural tendency; it is the political style most hospitable to the visionary quest. The relationship is ancient and indisputable—the politics of eternity has always automatically become communitarian politics. We see this in the life and thought of the Taoist sages, every one of them an anarchist outlaw. The monastic orders within every religious tradition have been assertions of the anarchist instincts. So too the pietist communitarianism of the late middle ages, the evangelical sects of the Reformation (especially among the "Everlasting Gospellers" of England—Blake's tradition), the Transcendental Utopias of nineteenth-century New England. The original Buddhists and Christians naturally constituted themselves as autonomous socialist communities. The same has been true of every contemplative school and mystery religion in history. The stronger the mystical sensibility, the stronger the longing for anarchist brotherhood and sisterhood.

In our own time as well, the two tendencies continue to move hand in hand. Gandhi's politics has proved to be prophetic in this respect. While much of Gandhi's energy went toward nation building, his mysticism made him inveterately hostile to the imperious demands of the national state. He was never at home in the Congress Party and refused throughout his lifetime to accept any official position in Indian government, even after independence. Rather, his bent was for the village community, handicraft technics, and the meditative communion of the ashram. It was on these that his

economic thought centered. Similarly, the irresistible need of
every young person who has been turned on to Zen, or Sufism,
or Meher Baba, the irresistible need of every adult whose
transcendent longings have been awakened by Gestalt or sensitivity training, is invariably to find like-minded others, to become this special group unto itself: the commune, the one
place in all the fierce, foolish world where men and women
may call their souls their own.

This is a great and hopeful point to ponder, especially
when we weaken toward a "political realist" cynicism. The
clear lesson of history is that whole and healthy people who
have tasted the visionary splendors are a poor material for
mass movements or armed collectivities. They simply have better things to do with themselves than play power politics.
True, they want control of their own lives; they want independence—which must not be mistaken for isolation or total
economic self-sufficiency, goals that may be of dubious value.
But beyond that, they want the peace and personal intimacy
that alone allows for spiritual growth. And that means the
life of small, congenial groups. As the Old Gnosis comes back
to mind in our time, once again people become—like most
religious communitarians of the past—pacifist and anarchist.
They disaffiliate, decentralize, cultivate non-violent relationships, look after their own needs. That is the natural style of
the visionary commonwealth.

It is easy to make light of the mystic and religious element
in these communitarian experiments, even to write them off
as an outlandish epiphenomenon. But I think that is dead
wrong. The visionary strain is the heart of the matter; it is
the best assurance of a sane, humanitarian politics, and certainly the most durable base on which to build communities.
It gives them a creative center and a positive meaning. It
makes the common life a withdrawal *to* and not merely a
flight *from*. Nor is it very perceptive to reject the visionary

commonwealth as being politically irrelevant and so irresponsible. For one thing, no community today can ever remove itself so far from the urban-industrial network that it can for very long avoid fighting for its privacy, freedom and peace of mind, for fresh air, pure water, self-determination. There is no wilderness remote enough to isolate the most determinedly apolitical drop-out more than temporarily. And wherever the community takes up its fight, it gives new life to those values of personal liberty and dignity which the artificial environment has all but obliterated. Even if the visionary commonwealth is never more than a relative handful in the city and the wilderness, its role is apt to be like that of the medieval monastics: to exemplify an ideal of life by which the many may judge themselves and the world. The power of such a living example must never be underestimated. Certainly, if over the next few critical generations there survives in the collective memory anything like a decent sense of what it means to be a free and fulfilled human being, it will be due to the standard that has been set and defended by the communitarian minority.

We must remember, when we talk politics in the technocratic society, how important the fine art of psychic pressure and leverage has become. Our economy today is wholly dependent upon inventing what the hucksters cutely refer to as "needs people never knew they had." Our political life is similarly dependent on a subtly engineered conviction that all human aspirations can be gratified within a perfected urban-industrialism—and *only* there. Unless people remain obsessed with acquisitiveness, fixated on their selfish material needs, convinced of their own absolute incompetence and equally convinced of the technocracy's omnipotence, the artificial environment will begin to dissolve like a house of sugar candy in hot water. The visionary commonwealth is in fact and by example exactly such a solvent of the social order.

Why tribe? Clearly because we are dealing with a definite, tightly integrated constellation of perceptions and values: egalitarian social ethics—the sense of organic harmony—the need for visionary self-discovery. Wherever this constellation succeeds in reshaping the consciousness of people, the Great Society begins to disintegrate into communitarian cells; into cults, fraternities, religious collegia, small congregations of the saved. The metropolis, the nation-state, the empire . . . for men and women desperate for the health of their souls, such depersonalized collectivities have never been a place they could call home; even less so the corporation, the bureaucracy, the trade union, the party. These can only for a time put on the mask of Big Brother and counterfeit the ethos of community. Stalin and Mao may posture as heavy fathers of the nation; American corporations may pretend to be one big happy family; the fatherland may try to disguise itself as a Gothic tribe. But such deceptions soon break down under the weight of their own lies. Nothing better may replace them, only ugly, angry cynicism. But the deception is too difficult to maintain with conviction.

So now we see our own technocratic America beginning to sprout with communitarian ventures, almost all of them shot through with a mystical sensibility that determines family pattern, diet, architecture, work ethic, group ritual, education, relations with land, wildlife, and neighbors. Alicia Bay Laurel's *Living on the Earth* is a bright example of what I mean. Not a chore or a job in the commune but has its transcendent resonance, its quiet Zen lyricism.

Or search the burgeoning letters columns of *The Mother Earth News* and there the same themes are sounded over and again by lost souls in every lonely corner of the land asking for, offering help. One writes from Arizona:

> We have a going project in action now and won't turn down anyone who really wants to live in a spirit-

led environment of doing and learning. No drugs, dope
or dopes. We have signed contracts for organic produce.
Others pick, crate, and truck it; we grow it. We are a
co-op, not a commune, and we like yoga and everything organic, try to be Christ-like, and do not believe
in killing men or animals.

Another writes from New York City:

> I am a teacher of Freedom struggling with the Board
> of Education in a dying city. Using sheer will power,
> my wife and I manage to keep healthy by doing yoga,
> eating organic foods, adhering to a mucousless diet
> and the placation of love and Tantra Yoga. We have
> $1,000 to share and would like to know of a co-
> operative in Nature composed of people and fellow
> seekers of a natural life.

Another from California:

> We'd like to start a small village community with
> private homes for each family and shared labor,
> costs, food, property, affection and friendship, organic
> living and growing (we're not vegetarians though), no
> drugs, lots of natural highs.

Another from Massachusetts:

> Our fellowship is commited to spiritual quest and
> growth, unbounded by creeds and doctrines, open to
> truth wherever it may be found. Since we began three
> years ago, a few of us have shouldered all of the
> expense, done all of the work, and used our own
> homes for the endless stream of seekers. Now there
> is a definite need for a center where our efforts can be
> pooled and our resources made more widely available.

And another from Canada:

> We are in the process of building a planned com-
> munity about 35 miles outside of Edmunton. Right
> now we have 100 acres of rolling, partially cleared
> land bordered by a river and access to some old rail-
> way stations. As far as personal assets go, we have some
> skill in crafts and several of us are equipped to handle
> gestalt encounter groups, yoga meditation, and mas-
> sage classes. We envision a total-environment com-
> munity whose interaction with the city could supple-
> ment our source of income and provide a benefit to
> city-dwellers seeking a new lifestyle.

By tens and by hundreds they write in to this and a score of
similar journals and with each issue their numbers grow:
teachers, dentists, social workers, junior executives, dropped-
out students, people who have taken their life up in their
hands and carried it out of the artificial environment (though
not necessarily out of the city) in a noble act of defiance. I
can think of forty reasons why none of their projects can possibly succeed and forty different tones of wry cynicism in which
to express my well-documented doubts. But I also know that
it is more humanly beautiful to risk failure seeking for the
hidden springs than to resign to the futurelessness of the wasteland. For the springs are there to be found.

Perhaps their experiments do fail, and fail more than once.
Surely one has to be American beyond all redemption to
think failure is life's worst indignity. After all, the people and
their needs live on, and as their experience accumulates, their
resourcefulness grows. How can one doubt but that the communities will continue to push their way up like wildflowers
through every crack in the suffocating pavements? The tribes
and the bands, the clans and the free communes are forming
again, even in the belly of the monster.

And this is how the only revolution that can undo the

technocracy begins. Where we confront the millionfold consensus of urban-industrial culture, there is no Winter Palace
to be once and for all stormed by a party of iron discipline.
Nor does it make much sense to bomb well-insured capitalist
property, at the risk of killing a few bottom-dog janitors each
with a half-dozen kids at home. Urban-industrialism may be
at a dead end, unable to stave off its chronic, organizational
breakdowns, unable to throttle back its own suicidal dynamism. Even so, the technocracy cannot be overthrown; it can
only be displaced, inch by living inch. It is as Martin Buber
once wisely said:

> Revolution is not so much a creative as a delivering
> force whose function is to set free and authenticate
> —i.e. . . . it can only perfect, set free, and lend the
> stamp of authority to something that has already been
> foreshadowed in the womb of the prerevolutionary
> society.

For Buber, the hassidic sage, that "something" was the
kibbutz, and beyond it, the commonwealth of free societies
formed within the dying husk of the old order, there, waiting . . .

BUT WHERE ARE THE BLUEPRINTS?

A visionary commonwealth, then: a confederated community
of communities.

But what *specifically* would it look like, this bizarre post-
industrial alternative? How *exactly* would it hang together
and function?

I think only a fool would pretend he could answer that

question in any significant detail. Not that I haven't, in the privacy of my own head, done more than a little Utopian brainstorming about the world I think I see on the far side of the urban-industrial wasteland.

About the proper mix of handicraft labor, intermediate technologies, and necessarily heavy industry.

About the revitalization of work as a self-determining, non-exploitative activity—and a means of spiritual growth.

About a new economics elaborated out of kinship, friendship, and co-operation.

About the regionalization and grass roots control of transport and mass communication.

About non-bureaucratized, user-developed, user-administered social services.

About the relevance of women's liberation and extended families (or Huxley's "mutual adoption clubs") to population balance.

About labor-gift and barter exchange systems in the local economy.

About the commune and neighborhood as a basis for personalized welfare services.

About the role of neighborhood courts in a participative legal system.

About the society-wide co-ordination of worker-controlled industries and producers' co-operatives.

About credit unions and mutual insurance as an alternative to the big banks and insurance companies.

About de-urbanization and the rehabilitation of rural life by way of an ecologically diversified organic homesteading.

About non-compulsory education through free schools, folk schools, and child-minding co-ops.

These and countless other tangled problems of decentralism and communitarianism have suffered my own amateurish efforts at social invention. And of course they have received some brilliant attention by far more gifted minds. Anarchist socialism can boast a sizable body of imaginative theory and practical proposals. But I do not intend to rehearse these here. Not for lack of space; but because I have come to the conclusion that such theoretical conjecture, while personally engaging for me, is politically all but meaningless.

This book has talked much about new forms of consciousness; it may seem odd that it finishes by saying little about new forms of society and economy. But this emphasis is deliberate and, in fact, expresses what I believe to be a practical attitude toward political change. There are two reasons why I am so sparing in the discussion of social and economic alternatives. The first concerns the problem of motivation; the second, the meaning of democratic participation.

THE PERSON FIRST

The fundamental question of radical politics has always been, why do the people obey unjust authority? Sometimes the answer is as obvious as the threat of starvation or a bayonet held at the throat. But not always. As this book has sought to show, there are far subtler, more effective forms of power. Those who reside in the mainstream of the technocratic society obey because they are trapped in a diminished reality which not only closes out their vision of "realistic" alternatives, but persuades them that discontent about anything other than superficial inconvenience is inadmissible, a sign of unfortunate maladjustment or a failure of reason. Obstreperous blacks and other minorities may be kept in line by brute intimidation; but that is not what is keeping middle America loyal. The historical forces and cultural ideals that shape their consciousness to suit the urban-industrial imperatives are as subtle as they are formidable. Against these, not all the theoretical clarity in the world can count for much. But where the motivation for change exists, change happens though there are no theoretical landmarks along the way at all.

Certainly it has been my experience that those who demand the complete blueprints of a postindustrial alternative are only looking for as many academic bones of contention as possible —and finally for an excuse to turn off and rest content with the conventional wisdom. They are not ready to change their lives and the most studied Utopian prospectus will not bring them around. They will always find loopholes. I have had my entire viewpoint dismissed out of hand because I could not, on the spot, produce a communitarian substitute for computerized bookkeeping in the New York City welfare system— which "obviously" had to continue operating. And if I couldn't solve that one, what point was there in going any further? On the other hand, those I meet who are busy working to change their lives and their community from the ground up could not be less interested in the theoretical fine points that occupy more reflective types like me. They are too busy with the job at hand . . . and seem to be making more of a good difference in the world than I am.

The great trick is to discover what it is that holds people fast to the status quo and then to undo the knots—perhaps even on a person-by-person basis. It is a matter of recognizing that the future grows out of the here and now; and that people who are not here and now free and eager for change will have nothing to do with inventing better futures. There are questions that must, therefore, be worked deeply into awareness before social dependents become true citizens. What are you, and what do you want to become? What prevents you from becoming this other, better you? Why does change make you afraid? What are your true needs? *What are you in the world to do?* Are you in charge of your life, and if not, who is? Gradually, gradually, the whole person must be brought forth to answer.

These are at once personal and political questions; that is what it means to be involved in the psychological dimension of politics. What happens to people in any serious therapeutic exploration of their identity shapes the course of social change. Debating possible futures, discussing how we shall remake the world at large are unmotivating abstractions. They do not raise up the will to alter one's life; indeed, they may make personal decision seem puny in the great historical course of things and so encourage drift and adaptation. But to challenge people to set their own priorities, to confront them with the fears, hatreds, and hang-ups that betray these priorities: this is where the politics of the visionary commonwealth begins. Its field of play is the individual soul.

Such a profoundly personalist style of politics is already well developed on the new radical fringe and has, by way of the Human Potentials Movement, begun to infiltrate middle America. In a society as madly confused as ours is about what is real and meaningful, that style may have more to do with releasing the energies of change than all the ideology or futurist brainstorming one might muster. I have found myself in discussions with people whose whole loyalty to the existing order, if I should take them at their word, rests on a stereophonic radio-phonograph or the convenience of Bird's-Eye frozen food. They seem not to be able to contemplate their existence without such baubles—so trivial and cockeyed have their priorities become. In the absence of a vacuum cleaner, life could not go on. Clearly, what is *seriously* wrong with them is the very seriousness with which they take the trivialities of their life. In T. S. Eliot's words, they are "distracted from distraction by distraction." Having sold their souls for an electric dishwasher, what can they do but pretend the foolish thing is worth the price? Most of the rewards and conveniences of the swinging society are insidiously distracting nonsense; just as the status such a corrupted society offers those who win its sundry rat races is a hollow folly. But those who

cannot see beyond such trifles, who are not even in touch
with the attendant guilt and discontent that secretly eat at
their organism, would not turn from the artificial environment, even if we presented them with a whole new world
next door, alive and prospering. They are hooked too deeply;
the problem is to find where the hook has lodged and to work
the barbs free.

But psychic exploration is not the only way to awaken the
will to change. Even more important is the example of those
who have already found the resourcefulness to change their
lives and have fulfilled themselves in doing so. Nothing counts
more heavily against the technocracy than a successful deser-
tion, for there is no underestimating the influence of an authentically happy disaffiliate in a society of affluent self-con-
tempt. Every drop-out who drops into a freer, more joyous,
more self-determining style of life—a style of life that *works*—
breaks the paralyzing official consensus.

Even if one only goes a few steps out of the mainstream to
redesign some small piece of one's life—to organize a free
school or a free clinic, to build a labor-gift exchange or to
pool tools and resources with neighbors for the solving of a
problem—it is a sign to one's fellows that something better is
possible, something that does not have to await the attention
of experts but begins here and now with you and me. In
changing one's own life one may not intend to change the
world; but there is never any telling how far the power of
imaginative example travels.

This touches on the second reason why I have no interest in
blueprinting an alternative social order here. If one believes
in the validity of a participative democracy (and what other
kind of democracy can there be?) then it is little more than
academic presumption to begin unloading a host of institutional schemes in the abstract. It is people in the process of
changing their homes, neighborhoods, cities, regions who are
most apt to know best what they need and what works. And

if they don't know, they will only learn from their own failures. Nothing but responsibility for their own lives makes people grow up and get competent. The resourcefulness of ordinary people whose citizenly instincts have been awakened and put in touch with the real problems of their community can indeed be amazing. Their experienced judgment always counts for more than the most prestigious expertise.

Among most young radicals there is very little patience with purely academic experts who know about things "in general" but not "in person." And that is all to the good. For here again we confront the difference between the two ways of knowing. The involved knowing of those who are on the scene and in the thick is invariably more practical than the theoretical knowing of the distant specialist. Involved knowing possesses the resonance of all the imponderable and ineffable factors that make up the "feel" of the situation.

It is when I am in that situation that I may most properly bring my peculiar ideas to bear for what they are worth. But across the distance of these many pages, what would be the reality of my proposals? Drawing up abstract social prescriptions runs the risk of becoming an expert's game; and then it belongs to the technocracy, not its opposition.

AND THE REST OF THE WORLD . . . ?

I know there are those who fear that any effort to scale down urban-industrialism will leave us with a world of starving millions. The population explosion has become for many the iron imperative for all-out industrial expansion, rather as if the growth and technological sophistication of the richly developed societies were somehow automatically of benefit to the world's poor. This comforting illusion is the exact reverse of the truth; but it is a deception the technocracy has every reason to promulgate. It conveniently casts technician, research scientist, and industrial elite in the heroic role of world saviors; thus, what is best for them is best for mankind. And what is best for them is the rapid, global extension of the artificial environment.

To question this proposition is not to deny that there are many useful contributions that scientist and technician can make to the improvement of life. But it is to insist emphatically that their service within the context of urban-industrialism and its technocratic politics is no service whatever to the world's poor. That ought to be clear to any American with eyes to see. For even in our own land, where the level of productivity threatens to bankrupt the environment, the existing abundance—which is already more than enough to give us a healthy and secure population—is still not fairly shared out. It sinks down to a level that guarantees widespread docility and acquiescence, and there begins to fatten limitlessly; it goes no further. It serves to oil the vast majority of white collar and blue collar America into the system. But beyond that, the hard-core, powerless poor are always with us, scattered about in the forgotten pockets of the society. They receive little more than they can win for themselves by organization and obstreperous militancy.

How naïve, then, to believe that the poor outside the affluent societies have anything more to expect from our prosperity or are in any way dependent on its increase. It is by now an open scandal that the aid and know-how America exports to the underdeveloped countries primarily caters to the needs of our own overseas investors and supports the policies of the American military and paramilitary agencies. Locally and secondarily, it serves the interests of whatever the CIA and World Bank have decided is a "reliable" political and/or entrepreneurial elite: meaning, a rich few who see things America's way in countries made up of a poor many who usually don't. And from these reliable elites, with their one-party politics, their chronically suspended constitutions, and their ponderous secret police establishments, the wealth trickles down like frozen molasses. The west helps the third world to develop its economies about as selflessly as the Russians help their Eastern European satellites with their development—and with the same motives at heart.

Certainly our megatechnics is of no use to tribal or village-based traditional societies. Where it descends upon them, especially under foreign control, it only crushes local structures of life, depletes resources, and initiates hasty migrations to the cities that end in the desolation of shantytowns: a ring of human dilapidation surrounding a make-believe metropolis of high-rise towers built to dazzle tourists and keep the bureaucrats air-conditioned. Even where the big technology is brought in under authentic national auspices, it disrupts more than it enriches—as witness the classic fiasco of the Aswan high dam project in Egypt. The poor countries could much more make do with labor-intensive intermediate technologies that adapt to existing skills and strengthen grass roots social structure. A cheap and simple Humphery pump that runs on the methane gas produced from animal dung can do more to improve living standards in many poor societies than the fast-breeder reactors which may finish by lowering ours. But far and away what the wretched of the earth need to improve their material lot is what the poor of our own country need. Nothing technological, but something through and through political. They need control over their own communities. Only that will permit them to set their own priorities and so undertake a development which is more than one-crop economies, foreign-owned assembly plants, and a glittering façade of Hilton hotels.

Even then, many third world societies may be weighed down by burdens enough, by their own nationalist phobias and manias, their homegrown corruption and incompetence, their foolish zeal to imitate our mad standard of affluence, their weakness for dictatorship. The underdeveloped societies are neither angelic nor infallibly wise; but they do know their needs better than the power elites of west and east ever will. And it would be absurd to think that we have anything to teach them about freedom, justice, or economic intelligence until we put our own house in order. Certainly they will not be of a mind to take counsel from us while our Big Power politicking cheats them of self-determination, and the avarice of our corporations continues to arrange their economies to meet the needs of distant investors and consumers. The greatest single contribution America could make to the development of the poor countries would be to abolish the CIA tomorrow . . . and the Chase Manhattan Bank the day after.

Urban-industrialism is indeed expanding to encompass the globe; ready or not, people everywhere are being integrated into the network. But the benefits accrue to the bastardized technocracies that drive that expansion forward—and to the home populations whose acquiescence the technocrats bribe by ever increased affluence. The notion that the economic problems of the poor countries are going to be solved by an automatic overflow of abundance and know-how is a shabby lie. Long before that abundance overflows, the inordinate high consumption of the world's fat nations will have bled white the environment off which all the nations must live; and the first to suffer will be the poorest. What we must come to see is that the expansion of urban-industrialism has no part to play in feeding the hungry. Quite the contrary. The urban-industrial dominance is the disease, not the medicine.

There is of course an absolute limit to how many people our earth can support. And if we reach it, not even superindustrialism will prevent disaster. This is a real problem and I respect its importance. Just as I recognize that population restraint can be of great economic value in the world as a whole, and especially in the poor and highly congested societies. But these demographical considerations have come to be used in the wealthy nations in a thoroughly dishonest way. They allow us to trace world poverty to a "population crisis" that can supposedly be solved *without cutting back on our own maniacal growth.* We ignore the cause of world poverty and occupy ourselves with symptoms. We tell ourselves that the problem is *their* population and underdevelopment, never our living habits. And for *their* problem, we insist there must be some purely technological solution . . . if only *they* were not too backward to take advantage of it. But the simple, fearful truth is: our overdevelopment has far more to do with the world's miseries, past, present, and future, than the supposed overpopulation of the poor.

The people of the United States today (about 7.5 per cent of the world's population) consume some 30 per cent of the non-renewable resources produced each year, including 37 per cent of the energy, 25 per cent of the steel, 28 per cent of the tin, 33 per cent of synthetic rubber. They eat far more than their share of the world's protein and produce most of the world's waste and pollutants. Moreover, the United States projects across the globe a standard of consumption which the world at large could only emulate by achieving an annual production at levels like sixty billion tons of iron and fifty million tons of tin . . . an impossible two to four hundred times the present output. Any discussion of world poverty that does not come round to demanding a radical change in our habits of consumption and waste, our tastes, our profligate standard of living, our values generally is a hypocrisy. There are no technical answers to ethical questions.

Those who anguish over a starving mankind on the easy assumption that there just is not enough land and resources to feed the hungry might do well to pay a special kind of visit to their local supermarket. Not to shop, but to observe and to meditate on what they see before them and have always taken for granted. How much of the world's land and labor was wasted producing the tobacco, the coffee, the tea, the refined cane sugars, the polished rice, the ice creams, the candies, the cookies, the soft drinks, the thousand and one non-nutritional luxuries one finds there? The grains that became liquor, the fruits and vegetables that lost all their food value going into cans and jars full of syrups and condiments, the potatoes and corn that became various kinds of chips, crackles, crunchies and yum-yums, the cereals that became breakfast novelties less nourishing (as a matter of scientific fact) than the boxes they are packed in, the wheat that became white breads and pastry flours . . . How many forests perished to package these non-foods? How many resources went into transporting and processing them? (And the less nutrition, the more processing.) How much skilled energy went into advertising and merchandising them? There they stand in our markets, row upon row, aisle upon aisle of nutritional zero, gaily boxed and packed, and costing those fancy prices we then gripe about as the high cost of living. Is it not amazing how much floor space they take up and how much of our diet they comprise? (Subtract the room taken up by the detergents, paper-goods luxuries, cosmetics and toiletries, and what would there be left of most supermarkets?) And how much more land was used up for the animal feed and grazing that support our extravagant (and nutritionally inefficient) meat-eating habits? How much of this phony food does nothing more than lay on the fat we must then join an expensive gym to work off?

Then on the way home, ponder the land areas we have used up for streets, freeways, and parking space—all of it capable of producing food, but now sacrificed to the needs of traffic. Consider how much more of it is covered over by stores, factories, warehouses, shopping centers, and dumping grounds which exist only to process, store, and merchandise consumer goods that are of less true social value than the land they take out of cultivation. In some cities, the used car lots alone could feed whole neighborhoods. Consider too the amount of arable soil we give up to the wasteful urban pattern of one-family private yards, patios, and swimming pools. Think how much of this could be reclaimed and consolidated into productive neighborhood commons where urban dwellers might grow a substantial portion of their own food—as well as reaping the benefits of a revitalized community life. For that matter, consider the rich American farmlands which politically well-connected agrindustrialists are subsidized each year (currently to the tune of $2 billion) to hold out of production. And once home, note the organic wastes we liberally wash down the disposal or cast away in plastic sacks because we are too fastidious to sort out and recycle our garbage—and remember that all of it is the world's best fertilizer.

Much the same mad waste of resources can be found in every other walk of life: our clothes, appliances, household furnishings, automobiles, airplanes, entertainments—and of course most glaringly in the world's military pyramid-building. The space programs and weapons systems of the great powers alone burn up enough wealth and talent to underwrite the intelligent development of whole nations. *This* is why there may well be world famine without precedent in the next generation—on a scale far surpassing the fifteen million people who already die of malnutrition each year in the obscure and exploited corners of the earth. So that we in the rich nations can enjoy bad nutrition and tooth decay; so that we can have somewhere to park our cars; so that we need not soil our fingers with our own garbage; so that we can boast history's vastest military overkill. It is out of such routine extravagances that the technocracy weaves its spell over our allegiance . . . and then assures us we are the hope of the world.

THE NEXT POLITICS

Environmental collapse, world poverty, technocratic elitism, psychic alienation, the death of the soul. When I look about me to discover somewhere in the world a politics that goes to the root of these problems, I find it no place but in the range of fragile experimentation I have here called the visionary commonwealth. Here alone are people living out real solutions, people who have integrated the great ethical issues of the time into their very eating habits. Here is the brave, radical break with urban-industrialism that promises—though not overnight, or without constant pressure on the wrong-headed world—a new ecology, a new democracy, a new vitality of spirit. This alone looks to me like the necessary next politics. Whatever else I see happening is little more than propaganda or another myopic effort at expert manipulation.

If that next politics catches fire, we shall doubtless in the short run require a transitional and therapeutic technology to help us in disassembling urban-industrialism. There must be techniques for intelligently scaling down the cities and industrial plant and unscrambling the many interlocking necessities the artificial environment has imposed. It will take no little technical wit to dig us out of the patterns of life we are now trapped in; even so, there are apt to be many collective withdrawal pains as we unhook from our urban-industrial addictions. But the criterion of a therapeutic technology will be that it leaves us always less expert-dependent, more decentralized, more communitarian than we were before. It proceeds in the spirit of contrition and its resolve is to put itself out of business.

I think we are beginning to find the people we need for

the task: dissenting young technicians, dropped-out professionals, young scientists who are well away into Tantric sadhanas, people's architects, advocacy city planners, hip artisans, ecological activists brimming over with better possibilities. Here are sharp minds that have seen through the mystique of expertise and the artificial environment. They have learned to solve problems *with* people and not *for* them. They have access to the right skills and tools. Above all, they have their eyes on the visionary commonwealth.

Even with their help, of course, unmaking the artificial environment cannot help but to seem a mind-boggling project —as do all revolutions from a distance. Where does one even begin? But the answer is, we have already begun, here and there, in courageous little ways, with crafty little improvisations. There is a visionary commonwealth already in our midst, and one need not look far to find it in one form or another. Even the mass media know it is there, though their publicity can do more harm than good. None of these experiments began because people discovered the ground plan for a whole new social order. Rather, they started with something else that lent the impossible complexity of the revolution a startling simplicity. They did not start with people asking, how do I save the technology? but with the more pertinent question, how do I save my soul? When that question has been pressed to the deepest level of the self, then—suddenly —we are at the threshold of a new reality where the necessities and inevitabilities of the technocratic society look a deal less commanding.

CHAPTER 13

Apocatastasis

It is the vision of apocatastasis, the reversal . . . the transformation of the demonic forces into the celestial.

Judith Malina and Julian Beck

In Gnostic mythology, there is a recurrent motif which tells how the soul, glimpsing a reflection of the divine light in the darkness below and mistaking it for its original, pursued the beckoning image into the depths and there became lost. The drama of everyman's spiritual travail may be in that myth; but in a peculiar and collective way, the grand tragedy of the urban-industrial epoch is there as well. We too have lost our way in the abyss, searching for divine goods dimly reflected there. For us, the entrammeling descent has been the pursuit of total human fulfillment through the mastery of history and matter. Committed to saving the soul by unlimited secular progress, we have become easy prey for totalitarian and technocratic Grand Inquisitors. Determined to build the New Jerusalem with dynamos and computers, we have finished as prisoners of the artificial environment.

Any discussion of the contemporary world that does not

appreciate this interplay of the demonic and the ethical in the history of urban-industrialism cannot help being shallow, either in its optimism or its despair. It will miss the terrible ambiguities that bind our good and our evil together as creatures of one flesh.

Blake, the isolated and unheeded prophet of our age and himself an avid student of the Gnostic tradition, saw more deeply than anyone into this tragic irony. For him, industrial society was "Babylon builded in the Waste, founded in Human desolation." And yet what a marvel it was, and what a religious zeal fired its builders. They were not merely raising up a new social order, they were remaking the universe at large, imprisoning heaven and eternity in the chains of their social need. It was the process historians would later call the "secularization" of western culture; Blake wrote never a word about it that was not touched with awe and horror.

> . . . immense in strength and power,
> In awful pomp and gold, in all the spacious unhewn stones of
> Eden,
> They build a stupendous Building on the Plain of Salisbury,
> with chains
> Of rocks round London Stone, of Reasonings, of unhewn
> Demonstrations
> In labyrinthine arches . . . thro' which
> The Heavens might revolve and Eternity be bound in their
> chain.
> Labour unparallell'd! a wondrous rocky World of cruel
> destiny,
> Rocks piled on rocks reaching the stars, stretching from pole
> to pole.

And still, for all its magnificence, Blake called it "a building of eternal death, whose proportions are eternal despair."

The architect of that industrial colossus Blake identified as "Mighty Urizen," the god of mad rationality and purposeless power whose other name (in the mythology of Blake's visionary epics) was Satan. For mankind beneath the influence of this deity, "obscure, shadowy, void, solitary," Blake could foresee only the death of nature and of the soul. He called Urizen's affliction—as I have in this study—single vision; touched by its poison, man becomes

> . . . self-exiled from the face of light and shine of
> morning,
> In the dark world, a narrow house! He wanders up and down
> Seeking for rest and finding none.

We have since become almost flippantly familiar with that sickness of the spirit under the name of "alienation," and have watched it spread across the earth in the wake of European cultural and political expansion. It is the psychic Black Plague of our time, inseparably attached to the urban-industrialization of the world. We who belong to the white middle-class west are the prime infectious agents of this pandemic. And thus far, the only treatment to be widely applied—the quackery of totalitarian mass movements—has proved deadlier than the disease.

We are not the first people in history to suffer the psychic corrosion of alienation. As the experience of having strayed from the sacred sources of life, it must be as old as the human mind. Christian theology knew it as ultimate fallenness, the despair of the damned. In the Hermetic tradition, alienation was seen as the soul's entrapment in the *massa confusa,* the realm of the self-consuming dragon, the sanity-shattering chaos of the *nigredo.* So too, in his study *The Gnostic Religion,* Hans Jonas has shown how the Gnostic vision of a demonized nature long ago anticipated the darkest terrors of existentialist nihilism.

> Under this pitiless sky, which no longer inspires worshipful confidence, [the Gnostic] becomes conscious of

his utter forlornness. Encompassed by it, subject to its power, yet superior to it by the nobility of his soul, he knows himself not so much a part of, but unaccountably placed in and exposed to the enveloping system. And, like Pascal, he is frightened. His solitary otherness, discovering itself in this forlornness, erupts in the feeling of dread.

No Sartre or Beckett has ever drawn us a bleaker picture of the human condition than the Gnostic cosmology.

But there is a difference. Until our own time, alienation has always stood in the shadow of salvation; it has been the falling rhythm of the soul's full cycle. It carried with it implications of transcendence. Ours is the first culture so totally secularized that we descend into the nihilist state without the conviction, without the experienced awareness that any other exists. I am not close enough to the churches to say how far beyond the level of Sunday school platitudes the clergy and their flocks press the discussion of Christian eschatology. But if that discussion goes more than skin-deep, it is abundantly clear from the character of social and cultural life throughout the west that it has been well quarantined within the congregations. Where public affairs begin, the churchgoing millions are at one with the atheist existentialist few: in body, mind, and deed they live the conviction that salvation will be found nowhere but in the collective, historical process—in making, doing, and improving. That is where their effort and attention go. Time and matter have trapped their vital energy; secular enterprise consumes it totally. Christian faith—the willful belief of the unbelievable—was never better than a poor substitute for sacramental experience; but even dutiful belief in a transcendent dimension of life has long since degenerated into mere opinion, socially irrelevant, even if privately engaging.

But it is not simply that transcendence has faded from our awareness. For many committed intellectuals and radical activists—those who have spearheaded the struggle for liberal and social democracy—it has been imperiously crowded out by the demands of conscience. In the moral conviction of these crusaders without a god, a science-based humanism and the left-wing anti-clerical legacy have combined to make religion an intolerable distraction from social responsibility. And how the religious, who come to the cause so late in the day, have learned to blush and cringe before the moral fire of militant humanism! At least since the days of Danton and Saint-Just, it has gone without question among increasing numbers of politically engaged people that only the struggle for progress, the struggle for justice are *real;* they must have *all.* To yield to the transcendent longings is selfish indulgence. "If God existed," said Bakunin, "we should have to abolish him." In brief, our ethics is at war with religion. Ours is a culture alienated in fact and *on principle.*

That is unique—terrifyingly unique. Never before have those who would speak for the transcendent ends of life had so little cultural purchase. In times past, the saints and sages have had to suffer the hypocrisy of the world, and its neglect; but their vision was never denied its validity or righteously eclipsed. They have never had to apoligize for their knowledge of God or hide it away like a guilty secret.

But what choice does urban-industrial culture leave to a genuine religious sensibility if it wishes to avoid the lunatic fringe on the one hand, and self-serving bourgeois mediocrity on the other? Nothing but to immerse itself in the social gospel, to exhaust itself in a secular ethics. Wherever in the world today religion bids for intellectual reputability, it is by reducing itself to a dense residue of passionate ethical exhortation. That was the course the Deists chose in the age of Newton, relinquishing to the New Philosophy all knowledge of reality beyond the moral impulse; it remains the strategy of every embarrassed clergyman scrambling for "relevance" in the modern world and the acceptance of proudly alienated culture makers.

Granted, moral action is more becoming to the religious life than endless, arid theological nit-picking—the peculiar vice of Christianity; better too than sinking to the level of a middle-class social club or a Billy Graham theater piece. But *none* of these is religion; all are expressions of alienated consciousness, the social gospel no less than the rest. So Blake recognized in taking up his "mental fight" with the Deists. As the brave ally of Tom Paine and the revolutionary forces of his time, Blake took second place to none in his hostility toward aristocratic privilege and capitalist oppression. But whom did he mark out as the prime antagonists of Poetic Genius and the Divine Vision? Not obvious villains and godless scoundrels—Blake wastes little time on easy targets. But Bacon, Newton, Locke, Voltaire, Rousseau, Gibbon . . . the noblest spirits of Enlightenment and natural religion. It is with such giants that Blake tangles. Why? Because it is with them that the denaturing of visionary imagination begins. With them, alienation initiates its climb to supreme virtue. In the name of Reason, Progress, Humanity—the total secularization of mind and energy.

That is why Blake called Deism "the Religion of Satan." Not because it was the faith of wicked men. On the contrary, the very purpose of natural religion was to salvage Christian ethics within Newtonian nature. It was indeed the first step toward that intrepid secular humanism which boasts so proud a history of reform and revolution, and from which the social gospel has taken its inspiration as the minimally religious alternative to the godless ideologies. Yet beneath the ethical cover of Deism, humanism, and the social gospel, single vision has worked its way deep into the bloodstream of modern culture. Hence Blake's titanic effort to integrate radical politics with the Old Gnosis. He knew intuitively that in the long evolution of human consciousness, ethical principle has grown up out of a religious soil, that human fellowship is the moral aspect of that transcendent Oneness whose root meaning is known only by visionary experience. And Blake would not part the soil from the fruit, lest in time the fruit wither. That is what makes his political intelligence (like that of Tolstoy, Gandhi, Buber) so much keener than that of Marx and the secular ideologues. Knowing what horrors follow when the discipline of the sacred has been lost, Blake could discern "the spirit of evil in things heavenly"—bomb physics and the human guinea pigs of Buchenwald emerging from the worldview of Newton and Pasteur, the behavioral reductionism of Watson and Skinner springing from the humane aspirations of Bacon and Locke, the Frankensteinian nightmares of modern science and technics arising from Promethean dreams of glory.

This is a cultural lineage that even now few humanist intellectuals are prepared to recognize as part of their tradition. Instead, they forcibly ignore it, like a respectable family struggling to conceal a streak of criminal insanity in the blood. They insist that our science and technics need only recover a proper sense of "social responsibility," and all will be well. They argue that by measures of institutional and professional reform—or perhaps by moral exhortation alone—urban-industrial society can yet be "humanized." For obviously it cannot be humanism itself that requires critical examination; it is simply that society is not yet humanistic enough. So they produce eloquent pleas and ingenious schemes for a "humanistic" psychology and psychotherapy, a "humanistic" sociology, a "humanistic" economics, linguistics, literary scholarship, anthropology, technology, city planning, social welfare, medical science; and on the far left, a "humanistic" Marxism. Year after year—and for how many years already!—these bold proposals sound across the pages of the best journals like clarions of a new dawn. Volumes of hotly dissenting humanist opinion pile up on the bookshelf, brilliant

critiques of reductionism, mechanism, behaviorism, structural-
functionalism: daring revisions that finally break through,
with great self-congratulations, to some minor human truth
that Shakespeare or Sophocles long ago salted away in a
casual epigram and would never have imagined needing to
document or defend. Strange, is it not, how we now have
whole libraries of heavy research in the humanities and social
sciences—including the work of our humanist scholars—
that add up to less wisdom, less living insight than many of
our youth can find in the words of illiterate primitives like
Black Elk or Carlos Casteneda's Don Juan, and surely less
than any of us would find in a single dialogue of Plato, a single
essay of Montaigne, a single Buddhist sutra?

Can one help concluding that there is something more
radically corrupted than humanist intellectuals suspect about
a standard of intellect which requires a lifetime of professional study and strenuous debate, much ornate methodology
and close research to produce at last a meager grain of human
understanding, cautiously phrased and nearly drowning in its
own supporting evidence? That people are very likely not machines . . . that love is rather important to healthy growth
. . . that "peak experiences" are probably of some personal
and cultural significance . . . that living things have "goal-
oriented needs" . . . that human beings have an emotional
inside and are apt to resent being treated like statistical
ciphers or mere objects . . . that participating in things is
more rewarding than passively watching or being bossed
about . . . how many books do I take up each year and
abandon in anguished boredom after the first two chapters, because here once again is some poor soul offering me a ton of
data and argument to demonstrate what ought to be the axioms
of daily human experience? If our paleolithic ancestors were
presented with these "controversial new findings," surely far
from applauding our deep-minded humanism, they would
only wonder "where along the line did these people become

so stupid that they now must prove to themselves from scratch that $2+2=4$?"

In a recent essay, the humanistic psychologist Sigmund Koch confesses to being plain *tired* of the bone-wearying struggle he has had to wage in his profession against the behaviorist counterfeiters, and must still wage. "Yes, still. . . . I have given half a career as a psychologist," he laments, "to the detailed registration of scholarly error over the phenomenon—and strange time course—of behaviorism. It has been a tiresome role . . ." No doubt. And yet reductionist intellect, like Dr. Frankenstein's monster, refuses to die; it stalks on across the landscape trouncing everything in its path. Why is it the humanists cannot deal the monster its death blow? Is it perhaps because they know that their own life's blood—*their* tradition, *their* dearest values—courses through the monster's body, and therefore they dare not strike? Professor Koch comes close to the heart of the beast when he asks, "What does behaviorism mean? I mean in a human way."

> Really very simple: behaviorism is the strongest possible wish that the organism and, *entre nous,* the person may not exist—a vast, many-voiced, poignant lament that anything so refractory to the assumptions and methods of eighteenth-century science should clutter up the world-scape.

For where, after all, do the humanists think the behaviorist's debased, manipulative caricature of human nature and society springs from? Where do they think the dehumanizing forces originate which corrupt the academic and intellectual traditions they now must strain to rehumanize? Where do they think the strange idea comes from that knowledge can legitimately be detached from wisdom, that specialized research can be a suitable substitute for integral and participative experience? Above all, where do they think the reductionist scholars and scientists draw the influence and conviction which allows them to brush aside humanist moralizing so effortlessly?

The answer is that intellect in urban-industrial society—*including humanist intellect*—is the captive of single vision; and the heart of single vision is that very science of nature from which humanism historically and still today takes inspiration for its project of secularizing value and culture. Humanism, for all its ethical protest, will not and cannot shift the quality of consciousness in our society; *it has not the necessary psychic leverage.* Indeed, it stands full square upon the stone that must be overturned. After all, the reductionists who see nature as a machine and the human being as a robot are not apt to regard moral indignation as anything more than a queer quirk in the robot's electro-bio-psycho-chemico-physical feedback apparatus. And who are the humanists to talk to them of the reality of soul or spirit?

Burdened as they are by single vision, the secular humanists simply do not see the crucial links that bind them to reductionist intellect. They cannot trace alienation back to its germ in the objectified worldview of natural science. They cannot see how the blight that lays waste our life and our culture takes its course from the physics of Newton, Einstein, and Bohr, from the biology of Darwin, Crick, and Watson. They cannot see how the deadly chill of Pavlov's psychology is able to shelter within the high moral flame of "scientific socialism." They do not know that when nature dies beneath Urizen's scalpel, the human soul dies with it. For between mankind and nature there is no conveniently dichotomizing line the humanists can hold against the reductionist advance. Finally and inevitably, the picture we accept as a valid depiction of the molecules and galaxies will be our own self-portrait.

"The spirit of evil in things heavenly . . ." But within the last few generations, as alienation has come to be recog-

nized as a chronic condition of urban-industrial life—a state
of sick normality—many intellectuals and artists, with the
trendier critics and slick journalists not far behind, have become almost chummy with that "spirit of evil." There has
developed a bizarre virtuosity in the varieties of nihilism;
whole schools of art and literature now specialize in its iconography and modish nuances, lending it the dignity of being
"our twentieth-century way of life." Accordingly, clever,
highly literate people now toy with the latest fashions in
alienated living. They watch keenly for crisp, new analyses and
elaborations and insights; and if these are not forthcoming, they
grow bored with the scene and insist that we go on to the *next*
subject of discussion. It is rather like getting so used to living
with death camps and political terrorism that it all becomes
too tiresome to talk about. Already our novelists, painters,
playwrights, and film makers must resort to apocalyptic extremes to express in some arrestingly novel way the ingrained
death-in-life of normal middle-class society. A madhouse imagery of mass murder, cannibalism, necrophilia, bestiality,
Grand Guignol fills their work. They waste their talent in a
worthless competition to be the first with the most extreme.
Worst of all, they forget that art has any other function than
to mirror the horrors. Within the last several years, most of
the experimental little theater productions I have seen have
been so routinely taken up with breakdown-of-communica-
tion, dehumanized encounters, casual sadism, sexual mayhem
that I begin to wonder if perhaps these young writers and
actors and directors do not too much relish the decay they
deal in. They have become so greedy-eager to work out all the
permutations of the horrible. And then, "Ah yes," say the
connoisseurs, "that was a strong statement . . . though perhaps with a bit too much theater of cruelty in the second
act—and Artaud was *last* year."

When I was at college (the middle fifties) I learned the
death of God like a data point in freshman survey courses. I

took exams on "contrasting concepts of the absurd—time limit twenty minutes." I was taught to admire the latest refinements Beckett and Ionesco had wrought upon the existential vacuum. Modern man, I dutifully noted, is in search of a soul, and the age is an age of longing. But sophisticated minds must know better than to expect that search and that longing to find gratification. There might be private strategies of consolation (like Santayana's cultivation of an aesthetic religiosity), but the first fact of public life was alienation—and alienation was here to stay. Except perhaps in economic affairs. There a strong left-wing commitment permitted one to speak of eliminating the worker's "alienation" from the means and fruits of production—a much reduced Marxist usage of the term, which, of course, had nothing to do with the spiritual life. Of the needs of the spirit one simply did not speak; the very word was without a negotiable meaning in educated company. This, I rapidly learned, was the most intellectually intolerable aspect of personality and accordingly the most repressed. One might discourse in luscious detail about one's sex life in fact and fantasy; but how gauche, how offensive to introduce anything even vaguely religious into serious conversation—unless with a fastidious scholarly detachment . . . as a point of fact . . . about other people . . . in other times and places.

But what was all this clever confabulation with the alienated life but the cultural expression of urban-industrial social necessity? For the sake of the artificial environment, the soul *had* to die. The transcendent impulse that cried out in me for life and a dignified space in the world *had* to stay jailed up in my head as personal fantasy. Either that or be gunned down on sight for subversive activity. God—any god who was more than a presidential platitude—had become an enemy of the new industrial state. This was why secular humanism had become the orthodox intellectual style of the age; why Marxism had become the orthodox radicalism. Neither took issue with science or technics or the psychological mode they demand. Neither broke with the artificial environment. Both served the needs of technocratic politics.

How long could this principled repression of the visionary energies go on? How long before there came a generation which realized that a wasteland is no place to make one's home?

No doubt there are ways and means to ameliorate, at least temporarily, the most dangerous excesses of urban-industrialism and the technocratic politics it breeds. But for the disease of single vision there can be no ad hoc reform, no quick technological fix. And it is single vision that underlies the despair, the anomie, the irresponsible drift, the resignation to genocide, the weakness for totalitarian solutions, which make radical, enduring change in our society impossible. Until we find our way once more to the experience of transcendence, until we feel the life within us and the nature about us as sacred, there will seem to us no "realistic" future other than more of the same: single vision and the artificial environment forever and ever, amen.

That is why the politics of our time must reopen the metaphysical issues which science and sound logic have for the last two centuries been pleased to regard as closed. For to expound upon social priorities or the quality of life without confronting those issues is the very folly of alienation. It is, once again, the half person prescribing the whole person's needs. But it is *experience* that must reopen those issues, not academic discourse. We must learn once more to discriminate experientially between realities, telling the greater from the lesser. If there is to be a next politics, it will be a religious politics. Not the religion of the churches—God help us! not the religion of the churches—but religion in the oldest, most universal sense: which is vision born of transcendent knowledge.

"Be realistic. Plan for a miracle," reads a hip maxim of the

day. What miracle? The Buddha once said there is only *one*
miracle. He called it "the turning about in the deepest seat of
consciousness." *Paravritti.* The sharp reversal—like coming out
of crash dive at the last minute. Not a turning back of the
clock—which is never possible personally or socially—but a
saving return from the depths. The prophet's return from the
speaking solitude of the wilderness. Ishmael's return from the
demonic voyage. Or the return of the mad from their secret
self-annihilation. A *wise* return, which brings back the full
experience of the outward journey.

The apocatastasis: the great restoration. Since its earliest
days Christian thought has been haunted by this strangest
and most beautiful of all heresies. Where does it come from?
Out of the old mystery cults and the orient, by way of Plato
perhaps. A memory of the great cycle in which history turns
like a wheel around the hub of eternity. The teaching speaks
of another world that is destined to inherit from this fallen
creation and which is, in fact, paradise regained. And between the two worlds, the fire of perdition is no more than
the interval of terrible instruction that burns the soul's gold
free of its dross. Hell having been universally harrowed, even
Satan and his reprobate band (so the heresy teaches) will
turn from their infernal obsessions and find their way to
original unity.

In the Gnostic myth, the apocatastasis is the illumination in
the abyss by which the lost soul, after much tribulation, learns
to tell the divine light from its nether reflection. So a new
reality replaces (or rather *embraces*) the old and draws the
fallen spirit up, wiser than if it had never fallen. For us, this
means an awakening from "single vision and Newton's
sleep," where we have dreamt that only matter and history
are real. This has been the bad, mad ontology of our culture,
and from it derives that myth of objective consciousness
which has densified the transcendent symbols and persuaded
us to believe in the reality of nothing that cannot be weighed

and measured—not even our own soul, which is after all a subtle dancer. So long as that myth rules the mind, not even the most humanely intentioned among us will find any course to follow but roads that lead deeper into the wasteland. But the mind freed of that myth may begin to find a project as vast as repealing the urban-industrial dominance not only feasible but necessary.

It would be preposterous to think that anything I write here, anything that any one perosn says or writes, demands or pleads for, could bring about the apocatastasis. Such a spiritual regeneration happens of its own mysterious accord or not at all. And of course it is happening. The fact that these words find their way into print now—as they could not even ten years ago—is a manifestation of that happening. Though whether the reversal will happen soon enough and on a sufficient scale there is no telling. That is the cruel edge of the adventure.

The signs of regeneration can be seen all about us in the heightened appetite for experience, the often indiscriminate passion to explore every forgotten reality of the self and nature. Listen, and you can hear that appetite eating away at its exotic diet of dreams, ecstasies, old mysteries, and quaint personal awakenings; you can detect it in the mode of the music, in the tones and gestures of ordinary people, in the rhythms of their breathing. The outlaw young in their counter culture, the restive middle Americans in their Growth Centers have become a participating audience for all the long-neglected artists, psychologists, and philosophers of the Extraordinary.

And this is—potentially—the beginning of the end for the old Reality Principle and the artificial environment that strives to become its perfect embodiment. Gradually the realization dawns that *all* the realities men and women have known are real, each being the discovery of a human potentiality. The scientist's reality together with the mystic's, the technician's together with the poet's. Even the madman's reality is real, and not only to the mad. For have we not, in the twentieth century, found our way back to the mythic and visionary origins of culture in large part by following the mad through their dark, internal country? "Breakdown," R. D. Laing has observed, "may also be breakthrough," a torturous return to the source of the transcendent symbols. Here is one of the strangest adventures of our time: the rediscovery by psychoanalysis of universal truths beneath the wreckage of personal nightmare and neurosis.

It is as Robert Duncan has said: we are gathering together a new symposium where all are invited to participate.

> To compose such a symposium of the whole, such a totality, all the old excluded orders must be included. The female, the proletariat, the foreign; the animal and vegetative; the unconscious and the unknown; the criminal and failure—all that has been outcast and vagabond must return to be admitted in the creation of what we consider we are.

In the new reality game, all these pieces are on the board, and any conception of Reason or Sanity that demands a smaller, more conveniently manageable field of play will be overturned. Too many have now learned that the Reason which represses any part of the Whole is only insanity's mask.

To be mad, as the world judges, is to be trapped in a narrow and lonely reality. To be sane, as the world judges, is to be trapped in a reality no less narrow, but heavily populated. But there is also the higher sanity, which is neither the going consensus nor the latest compensatory excess. Its health is freedom from all traps; its sign is the knowledge of many realities. All realities are real; but sanity's reality is vaster, more various, more vividly experienced in all its sectors, and more judiciously ordered. It is a spectrum, and not a single color worn like a uniform and flown like a crusading banner. The

higher sanity can taste of all realities, but respects the ontological priorities.

Here and now, as we restore the orders of reality, we are
in the stage of closing up all the traditional dichotomies of
western culture which have served as the bulwarks of the old
Reality Principle. Spirit-flesh, reason-passion, mad-sane, objective-subjective, fact-value, natural-supernatural, intellect-
intuition, human-non-human . . . all these familiar dualisms
which have divided the spectrum of consciousness vanish as
we create the higher sanity. The dichotomies are healing
over like old wounds. Even science, in its awkward single-
visioned way, has been led to continuities that baffle traditional assumptions. It can no longer draw hard lines between
matter and energy, organic and inorganic, man and lower
animal, law and the indeterminate, mind and body. What is
this but a final cold reflection of the visionary Whole, the
Tao, the One, at last appearing in the alienated mind where it
reaches the end of its tether?

In the society generally, this closure of the dichotomies appears as a ransacking of all the excluded human traditions. It
is as if the repressed collective unconscious of our culture
were being turned inside out before our very eyes. Everything
once forbidden and outcast now makes its way into paperback
editions, comic books, poster art, pop music. A dizzying spectacle. A necessary stage. Easy enough to ridicule the excesses.
They are apt to be with us for some time to come. Perhaps
there will always be people undergoing at some interval in
their lives the same ungainly traumas of liberation, desperately
trying this and that. There will surely always be fourteen-
year-olds coming along the way, absolute beginners. But the
fair questions to ask are: how did the traumas resolve themselves . . . where are the fourteen-year-olds ten years later
. . . what was learned by the failed experiments? These exotic samplings and improvisations—even where they abandon

caution—are essential to the personal and cultural search for wholeness. Though of course the whole, as a disciplined creation, must finally become more than a chaos of possibilities. Just as the finished painting must be more than the well-heaped palette.

Only one dichotomy will remain, the inevitable distinction between more and less. There must always be this tension between those who would have sanity be less than the whole, and those who would have the whole. Where this book, for example, has taken issue with single vision, it has been with the *exclusiveness* of "Satan's mathematic holiness." Not, in turn, to exclude it, but to find it its proper place in a science of rhapsodic intellect. Between those who are still locked in the box of the Reality Principle and those who have escaped it, there will always be the tension of disagreement. For Jack In-the-Box will insist there is nowhere to be but where he is. Jack Out-of-the-Box will know otherwise. It is the inevitable contrast of sensibilities between the free and the imprisoned mind—and only the *experience* of more will ever overcome anyone's allegiance to less.

To argue as I do that urban-industrialism is a failed cultural experiment and that the time is at hand to replace it with the visionary commonwealth amounts to a strict denial of the secularized myth of progress as we have learned it from our forebears of the Enlightenment. That is a bitter pill. It declares many generations of hardship and effort to have been a catastrophic mistake. For those who are not in touch with other, more fulfilling realities, such an admission is bound to seem an intolerable humiliation. But I hope I have made clear that I am not, as has become so much the morbid fashion among western intellectuals since the *fin de siècle*, rejecting the pursuit of secular progress in favor of wholesale cynicism. Such cynicism, being legitimately unacceptable to society at large as a basis for life, has only increased the desperation with which the millions cling to that myth despite their inadmissible misgivings. We must remember Blake's warning.

> Man must & will have Some Religion: if he has not the Religion of Jesus, he will have the Religion of Satan & will erect the Synagogue of Satan, calling the Prince of the World, God, and destroying all who do not worship Satan under the name of God.

True enough, no one who is not lying himself blind to the obvious can help but despair of the well-being that a reductionist science and power-ridden technology can bring. Nothing humanly worthwhile can be achieved within the diminished reality of such a science and technics; nothing whatever. On that level, we "progress" only toward technocratic elitism, affluent alienation, environmental blight, nuclear suicide. Not an iota of the promise of industrialism will then be realized but it will be vastly outweighed by the "necessary evils" attending.

But there is another progress that is not a cheat and a folly; the progress that has always been possible at every moment in time. It goes by many names. St. Bonaventura called it "the journey of the mind to God"; the Buddha called it the eightfold path; Lao Tzu called it finding "the Way." The way *back*. To the source from which the adventure of human culture takes its beginning. It is *this* progress which the good society exists to facilitate for all its members.

The higher sanity will find its proper politics when we come to realize in our very bones that we have nothing to add to the splendor of the Old Gnosis and can make no progress "beyond it." We can do no more than return to it, borrow from it, reshape it to suit the times. This is to recognize that all the resources of the spirit human beings have ever needed to work out their destiny have always been with them . . . *in* them . . . provided; all they have needed to be beautiful and dignified, graceful and good. *In this sense,* there is nothing to do, nowhere to get. We need only "stand still in the light." This is something that must be emphasized not only to the technocrats with their ingrained contempt for traditional wisdom, but also to the young media-freaks and acid heads with their bizarre passion for an electrochemical epiphany. For they seem not to realize how pleased Westinghouse, Du Pont, and RCA would be to wire them up for skull-flicks and throw the switches. Anything to keep the public grateful and distracted.

Technologically speaking, there is indeed a course of history, obviously linear and cumulative. Its measure is increase of material power and, within a discipline of the sacred, that historical potentiality must also be unfolded. But the Old Gnosis needs no history; it is whole in every moment of time. The Romantics, in their struggle against single vision, thought they saw such a timeless self-fulfillment in the delights of infancy. Certainly they, with most artists, found it in their work, in the stasis that comes of capturing a symbol's transcendent meaning.

But such symbols are with all of us everywhere and at all times; not only in the language and imagery of our cultural making, but in every most ordinary moment, every least scrap of the world around us, in the rhythms of our own body, in the lights and airs that fill the sky, in the things and creatures with which we share the earth. It is the presence of transcendent symbols instructing, nurturing, brightening life at every turn that makes the world at large a magical object and human culture a whole from its most technologically primitive origins to the present time. Here we find what can alone give meaning to our historical project: the eternity that seeks its reflection in the mirrors of time.

NOTES AND ASIDES

*Publisher, date, and place of publication are
given only with the first citation of each book.*

The Artificial Environment

page 3
Henry David Thoreau, from his essay *Walking and the Wild.*
page 5
J. Bronowski, *Science and Human Values,* New York, Harper
Torchbooks, 1965, p. 112. But for other views on the primi-
tives less distorted by such easy ethnocentrism (and much
more to my liking) see Stanley Diamond's excellent essay,
"The Search for the Primitive" in Ashley Montagu, ed., *The
Concept of the Primitive,* New York, Free Press, 1968; Irven
DeVore and Richard B. Lee's anthology *Man the Hunter,*
New York, Aldine Publishing Co., 1969; and Dorothy Lee,
Freedom and Culture, Englewood Cliffs, New Jersey, Pren-
tice-Hall, 1959.
page 9
The statistics on urbanization are those of Professor Kingsley
Davis of Princeton. They are cited in Lord Ritchie Calder,
"Polluting the Environment," *The Center Magazine* (Center
for the Study of Democratic Institutions—Santa Barbara,
California), May 1969.
page 10
The work of the Environmental Systems Group at the Univer-
sity of California at Davis offers some examples of a more
skeptical approach to urban economics. See the article by
Kenneth E. F. Watt, one of its members: "The Costs of Urbanization," in *The Ecologist* (London) February 1972.

page 14
Buckminster Fuller, *Operating Manual for Spaceship Earth,* Massachusetts Institute of Technology Press, 1969, p. 91. One cannot help but be ambivalent about Fuller. He is in some ways a marvelous maverick with much of the charm of the Connecticut Yankee about him. But he lacks an organic sensibility and I would not be surprised to hear him announce someday that he had invented a better tree. All his solutions to social problems are technical gimmicks, and one has to be pretty naïve (or hopelessly technocratic) to swallow such a prescription.

page 14
J. Bronowski, *Science and Human Values,* p. 113.

page 16
On the extermination of the Brazilian Indians—by the official Indian Protection Service no less—see the report by Norman Lewis in the *Sunday Times Magazine* (London) February 23, 1969. Information is also available from Survival International (36 Craven Street, London W.C.2), which is a good source on the plight of primitive people everywhere.

page 17
The world could surely use a hard critical study of the ethics and economics of the tourist trade. It is one of the great evils in which millions of innocently intentioned people have become implicated and one of the most destructive forms of pollution. Many third world nations are now spending more money to finance roads, hotels, and vacation facilities for the tourists than they will ever make up from the trade.

page 19
Emmanuel Mesthene, quoted in Victor Ferkiss, *Technological Man,* New York, Braziller, 1969, p. 20. Professor Mesthene was head of the Harvard University Program on Technology and Society. See his book *Technology and Social Change,* Indianapolis, Bobbs-Merrill, 1969, for a report on the program's activities.

page 22
Alvin Toffler, *Future Shock,* New York, Random House, 1970, pp. 266–67. The book is a fast cruise over the glossy surface of the artificial environment, finishing with a facile endorsement of urban-industrialism.

CHAPTER 2

Citadel of Expertise

page 28
Saint-Simon, from *L'Organisateur* (1819) in *Oeuvres de Saint-Simon et Enfantin*, Paris, 1869, Vol. IV, pp. 156–58.

page 32
Jacques Ellul's *The Technological Society*, New York, A. A. Knopf, 1964, pp. 338–39. Ellul is far too pessimistic in this work for my tastes. But as a sketch of the urban-industrial trap seen from its grimmest angle, the book is unsurpassed.

page 33
John Ziman, *Public Knowledge: The Social Dimension of Science*, Cambridge University Press, 1968, pp. 28, 74. An excellent little book on the professional practice of science.

page 36
Simon Ramo, *Cure for Chaos: Fresh Solutions to Social Problems through the System Approach*, New York, David McKay, 1969, p. 15.

page 37
Ibid., p. 116. For a critical study of systems analysis, see Robert Boguslaw, *The New Utopians: A Study of Systems Design and Social Change*, Englewood Cliffs, New Jersey, Prentice-Hall, 1965.

page 40
E. J. Mishan, *The Costs of Economic Growth*, London, Pelican Books, 1969, p. 27. First published in 1967, this shrewd critique of "growthmania" is one of the first voices of the new zero-growth economics.

page 41
Jean Meynaud, *Technocracy*, trans. by Paul Barnes, New York, Free Press, 1969, pp. 209, 248.

page 42
Veblen's famous appeal for technocratic government was *The Engineers and the Price System*, New York, Viking Press,

1933. For a good, if rather diffuse survey of the ideal, see
W. H. Armytage, *Rise of the Technocrats,* University of To-
ronto Press, 1965, which reaches back to Francis Bacon.

page 43

Howard Perlmutter, "Super-Giant Firms in the Future," in
Wharton Quarterly, Winter 1968. On the global expansion of
the corporations and its effect on economic policy in foreign
countries, see Christopher Tugendhat, *The Multinationals,*
London, Eyre and Spottiswoode, 1971. Also see Andrew Jack-
son and Gerald Newbould, *The Receding Ideal,* Liverpool,
England, Guthstead, 1972, on mergers and corporate giants.

page 44

On the ethos and power of the modern corporations, see John
K. Galbraith, *The New Industrial State,* Boston, Houghton
Mifflin, 1967. Richard Barber's *The American Corporation:
Its Power, Its Money, Its Politics,* New York, Dutton, 1970,
and Paul Dickson's *Think Tanks,* New York, Atheneum,
1971, are good basic guides.

page 52

The formula for I.Q. is from Arthur R. Jensen's "How Much
Can We Boost I.Q. and Scholastic Achievement?" in *Harvard
Education Review,* Winter 1969. The formula for the balance
of payments is from E. J. Mishan, *The Costs of Economic
Growth,* Appendix B.

page 65

The "electronicized desk" is in fact an example of what a systems analyst takes a great educational idea to be. See Simon
Ramo, *Cure for Chaos,* p. 40.

page 65–66

Herman Kahn, quoted in *The Observer* (London), September
28, 1969.

page 69

The quotations from Alvin Toffler are from his introduction to
Kurt Baier and Nicholas Rescher, eds., *Values and the Future,* New York, Free Press, 1969. The anthology is a good introduction to the futures industry, complete with zany questionnaires and computer games. In his *Future Shock,* Toffler
tries to suggest that he is opposed to technocratic politics. But
that is a contradiction in terms. The precise, canonical definition of a technocrat is: anyone who thinks like Alvin Toffler.

CHAPTER 3

Waking Up, Being Real

page 74
William Blake, from *Jerusalem.*
page 75
For a review of Freud's thought on the Reality Principle, see
Pat Radford, "Principles of Mental Functioning," in *Basic
Psychoanalytical Concepts of Metapsychology,* London, George
Allen and Unwin, 1970.
page 78
The quotation from Ryle appears in a discussion of his *The
Concept of Mind,* in *The Listener* (London) January 21,
1971. The best basic survey of dream and sleep research is
Ann Faraday, *Dream Power,* New York, Coward-McCann,
1972.
page 79
A prediction that sleep would soon be replaced by the use of
drugs was made by Dr. Nathan Kline of Rockland State
Hospital, New York, in April 1969—and reported by the
Associated Press.
page 83
Alfred Kroeber, *Anthropology,* New York, Harcourt Brace,
1948, rev. ed., p. 298.
page 83
On Senoi dream theory, see Kilton Stewart, "Dream Exploration Among the Senoi," in Theodore Roszak, ed., *Sources,*
New York, Harper and Row, 1972.
page 84
Lewis Feuer, *The Scientific Intellectual,* New York, Basic Books,
1963.
page 89
For a discussion of recent research on pheromones, see Alex
Comfort, "Communication May Be Odorous," in *New Scientist* (London) February 25, 1971.

page 92
The verse passage is from Traherne's poem *My Spirit*. The prose is from the second section of his *Third Century*.

page 94
On the evolution of the forebrain and its increasing disconnection from the rest of the organism, see A. T. W. Simeons, *Man's Presumptuous Brain*, New York, Dutton, 1962. On the anatomical and characterological aspects of erect posture, see Moshé Feldenkreis, *Body and Mature Behavior: A Study of Anxiety, Sex, Gravitation and Learning*, London, Routledge and Kegan Paul, 1949.

page 95
Freud's later and darker speculations on the death instinct are the subject of Norman O. Brown's *Life Against Death*, Wesleyan University Press, 1959.

page 97
Kroeber, *Anthropology*, p. 301.

page 99
See Roderick Seidenberg, *Posthistoric Man*, University of North Carolina Press, 1950.

page 100
Abraham Maslow's "eupsychian network" appears in his revised edition of *Toward a Psychology of Being*, New York, Van Nostrand, 1968. For another, updated guide to Growth Centers, see the appendix to Roszak, ed., *Sources*.

page 101–2
The passage is from Shelley's essay "On Life."

page 105–6
Jacques Monod, *Chance and Necessity*, trans. by Austyn Wainhouse, New York, A. A. Knopf, 1971, pp. 170, 172. Monod's book is unflinching single vision pressed to its annihilating conclusion. It is, I think, the best and most candid recent statement of where the mainstream scientific tradition leads. See my review in *Book World*, October 15, 1971.

page 107
The lines from Blake appear in a letter to Thomas Butts written in 1802. See *Blake: Complete Writings*, edited by Geoffrey Keynes, Oxford University Press, 1969, p. 818.

CHAPTER 4

The Sin of Idolatry

page 109
Chief Dan George of the Pacific Northwest, "My People," *The Mother Earth News,* No. 10, July 1971.
page 114
Edwyn Bevan, *Holy Images,* London, George Allen and Unwin, 1940, pp. 20, 23.
page 115
The American Indian is quoted in Emile Durkheim, *The Elementary Forms of the Religious Life,* trans. by J. W. Swain, New York, Macmillan, 1915, p. 199. Durkheim's book as a whole is the classic refutation of the Christian stereotype of idolatry. His scholarly deduction of an immanent sacred force (*mana, wakan*) at the root of religious consciousness is one of the great insights of modern thought.
page 115
Owen Barfield, *Saving the Appearances,* London, Faber, 1957, pp. 111, 114. The interpretation of idolatry developed in this chapter draws heavily on this excellent, but much neglected book. Barfield's line of thought, however, leads to a renewed Christian commitment; mine obviously does not—though I find much to sympathize with in Barfield's occult reading of Christianity and in that of his mentor, the gifted Austrian mystic Rudolf Steiner.
On the use of images in Tantric *puja,* Philip S. Rawson comments: "By concentrating on the actual icon one can awaken its inner image in the mind for inward meditation and worship. . . . No physical image can . . . be any more than a reflection of the true transcendent image whose sphere of existence is the MIND-mind. What one worships that one becomes. . . . Among many Tantrikas it is customary to make temporary images which can be disposed of at home or thrown away into water, so as to prevent what the physical eyes have seen impeding the transformation of the visual image into an

inner presence." *Tantra*, London, Arts Council of Great Britain, 1971, p. 20. As Rawson puts it, the Tantric icon is "a roosting place" for the divine.

page 116–17

Calvin's analysis of idolatry appears in Book I, Chapter 13, of *The Institutes of the Christian Religion*.

page 120

For an astonishing example of how shamanism within a robust tribal context can alter and enrich the perceptual powers, placing them in touch with extraordinary realities, see the curious incident described in the *Report of the Canadian Arctic Expedition, 1913–1918*, Vol. XII, Ottawa, 1922, p. 194. At a shamanic séance attended by the expedition anthropologist, every member of this Copper Eskimo tribe *saw* (quite matter-of-factly) the shaman Higilak turn into a polar bear as part of the rite, and insisted on this as "incontestable fact" under questioning. The anthropologist saw no such thing and interpreted the event as a collective hallucination. Since the empirical consensus was wholly against him— and since Eskimos are surely better authorities on what is and is not a polar bear—I gather we must conclude that his interpretation is wrong.

page 122–23

Lactantius, *The Divine Institutes*, trans. by W. Fletcher, in Alexander Roberts, et al., ed., *The Ante-Nicene Fathers*, Grand Rapids, Michigan, W. B. Eerdmans Publishing Co., reprinted from the edition of 1867–97, Volume VII, p. 49.

page 125

Calvin's thought on the eucharist appears in *The Institutes of the Christian Religion*, Book IV, Chapter 17.

page 125

William Perkins' thought is summarized in Frances A. Yates, *The Art of Memory*, London, Routledge and Kegan Paul, 1966, p. 278.

It is interesting to note a vivid echo of this rejection of visual imagination in contemporary science. There too we have puritans like Ernst Mach and his followers, who have rejected the pursuit of visual models in physics as "image-worship." Erwin Schrödinger summarizes this trend by remarking, "the desire to visualize, so we are told, means wanting to know how Nature is really constituted, and that is metaphysics—an expres-

sion that in present-day science is mainly used as an insult."
What Is Life? New York, Anchor Books, 1956, p. 195.
page 126
Ernst Lehrs, *Man or Matter: Introduction to a Spiritual Under-
standing of Nature Based on Goethe's Method,* rev. ed., New
York, Harper, 1958. See his Chapter 9 on the sudden de-
cline of levitational theory in seventeenth-century science.
page 128
Lynn White, *Machina Ex Deo,* Massachusetts Institute of
Technology Press, 1969, p. 86.
page 136–37
Mammon's speech appears in Book II of *Paradise Lost.*
page 138
Ernst Cassirer's much celebrated contribution to the philosophical examination of symbolism (*The Philosophy of Symbolic
Forms, An Essay on Man,* both published by the Yale
University Press) does far greater justice to the cultural importance of symbols, especially in art and myth, than the
more logical and mathematical styles of philosophy. Still,
his identification of science as the highest stage in the evolution of symbolic forms leads him to very different conclusions
than I draw here—especially with respect to the symbolic
perception of nature. Cassirer, a neo-Kantian, limits himself to the role symbols play as noetic structures of the mind;
I am more concerned to find the meaning of Blake's conviction that "Every Natural Effect has a Spiritual Cause."
page 139
Ananda Coomaraswamy, "The Nature of Buddhist Art," in
Figures of Speech or Figures of Thought, London, Luzac and
Co., 1946, p. 193. An excellent discussion of the idea of symbolism I am following in this book.
page 140
Joseph Epes Brown, *The Spiritual Legacy of the American
Indian,* Wallingford, Pennsylvania, Pendle Hill Pamphlets,
1964, p. 25. Also see Brown's fuller study, *The Sacred Pipe,*
University of Oklahoma Press, 1953.
For a striking example of how even liberal Christian thought
continues to misperceive and denigrate the sacramental awareness of primitive religions, see the discussion of "The Disenchantment of Nature" in Harvey Cox, *The Secular City,* rev.

ed., New York, Macmillan, 1966. I agree with Cox that secularization is an outgrowth of Judeo-Christianity. But unlike him, I think the religion of alienation was an unnecessary extreme which has by now long since outlived whatever service it may once have performed. It is saddening to see how its apologetics go marching on.

CHAPTER 5

A Dead Man's Eyes

page 142
Francis Bacon, from the preface to *Novum Organum.*
page 146
On Bacon's debt to the alchemical tradition and for a keen study of his thought as a whole, see Paolo Rossi, *Francis Bacon: From Magic to Science,* trans. by Sacha Rabinovitch, University of Chicago Press, 1968.

On his borrowings from Aristotle, see Robert Larsen, "The Aristotelianism of Bacon's *Novum Organum," Journal of the History of Ideas,* October 1962.
page 150
The quotations from Bacon throughout this chapter, unless otherwise specified, are from the standard English edition: James Spedding, Robert L. Ellis and Douglas D. Heath, eds., *The Works of Francis Bacon,* 7 vols., London, Longmans, 1870. The *Novum Organum* appears in Vol. IV of the series.
page 150
"this Instauration of mine . . ." Bacon, *Works,* IV, p. 21
page 151
"You will never be sorry . . ." Quoted in Benjamin Farrington, *The Philosophy of Francis Bacon,* Liverpool University Press, 1964, pp. 114–15.
page 151
Max Gluckman, *Politics, Law, and Ritual,* New York, Mentor Books, 1965, p. 60.

page 153

On the critically important role of the textbook in science, see John Ziman, *Public Knowledge,* p. 70. Ziman draws here on similar thoughts in Thomas Kuhn, *The Structure of Scientific Revolutions,* University of Chicago Press, 1962.

page 157

"building in the human understanding . . ." Bacon, *Works,* IV, p. 110.

page 157–58

George Thomson, *The Inspiration of Science,* New York, Anchor Books, 1968, p. 9. Also see P. B. Medawar, *The Art of the Soluble,* London, Methuen, 1967, p. 132, where the author argues that there is no single method at all.

For a good critical discussion of the theories of scientific method, see J. R. Ravetz, *Scientific Knowledge and Its Social Problems,* Oxford University Press, 1971, especially pp. 169–80.

page 158

Michael Polanyi's *Personal Knowledge,* University of Chicago Press, 1959, is a key work to which I am much indebted. It should, however, be supplemented by J. R. Ravetz (see previous note).

page 159–60

"Certainly if in things . . ." Bacon, *Works,* IV, p. 40.

page 160

Rossi, *Francis Bacon,* pp. 16–18.

page 164

"The command over things natural . . ." Bacon, "Sphinx, or Science," *Works,* VI, p. 757.

page 164

David S. Landes, *The Unbound Prometheus,* Cambridge University Press, 1969, p. 61. This conclusion has been challenged with respect to the technology of the steam engine by Milton Kerker in his article "Science and the Steam Engine," *Technology and Culture,* Vol. II, No. 4, Fall 1961, pp. 381–90. But even if Kerker is right, it is still a long way from Bacon to the first economically significant engine produced by Watt and Boulton. For a survey of the problem that seeks to press the relevance of science to early technology as far as possible—but comes to a modest and ambivalent conclusion—see A. E. Musson and E. Robinson, "Science and Industry in the Late 18th Century," *Economic History Review,* December 1960, pp. 222–44.

page 166
"For first, the object of the natural history . . ." Bacon, *Works,*
IV, p. 28-29.

page 166
Compare Bacon here with Vannevar Bush testifying before
Congress in 1945: "Basic research is a long-term process—it
ceases to be basic if immediate results are expected on short-
term support. Methods should therefore be found which will
permit the agency to make commitments of funds from current
appropriations for programs of five years' duration or longer."
Quoted in Daniel S. Greenberg, *The Politics of Pure Science,*
New York, New American Library, 1967, p. 147.

page 169
Clark L. Hull, quoted in Floyd Matson, *The Broken Image,*
New York, Braziller, 1964, p. 64.

page 169
The use of human beings as rather less than voluntary guinea
pigs continues. In 1969 Dr. Austin R. Stough was discovered to be in business testing drugs produced by leading
pharmaceutical companies on prison inmates in Oklahoma,
Arkansas, and Alabama, some of whom died during the experiments—mainly due to hepatitis. See Walter Rugaber's
reports in the *New York Times* during July 1969. See also
M. H. Pappworth's *Human Guinea Pigs: Experimentation on
Man,* London, Routledge and Kegan Paul, 1967. In 1971
Senator Edward Kennedy revealed that the University of Cin-
cinnati has been making total body radiation experiments on
terminal cancer patients of an underprivileged background
as part of a Pentagon research project. The experiments
produced severe discomfort and vomiting, but patients were
not warned of the results because, as one doctor remarked,
"nausea is a very subjective thing." See the *New York Times,*
October 12, 1971.

page 170
Rossi deals at several points with the influence of Machiavelli
on Bacon's political thought. The effects are especially noticea-
ble in Bacon's essays "Of Empire" and "Of the True Greatness of Kingdoms and Estates" as well as in the hard-boiled
tone of the literary fragment "Of the True Greatness of
Britain." On this Machiavellian slant to Bacon's thought,

see Leo Strauss and Joseph Cropsey, *A History of Political Philosophy,* Chicago, Rand-McNally, 1963, pp. 324–42.

page 172–73

Charles Gillispie's *The Edge of Objectivity,* Princeton University Press, 1960, has been a controversial contribution to the history of science. I find it a uniquely cogent effort to trace out the mainstream of scientific thought since Galileo—though I suspect it is more rigorous in its presentation of the overall paradigm of scientific thought than more humanistically inclined scientists find comfortable. The book must be read in company with Thomas Kuhn's *The Structure of Scientific Revolutions.* Kuhn's justly praised work leaves open the question of what holds together all the many paradigms of the several sciences and gives them the general identity of "science." Gillispie seeks to suggest the minimal condition which all the paradigms must meet; he calls that condition "objectivity," an intellectual standard which ruthlessly excludes all theory or speculation that reads purposiveness, ethical meaning, or personal communion into nature. Whatever else Gillispie may be wrong about, on this critical point he is right about the course scientific sensibility has followed since the seventeenth century.

page 173–74

"I humbly pray . . ." Bacon, *Works,* IV, p. 20.

page 175

From the *Saturday Review of Literature,* March 16, 1957. If the scientific community were to take Fromm's viewpoint to heart, I daresay most of our psychologists, political scientists, sociologists, economists, and a good many biologists and medical researchers would be out of work.

There are excellent discussions of Bacon's contribution to science in Joseph Haberer, *Politics and the Community of Science,* New York, Van Nostrand-Reinhold, 1969, Chapter 3, and, especially in Lewis Mumford, *The Pentagon of Power,* New York, Harcourt Brace Jovanovich, 1970, Chapter 5. Also see Loren Eiseley, *Francis Bacon and the Modern Dilemma,* University of Nebraska Press, 1962, and Moody E. Prior, "Bacon's Man of Science," *Journal of the History of Ideas,* Vol. XV, 1954.

CHAPTER 6

Fair Bait . . . Cruel Trap

page 178
Arthur Eddington, *Philosophy of Physical Science,* Cambridge University Press, 1949. The quotation is from the final chapter, which is a wise comment on the ethical meaning of science.
page 179
On the underlying assumptions of the new science, the classic study is E. A. Burtt, *The Metaphysical Foundations of Modern Science,* New York, Anchor Books, 1954.
page 181
F. S. C. Northrup, *Man, Nature, and God,* New York, Pocket Books, 1963, p. 140.
page 182
On Bohr's use of indeterminacy and the motivations of Max Delbrück and his colleagues, see Gunther S. Stent, "That Was the Molecular Biology That Was," *Science,* April 26, 1968.
page 182
Schrödinger's views on biology are well expressed in a famous essay, "What Is Life?" (1944), in the collection *What Is Life?,* New York, Anchor Books, 1956.
For an interesting effort to harness Bohr's principle of complementarity to humanistic purposes, see Thomas Blackburn, "Sensuous-Intellectual Complementarity in Science," *Science,* June 4, 1971.
page 182
Floyd Matson's *The Broken Image,* an excellent book in many respects, is vulnerable on more than one count. I suppose the behaviorists might insist that the Newtonian image still holds for the world of everyday experience and so can be legitimately applied. Or they might argue that their new, sophisticated statistical methods are quite in step with the mathematical style of the new physics.

page 183
Gillispie, *The Edge of Objectivity,* p. 517.

page 183
Einstein seems to have finished his life as sad-faced and stoical in his vision of nature as any. For him, too, religion was the "merely personal," an unworthy domination of life by "wishes, hopes, and primitive feelings." His conversation with Rabindranath Tagore in 1930 shows how chillingly inhuman his vision of nature was. See Appendix II of Tagore's *The Religion of Man,* Boston, Beacon Press, 1961.

page 184
See Joseph Needham, *Man a Machine,* London, Kegan Paul, 1927, p. 93. The book takes its title from La Mettrie's famous eighteenth-century work, one of the most sweeping efforts to produce a behavioral-physiological reduction of human nature. Aram Vartanian has done an excellent edition of the book: *La Mettrie's L'Homme Machine, A Study in the Origins of an Idea,* Princeton University Press, 1960.

page 184–85
See Koyré's essay "The Significance of the Newtonian Synthesis" in *Newtonian Studies,* Harvard University Press, 1965.

page 185
The background of Newton's religious thought is a complex brew of theology, alchemy, and occult studies—though only a cautious Deism ever slipped into his science (as in Query 28 of *The Opticks*). On these more eccentric aspects of Newton, see Frank Manuel, *A Portrait of Isaac Newton,* Harvard University Press, 1968; and Margaret Lewis Bailey, *Milton and Jakob Boehme,* Oxford University Press, 1914. Boehme's work was a definite influence on Newton, even drawing him into laboratory experiments in alchemy. Bailey thinks Newton "did but reduce to a mathematical form the central principles of nature revealed in Boehme." If that is true, then much was lost in the mathematical translation —in fact, everything that would not pass through the filter of an objectified psychology. The bulk of Newton's alchemical notes remain unedited, untranslated, and unexplored.

page 187
The passage is from Nietzsche's *Genealogy of Morals,* Section 25, trans. by Horace B. Samuel.

page 188
Francis Crick, *Of Molecules and Men,* University of Washington Press, 1966, pp. 87, 93.

page 197–98
Charles Gillispie, "Remarks on Social Selection as a Factor in the Progressivism of Science," *The American Scientist,* Winter 1960.

page 200
Descartes, *Philosophical Essays,* trans. by Laurence J. Lafleur, New York, Library of Liberal Arts, 1964, p. 179.

page 201
For an interesting extension and critique of Kuhn's well-known thesis, see S. B. Barnes, "Paradigms, Scientific and Social," *Man* (London), March 1969.

page 203
It is amusing to note how Descartes, sensing the revolutionary democratic implications of his method, seeks to cover himself at one point in the *Discourse* by way of some feeble qualifications. The method, he claims, is really for those "whom God has more bountifully endowed." Why? Because there do seem to be "mischievous spirits" in society, and "once they have taken the liberty of doubting their established principles, thus leaving the highway, they will never be able to keep to the narrow path." Descartes' own politics were extremely conservative and excluded reform as "folly." But these qualifications have no philosophical depth to them; they are simply gestures of loyalty offered in behalf of a philosophy whose potential subversiveness Descartes must clearly have recognized.

page 208
See, for example, Popper's *The Open Society and Its Enemies,* Princeton University Press, 1966, 2 vols., 5th ed., or Robert K. Merton's "Science and Democratic Social Structure" in *Social Theory and Social Structure,* Glencoe, Free Press, 1957. For an excellent critique of Merton and his followers, see S. B. Barnes and R. G. A. Dolby, "The Scientific Ethos: A Deviant Standpoint," in *Archives of European Sociology,* XI, 1970.

page 208–9
Karl Pearson, *The Grammar of Science,* London, Everyman, 1937 (first published 1892), pp. 11, 13. The italics have been

added to emphasize that what Pearson values in science is its objectivity, and that he takes the scope of objectivity to be universal. The passage as a whole is a classic celebration of technocratic politics.

page 210
The translation of Halley's Latin original is by L. J. Richardson in Florian Cajori's edition of *Sir Isaac Newton's Mathematical Principles of Natural Philosophy,* University of California Press, 1947.

page 217
Gillispie, *The Edge of Objectivity,* pp. 155-56.

CHAPTER 7

Science *in Extremis*

page 220
José Ortega y Gasset, from *The Mission of the University,* New York, Norton, 1966.

page 225
The quotation from Peter Kapitsa, the leading Soviet physicist, appears in J. R. Ravetz, *Scientific Knowledge and Its Social Problems,* p. 32.

page 225
No attempt here to document the bigness of contemporary science or its complex interrelationship with government and economy. For those who want the facts and figures, see Derek De Solla Price, *Big Science, Little Science,* Columbia University Press, 1963; Michael Reagan, *Science and the Federal Patron,* Oxford University Press, 1969; Daniel S. Greenberg, *The Politics of Pure Science,* New York, New American Library, 1967; Alvin Weinberg, *Reflections on Big Science,* Massachusetts Institute of Technology Press, 1967; Robin Clarke, *The Science of War and Peace,* London, Jonathan Cape, 1971; and J. R. Ravetz, *Scientific Knowledge and Its Social Problems.*

page 228
Kingsley Davis, quoted in Michael Reagan, *Science and the Federal Patron,* p. 188.

page 230
Kenneth Boulding "The Diminishing Returns of Science," *New Scientist* (London), March 25, 1971. Also see Sir Macfarlane Burnet's somber reflections on the same theme in *Dominant Mammal,* London, Heinemann, 1971.

page 232
Kroeber, *Anthropology,* p. 298.

page 237
Joseph Needham, *The Grand Titration,* London, George Allen and Unwin, 1969, pp. 144, 145.

page 238
Haberer, *Politics and the Community of Science,* pp. 150, 155. Haberer offers a grim picture of scientific acquiescence to the Nazis.

page 239–40
J. Shapiro, L. Eron, J. Beckwith, letter in *Nature,* December 27, 1969, p. 1337. The letter replies to an editorial in *Nature,* November 29, 1969, pp. 834–35, which raises the argument that the position these dissenting biologists take would endanger scientific progress. Indeed it would. It takes time away from research to consult one's conscience.

page 240
Buonarrotti quoted in Lewis Feuer, *The Scientific Intellectual,* p. 279.

page 241
Daniel Moynihan in Daniel Bell, ed., *Toward the Year 2000: Work in Progress,* Boston, Beacon Press, 1968, pp. 173–74. Michael Reagan, *Science and the Federal Patron,* also makes a strong plea for greater government subvention of social science.

page 241
On Project Cambridge, see Joseph Hanlon, "The Implications of Project Cambridge" in *New Scientist* (London), February 25, 1971. According to a report in the *Times* (London) for November 23, 1969, the air war in Vietnam has been carried out by just such advanced computer gaming techniques. The computer chooses the targets and the levels of bombardment.

It even gives "a calculable but never calculated chance of killing civilians in the process." A similar technique called Project Phoenix has been worked out for selecting individual Viet Cong sympathizers for assassination. But perhaps these are only crude examples of what Project Cambridge intends, since obviously enough the technique proved to be a fiasco in Vietnam.

page 246
Comte, quoted in Floyd Matson, *The Broken Image,* p. 33.
page 247
B. F. Skinner, *Beyond Freedom and Dignity,* New York, A. A. Knopf, 1971, p. 58.
page 252
Abraham Maslow, *The Psychology of Science,* New York, Harper and Row, 1966, p. 42. An essential, but much neglected book in the reconstruction of scientific intellect; perhaps Maslow's finest effort. Also see Viktor Frankl, "Nothing But —On Reductionism and Nihilism," in *Encounter,* November 1969.
page 256
Erwin Schrödinger, *What Is Life?,* p. 133.

CHAPTER 8

Romantic Perversity

page 277
Shelley, from *A Defense of Poetry.*
The literature on Romanticism is far too great to be more than skimmed here—and not much of it is directly related to the issues that concern me in this chapter. C. M. Bowra, *The Romantic Imagination,* New York, Galaxy Books, 1961, is solid and scholarly, but does not ultimately see the contemporary philosophical value of its subject. M. H. Abrams, *Natural Supernaturalism: Tradition and Revolution in Romantic Literature,* New York, Norton, 1971, is filled with

insight especially on the religious continuities in the movement, but seems sadly out of sympathy with the poets it discusses; rather as if Romanticism were over and done with. Alethea Hayter, *Opium and the Romantic Imagination*, University of California Press, 1971, is a good survey of the range of exotic experience which the Romantics investigated. Jacques Barzun's *Romanticism and the Modern Ego*, Boston, Little Brown, 1944, is a spirited defense of the Romantics against the academic establishment. By far the most perceptive studies of the deep philosophical meaning of Romanticism are Owen Barfield's *Romanticism Comes of Age*, Wesleyan University Press, 1966, and Charles Davy's *Toward a Third Culture*, London, Faber, 1961.

page 283
On Rimbaud's theory of poetry and its background, see Enid Starkie, *Arthur Rimbaud*, New York, New Directions, rev. ed., 1968.

page 294
Descartes' dream of the angel of truth is recounted in Laurence J. Lafleur's introduction to Descartes' *Philosophical Essays*, New York, Library of Liberal Arts, 1964.

CHAPTER 9

Mind on Fire

My reading of Blake is much indebted to Kathleen Raine, *Blake and Tradition*, 2 vols., Princeton University Press, 1968; Samuel Beer, *Blake's Humanism*, New York, Barnes and Noble, 1968; Désirée Hirst, *Hidden Riches: Traditional Symbolism from the Renaissance to Blake*, London, Eyre and Spottiswoode, 1964; and Northrup Frye, *Fearful Symmetry*, Princeton University Press, 1947. D. V. Erdman's *Blake: Prophet Against Empire*, Princeton University Press, 1954, is a thorough discussion of Blake's politics. Also of singular value in understanding the tradition behind Blake is Hans

Jonas, *The Gnostic Religion,* 2d ed., Boston, Beacon Press, 1963.

Melvin Rader's *Wordsworth: A Philosophical Approach,* Oxford University Press, 1967, is helpful on the epistemology and psychology of the poet's work.

The two best philosophical studies of Goethe's scientific vision are Ernst Lehrs, *Man or Matter: Introduction to a Spiritual Understanding of Nature Based on Goethe's Method;* and Rudolph Steiner, *Goethe the Scientist,* New York, Theosophical Press, 1950—though in the latter it is often difficult to tell where Goethe leaves off and Steiner begins.

The basic scholarly survey of Goethe's scientific work (and a highly critical one) is Rudolf Magnus, *Goethe als Naturforscher,* Leipzig, 1906.

A good selection of Goethe's scientific writing can be found in *Goethe's Botanical Writings,* trans. by Bertha Mueller, University of Hawaii Press, 1952. Goethe's *Farbenlehre* and other writings on color can be found well edited and beautifully illustrated in Rupprecht Matthaei, ed., *Goethe's Color Theory,* New York, Van Nostrand-Reinhold, 1971. Most of my quotations from Goethe's work on plants and colors are from these books.

H. O. Proskauer, *Zum Studium von Goethe's Farbenlehre,* Basel, Zbinden Verlag, 1968, is a sound introduction to Goethe's color research.

Charles Sherrington, *Goethe on Nature and on Science,* Cambridge University Press, 1949, is a brutal criticism of Goethe's scientific work by a leading scientist.

R. D. Gray, *Goethe the Alchemist,* Cambridge University Press, 1952, and *Goethe: A Critical Introduction,* Cambridge University Press, 1967, are extremely good. G. H. Lewes, *The Story of Goethe's Life,* Boston, Houghton-Mifflin, 1898, retains much value, especially on Goethe's science.

The essay on Goethe's science in Erich Heller's *The Disinherited Mind,* New York, Meridian Books, 1959, is excellent; even more so is L. L. Whyte's "Goethe's Single View of Nature and Man," in *German Life and Letters,* new series Vol. II, July 1949. Whyte's writings as a whole are a brilliant extension of Goethe's vision to contemporary science. For a brief, recent summary of his thought, see his essay, "Toward a Science of Form," in *Hudson Review,* Winter 1970–71.

For some contemporary works in which the Goethean spirit lives on, see Adolf Portmann, *New Paths in Biology,* New York, Harper and Row, 1964; E. L. Grant-Watson, *The Mystery of Physical Life,* New York, Abelard-Schuman, 1967; Theodor Schwenk, *Sensitive Chaos,* London, Rudolf Steiner Press, 1965. Also several of the essays collected by Arthur Koestler and J. R. Smythies in *Beyond Reductionism: New Perspectives in the Life Sciences,* New York, Macmillan, 1970.

The bulk of the quotations from Wordsworth are from *The Prelude,* with a few from *The Excursion.* The translations of Goethe's poems are my own and occasionally violate the meter, which in the original is always as strict as it is graceful. Most of the quotations from Blake are from his three prophetic epics, *Vala, Milton,* and *Jerusalem.* The various published versions of Blake's *Vala* are guesswork reconstructions from the poet's chaotic, unpublished notes. For an exhaustive examination of the literary remnants and a facsimile edition, see G. E. Bentley, ed., *Vala, or the Four Zoas,* Oxford University Press, 1963.

page 343
L. Pearce Williams, *The Origins of Field Theory,* New York, Random House, 1966.

CHAPTER 10

Uncaging Skylarks

page 346
Goethe, from *Faust.*
page 348
On Leonardo's ambiguous ruminations about flight, see C. H. Gibbs-Smith, *Leonardo da Vinci's Aeronautics,* London, Her was obsessed with birds from his childhood; he studied them technological—"the cry of a poet, not a scientist." Leonardo nardo's vision of flying may have been as symbolic as it was Majesty's Stationery Office, 1967. Gibbs-Smith believes Leo-

throughout his lifetime with great love, and would often buy caged birds in the market of Florence to set them free. But none of his ornithopters were the least practicable. They were more like a technician's hymns and meditations upon an unattainable ideal.

page 353
Coleridge, from "The Statesman's Manual," in Shedd, ed., *Complete Works of S. T. Coleridge,* New York, Harper and Bros., 1871, Vol. I.

page 354
Carlos Casteneda, *The Teachings of Don Juan: A Yaqui Way of Knowledge,* University of California Press, 1968, pp. 93–94.

page 356
Mircea Eliade gives special attention to the vision-flight in his *Shamanism,* Princeton University Press, 1964.

page 356
My thoughts on language here draw on Owen Barfield's theory of poetic diction. Barfield argues that language traces back to richly comprehensive "single meanings" which are intuitions of "living unity." Language grows by metaphorical extension because "these poetic and *apparently* 'metaphorical' values were latent in meaning from the beginning." Barfield agrees with Emerson that "as we go back in history, language becomes more picturesque, until its infancy, when it is all poetry" —an idea which also appealed to both Shelley and Wordsworth. See Barfield, *Poetic Diction,* London, Faber, 1952.

page 368
I had written this section on the two forms of seeing as one finds them discussed by Goethe before I came across the same distinction in Carlos Casteneda's recent book *A Separate Reality,* New York, Simon and Schuster, 1970.

page 375
On technics within the magical worldview, see Eliade's study *Myths, Dreams, and Mysteries,* New York, Harper and Row, 1961.

page 376
V. Gordon Childe, quoted in H. J. Muller, *Children of Frankenstein,* University of Indiana Press, 1970, p. 17.

On the understanding of symbolism I deal with in this chapter, I much recommend Kathleen Raine's essay "Symbolism" in

Defending Ancient Springs, Oxford University Press, 1967, which compresses the entire idea into a few beautifully written pages.

CHAPTER II

Rhapsodic Intellect

page 380
Zosimos the Panopolitan is one of the earliest Hermetic philosophers. The quotation is from John Read, *Prelude to Chemistry,* London, G. Bell, 1936.
page 389
Jung's *Alchemical Studies,* in *Collected Works,* Vol. 13, Princeton University Press, 1968, is the most influential work of modern scholarship on alchemy. But a far more authentic reading of the tradition can be found in Titus Burckhardt, *Alchemy,* London, Stuart and Watkins, 1967. Also see Mircea Eliade, *The Forge and the Crucible,* New York, Harper Torchbooks, 1971, and Jack Lindsay, *The Origins of Alchemy in Graeco-Roman Egypt,* London, Muller, 1970.
page 392
The *Gloria Mundi,* quoted in Read, *Prelude to Chemistry.*
page 393
Rawson, *Tantra,* p. 7.
page 397
Bronowski, *Science and Human Values,* p. 95.
page 399
Gillispie, *The Edge of Objectivity,* p. 198.
page 402
Ian McHarg, *Design with Nature,* New York, Natural History Press, 1969, p. 68.
page 406
Seyyed Hossein Nasr, *The Encounter of Man and Nature,* London, George Allen and Unwin, 1968, p. 95. A brilliant and important book—except, I think, for a weak treatment of evolutionary theory in the last chapter.

page 407
Stephen Toulmin, *The Philosophy of Science,* London, Hutchinson University Library, 1967, Chapter 4.
For the discussion of the Hermetic tradition developed in this chapter, and its relationship to a rhapsodic natural philosophy, I am much indebted to Betty Roszak for the benefit of her reading and interpretation.

CHAPTER 12

The Visionary Commonwealth

page 413
Martin Buber, from *Paths in Utopia,* Beacon Press, 1960.
page 415
See, for example, Soleri's book, *Arcology: The City in the Image of Man,* Massachusetts Institute of Technology Press, 1969, where the proposal is that we concentrate whole cities into hivelike megastructures—in order to save open space. But how long would it take to get out of one of these city-sized skyscrapers in order to visit those open spaces? The arcologies would in fact be the society E. M. Forster imagined in his story "The Machine Stops." The problem is not, of course, that such cities will ever be built; but that they express and dignify the sensibility which is the real problem facing us.
page 421
See Mumford's wise discussion of plenitude in *The Pentagon of Power,* pp. 393–94.
page 421
Robin Clarke, *The Science of War and Peace,* p. 321.
page 428
For a brief guide to communitarian activities in America, see the "Survival Kit" section of my anthology, *Sources,* New York, Harper and Row, 1972. The final edition of the *Whole Earth Catalog* was published by Random House in 1971. *The Mother Earth News* carries on the story; it can be obtained

from P. O. Box 38, Madison, Ohio 44057, and is by far the best way of keeping up with organic homesteading, communes, voluntary primitivism, etc. A beautiful publication; basic reading for the sane society.

page 428

Alicia Bay Laurel, *Living on the Earth,* New York, Random House, 1971.

page 432

An excellent recent collection of anarchist writings is George Benello and Dimitri Roussopoulos, eds., *The Case for Participatory Democracy,* New York, Grossman, 1971.

page 438

For example, a Latin American developer defending Brazilian economic policy in Amazonia writes to the *Times* of London (November 29, 1971) to castigate "those latter-day Luddites, the American environmentalists." He argues that "the most serious problem facing the emerging nations today is the malnutrition of millions of human beings caused by the underdevelopment of their natural resources." Accordingly, "Who . . . would claim to be qualified to make the value judgement that the ecology of a forest glade is more worthy of preservation than a rat-infested slum is worthy of eradication? . . . Whatever public works are necessary to reduce the misery of hunger will be welcomed by the majority of the people. After all, 99 per cent of all the species which have existed on earth are already extinct." But apparently the problem of poverty is not urgent enough in Brazil to warrant an even remotely equitable redistribution of income or political power. And as we have learned in America, until such redistribution takes place, the poor get poorer and the rich get richer, no matter how much of the landscape we tear up.

page 441

The figures are U.N. statistics quoted by Paul Ehrlich and J. P. Holdern in "Impact of Population Growth," *Science,* March 26, 1971. Also see G. R. Taylor, *Doomsday Book,* New York, World, 1971, p. 292.

page 442

Vegetarians claim that 1.64 acres of average land will support four of them, but will graze only enough livestock to feed one meat-eater. Moreover, in the process of converting grass or fodder into beef for meat-eaters, about fifty per cent of the protein is lost—or rather burned up by the cattle. In a crowded and poorly fed world, meat is indeed a luxury.

CHAPTER 13

Apocatastasis

page 446
Judith Malina and Julian Beck, from *Paradise Now,* New York, Random House, 1971.

page 454
See Koch's essay in Marjorie Grene, ed., *The Anatomy of Knowledge,* University of Massachusetts Press, 1969. The book is a product of the Study Group on Foundations of Cultural Unity, of which Michael Polanyi is a leading member.

page 461
Robert Duncan, "Rites of Participation," in Clayton Eshleman, ed., *Caterpillar Anthology,* New York, Anchor Books, 1971, p. 24.